A GENTLEMAN AND A THIEF

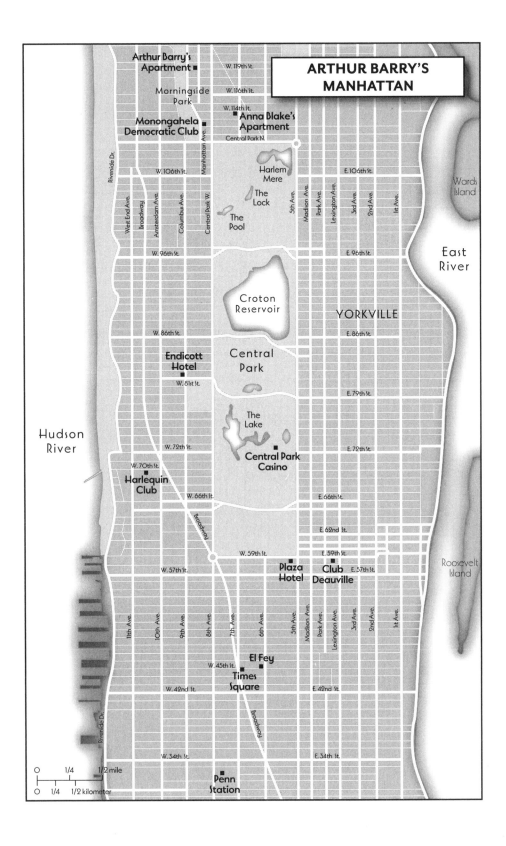

A GENTLEMAN AND A THIEF

The Daring Jewel Heists of a Jazz Age Rogue

DEAN JOBB

ALGONQUIN BOOKS
OF CHAPEL HILL 2024

Published by
ALGONQUIN BOOKS OF CHAPEL HILL
Post Office Box 2225
Chapel Hill, North Carolina 27515-2225

an imprint of Workman Publishing
a division of Hachette Book Group, Inc.
1290 Avenue of the Americas
New York, NY 10104

The Algonquin Books of Chapel Hill name and logo are registered trademarks of
Hachette Book Group, Inc.

Printed in the United States of America.
Design by Steve Godwin.
Maps by Mary Rostad.

The publisher is not responsible for websites (or their content) that are not owned
by the publisher.

Library of Congress Cataloging-in-Publication Data
Names: Jobb, Dean, [date]– author.
Title: A gentleman and a thief : the daring jewel heists of a Jazz Age rogue / Dean Jobb.
Description: First edition. | Chapel Hill, North Carolina : Algonquin Books
of Chapel Hill, 2024. | Includes bibliographical references and index. |
Identifiers: LCCN 2024005157 | ISBN 9781643752839 (hardcover) |
ISBN 9781643756110 (ebook)
Subjects: LCSH: Barry, Arthur | Jewel thieves—United States—Biography. |
Jewelry theft—United States—History—20th century. | Escapes—United
States—History—20th century.
Classification: LCC HV6653.B38 J63 2024 |
DDC 364.16/2873927092 [B]—dc23/eng/20240329
LC record available at https://lccn.loc.gov/2024005157

10 9 8 7 6 5 4 3 2 1
First Edition

For Kerry

For what it's worth, I never stole from anybody who would go hungry.
—Cary Grant as John Robie in *To Catch a Thief*, 1955

~~~~~~~~~~~~~~

I only robbed the rich. If a woman can carry around a necklace worth $750,000, she knows where her next meal is coming from.
—Arthur Barry, 1932

CONTENTS

A NOTE TO READERS

WHILE MANY OF Arthur Barry's crimes are so audacious that they read like fiction, they are fact. Every statement within quotation marks in the pages that follow is drawn from newspaper reports, interviews Barry granted over the years, court files, prison records, histories and memoirs of the Jazz Age, and documents found in archives as far afield as Wyoming and Southampton, England. No quotations have been altered; no details have been added or embellished. All scenes and events unfolded as described. Where there were differing accounts of conversations or what happened, I relied on what was said at the time, rather than what Barry and others remembered or asserted long afterward. An essential element of true crime, after all, is truth.

A GENTLEMAN AND A THIEF

PRINCE CHARMING

Long Island and Manhattan • 1924

A MAN IN A tuxedo and winged collar navigated a room filled with black-clad men and elegant women in Parisian gowns, sparkling with jewels. He docked alongside a group of guests who had formed a cordon around a punch bowl. Someone offered him a drink, and as names were exchanged the newcomer identified himself as Gibson. Dr. Gibson. He had thick black hair, blue eyes, and the chiseled good looks of the matinee idols seen—but not yet heard—in the movie houses. Some guests may have done a double take as he passed; he was a dead ringer for the British actor Ronald Colman, who had been catapulted to Hollywood stardom the previous year in *The White Sister*, starring opposite silent-era legend Lillian Gish.

One of the punch bowl's defenders was short and slim, with sandy hair, and needed no introduction. His boyish face was tilted slightly downward, betraying his shyness, and his puppy-dog eyes had been staring out from the pages of every newspaper in the United States for days. Gibson, who scoured the society pages of New York City's papers as meticulously as a prospector in search of gold or precious jewels, had recognized him from across the room. Edward, the Prince of Wales, was almost a week into a much-ballyhooed American holiday. Eager for a break from his royal duties, the heir to the British throne had headed for "that slender riotous island," as F. Scott Fitzgerald would describe it in his soon-to-be-published novel, *The Great Gatsby*, "which extends itself due east of New York." Long Island.

The September 1924 royal holiday coincided with a late-summer heat wave. The prince was the guest of honor at dinners, dances, and cocktail parties in the imposing mansions of the island's elite. He went riding and played polo on their manicured grounds. He boarded their yachts to skim the waves of Long Island Sound. He golfed their private courses and plunged into their swimming pools. A fox hunt with a pack of about a hundred hounds was organized, to make him feel at home. "Never before in the history of metropolitan society," claimed a columnist for the *New York American*, "has any visitor to these shores been so persistently and so extravagantly feted."

Standard Oil executive Harold Irving Pratt and his wife, Harriet, threw a garden party for the prince and two hundred guests at Welwyn, their country estate at Glen Cove, which overlooked the sound and was considered "one of the show places of Long Island." But they were soon upstaged by Clarence H. Mackay, a financier and heir to a mining fortune, who hosted a dinner and dance for the distinguished visitor and almost one thousand worthies at Harbor Hill, a replica French château with six hundred acres of grounds. A platoon of workmen spent days trucking in potted orange trees and installing strands of yellow electric lights, transforming the outdoor dining area into "a fairyland" fit for a prince. "A royal fete for a royal guest," gushed Washington, DC's *Evening Star*.

Not to be outdone, iron and steel magnate James Abercrombie Burden handed the prince the keys to Woodside, a Georgian mansion near Syosset that could have been transported intact from the English countryside. One New York newspaper gave it a new name: Burden Palace. The prince and his entourage were also free to drive the automobiles Burden kept on-site, a fleet that included five chrome-grilled, bug-eyed Rolls-Royce limousines.

The Cedars, the estate of Oklahoma oilman Joshua S. Cosden and his wife, Nellie, in Sands Point, however, turned out to be the biggest draw for the prince. The mansion, overlooking a wide white-sand beach, was a rambling, colonial-style confection of porches and columned verandas, with two tiers of dormers and eyebrow windows peeking out from its barnlike gambrel roof. Its owners offered the prince something the Burdens, Pratts, and other Long Island hosts could not: familiar faces. His cousin Lord Louis Mountbatten and his wife, Lady Edwina, along with his close friend Jean Norton, wife of the future Lord Grantley, were staying at The Cedars.

The Prince of Wales in 1924, the year of his Long Island visit (Author Collection)

When the Cosdens hosted a late-night party in early September, the prince and his aides commandeered one of the Burden cars and drove over. It was there, in the midst of what one press report termed a "small but jolly" gathering, that Gibson met the prince. Gibson also caught a glimpse of the Mountbattens—the "dark, handsome naval officer," he recalled, and the "lovely Lady Mountbatten, a pearl of international society"—as they chatted with other guests.

The party was the kind of modest, laid-back gathering the prince had been craving since his arrival. This was a holiday, not an official visit; his only commitment was to attend an international polo championship being staged on Long Island, to cheer on the British team. Edward had been traveling the world as Britain's goodwill ambassador—cutting ribbons, making speeches, and shaking hands to shore up wartime alliances and drum up trade deals. He wanted a break. "He is here to play," one of his aides, Tommy Lascelles, reminded the reporters and photographers documenting his every move. "His royal highness is entitled to some time to enjoy himself."

The prince was the first of what would become a twentieth-century phenomenon: the royal celebrity. And he was furious to discover that American journalists were more aggressive and relentless than their British counterparts. "These Yank pressmen are b––s," he griped to his private secretary in unroyal language. "One does resent their d––d spying." The most eligible bachelor on the planet had turned thirty in June, and the American papers were obsessed with the notion that "Prince Charming" had come to their shores in search of a bride. "Would you marry an American girl if you fell in love with one?" was one of the first questions a reporter fired at him when he reached New York on board the liner SS *Berengaria*. And there were plenty of candidates eager to meet him or to catch his eye. ARMY OF LOVELY WOMEN SEEK HIS PRINCELY SMILE, shouted a headline in the New York *Daily News*. Hundreds of women "forgot decorum," as one journalist put it, and stood on their seats at Belmont Park to catch a glimpse of him as he watched the thoroughbred races from the judges' box.

When Gibson first spotted the prince at the Cosdens' party, an older woman was monopolizing the guest of honor's time, no doubt extolling the beauty and virtues of a daughter or niece. The prince had been listening politely, a cocktail in his right hand and his left arm gracefully folded against the small of his back. But it was not the woman vying for the prince's attention that caught Gibson's eye; it was the expensive jewelry adorning the necks and wrists and fingers of so many others. "I'm a judge of that sort of thing," he admitted, "and I couldn't help but admire what they wore." Years later, he still remembered an antique Chinese piece he spotted that night, fashioned from hand-hammered gold and set with a single diamond.

Someone in the prince's group suggested they "get away from the women" for a while. Gibson piped up and suggested "a sortie to gayer places," that they drive into Manhattan and "see the town." Gibson offered to be their guide.

A couple of the men surrounding the prince objected, and the idea was dropped. But Edward was not willing to pass up the opportunity to sample New York's nightlife. "Wales does things spontaneously and when he chooses," noted one of the American journalists covering his visit. "That is part of his charm." The prince took his new acquaintance aside. For once, he was free of the reporters who relentlessly shadowed him. This was his chance to see New York as a tourist, not as a future king.

"Dr. Gibson," he asked, "is that little lark still on?"

～～～～～～

"Hello, suckers!"

Those were the first words most patrons heard after they climbed a flight of stairs and slipped inside one of New York's most famous speakeasies, a greeting shouted over the din of the crowd by a brash blue-eyed blond woman who was clearly in charge. The awning over the entrance door below, on West Forty-Fifth Street, identified it as the El Fey Club, but everyone in New York called it Texas Guinan's place. Mary Louise Cecilia Guinan was a former vaudeville and movie star who had reinvented herself as a nightclub manager. Texas-born, which explained her nickname, she had appeared in *The Gun Woman*, *Code of the West*, *The Wildcat*, and dozens of other westerns.

When bootlegger Larry Fay opened the El Fey earlier that year, he hired Guinan to recruit musicians and dancers, emcee the floor shows, and welcome customers with her cheeky trademark greeting. A "formidable woman," was the verdict of critic and journalist Edmund Wilson, "with her pearls, her prodigious glittering bosom, her abundant and beautifully bleached yellow coiffure, her bear-trap of shining white teeth." A saucy Mae West prototype, she presided over her domain, mused one journalist who dropped by, "like a gorgeous tamer who had just let herself into a large cage of pet tigers."

As many as two hundred could be packed into the club's narrow, smoke-filled room, but no more than a half dozen couples could sardine onto the tiny patch of dance floor. A jazz band and Guinan's outsized personality attracted the likes of actor Al Jolson, boxer Jack Dempsey and, on this night, a future king of England. Guinan, ever the cheeky self-promoter, would later boast to audiences that she had once hosted the world's most famous prince, "a little fellow who never had a backyard or a dirty face."

The prince had convinced a few of his companions to join Gibson on the lark. Their destination was Broadway. The White Light Belt, New Yorkers called it, or simply the Big Street. The grid of avenues and cross streets of the theater district—an area known as the Roaring Forties, with the El Fey at its epicenter—was jammed with restaurants, nightclubs, and cabarets. This was where "society, the stage, the movies and the wealth and the fashion of the town go," noted the *Daily News*, "in the hours when the gay set is at its best." Alcohol flowed as if Prohibition had never become the law of the land. To stymie the federal agents who conducted periodic raids, the El Fey stashed its liquor in the building next door, passing bottles into the club as needed through a hole in the wall that could be concealed with a loose brick.

The El Fey was known for the young, scantily clad dancers who performed and, between numbers, mingled with the men in the audience. "It was a bacchanalian feast, a Roman orgy, a politician's clambake, all rolled into one," recalled one of Guinan's friends, the theater producer and publicist Nils T. Granlund. A newspaper illustrator would later imagine the prince and Gibson seated at a table and offering toasts to a lineup of bob-haired showgirls in low-cut outfits, one of them wearing a top hat presumably plucked from the royal head. The caption: "Princely Fun."

At the El Fey and other stops, Dr. Gibson would recall, the prince's companions referred to him as Mr. Windsor, "a high-ranking member of the British diplomatic corps." The subterfuge suited the prince's guide. He wasn't a doctor, and his name wasn't Gibson.

Broadway in the 1920s (Author Collection)

They hopped from the El Fey to what Gibson billed as "a swell spot" on East Fifty-Ninth Street. The Club Deauville's "atmosphere of mystery," press reports noted, attracted "many socially prominent New Yorkers." Members of the house orchestra, Clark's Hawaiians, navigated between tables as they took requests and played music from the islands. It was a slow night, with only a few tables occupied and the occasional couple fox-trotting around the dance floor. Someone offered the prince a lei, which he draped around his neck. He praised the fine tenor voice of one of the singers, then asked the band to play his favorite Hawaiian song, a chart-topping hit that year called "Aloha 'Oe" ("Farewell to Thee"). Gibson grabbed a seat beside the prince, and they chatted, about nothing in particular—Broadway shows, popular tunes of the day, how Prohibition made it so hard to find decent liquor, even in fun-loving, booze-soaked New York. Gibson helped himself to champagne but noticed that the prince drank little. A third stop was the Florida Club, on West Fifty-Fifth Street, where a piano was set up in the middle of the room and the group took in a musical review.

The two men hit it off. The prince struck Gibson as "a real fellow. A real sport." They were almost the same age. Both were unmarried, and both had served in the war—Gibson as a medic in the US Army, the prince as an officer in the Grenadier Guards, who toured front-line trenches to boost morale. Gibson's posh accent masked his working-class roots in Worcester, Massachusetts. He seemed to know everyone who mattered, dropping names of the rich and famous with ease. His wit, charm, and flawless manners were those of a well-educated, well-bred member of a family that was wealthy and important. And in a tux—the work clothes of his trade—he looked the part, too. For a nighttime foray like the one to the Cosden estate, Gibson "dressed faultlessly in evening clothes," his future wife, Anna Blake, would note. "He always looked handsome in them."

Gibson said his goodbyes around half past five, barely an hour before sunrise, hailed a taxi, and returned to his Manhattan apartment. The prince and his companions piled into their car for the thirty-five-mile trek back to the Burden estate.

The royal tour of Manhattan's nightlife was soon the talk of the city. The borrowed car was spotted near Texas Guinan's, on a street off Broadway. A suspicious journalist traced the plates and discovered it belonged to the prince's host. "He went in disguise to one of the white light jazz palaces on Broadway," noted one account. "Nothing could prevent his instinct for fun bringing him into close view of the twinkling lights and engaging characters of New York's night life."

A KING-IN-WAITING HAD managed to enjoy a few fleeting hours of freedom by pretending to be Mr. Windsor. He never suspected that his guide had been playing a part as well.

Gibson had not been on the guest list for the Cosdens' party. Before meeting the prince that night, he had parked his red Cadillac coupe on a secluded lane at the edge of the estate, bypassing the fieldstone gatehouse at the entrance to The Cedars. He crouched in the shrubbery in his tux until he saw an opening, then emerged—"as spick and span in my dress clothes as any guest," he later boasted—to mingle with people chatting and drinking nearby on a brick terrace. As a waiter passed, he scooped up a cocktail and joined the conversation.

He soon slipped into the darkness and wandered alongside the mansion until he found a secluded spot. He climbed a rose trellis to the roof of a porch. Above him was a second-floor window, left open on the warm summer night. Grasping the ledge, he hoisted himself inside.

He pulled on a pair of white silk gloves, ensuring that he left no fingerprints, and crept from bedroom to bedroom. He checked the tops of dressing tables and quietly slid open bureau drawers. He could hear muffled voices and music from the party below. If anyone came upstairs and spotted him in the hallway, he knew what to do—he would pretend to be lost or drunk, or claim he was looking for the bathroom.

He could find no jewelry worth taking. The fortune in gems he had come for was either locked away or on display downstairs. He returned to the open window and was about to climb out when he realized a few guests had gathered under the porch while he was inside. A waiter was refreshing their glasses, and they appeared to be in no hurry to move along. There was only one other way out. He followed the hallway to the main staircase and descended into the heart of the party. When a young woman coming up the stairs smiled at him as they passed, he was certain he looked like any other guest.

Gibson's real name was Arthur Barry, and he was one of the most brazen and successful jewel thieves in history. He was a bold impostor, a charming con artist, and a master cat burglar rolled into one. During the Roaring Twenties, with the posh estates of Long Island and New York's Westchester County as his hunting grounds, he swiped diamonds, pearls, rubies, emeralds, and other glittering gems worth almost $60 million today. His victims included a Rockefeller, bankers and industrialists, Wall

Street bigwigs, and an heiress to the Woolworth five-and-dime store fortune. A skilled "second-story man," Barry could slip in and out of bedrooms undetected, sometimes as the occupants were sleeping inches away, oblivious to his presence. He hobnobbed with celebrities and millionaires as he cased their mansions and planned some of the most audacious and lucrative jewel heists of the Jazz Age. He outfoxed investigators, eluded the posse of police and private detectives trying to hunt him down, and staged a spectacular prison break to reunite with the woman he loved. He was touted in the press as a "Prince of Thieves" and an "Aristocrat of Crime." *Life* magazine would proclaim him "the greatest jewel thief who ever lived."

Barry smoothed his hair into place, straightened his bow tie, and headed for the punch bowl to launch his night on the town with the prince. He now knew the upstairs layout of the Cosden mansion. He would be back.

1

"A GRAND LIFE"

~~~~~

ONE

THE COURIER

Worcester, Massachusetts • 1896–1913

T HE TEENAGER WAS traveling alone on a southbound train that rattled and clanged toward New Haven. A cap shielded his eyes, and
a large black suitcase was clamped between his knees. Arthur Barry
was big for a thirteen-year-old. He had an athlete's thick build and stood
almost five foot eight, the height he would be for the rest of his life. Other
passengers who had climbed aboard at the station in the factory town of
Worcester, Massachusetts, likely thought he was on his way to college.
None could have guessed what was in the suitcase he seemed to be guarding with his life.

The case and its contents belonged to Lowell Jack, a retired
safecracker—a peteman or yeggman, in the slang of the day—who was
reputed to be one of the best. He had robbed businesses and banks all over
New England, drilling holes in the doors of safes and gingerly pouring
in enough nitroglycerin to blow them open. He was "of the dangerous
class," noted a newspaper account that lumped him in with a select group
of notorious thieves, all named after their hometowns—Portland Fatty,
Pawtucket Johnnie, Philadelphia Slim—and "all having prison records."
Jack's most dangerous days, however, were behind him. He was too old to
break into buildings and blow up safes, let alone to scamper away with the

loot. His retirement pastime was supplying nitroglycerin to a new generation of yeggmen.

The "soup," as the safecrackers called it, was simple to make. Jack heated dynamite in a bucket of water on a kitchen stove, extracting the nitro as an oily yellow-tinted liquid that flowed like ink. It was a risky business. If the water reached too high a temperature, the nitroglycerin could explode. And in liquid form, nitro was extremely volatile. If it was shaken or bumped, or its container was dropped, the explosion would be deadly. Jack carefully poured the nitro into a thick-walled glass bottle, then nestled it in a suitcase stuffed with cotton. It was enough padding, he reckoned, to absorb any shocks or jolts.

Delivering his product to safecrackers across New England and beyond was the next challenge. He needed a reliable courier, someone railroad conductors, ticket agents, and nosy policemen would never suspect was carrying high explosives. Someone like Arthur Barry.

He had met the youth several times. Arthur had a part-time job delivering coffee and sandwiches for a restaurant and had brought food to Jack's apartment turned bomb factory.

"Son," he said to him at some point in 1910, "how would you like to make five dollars?" That would be almost fifty dollars today. Jack explained that he needed a package delivered to a customer in New Haven. All Arthur had to do was to take it there by train.

He handed the suitcase to his new employee.

"Don't drop it. In fact, don't shake it too much," he cautioned. "And try not to bump into anybody on the train."

———

ARTHUR'S HOMETOWN WAS one of New England's industrial powerhouses. Located fifty miles due west of Boston, Worcester at the dawn of the twentieth century was the second-largest city in Massachusetts and close enough to the state's geographical center to be the self-proclaimed Heart of the Commonwealth. Worcesterites had been in the thick of things since the Revolutionary era. A young John Adams, the future president, taught school there in the 1750s and discovered a town "immersed in politics" and primed for the impending rupture with Britain. The Declaration of Independence was read in public for the first time in New England from the steps of one of its churches. In 1854, when a man who had escaped enslavement was arrested in Boston and faced extradition to the South, almost one thousand people from the Worcester area converged on the city to protest, giving the abolitionist movement a shot in the arm. And a canal to the sea and a railway link to Boston put Worcester at the vanguard of New England's nineteenth-century industrial revolution. The population, approaching 100,000 when Arthur was born, would balloon to almost 150,000 by the time he reached his teens.

Worcester, Massachusetts, in the early 1900s (Worcester Historical Museum Collection)

The downtown core was nestled in a serpentine valley, but the streets and tenements of new neighborhoods spilled onto the slopes of surrounding hills like a relentless tide rising against a shoreline. The newcomers were a hodgepodge of nationalities: Poles, Scots, Germans, and Swedes; Italians and other immigrants from the Mediterranean; French Canadians who had migrated south; Irish castoffs like the Barrys. They came for the factory jobs. Worcester's smoke-belching mills, tanneries, and foundries churned out everything from textiles and shoes to firearms and railcars. Washburn & Moen's sprawling works was the leading producer of wire, cable, and fencing in the United States. The Royal Worcester Corset Company boasted one of the largest female workforces in the country. Irish newcomers, most of them unskilled laborers, toiled "at the city's worst jobs," the historian Timothy Meagher noted in an account of Worcester's Irish community, supplying the muscle needed to keep the factories humming.

Arthur's father had been born in Cork in the late 1850s. Thomas Barry's parents died before he reached the age of ten, and he emigrated to America as a youth. When he married in the fall of 1880 at twenty-three, he was living in Worcester and working as a plumber. His bride, Bridget Walsh, an Irish-born servant, was twenty. They posed for a studio photograph about that time. Thomas, square-jawed, walrus-mustached, and uncomfortable as he sat in his Sunday-best suit, stared down the camera as if it were an intruder. Bridget stood at his side in a flowing dress with frilled collar and cuffs, her pinned-back dark hair revealing her delicate features; she seemed more at ease as she rested her right hand reassuringly on his shoulder.

By 1890, the Barrys had four children and were living in an apartment block at 81 Ward Street in the Vernon Hill neighborhood on the city's east side—"the poor, workaday part of Worcester," as a journalist later described it. Thomas now worked as a laborer at Bowler Brothers, brewers of Matchless Porter and Extra Seneca Lager. Arthur, born on December 10, 1896, was the sixth of the couple's nine surviving children—four others died in infancy.

Each Sunday, the Barrys attended Sacred Heart on Cambridge Street, a cathedral-like church with a spectacular arched stained-glass window dominating a facade of red brick trimmed in white stone. When he was old enough, Arthur served as an altar boy. He filled cruets with wine, then pulled on a starched white linen surplice over his black cassock so he was ready to assist the priest during Mass. One of his tasks, he remembered, was ringing "the sweet-toned bell" that signaled each stage of the Communion rites. He later sang in the choir. For a time, his father and mother hoped he might enter the priesthood. The calling attracted so many of Worcester's young Catholics that the local diocese could not find parishes for them all. Not Arthur. "I didn't take to the idea," is how he put it.

His first school was Millbury Street Schoolhouse No. 4, a brick-walled, slate-roofed hulk that dwarfed its young occupants. Built to accommodate the children of Worcester's growing workforce, it had opened its doors only a few years before Arthur began making the five-minute walk down Ward Street to his classes.

Thomas and Bridget Barry and their children. Arthur is on the right, beside his mother (Mary Schumacher)

Sometime before 1905, Thomas Barry changed employers. He was taken on as a laborer at Worcester Brewing Corporation, a smaller operation, where he would be eventually promoted to foreman. He moved his family as well, into a newly built tenement around the corner. The building at 32

Perry Avenue was one of the city's many "three-deckers"—large wood-frame structures that were common in New England's industrial cities, with three full floors and more space for the growing Barry clan. In Worcester, the tenements were built on narrow lots, but they extended well back from the street, creating a flat with a large living area on each floor. Row after row of them straddled the hillside, and peeling paint combined with shoebox-shape monotony to create an eyesore. The image-conscious Worcester Board of Trade dismissed the buildings as an "architectural monstrosity" and "a blot on any landscape."

In the early twentieth century, however, Vernon Hill was a good place to raise children, recalled the playwright, screenwriter, and journalist Samuel Behrman, who was about Arthur's age and grew up in a three-decker a half mile from the Barry home. With kids everywhere, and two other families living in each building, it was easy to find playmates. There were apples, pears, and cherries to be picked from backyard trees. Each tier had balconies—residents called them "piazzas"—front and back. "The contemplative and withdrawn could sit on the back piazzas and look at the fruit trees," Behrman noted, "the urban and worldly could sit on the front piazzas and survey the passing scene." Arthur was no doubt one of the kids drawn to a front balcony.

The Barrys were "a fine and close-knit family," Arthur recalled. His parents were "firm but fair" as they meted out discipline, and his father's take-home pay was "low but adequate." His father drank—Arthur later described him as "moderately alcoholic"—but there was "no more than the usual amount of friction" within the family. One household rule stuck with him: never tell a lie. "We knew we'd be punished far more for lying than for telling the truth, no matter what the truth was," he told an interviewer. Not once, he claimed, had he ever lied to his parents. This, of course, was a lie.

———————

IT'S NOT CLEAR how many suitcases Arthur delivered for Lowell Jack before he realized he was carrying bombs—and hair-trigger ones at that. He "enjoyed the intrigue," he recalled, and had sensed from the start that "the transaction was outside the law." Jack began sending him farther afield—to Boston; into New York State to supply customers in Albany, Syracuse, and Rochester; and as far west as Cleveland. It was, Arthur recalled, "a grand life." On the days he was traveling, his parents assumed he was in school. When longer trips required overnight stays, he lied and assured them he was spending the night at a friend's house.

Soon, Arthur was being hauled before judges for minor offenses. In September 1910, about the time he became a courier for Lowell Jack and three months before he turned fourteen, two patrolmen caught him smashing the globes of electric streetlamps—"amusing himself by putting the lights out of commission," as the arresting officers put it. He was convicted of vandalism, fined three dollars, and written up in the *Worcester Daily Telegram*. A few weeks later, he paid another three-dollar fine for discharging a firearm; the type of gun, how he obtained it, and where he fired it are a mystery. In April 1912 he was again convicted of discharging a firearm, and this time, as a repeat offender, the fine was bumped up to seven dollars. Worcester police considered him "a pretty bad boy."

Arthur would one day attribute his early descent into a life of crime—his "downfall," as he called it—to his size as a youth. He was bigger, and looked years older, than friends and classmates his age. He preferred the company of older teenagers and adults. He started drinking beer and wine at age seven and smoking at fifteen. At sixteen, he was gambling—"excessively," he later admitted—on card games and dice rolls. Running nitro for Lowell Jack brought him into contact with plenty of shady characters. And in Irish enclaves such as Arthur's Vernon Hill neighborhood, observed Timothy Meagher, "crime flourished." The Worcester Police Department had added thirty officers to its roster of ninety patrolmen during the 1890s to meet "an urgent demand . . . for increased police protection," noted an account of the force's history. Vernon Hill backed onto Union Hill, an area that was a "byword," wrote one historian, "for poverty, disorder, fights, and youth gangs," and the *Worcester Spy* condemned its back lanes as "lurking corners for filth and vice." Another city newspaper described the nearby Oak Hill neighborhood as a "hot-bed of drunkenness and rum-fights."

Sometime that year, Arthur shadowed a middle-aged couple who owned a dry goods store and memorized their routine: Each evening, he noted, they closed the store and took home the day's earnings. The money would be deposited the next day, when the banks reopened. Several times, while they were at work, he entered their empty house through an unlocked window. He moved from room to room, getting a feel for the layout as he hunted for the hiding place where the cash was kept overnight. He opened a desk drawer and was sure he detected the faint odor of well-handled paper money. He returned that night, entered through the same unlocked window, grabbed a stack of banknotes from the drawer, and slipped back out through the window. His take was about one hundred dollars, a small fortune for a teenager. He could order a roast turkey dinner at a restaurant for thirty-five cents; a decent watch would set him back less than five dollars. His haul was the equivalent of almost $3,000 today. "I wish I could remember," he would wonder aloud years later, "how I actually got up the nerve to enter a house and take property."

His patience and dry runs had paid off. And after carrying around enough high explosives to blow him sky-high, breaking into a house—even one that was occupied—seemed easy. If he had made a noise and roused the homeowners, he was confident he could have escaped. "If they had awakened, the advantage would have been all mine," he explained as he remembered that night. "I was wide awake, they were groggy. I knew what was behind every door as well as they did. I could have been halfway down the block before they got organized."

He had pulled off his first burglary. The job had been so meticulously planned and carefully executed, one journalist later noted with admiration, it was as if he had been "preparing to steal the British Crown Jewels." He was fifteen.

His parents, unable to control him or keep him out of trouble, took a drastic step in the summer of 1913. They went to court and had him declared a "stubborn child" under a Massachusetts law that allowed the courts to intervene to help parents unable to cope with a disobedient and unruly teenager. It was a polite way of saying he was a juvenile delinquent. Arthur could have been sent to a reformatory but instead was released on probation, on the condition that he behave and remain in the care and custody of his father and mother.

Arthur ignored the close call. A few weeks later, a frantic Bridget Barry contacted the Worcester police to report that Arthur had locked her out of the family home. A patrolman was sent to arrest him for breaching the terms of his probation. When Arthur struggled with the officer and tried to run away, he was handcuffed. A search of his pockets turned up packs of cigarettes stolen from a tobacco store the previous night. The arrest and scuffle made the front page of the *Worcester Evening Gazette*. He was charged, along with two other youths, with breaking into the store and stealing the cigarettes. The case went to trial in juvenile court, but the local papers do not appear to have reported the outcome. In June 1914, Arthur failed to appear before a Worcester judge to answer to a charge of breaking and entering.

A bad boy had found his calling.

~~~~~~~~~~~

BEFORE DISPATCHING ARTHUR on one of his nitro deliveries, Lowell Jack took him aside. The teenager who no longer listened to his parents would never forget the advice he was offered, crook to crook.

"Always be courteous, my boy, particularly to the police," he told his protégé. "Be gentlemanly and be sincere. It will save you countless inconveniences, and maybe a few trips to the clink."

Arthur would become a gentlemanly thief. But it would be years before he heeded Jack's advice and learned how to deal with the police. And how to stay out of jail.

TWO

A "BIG-TIMER"

Massachusetts and Connecticut • 1914–17

RTHUR BOLTED FROM the railyard and ran until he reached an intersection. A thick fog shrouded the empty streets, making it hard to tell if the cops were still after him. It was an hour before dawn and he was in Pittsfield, Massachusetts, a city of more than thirty thousand nestled among the Berkshires and only a few miles from the New York State border. He was a hundred miles from home.

He was on his way back to Worcester from Cleveland on that August morning in 1914, after delivering a batch of Lowell Jack's nitroglycerin. Short of money, he had decided to ride "blind baggage"—hop a freight—for the trip home. When the Boston and Albany Railroad train stopped in Pittsfield to pick up mail, Arthur climbed down from his perch between two boxcars to stretch his legs. Then he heard shouts.

A police officer and a railroad worker were running toward him. Arthur raced through the railyard, zigzagging between boxcars to give them the slip. When he reached an adjacent street, he stopped at the intersection to catch his breath. On the opposite corner, another policeman materialized from the fog. Arthur turned and ran as patrolman John Sullivan pulled his revolver and fired a warning shot into the air.

Arthur kept running, turning onto side streets and ducking into dark alleys. He struggled to keep his footing as he scrambled over the Pittsfield

Electric Company's coal pile. He turned down an alley and came face-to-face with another officer, John O'Connor, who had heard the gunshot and joined the chase.

Arthur heaved himself over a fence and dropped into the backyard of a house as O'Connor squeezed off two more warning shots. Within moments, Sullivan had Arthur cornered in the yard. He pointed his revolver at Arthur's chest.

"The next one," he warned, "will be to kill." Arthur, panting and dripping with sweat, surrendered.

Sullivan and O'Connor marched him to police headquarters, an aging and forbidding building with dungeon-like, iron-barred windows. It was barely a block away. Arthur, in Pittsfield for the first time, had been running toward the station house. He sat for hours on a bench, awaiting the arrival of another officer, who was investigating a break-in at a clothing store near the railyard. Arthur matched the description of a man seen fleeing the scene. He had not been hunted down and arrested at gunpoint for riding a freight train. He was a suspect in a burglary.

~~~~~~~~~~~

LESS THAN AN hour earlier, at about four o'clock, officer Charles Barry had been walking his beat when he spotted a figure on a ladder at the back of Brown's drugstore. A man was trying to open an upper-story window. As the patrolman approached, he stepped on a board that creaked under his weight, betraying his presence. The man jumped from the ladder and fled into the railyard.

Officer Barry alerted other patrolmen and gave them a description of the suspect. Sullivan and O'Connor searched the railyard and the surrounding streets. Peering through the fog, Sullivan spotted two men walking down the tracks, one of them carrying a suitcase. They split up when they heard the officer approaching, and Sullivan searched for them among the boxcars and behind buildings on the nearby streets. Then he saw a young man standing on a street corner. Arthur matched the description of the burglar. The chase was on.

Back on West Street, Officer Barry discovered that someone had smashed a window and entered the Boston Bargain Store, steps from where he had seen the man on the ladder. An expensive suit, a pair of shoes, a suitcase, and a watch were missing, worth a total of almost $500 today. The burglar had changed into the stolen clothing, leaving behind an old suit and shoes.

Officer Barry returned to the police station. Despite the fog and the darkness, he was certain Arthur was the man he had seen on the ladder. Arthur admitted he had been in the railyard but insisted he knew nothing about the break-in. And he was not wearing or carrying any of the stolen items. Sullivan's sighting of the men on the railroad tracks, however, suggested that an accomplice, who was still at large, had made off with the stolen goods and the suitcase. Arthur was charged with breaking and entering and larceny.

Later that morning, on a day that German troops poured into Belgium as the Great War began and the first ship navigated the Panama Canal, Arthur appeared in court. He stood in the prisoner's dock in the Berkshire County Courthouse—an austere pile of local white marble with just enough Italianate flourishes to give it style as well as gravitas—and pleaded not guilty. A reporter for the local paper sized up Arthur and guessed he was twenty-five; he was just seventeen. Asked to identify himself, Arthur said he was Frank J. Walsh from Boston. District Court Judge Charles Hibbard delayed the proceedings, to give the police a few days to establish whether he had a criminal record. To ensure that the suspect remained in custody, the judge set bail at an impossibly high figure—$500, or more than $13,000 today.

That night was the first Arthur spent behind bars, in a six-by-ten-foot cell at the Pittsfield Jail, a sprawling brick-walled relic of the Civil War era. If he stretched out his arms, his fingertips would touch the wall on either side of the spartan cell. He would be locked up for ten days as he awaited trial.

The Pittsfield police contacted the authorities in Boston and discovered there was no record of a Frank J. Walsh. He finally provided his real name and home address. He also admitted being prosecuted in Worcester as a stubborn child.

Despite being caught in a lie, Arthur insisted he was innocent. And the case against him was weak. The stolen watch was found on the route he had taken as he fled from Officer Sullivan, but there was no evidence he had discarded it. It was his word against the sworn testimony of Officer Barry.

The patrolman was convinced Arthur was the man he had seen on the ladder, and this was all the evidence Judge Hibbard needed to convict him of attempted breaking and entering. A journalist, likely the one who had been wrong about Arthur's age, noted he was "of good appearance" and "neatly dressed" as he appealed to the judge for leniency—echoes of the dapper man who would one day fool millionaires and royalty. The judge, however, said Arthur's attempts to mislead the authorities ruled out a light sentence. And the youth appeared to have lost the support of his family. While his father had been notified of his arrest, he had not shown up. Arthur offered an explanation: his father was in poor health—"a rheumatic cripple," he said—and unable to travel to Pittsfield for the hearing.

The judge imposed the maximum sentence—up to five years in the Massachusetts Reformatory. The harsh penalty, Pittsfield's *Berkshire Eagle* newspaper would later note, "marked the end of his amateur days and his debut as a 'big-timer.'"

Arthur was telling the truth. The store had been broken into before his train had stopped in Pittsfield. One of the most accomplished burglars in history had been wrongly convicted of the very crime that would make him famous.

ARTHUR WAS IN handcuffs when he arrived at the reformatory. The massive building, about twenty miles west of Boston, in Concord, looked like an architect's attempt to graft a chapel onto a military barracks. An eight-sided central rotunda, topped with a tower, loomed over the outstretched, high-windowed wings that housed tiers of cells. Once inside, newcomers were processed with assembly-line efficiency. Arthur's height and weight were recorded. He signed a form authorizing staff to open his mail. He handed over his pocket money, to be returned upon his release. His hair was cut short—"ruthlessly shorn away," as one prisoner put it. He pulled on

a prison-issue uniform. His mug shot was snapped, and his Bertillon measurements were recorded—the width of his head, the length of his middle
finger, his left foot, and other body parts—to identify him if he broke the
law again. Fingerprints were being hailed as the criminal identification
system of the future, and his were likely inked for the reformatory's files.
His brick-walled cell, with an iron-grate door, was barely large enough for
a bed, wash basin, toilet, and a small table and chair.

The Massachusetts Reformatory, Concord (Author Collection)

The Concord Reformatory, as it was known, had opened almost four
decades earlier as an alternative to the state prison for youths, men convicted of minor crimes, and first-time offenders. "Correction of waitward-
ness and education along lines adapted to the boy's special needs and
capabilities must be always kept in mind," one writer said of the institution. "They are there to learn, rather than to be punished." And they were
there, explained one Massachusetts juvenile court judge who sent his share
of young offenders to Concord, because "the influence of the home, the
school and the church has been a failure." The reformatory was seen as the
last chance to save wayward youths from a life of crime.

Arthur settled into a regimented routine of work, training, and instruc-
tion. A bell—"the hated bell," one inmate called it—jarred him awake every

weekday at half past six. The reformatory's workshops turned out shoes, clothing, and furniture for hospitals and other public buildings. Inmates could learn an array of trades, from printing and engraving to bricklaying, carpentry, and plumbing. They farmed the surrounding fields to put vegetables on the dining hall's tables.

At the end of the workday, however, the reformatory resembled a boarding school with locked doors. Inmates attended evening classes—a "school of letters," the staff called it—to upgrade their education. They were encouraged to borrow books from the library's six-thousand-volume collection, which featured inspiring works about "men who have fought the battles of life," noted chaplain Robert Walker, "and won." Guest speakers turned up to lecture on an array of subjects—beekeeping, coal mining, hiking in Norway, life in faraway Siberia. Dozens of inmates joined societies that met twice a month to discuss such weighty matters as ethics, literature, and temperance. Staff and prisoners collaborated to produce a sixteen-page weekly newspaper, featuring poems and stories written by inmates and a column of "News from the Outside World." Sports and military-style drills promoted fitness and instilled discipline.

A darker, grittier reality, however, lurked below the surface. Some Concord inmates were beyond redemption and took "pride in their criminal tendencies," noted one state legislator, and "will corrupt others if they can." The facility held about seven hundred inmates while Arthur was incarcerated there, ranging in age from fifteen to thirty-six. Most, like him, were serving time for burglary or theft, but a handful had been convicted of assault, robbery, sexual offenses, or arson, and nothing was done to separate the young and impressionable from the streetwise and incorrigible.

A politician who toured the facility was outraged to discover "a boy in short trousers in the company of habitual criminals." And this core of hardened crooks often scuttled the rehabilitation efforts underway in the workshops and the classrooms. The reformatory, in one newspaper's opinion, was little more than "a school for the education of criminals." Former prisoners who landed back in court for new crimes were described in the press as Concord "graduates." One teenager assured a judge that inmates devoted "most of their leisure time to planning criminal work to be done when released." If Arthur wanted to learn how to be a better burglar and thief, Concord offered plenty of teachers.

———————

HE WAS ELIGIBLE for release on parole in March 1915, after serving seven months. Inmates who behaved, followed the rules, and learned a trade or furthered their education could earn their freedom. Arthur was summoned for an interview. His work history and conduct while in custody were assessed, including whether he had borrowed books from the library and attended religious services on Sundays. The parole board refused to release offenders who did not have a job, a place to live, and someone to supervise them. "A man coming out of prison in good times or bad," warned one parole board member, "will quickly be open to severe temptations of the underworld when he cannot get a job at once."

Arthur's parents had visited him at Concord—he assured them he was innocent of the Pittsfield burglary—and confirmed he could live with them. One of his brothers, who ran a liquor business, agreed to hire him to do clerical work. Somehow, amid his brushes with the law and his time behind bars, Arthur had earned a high school diploma. Parole was granted.

He stayed out of jail for a year and a half. His only run-in with the police in 1915 was a ten-dollar fine for drunkenness. A car accident that fall put him back in the local papers. He was walking with a girlfriend after dark when a driver, blinded by the headlights of an oncoming vehicle, swerved to the side of the street and struck them. The driver bundled them into his car and sped to the home of a doctor; they were both badly bruised but suffered no broken bones.

Arthur was arrested in September 1916, for violating the conditions of his parole. Details of his latest infraction were not reported in the press, and he never discussed his time in the reformatory. He was sent back to Concord to resume serving his five-year term. He was about to turn twenty. If he served his full sentence, he would be twenty-four by the time he was released in early 1921.

The war raging in Europe appears to have been his ticket to freedom.

By 1916, all Concord inmates were required to take part in military drills, possibly in preparation for the day the United States might be drawn into the war. "We do not attempt to make soldiers," chaplain Robert Walker explained, "but we are making fine examples of physical, mental and moral manhood." The chaplain was impressed by "the spirit of patriotism" among the inmates. "They have heard the call of youth to the defense of humanity," he noted, "and are eagerly awaiting the opportunity to respond in service, military or industrial, as occasion shall demand, upon their release."

Barry worked at the Remington Arms factory in Bridgeport, Connecticut
(Library of Congress Prints and Photographs Division)

After the United States declared war on Germany in April 1917, Arthur was among Concord's fine examples of manhood eager to do their part. By June 1917, nine months after his return to the reformatory, he was again free on parole. He was hired by the Remington Arms-Union Metallic Cartridge Company in Bridgeport, Connecticut, a major producer of rifles, handguns, ammunition, and bayonets for the US Army and for Britain, Russia, and other allies. He was assigned to the drop forge department, where machines hammered red-hot ingots into shape. Workers, as a visitor who toured the plant that summer noted, seemed oblivious to the "terrific heat" from the furnaces and molten metal.

Arthur's job was to inspect the components produced, looking for flaws. A defective firearm or round of ammunition could maim or kill the user, and the company employed an inspection staff of several hundred. By 1917, the vast complex, with a million square feet of production area and a work-force of almost twenty thousand, was producing five thousand rifles for the Russian army—and millions of cartridges—every day. The company paid high wages and introduced an eight-hour workday to retain employees and reduce the risk that strikes would disrupt production. Security was tight, to prevent sabotage; local militiamen stood guard, and Arthur flashed a small card bearing his employee number each time he entered and left the plant.

When Arthur registered for the draft on June 5, he noted on the registration form that he was helping to support his mother and his disabled father. And there was something else: He told the draft board he had been born in 1894, making him twenty-two instead of twenty. Providing his "true age and background," he later explained, would have revealed his criminal record in Massachusetts. While men convicted of minor offenses could be drafted or enlist, those convicted of burglary and other felonies were ineligible for military service. And Arthur was determined to get to the front as soon as he could.

THREE

FIRST-AID MAN

North Carolina and France • 1917–18

A LOOKOUT SPOTTED SOMETHING in the water. Could it be a periscope? The USS *Princess Matoika* had passed north of the Azores two days earlier, and the closer the ship steamed toward the French coast, the greater the risk of encountering a U-boat.

Alarms sounded. Crewmen rushed to the four gun batteries grafted onto the deck of the former passenger liner. Cannons thundered and belched smoke as a volley of six-inch shells hurtled toward the object. Explosions sent columns of water high into the air.

It was May 20, 1918, and Arthur Barry was in the midst of his first battle as a private in the United States Army. He was among the four thousand soldiers crammed onto the *Princess Matoika*, bound for the trenches of the Western Front. U-boats had forced the United States into the Great War—one had torpedoed and sunk the liner RMS *Lusitania* in 1915, killing more than 125 Americans. The final straw was Germany's declaration, at the outset of 1917, of open season on the ships of the United States and other neutral nations. The massive troopship, as Barry and everyone else on board knew, was a tempting target for any submarine lurking below. Crewmen and soldiers alike were ordered to sleep in their clothes. There had been an abandon-ship drill at the start of the voyage. If a torpedo struck, one of the sailors reckoned, they could get everyone into rafts and lifeboats and clear of the ship within five minutes.

The deck-shaking cannon blasts stopped after a few salvos. Only then was the enemy's true identity discovered. It was a bucket bobbing in the water.

~~~~~~~~~~~~

BARRY ENLISTED BARELY a month after registering for the draft. He traveled to New York and was processed at a recruiting station in Times Square on July 12, 1917. He did not tell his parents he was signing up and listed an older sister, Evelyn, as his next of kin. Recruits were subjected to a battery of written examinations—to gauge their knowledge of everything from grammar and spelling to arithmetic, geometry, and the structure of the US government—as well as psychological and aptitude tests. Barry's results pegged him for assignment to the medical corps as a "first-aid man," as medics were known in the Great War. He was dispatched to a base hospital for training, along with about three dozen other recruits. He practiced carrying injured men on stretchers. He learned how to prepare bandages and dress wounds. He inoculated long lineups of soldiers. There were lectures and examinations on anatomy and physiology.

Barry was assigned to the Forty-Seventh Infantry. Camp Greene, on a four-square-mile site on the outskirts of Charlotte, North Carolina, was chosen for the unit's training base. Buildings and roads were still under construction in the fall of 1917 as thousands of soldiers began arriving from New England and western states. The largest contingent was from Barry's home state. The camp was a sea of long, narrow barracks and cone-shaped tents perched on wooden platforms.

At some point, Private Barry dropped by a photographer's studio. For one image, he stood smartly at attention in his dress uniform, turning slightly to one side to show off the Red Cross insignia on his white armband. Brass disks stamped with the Medical Corps insignia—two snakes entwined around a winged staff—adorned his collar. For another shot, he faced the camera in a rumpled field uniform and puttee leggings, and had slipped off his brimless garrison cap to reveal a mop of dark hair parted in the center. "Barry possessed a wonderful personality," recalled a recruit

Barry in his army uniform (Tom Galliher/Findagrave.com)

from upstate New York who trained at Camp Greene and served with him overseas, "and was considered a hale fellow, well met."

The army established Camp Greene and other training sites in southern states, where the weather was mild and recruits could march and drill outside year-round. But the winter of 1917–18 would be the coldest in memory in many parts of the eastern United States, including the South. Frosts hit North Carolina in early October, an ominous herald of the punishing weather ahead. On one December day, thermometers in the state dipped to a record low of twenty-one below zero Fahrenheit. As 1918 began, "cold waves of increasing severity," a climatologist reported, "held the country in its icy grip."

Life was miserable for the recruits trapped in Camp Greene's tent city.

A succession of storms blasted North Carolina. Boots and wheels churned the camp's red-clay roads "into a sea of mud, which froze and thawed and froze again, to the continual discomfort of both officers and men," Second Lieutenant James Pollard recalled in an official history of the regiment. Outdoor training exercises were suspended for weeks, leaving only guard duty, work detail, and indoor lessons on bayonet fighting and handling rifles and machine guns to relieve the tedium. Much of the time, Barry and his comrades shivered in their eight-man tents. Swaths of the surrounding pine forest were chopped down for firewood. Tents caught fire, sending men scrambling into the cold night. "A modern sewage system," Pollard noted, "was lacking." Illnesses spread, and the men endured almost a month in quarantine after an outbreak of spinal meningitis.

The cold, the monotony, and the strict rules—forgetting to shave meant five days on kitchen duty—chipped away at morale. The YMCA fought back, entertaining the troops with vaudeville performances and publishing a camp newspaper filled with articles on recruitment drives and other matters of interest to "army men and their home folks." But when leaves were granted for forays into Charlotte, one diversion was not on offer. The city was "full of soldiers," a visitor scribbled on a postcard home in the spring of 1918, but there was "no liquor sold"—a statewide ban on alcohol had been in effect for a decade.

By the time field training resumed in March, the regiment was only weeks away from being sent overseas as part of the army's Fourth Division. There was a last-minute scramble to finish the practice trenches and rifle range needed to prepare recruits and draftees for the battles ahead. By the time the Forty-Seventh boarded trains bound for New York at the end of April, Barry had endured Camp Greene's mud and misery for more than six months. And now the war was about to become real.

~~~~~~~~~~~~

MEN IN KHAKI uniforms filled the decks of the *Princess Matoika* as the sleek two-funneled ship steamed out of New York Harbor on the morning of May 11. Rain sputtered from a somber sky that was as gray and dull as the liner's camouflage paint. In an ironic twist, soldiers who would soon fight the Germans were traveling in a German-built vessel that had been seized in the Philippines when the United States entered the war. It now carried double its pre-war capacity of two thousand passengers.

The ship carrying the Forty-Seventh joined a convoy of thirteen transports and an escort, the cruiser USS *Frederick*. The threat of a submarine attack and the battle with the bucket had put everyone on edge. Fresh water was rationed, and the overwhelmed kitchen staff could serve only two meals a day. Rough weather midway through the voyage left many men too seasick to care about the dining schedule. "I never saw so much water in my whole life," exclaimed a crewman fresh from the wheat fields of Kansas.

A cavalry of nine Allied destroyers intercepted the convoy for the hazardous final approach to the French coast. On May 21, after a ten-day crossing, *Princess Matoika* and the other transports reached the port of Brest, near the western tip of Brittany.

Trains were waiting to whisk them across northern France. "They were all anxious to go to the front and get it over with," a sailor on Barry's ship assured his folks in a letter home. But the sight of Red Cross trains disgorging men homeward-bound with horrible wounds—some with missing arms or legs, some blinded—dampened the enthusiasm of the new arrivals. They saw the savagery and slaughter that lay ahead.

"Never before," noted a Pennsylvania newspaper not long after the United States entered the war, "have the means of dealing death been so numerous or so ingenious, or so terrible." High-explosive shells. Rapid-fire machine guns. Poison gas. Flamethrowers. Bomb-laden airplanes and zeppelins. The first lumbering tanks. Shrapnel—fragments from exploding artillery shells—felled far more soldiers than bullets and inflicted ghastly wounds; the jagged metal "rips, tears and lacerates the tissues," noted one military surgeon. An American who volunteered to drive Red Cross ambulances early in the war, Leslie Buswell, published a book in 1916 to expose "the futility, the utter damnable wickedness and butchery" of the war. He held nothing back. The muddy shell craters of No Man's Land, he reported, were littered with "hundreds of mangled forms . . . arms, legs, heads, scattered disjointedly everywhere . . . some half rotted, some newly dead, some still warm, some semi-alive, stranded between foe and friend." Barry's gruesome, dangerous job was to charge into this hell on earth, oblivious to bullets and shells, to find those still alive.

First-aid men were part of every offensive, tending to wounded men where they fell. A Red Cross armband alone announced their role on the battlefield; otherwise, their uniforms and helmets made them indistinguishable from their fellow soldiers. They carried iodine to clean wounds, and bandages to stop bleeding. This early intervention was crucial, reducing the risk of infection and increasing the chances that even badly wounded soldiers might survive long enough to be transported by ambulance to a field hospital, a safe distance from the front lines, for surgery and treatment. Stretcher bearers collected the wounded; if none were available, first-aid men slogged through the mud to carry or drag them to safety.

Before being sent to field hospitals, casualties were stabilized and assessed at dressing stations in ruined buildings or trench dugouts. "A gloomy cavern lighted by two lanterns," was how a *Washington Post* correspondent touring the American front lines described one of the stations. A medic inside had pointed to a rough bench and two boxes that served as chairs. The primitive setup, he'd told the journalist, was "our operating table." Tetanus shots were administered. Splints were fashioned for shattered limbs. Triage weeded out those beyond saving. The Medical Corps also tended to wounded Germans, but only when there were no more Allied soldiers to bandage and carry to safety. "Ours come first," noted one stretcher bearer. "Fritz must wait."

The courage of the first-aid men astonished a *Boston Globe* journalist covering the war. "It is one thing to go over the top in a company," he noted in a dispatch from France. "It is something else again to go quietly out into the hail of bullets and pick up or bandage where he lies, a wounded comrade." Since the skill and quick actions of the first-aid men could mean the difference between life and death, they were held in high esteem within their units. They were often "the most popular man in the platoon or company," noted one US Army report, and earned a good-natured nickname: Trench Rats.

Casualty rates for medical units were shockingly high. Medics and stretcher bearers were easy targets for enemy artillery, machine gunners,

A team of first-aid men tend to a casualty (Author Collection)

and pilots. One group of first-aid men trying to establish a dressing station near the front lines was pinned down for hours as shrapnel and poison-gas shells exploded around them. In another battle, an exploding shell killed two stretcher bearers and the soldier they were carrying. Private Charles Holt of Brooklyn watched in horror as German biplanes strafed a battlefield, killing wounded soldiers and the medics trying to save them. The first-aid men could do little to fight back. They were issued two weapons—a .38-caliber Colt automatic pistol and a bowie knife—useful only for close combat. While some of those targeted may have been mistaken for combatants, such attacks were touted in the American press as proof of German barbarity. "A Red Cross," huffed one soldier from Connecticut, "means nothing to most Huns."

BARRY AND HIS medical corps comrades faced their first test at the end of July. The Americans spearheaded an offensive that pushed deep into German-occupied French territory north of the Marne River. At the village of Sergy, the Forty-Seventh faced the Fourth Prussian Guards, one of the German army's crack units. The Americans were shelled and sprayed with machine-gun fire as they forded a river and stormed into the battered village on the morning of July 29. The Guards counterattacked, were swept back, and attacked again. Sergy changed hands as many as nine times. Savage fighting littered the ruined streets with dead and wounded.

German soldiers were seen bayoneting injured Americans left behind during one of the retreats. Enemy machine gunners and snipers fired on stretcher bearers, and a German flier dropped a bomb on a truckload of wounded Americans. The infuriated Yanks were just as ruthless, taking few prisoners when it was their turn to counterattack. "It was simply hell," reported the commanding officer of one of the Forty-Seventh Infantry's medical units. Two of his fourteen men died in the battle, and six more were wounded. "Medical officers and enlisted men," James Pollard recorded in his account of the battle, "were brave almost to the point of recklessness in establishing and maintaining first aid stations well within the hottest zone of enemy fire."

Barry was in the thick of the fighting. He crawled on his hands and knees to reach a soldier who had been shot in the chest and leg. Barry hoisted him onto his back and ran to the American lines; the soldier's leg had to be amputated, but he survived. Barry—"a soldier who always volunteered for hazardous duty," said one of his commanding officers—made a dozen forays onto the battlefield to administer first aid or to carry or drag wounded men to safety. Then a shell exploded nearby, and a chunk of shrapnel sliced into his lower leg. It was a minor wound, and no bones were broken, but he had to be carried to a dressing station behind the front lines for treatment. Impressed with his "extraordinary heroism in action," his superiors recommended him for the Distinguished Service Cross, the army's second-highest decoration for bravery. "Barry repeatedly crawled into areas swept by shell and machine-gun fire to administer first aid to wounded soldiers," read the official citation, and "disregarded his own safety."

He was patched up and able to rejoin his regiment within days. The Forty-Seventh kept up the pressure on the retreating Germans, pushing them ten miles beyond Sergy to the village of Saint-Thibaut on the River Vesle. The regiment again faced the Fourth Prussian Guards on August 8, when a barrage of shells unleashed mustard gas on the American lines. Barry was temporarily blinded, suffered serious burns to his body, and inhaled the caustic gas, searing the lining of his nose and throat. He was evacuated to a hospital at Nemours, south of Paris, where doctors inserted rubber tubing into his nose and mouth to allow the damaged tissue to heal. Every hour for a week, he recalled, he endured a painful ritual as nurses cleaned and applied fresh bandages to his burned, blistered skin, to prevent infection. Back home, his name appeared in newspaper listings of casualties under the alarming headline WOUNDED, DEGREE UNDETERMINED.

As he recovered, Barry became restless. One afternoon, he hopped aboard a train bound for Paris with another patient, a sergeant from his regiment. They immersed themselves in the city's nightlife. They took in risqué shows at the Folies-Bergère, strolled down the Champs-Élysées, sipped cognac in the cafés of Montparnasse. Ernest Hemingway, who would soon haunt the same cafés as he launched his writing career, was serving as an ambulance driver on the Italian front when he was riddled with bullet and shrapnel wounds, just a few weeks before Barry was wounded. For Hemingway, it was a turning point in his life. "When you go to war as a boy you have a great illusion of immortality. Other people get killed not you," he would one day write. "Then when you are badly wounded the first time you lose that illusion and you know it can happen to you." The Paris spree suggested that Barry, too, was determined to make the most of his second chance.

After a fortnight, with no money left, they hitchhiked back to the hospital and were charged with being absent without leave. Before a court-martial could be convened, however, Barry left the hospital without permission a second time and rejoined his regiment at the front. Military officials never prosecuted him for the unauthorized leaves, and none of his superiors raised an eyebrow when he returned to duty. The jaunt to Paris, however, likely cost him the Distinguished Service Cross. Since he was AWOL when the medal was bestowed on other recipients, his name was withdrawn from the list of candidates for the award. "Don't know why I never received it," he deadpanned when he was asked about the honor years later.

That fall, the Forty-Seventh joined the Meuse-Argonne offensive, a massive Allied push to end the war. Even with the Germans in retreat, American casualties were appalling—more than twenty-six thousand killed in action. Barry's regiment was fortunate to be held in reserve during many battles and was rotated to the front during lulls in the fighting. The unit was camped near the ruined village of Montsec and was preparing to go into battle the next day when word spread of the armistice. "The men were doubtful at first," regimental historian James Pollard recalled, but when the official announcement was made on November 11, "they yelled and cheered as only Americans can." The rumble of distant artillery duels ceased, replaced by songs and laughter as men gathered around flickering bonfires, grateful to be alive.

The regiment had suffered more than 2,600 casualties, including 473 who were killed in action or died of wounds or disease. Five of Barry's fellow first-aid men were dead, and he was among the more than twenty others who had been wounded. The Forty-Seventh's division, the Fourth, "came in mighty green from the states," noted the American war correspondent Georges Seldes, "and fought like the best of them."

Barry's war was over. But his days in uniform, he soon discovered, were not.

FOUR

THE LONG WATCH

Germany • 1918–19

RTHUR BARRY LAUNCHED his invasion of Germany on November 20, 1918, barely a week after the armistice. The men of his division, the Fourth, crossed scarred battlefields and camped in ruined buildings that, only days before, had housed enemy soldiers. They marched along rutted roads littered with helmets and wooden-handled grenades—"potato-mashers," Allied soldiers called them—discarded as the Germans hastily withdrew from French territory they had held since 1914. The men of the Forty-Seventh Infantry reached the Moselle River and entered Germany on December 3. The Eifel mountains, heavy packs, and wet, bone-chilling weather slowed their advance. They reached their destination—the area around Adenau, a town about forty miles west of the city of Koblenz, spelled Coblenz in those days—on December 15. They had marched 225 miles, the distance from New York City to Washington, DC.

The Forty-Seventh was among the first American units ordered to occupy the Rhineland. As negotiators hammered out a peace treaty in Paris, Allied armies established a beachhead inside Germany's western border and took control of three bridges that crossed the Rhine river, including the crossing at Coblenz. A quarter million US troops were sandwiched between a British occupation zone to the north and French forces stationed to the south. Barry was billeted in Dümpelfeld, a village of a few hundred. The Rhineland, untouched by the war, remained a fairy-tale land of postcard-perfect hamlets, terraced vineyards, and white-towered mountaintop castles. "It made a picture for tired eyes," admitted one Fourth Division soldier.

For Barry and other men fresh from the adrenaline rush of battle, however, what the press was calling the Watch on the Rhine would be mind-numbing, tedious duty. They policed towns and villages and kept their fellow soldiers in line. They guarded public buildings. They asked for passes at checkpoints. Barry picked up enough German and French to feel comfortable speaking in either language.

Commanders prescribed a regime of training exercises, target practice,

American soldiers gather in a German village during the occupation of the Rhineland (Author Collection)

and athletic events to keep the men busy—and battle-ready, in case the armistice did not hold. Leaves were granted to boost morale, and soldiers fanned out on jaunts to London, Paris, and the South of France. One American pilot, desperate for some excitement, ducked his plane under the soaring arches of a Rhine bridge just to see if he could pull off the stunt.

For the Fourth Division, isolation compounded the boredom. While most American units were based in Coblenz and other major centers along the Rhine, the Fourth was scattered over eight hundred square miles of sparsely populated hinterland. It became known as the Forgotten Fourth, the Hard Luck Division. "War is hell but I believe peace is worse," complained one member of the division's military police. "We'd rather watch on the Mississippi or some other American stream."

Soldiers were ordered not to fraternize with residents, except when transacting business, but these rules were impossible to fully enforce since many soldiers were billeted in the homes of German families. The restrictions made day-to-day life a bureaucratic nightmare. Buying a glass of beer was not fraternizing, an American journalist was relieved to discover, but tipping the waiter was. "No man in American uniform was to speak, let alone have other relations, with any German man or woman," recalled George Seldes, who reported from the Rhineland. The real goal was to deter soldiers who wanted to "promenade with the blonde fräulein," as Seldes delicately put it. But the rules did little to keep soldiers away from young German women who were willing to trade sex for chocolates or a bar of soap.

What Barry and his fellow Rhine watchers wanted most of all was not beer or sex. They wanted to go home. By early 1919, US soldiers were boarding troopships at the rate of three hundred thousand every month, including draftees never sent into battle and units shipped overseas long after Barry's regiment arrived in France. "Men in fighting men's uniforms who had not fired a shot," sniffed Seldes, echoing the outrage of many of those marooned in Germany. Allied leaders, however, needed to maintain their military presence along the Rhine, to pressure the Germans into signing a treaty to officially end the war. "As their armed forces demobilized," the historian Margaret MacMillan noted, "their power was shrinking."

American morale plummeted. The "growing spirit of dissatisfaction" within the occupying army shocked journalist Edwin James. "Now that Germany is licked," he reported in a dispatch from Coblenz, "the vast majority of them want to get out of the army." General John Pershing, commander of the American Expeditionary Force, heard the grumbling for himself when he inspected the occupying forces in mid-March. At stop after stop, once the troops had paraded past the reviewing stand, shouts of "When do we go home?" erupted before the general could begin his pep-talk speech. Pershing refused to offer false hope. Some of them, he warned, might still be in Germany in 1920.

The last unit to assemble for Pershing's inspection was, fittingly, Barry's hard-luck Forgotten Fourth. Some of its far-flung units had to march forty miles over three days to reach the parade grounds near Cochem, on the Moselle River. Snow was falling as they pitched pup tents in the nearby forest, and a storm blew in overnight. Huge bonfires blazed in the darkness to defend against the cold. More than ten thousand men donned full battle gear and began assembling at nine o'clock on the morning of March 18 on a field surrounded by snow-covered mountains. The men of the Forty-Seventh Infantry, among the first to take their places, stood for five hours as a biting wind mounted a relentless attack. The sun had broken through the clouds, offering some warmth, by the time Pershing arrived at two in the afternoon.

After the troops marched past in formation, the general praised their "magnificent appearance" and thanked them for serving their country. He was confident, he said, that they would "be ready for and equal to the tasks . . . peace would be sure to impose." He likely repeated a line he had used during earlier reviews, urging them to "uphold their fine, clean records as soldiers when they become civilians." This time, though, there were no shouts from the ranks, no demands to know when the division would be sent home. Instead, men who had been shivering in the cold for hours took off their helmets, as a sign of respect, and cheered for their commander. "They presented a brave spectacle," Seldes told his readers.

The Fourth Division received its long-awaited orders to ship out at the end of May 1919. "Everybody was in a fever of excitement," noted James Pollard, the Forty-Seventh Infantry's historian, "over the approach of the day for which they had been waiting so long." Training ceased, and the men handed in their weapons—only to have their hopes dashed. There were fears the German government would reject a peace treaty that, among its humiliating terms, required Germany to pay massive sums to compensate the victors. The Allies needed leverage.

The Fourth Division was rearmed as part of a new military buildup. Plans were drafted for a full-scale invasion of Germany and a march to Berlin. French prime minister Georges Clemenceau, with American and British backing, vowed to strike "a vigorous and unremitting military blow" to "force the signing." The threat worked; German delegates formally signed the pact at the Palace of Versailles on June 28. The Fourth Division was finally bound for home.

The soldiers of the Forty-Seventh jammed the decks of the USS *Mobile* on the evening of July 26, eager to see the Manhattan skyline as the ship nosed into New York Harbor. But the ship was flying a yellow flag, a warning of contagious disease. A crewman had developed smallpox early in the voyage. Everyone on board had to be inoculated and spend several days in quarantine, to make sure they had not been infected. The delay was a final blow for men eager to get out of the army and return home.

When Barry and his comrades disembarked at Hoboken, New Jersey, the *New-York Tribune* described the regiment as "the most upset aggregation of returning troops" to arrive from Europe since the armistice. Cheering crowds and blizzards of ticker tape had welcomed earlier shiploads of veterans as they marched down Fifth Avenue. Barry and his comrades had returned "at the tail end of the homeward exodus from France, when soldiers no longer attract much public attention," the *Tribune* noted. "All the jubilation over peace," added journalist George Seldes, "had been spent by the American people on the first arrivals."

Private Arthur Barry's "honest and faithful service" earned him an honorable discharge from the army on the first day of August. Barry had been a hero on the battlefield, risking his life to save his comrades. He had been wounded. His army record was unblemished, officially at least. But he had been in trouble with the law before the war and had served time behind bars. He may have wanted to follow General Pershing's advice to keep his record clean as a civilian, but as America began to hurtle at full throttle into the Roaring Twenties, he would find it impossible to change his dishonest ways.

2

THE LADDER BURGLAR

FIVE

SECOND-STORY MAN

Manhattan and Westchester County • 1919–22

T HE MEN IN the first waves of soldiers sent home from France claimed most of the jobs as well as all of the glory. Arthur Barry returned to Worcester in the fall of 1919 but could not find work. He had no trade and a criminal record. Few factories and businesses were hiring—government contracts for munitions and supplies were canceled after the armistice, throwing tens of thousands out of work. And many of the city's employers refused to hire Irish Catholics—preferring, as one put it, a workforce of "thrifty, industrious, capable and law-abiding" Swedes. He went back to New York City to look for a job, brushing off his mother's objections and misgivings. "Time and again I pleaded with him to stay home," Bridget Barry recalled. "I thought his service in France would satisfy his craving for adventure, but it did not."

Times were tough. Wartime shortages and profiteering had driven up the cost of food, clothing, and other necessities. "The cost of living horror," the *New York Herald* complained, was imposing an "insufferable burden which is crushing the American people." The price of milk, butter, and eggs had almost doubled since 1914. Landlords jacked up rents. At least five thousand demobilized servicemen were looking for work in New York in August 1919, the month Barry was discharged, and two thousand more were joining them every week. A cartoon published in *Life* magazine,

depicting Uncle Sam greeting a returned soldier, captured their frustration. "Nothing is too good for you, my boy! What would you like?" The
soldier's answer: "A job."

Barry rented an apartment at 361 West 119th Street, in a row of drab
five-story buildings near Columbia University and only a half block from
Morningside Park. He crisscrossed Manhattan in search of a job. He
approached businesses in Brooklyn and the Bronx, and some days ventured as far as New Jersey. Employers wanted references, and the only
legitimate civilian job he had ever held had been the stint working for his
brother. No one needed a battlefield first-aid man in peacetime.

Fifth Avenue looking north from St. Patrick's Cathedral in the 1920s (Author Collection)

"New York is hard, cynical, ruthless," Ernest Gruening, editor of the
magazine the *Nation*, cautioned newcomers. "The city's philosophy is
everyone for himself—and the devil take the hindmost." F. Scott Fitzgerald
issued a similar warning in his first novel, *This Side of Paradise*, published
in 1920: "It's a bad town unless you're on top of it." To survive, Barry,
twenty-three that December, would have to become just as hard and

cynical and ruthless. He was determined to come out on top. And he was willing to steal to do it.

He weighed his options as if he were attending an underworld job fair. Safecracker? He knew how to handle explosives, thanks to his mentor, Lowell Jack, but he lacked the expertise to blow open safes. Bank robber? He would need accomplices, and he preferred to work alone. Mugger? He had no taste for confronting and accosting people on the streets, and threatening innocent passersby with a gun seemed to him to be "unprofitable and somehow disreputable." Burglar? Yes, that was it. He had meticulously planned his first break-in when he was a teenager. He knew how to slip in and out of homes without ever seeing his victims, let alone confronting them. And he would steal something worth the risk of being caught and sent back to prison: jewelry.

"The thought of violence repelled me," he later explained, and a jewel thief "could be a gentleman and put to use whatever cunning and imagination he might have." Even the slang term for burglar, *second-story man*— popularized by the title of writer Upton Sinclair's 1912 play about a thief who "climbs up porches and fire-escapes" to do his work—had a genteel ring to it. It was, Barry thought, "clean-cut and sportsmanlike" crime. If he was careful and did his homework, he could scoop up rings, necklaces, pins, and bracelets, and be long gone before anyone realized they had been robbed. It was as close to a victimless crime as he could imagine. "People rich enough to own jewels," he reasoned, "never had to worry about their next meal." And they would no doubt have an insurance policy to cover their losses.

It was the perfect way for "any smart man," as he put it later, to "clean up."

ONE DAY IN early 1920, he walked to the 125th Street station in Harlem and hopped aboard a northbound train. His destination was Yonkers, a prosperous city of about one hundred thousand on the Hudson River in Westchester County, about ten miles from Manhattan. He spent the morning wandering through posh neighborhoods on the outskirts of town, taking note of large homes with expansive grounds.

"I picked out a house that I knew belonged to wealthy people," he recalled. It was set back from the street, and a front porch would make it easy to reach the second floor.

He returned to Manhattan to buy a pair of gray silk gloves and a small flashlight. He rehearsed the job in his head as he took an evening train back to Yonkers. It was dark by the time he crept up to the house, and through a window he could see about a half dozen people at the dining room table. He climbed a pillar to a porch roof and tried a window. It was unlocked. He ducked inside and, as he suspected, he was in the master bedroom. He rifled a bureau, then opened the top drawer of a dressing table. A jewelry case inside contained a cache of earrings, pendants, and bracelets. Another drawer yielded jeweled cuff links and tie clasps. Barry filled his coat pockets and retreated out the window. He reckoned he was inside the home for no more than three minutes.

"I realized even then," he recalled, "that the trick is to work fast, go after the main stuff, and make a speedy getaway."

Back in his apartment, he pried each stone from its setting. Individual gems were impossible to trace, but the gold and platinum settings surrounding them were distinctive and could be identified. He tossed them into the Hudson River.

Now he had to find a buyer who would not ask too many questions about where the gemstones had come from and why he was selling them. New York's deputy police commissioner had circulated a bulletin to the city's gem dealers and pawnbrokers only a few weeks earlier, asking them to be on the lookout for a number of expensive pieces of stolen jewelry that might reach their counters. If Barry approached a buyer with a conscience, his first jewel theft could be his last.

The Canal Street end of the Bowery was the center of New York's diamond trade. "The strangest jewelry exchange in the world," claimed a reporter who dropped by in the spring of 1920, "a bee hive of activity." Buyers and sellers gathered in storefronts, but the haggling spilled out onto the sidewalk. Another journalist, Will B. Johnstone of New York's *Evening*

World, likened the brisk trading to a mini Wall Street. "Here," instead of stocks and bonds, "they gamble in jewelry." Barry needed a buyer willing to gamble on his haul.

He approached a counter at the back of a Canal Street store, produced a small diamond, and asked for an appraisal. The clerk valued the gem at $350. Barry spun a yarn about being given the stone by a friend, as collateral for a loan. His friend had not paid him back, and he wanted to sell it. The clerk offered him $125, and the deal was done.

"If you have anything to sell in the future," the clerk called out as Barry was leaving the store, "come in and see me."

He had found a fence. After several trips to the Canal Street store to sell individual stones, he had disposed of the entire haul for $2,500, more than many New York City schoolteachers earned in a year. A factory worker back home in Worcester had to toil for two years to make that much money. It was an incredible payoff for a few minutes' work, the equivalent of $32,300 today. And when Barry needed more money, he knew what to do.

"My conscience hurt me a little," he would one day acknowledge, "but that was the last time that it ever bothered me."

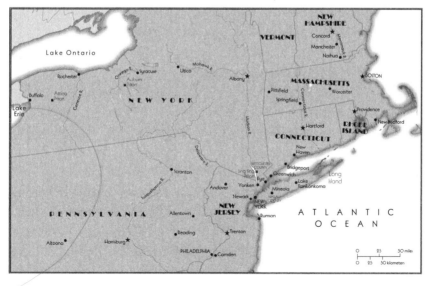

Sites of Barry's major heists, prisons, and other locations connected with his life.

THERE WERE AT least a half dozen jewel thefts from homes in Yonkers that fall. "The mysterious burglar is still a-burgling," the *Yonkers Statesman* reported in November, "and the police are still trying to tag him." The city's former mayor was among the victims. An enterprising insurance salesman tried to cash in, offering homeowners policies to protect their valuables amid the rash of break-ins. "Burglars," his advertisements asserted, "consider Yonkers a good field for operations."

The break-ins followed Barry's careful script. The burglar struck about the time the residents were having dinner. He climbed a porch to the second floor, entered a bedroom through an unlocked window, swiftly rifled bureau drawers for jewelry boxes and loose pieces, and fled without being seen. The largest single theft netted about $1,000, but the burglar sometimes managed to scoop up as little as one hundred dollars' worth of jewelry.

The following year, a burglar with an identical modus operandi began to target estates in the posh Ardsley area, less than ten miles upriver. The village of under a thousand boasted "spacious pieces of property," noted the *New-York Tribune*, and was home to stockbrokers, bankers, and businessmen who commuted to offices in Manhattan. In October 1921, someone slipped into the mansion of banker Edward Thalmann while he was dining with his family and made off with two boxes of jewelry valued at $10,000. No one heard the burglar, and the theft was not discovered until the following day. Soon, residents reported sightings of a prowler in the village.

On the last evening of February 1922, a maid ascended the stairs at the mansion of Henry Graves III and his wife, Margaret. A millionaire by the age of twenty-five, Graves was an executive of the New York Trust Company and grandson of the founder of the Atlas Portland Cement Company, supplier of much of the cement used to build the Panama Canal. The couple was at the dining table, but when the maid entered a bedroom and saw a man inside, standing in front of a bureau, she assumed it must be her employer.

"Oh, excuse me, Mr. Graves," she apologized as she backed out of the room. The man smiled, then shielded his face and bolted for the window. He dropped a jewelry case as he jumped through, landed on a porch roof, and scrambled down a ladder.

The startled maid screamed.

Graves phoned the police in nearby Dobbs Ferry, grabbed a revolver, and rushed outside. He thought he saw a figure in the darkness, running through the shrubbery, and fired a round. The gunshot alerted his neighbors, and a posse of chauffeurs used their automobile headlamps to illuminate the grounds as police officers tried to follow the burglar's trail. The state troopers who patrolled Westchester County's highways were alerted, but the culprit escaped. The thief's haul included rings set with large diamonds, and solid gold bracelets studded in diamonds and sapphires, worth an estimated $62,000. While everything was insured, Margaret Graves was devastated that some of the missing pieces were cherished wedding presents.

The crime had been well planned, the work of a professional. Police dusted the bedroom furniture for fingerprints but found none; the intruder, they concluded, must have worn gloves. Like the Yonkers burglar, he had struck at dinnertime and had worked with lightning speed. This careful thief was just as meticulous about his appearance. The maid described the man as wearing a stylish salt-and-pepper suit and a brown fedora, a hat that was just becoming fashionable thanks to the Prince of Wales, who often was photographed wearing one. It had taken the maid a few moments to realize she had interrupted a burglary, gaining the well-dressed man the precious seconds he'd needed to escape.

Graves was incensed. He had lost more than keepsakes; the break-in had threatened his family's safety. The couple's three children, all under the age of three, had been asleep upstairs as the burglar worked nearby. His neighbors' assistance in the search for the thief gave him an idea. Within days, he had organized a vigilance committee to protect the community if the brazen burglar returned. Armed watchmen were hired. Floodlights were installed above well-groomed lawns and gardens, turning night into day. Graves and some of his wealthy friends were appointed deputy sheriffs and mounted nightly patrols in their cars. Each man packed a pistol. They became known as the Gold Badge Squad, but one newspaper preferred a less flattering name for the group: Volunteer Thug Hunters.

Not long after the break-in, Graves, his brother Duncan, and another man were on patrol when the headlights of an oncoming vehicle blinded

Duncan, who was driving. He swerved, and the car skidded off the concrete roadway, sideswiped a stone wall, and slammed into a tree. Henry Graves and the other passenger, a young banker named Henry Wilson, were killed. The disastrous vigilante effort faded from the headlines.

Police in Westchester County would eventually identify Arthur Barry as the man responsible for the crime wave. The area's suburban estates became one of his favorite hunting grounds. He fit the maid's description of the man who robbed the Graves home. And dressing like a gentleman to steal from the wealthy would soon become one of his trademarks.

Within a month of the theft at the Graves estate, however, Barry must have thought his career as a second-story man was over. He was behind bars in another state, accused of a far more serious crime.

SIX

A SIMPLE ASSAULT

Bridgeport, Connecticut • 1922

A VOICE BELLOWED FROM the steps of Bridgeport's Schwaben Hall as two men emerged on a mild, cloudless April night. Two other men, who had left the dance there moments earlier, had already reached the street. LeRoy Gregory, one of the pursuers, was enraged; his friend, Peter Wagner, was struggling to hold him back. Gregory shouted at the men to stop. They ignored him, then split up and ran in different directions.

One of the runners suddenly wheeled around. He pulled a .25-caliber automatic revolver and fired from the hip. The muzzle flashed in the dim light. Five shots were heard, maybe six. Wagner, hit by two bullets, staggered and fell.

"Go, get them," he called to Gregory. "I'm all right."

A crowd of more than one hundred surged out of the hall and onto French Street. Wagner was bundled into a car and rushed to a hospital. Some of the wounded man's friends peeled off and ran after the assailants, chasing one of them to the railroad station before the man hopped a fence and vanished into the darkness. The police set up roadblocks at major intersections and on main routes out of the city. By daybreak, however, it was clear the gunman and his companion had escaped.

Bridgeport detectives soon had names and descriptions. Police in neighboring jurisdictions were asked to be on the lookout for Joseph Porter and Arthur Cummings, though there were doubts these were their real names. They were believed to be from New York City, the *Bridgeport Times* reported, and "thought to be members of a bootlegging ring."

Wagner underwent emergency surgery at St. Vincent's Hospital. One bullet had passed through his abdomen, the other had damaged his liver, stomach, and left kidney before breaking a rib and lodging near his spinal column. The bullet was removed, but the twenty-eight-year-old truck driver was "sinking rapidly," noted one press report, and "little hope is held out for his recovery." On April 18, 1922, five days after the shooting, he died of infection and other complications. Bridgeport police were now investigating a homicide.

A coroner's inquest and press reports revealed what had happened inside the hall before Wagner was shot. The man known as Porter asked Gregory's wife, Nina, to dance, unaware she was married. She declined. Porter, feeling snubbed, called her "a little bum." Bystanders pressed him to apologize. A crowd gathered, expecting a fight. Porter and Cummings retreated to the cloakroom, retrieved their hats and coats, and headed for the door. They wanted "to avoid trouble," according to a report in Bridgeport's other daily paper, the *Telegram*, "knowing as strangers they stood no chance in a free-for-all fight." Gregory, outraged when he learned of the insult, stormed after them to demand an apology. His fists, one witness noticed, were clenched. Wagner, fearing his friend would be outnumbered if punches were thrown, went with him. "Gregory forced the fatal shooting," the paper concluded, "by his stubborn attitude."

Bridgeport detectives soon located one of the fugitives. A week after Wagner died, Arthur Cummings was arrested in Worcester, Massachusetts, at the home of his sister, and charged with first-degree murder.

His real name was Arthur Barry.

THE POLICE NEVER revealed how they had identified Barry as a suspect. He had worked in a Bridgeport munitions plant during the war, and someone in Schwaben Hall that night may have recognized him. Barry admitted he was at the dance but denied carrying a gun. Porter, he insisted, had shot

Wagner. He did not know Porter's real name, he claimed, and he had no idea where he was. The police were buying none of it. Worcester's chief of detectives James Casey told reporters that Barry had been at the dance hall and "had an opportunity to fire the fatal shot."

Barry's extradition, however, was delayed. He was so ill that the arresting officers delivered him to a Worcester hospital for treatment. While press accounts did not reveal the nature of his illness, his condition worsened and, at one point, doctors debated whether to operate. He spent a week in the hospital, under police guard, before he was well enough to be taken back to Connecticut to face the murder charge, a capital offense. "The hangman's noose," as the *Bridgeport Times* grimly put it, was "staring him in the face."

Barry did not look or act like a man facing a possible death sentence when he appeared in a Bridgeport courtroom on May 8. The gallery was filled with Wagner's friends, who had lined up early in the morning to make sure they could claim a seat. Barry ignored the hostile crowd and "sat unconcerned," noted one reporter. As usual, he was a stickler for his appearance. His demeanor was "suave, debonair," his attire neat "but not flashy." The source of his confidence was the man seated beside him, George Mara. Barry's parents, who had once given up on him as a rebellious teenager, had retained one of Bridgeport's best lawyers to defend him. Mara was a Yale Law School graduate with a busy criminal practice and the right connections; he was a close friend and political ally of the local state's attorney, Homer Cummings, and had worked alongside him to organize the 1920 Democratic National Convention.

Coroner John Phelan released a damning report that found both Barry and Porter criminally responsible for Wagner's death: While they had reason to fear for their safety as they fled the dance hall, neither Wagner nor Gregory had been armed. Since the pair had not been in "imminent physical danger" of being seriously injured or killed, the shooting was unjustified.

The evidence implicating Barry, however, was weak. Mara went on the offensive. He demanded an early hearing to establish whether there was enough evidence to send his client to trial—a rare request by a defendant in a murder case, observers noted. The gambit left the prosecutor, Vincent Keating, with only a few days to cobble together his case.

Witnesses who testified at the pretrial session confirmed that Barry was in the dance hall before the shooting, but no one could place him outside or identify him as Wagner's killer. LeRoy Gregory was only a few feet away from the men during the confrontation, but the glare of a streetlight had obscured their faces. "He could not swear," he said, that Barry "was one of the men who did the shooting." Two other men who were outside Schwaben Hall witnessed the shooting, but neither one recognized Barry. Mara's cross-examination delivered the final blow to the credibility of the prosecution's star witness. After being questioned so many times, Gregory admitted to the defense lawyer, "he didn't know what he was saying half of the time."

Barry was elated. "The witnesses all exonerated me," he would later recall.

Keating tried to shore up his flimsy case. Barry had at least aided and abetted the crime, he argued as the hearing closed: "On the most favorable interpretation of the law this man is guilty." Mara stressed the prosecution's failure to produce a single witness who saw Barry outside the dance hall or firing a gun. Judge William Boardman, however, ordered Barry to stand trial for murder—apparently because there were no other suspects. Barry and Porter had been inside the hall and had left moments before shots were fired. "It would require a good deal of stretching," he believed, "to suppose others did the shooting."

Mara met with Keating's boss, his friend State's Attorney Cummings, a few days after the hearing. After lengthy discussions behind closed doors, Cummings announced the murder allegation against Barry would be dropped and replaced with a charge of manslaughter. Barry pleaded not guilty to the less serious offense, and his trial was set for September. Unable to raise the $2,500 required for his release on bail, he remained locked up in the Fairfield County Jail, a relic built in the 1870s, when Ulysses S. Grant was president.

By the time the case came up for trial, Mara had managed to whittle down the manslaughter allegation to one of the most minor offenses on the books. Barry appeared before a superior court judge on September 26 and pleaded guilty to simple assault. He was sentenced to an additional three months in custody and ordered to pay just under forty-three dollars in court costs. The *Bridgeport Times*, unable to hide its disdain at the outcome, reported that Barry "got off" with a "light sentence."

~~~~~~~~~~

ON A NOVEMBER morning, with his release date approaching, Barry crept along a dark corridor lined with tiers of prison cells. It was about five o'clock, almost two hours before dawn. Rasps of metal scraping metal could be heard as he sawed though the bolt on a door and entered an unoccupied section of the jail. Then, grasping the bars of the empty cells, he hoisted himself upward, floor by floor, until he reached a third-floor dormer window. He opened it and shivered as he climbed onto the roof—the temperature outside was uncomfortably close to freezing. He leapt to the ground and disappeared.

BARRY ESCAPES FROM COUNTY JAIL screamed a front-page headline in the *Bridgeport Times* on November 22. Connecticut state police and their counterparts in New York and Massachusetts were alerted, but Fairfield County's sheriff, embarrassed by the bold escape, had not made the news public for two days.

The Fairfield County Jail (History and Art Collection/Alamy)

The breakout—"my little prank," Barry later called it, chuckling as he recalled that night—had been meticulously planned. The empty cells and the windows to the roof, he realized, were the jail's weak points. He arranged for someone to smuggle in the saw. "I had friends on the outside," he noted. He made his move just before the day shift took over from the overnight guards.

"I knew when the guard made the rounds," he said, and he was sitting on his cot, smoking a cigarette, when the guard passed, so that he was sure he was seen. To buy himself time, he fashioned a dummy head out of bread he had squirreled away, added hair swept from the floor of the jail's barber shop, and positioned it on his pillow. A blanket stuffed under the covers simulated his body. Barry reckoned it took him no more than five minutes to reach the roof. The only hitch came when he hit the ground at an awkward angle. Nursing a dislocated shoulder, he hopped aboard a passing trolley before catching a train back to Manhattan.

One newspaper called the escape "one of the most daringly planned and executed in the history of the jail." A day later, two more prisoners followed Barry's route and escaped, prompting an investigation into security lapses at the facility.

Barry had earned the trust of his captors at the Fairfield jail and was serving as "head hall man" when he escaped. When inmates were locked in their cells for the night, Barry's door remained open so he could fetch water and other necessities for his fellow prisoners. It was a role reserved for someone serving a short sentence, someone unlikely to try to flee when freedom was within his grasp. Barry's release date had been only ten days away, but he had an incentive to risk an escape. The Worcester police had a warrant for his arrest—he faced a year-old accusation of stealing a car in his hometown—and planned to pick him up and put him back behind bars as soon as his sentence in Bridgeport expired.

"I wasn't guilty" of car theft, he insisted later, and he'd had no desire to be locked up again while he tried to prove his innocence. Barry had been in custody for almost seven months. He wanted to get back to the business of scoping out posh estates, planning burglaries, and stealing jewels. "I didn't want to linger in those parts any longer."

He likely was telling the truth when he said he did not shoot Wagner, but he was lying when he said he did not know his companion at the dance hall that night. The man known as Joseph Porter—Wagner's killer—was also from Worcester, and they had been friends since childhood. His real name was James Francis Monahan, and he may have delivered the saw to Barry.

Barry had risked a death sentence to hide his friend's identity. Monahan was eager to pay him back for his loyalty. They would later team up in an uneasy—and ill-fated—jewel-stealing partnership.

SEVEN

ALL THAT GLITTERS

Luxor, Egypt • 1922

T HEY STOOD AT the end of a dark, narrow passageway beneath the Valley of the Kings in Luxor, the final resting place of the great pharaohs of ancient Egypt. Archaeologist Howard Carter had been searching and digging and hoping for this moment for more than three decades. Lord Carnarvon, the British aristocrat who had been funding his expeditions for years, stood beside him. If they were right, the anterooms leading to the tomb of the boy king Tutankhamen, undisturbed for more than three millennia, were just a few feet away. Carter used an iron bar to poke a small opening in the plaster sealing the passageway. He held up a candle, and its flame flickered in a whoosh of escaping air. It took a few moments for Carter's eyes to adjust to the dim candlelight as he peered inside. Then, he saw them. "Strange animals, statues and gold," he would recall, "everywhere the glint of gold."

Carnarvon was growing impatient.

"Can you see anything?"

"Yes," Carter said at last, "wonderful things."

It was November 1922, the month Arthur Barry escaped from his Connecticut jail cell, and they had made one of the most important archaeological finds in history. The anteroom was crammed with everything a king might need in the afterlife. There were statues of exotic beasts, Egyptian gods, and Tutankhamen himself; beds and other furniture; the spoked wheels of dismantled chariots; and chests with more treasures inside. The furnishings, figures, and chariots were sheaved in gold and inlaid with obsidian, turquoise, royal-blue lapis lazuli, and other semiprecious stones.

In the months that followed, Carter's team entered more artifact-filled rooms until they reached the tomb itself, which yielded the king's mummified remains and his dazzling golden funerary mask. "Picture a heap of jewels worth a kingly ransom," wrote one of the first journalists who had a chance to look inside. "The gem-studded cavern of Ali Baba seems to have been a trinket shop in comparison."

Tutankhamen's treasure-filled tomb, discovered in 1922 (Author Collection)

There were more than five thousand items in the underground rooms, making it the only pharaoh's tomb discovered almost intact; others had been stripped of most of their treasures in ancient times. Thieves, however, had beaten Carter and Carnarvon to the prize. Many items were missing: gems stripped from their settings, gold decoration ripped from furniture, bronze tips snapped from arrows. Tut's tomb had been broken into at least three times shortly after the pharaoh's death, but the thieves had been caught or had grabbed only smaller items. When Carter swept the floor of one of the rooms after it had been cleared of artifacts, he discovered more discarded bits of jewelry and loose gems mixed with the dust.

They were proof that Arthur Barry's profession was one of the world's oldest.

~~~~~~~~~~~~~

HUMANS HAVE BEEN making and wearing necklaces, bracelets, and rings since the Stone Age. "In the beginning," author and lifestyle journalist Stellene Volandes has written, "there was jewelry." A stone bracelet and a ring of marble found in a Siberian cave, among the oldest known examples, were carved some forty thousand years ago. Shells, fish bones, and ivory were fashioned into jewelry long before the metalsmiths of Egypt and other ancient civilizations began transforming precious metals, gemstones, and beads of colored glass into miniature works of art.

Diamonds, formed from carbon deposits deep in the earth and brought to the surface in lava flows, have been mined for centuries in India's Golconda region, which produced the famous Koh-i-Noor and the Hope diamonds. The subcontinent was the world's main source of the gem until South African deposits were discovered in the 1870s. Rubies, varying in color from pinkish to blood red, were produced in present-day Burma for centuries before scattered deposits were discovered on other continents. Their dark-blue cousin, the sapphire, has been known since Roman times, and the largest examples have come from Sri Lanka. Deep-green emeralds—part of the gem family beryl, which includes lighter-hued aquamarines—were first mined in Egypt more than two thousand years ago. Pearls, formed inside oysters and other mollusks, are mentioned in both the New Testament and the Quran.

Jewels became potent symbols of wealth and power. They reigned as sparkling proof of imperial might, royal prestige, and the stability of monarchies. Emperors passed laws to protect the elite status of jewels. Julius Caesar, in awe of Cleopatra's collection of magnificent emeralds, decreed that only Rome's aristocrats could wear precious stones. Justinian, who ruled the Byzantine Empire in the sixth century, claimed the sole right to manufacture, possess, and wear emeralds and pearls. Many of the largest diamonds, rubies, and emeralds ever discovered were destined to adorn the crowns of kings and queens. Britain's imperial state crown, placed on Queen Victoria's head at her coronation in 1838 and worn when the sovereign opens sessions of Parliament, is studded with almost three thousand diamonds and features a large ruby that Henry V and Richard III wore on their helmets in battle.

Gems have built empires, funded wars, fomented revolutions, and created and destroyed nations. Spanish conquistadors steamrolled the civilizations of South America in a genocidal quest for gold, silver, and Colombia's rich emerald deposits. Rumors that the haughty and bejeweled Marie Antoinette had commissioned yet another expensive necklace helped stoke the public outrage that culminated in the French Revolution. The nineteenth-century scramble for South Africa's diamonds and gold ignited two wars between the British Empire and the region's Boer settlers.

Jewels—"the most non-essential of luxury objects," as *Town & Country* magazine has described them—also became weapons in the battle for social prominence. The rich and the aristocratic deployed them to flaunt their wealth and assert their status. They spent fortunes on gemstones and jewelry for one reason: they could. "One buys diamonds," the Parisian banker Georges Aubert noted in 1908, "because they are luxuries that not everyone can have."

What the wealthy and powerful owned, others were eager to take away. Pirates plundered Spanish treasure ships in the Caribbean. Invading armies looted treasuries and shrines. Robbers accosted well-heeled travelers, while burglars targeted jewelers and the homes of the rich. Prized pieces of jewelry disappeared or were stolen, sometimes resurfacing decades later in private collections or in the pages of auction house catalogues. "Precious stones have a strange lure," noted John D. Coughlin, New York's chief of detectives in the 1920s. "For them men and women lie, steal, suffer, kill and are killed more than for anything else on earth—not excluding love."

The allure of jewels—and the lengths owners will go to acquire them and thieves will go to steal them—has furnished plots to the most famous writers of crime fiction. Wilkie Collins's mid-nineteenth-century novel *The Moonstone*, one of the first detective mysteries, revolves around the theft of a rare yellow-tinted Indian diamond. In one of the earliest Sherlock Holmes stories, published in 1892, Arthur Conan Doyle's great detective describes fine gemstones as "the devil's pet baits" and "a nucleus and focus of crime." Every facet of a single large stone "may stand for a bloody deed," he tells Dr. Watson, from robbery to suicide to murder. "Who would think that so pretty a toy would be a purveyor to the gallows and the prison?"

In a story published in 1923, Hercule Poirot is dazzled by the magnificent jewels—"worn sometimes with more love of display than good taste," he notes—surrounding him during dinner at a posh Brighton hotel. It's enough to tempt even Agatha Christie's supersleuth. "The sight of so many jewels makes me wish I had turned my brains to crime, instead of to its detection," he remarks to his friend, Captain Hastings. "What a magnificent opportunity for some thief of distinction!"

THE ROARING TWENTIES was a perfect time to launch a career as a thief of distinction. "Diamonds are trumps," the *New York Daily Herald* declared at the dawn of the decade, "and everybody's playing them." The German occupation of Belgium toppled Antwerp as a diamond-cutting capital, allowing New York to emerge as a leader in the industry, with hundreds of skilled craftsmen at work. Demand for other gems was soaring. "People who made money freely during the war are reaping the benefits and decking themselves with priceless jewels," observed a newspaper in Palm Beach, Florida, the winter resort of New York's rich and famous. "It is nothing short of hysteria, the way everybody is buying jewelry," the editor of the *Jewelers' Circular*, the industry's bible, told the *New York Times*. "And it is not cheap jewelry, either. It is the real jewelry—jewelry that enables one to carry a fortune in one's hand."

Pearls, too, were trumps. They encircled the necks of society's power players, women who were rich enough—or had husbands who were rich enough—to squander a fortune on a single piece of jewelry. Perfectly matched strands of perfectly shaped natural pearls were so valuable that the New York financier Morton Freeman Plant handed the deed to his Fifth Avenue mansion to French jeweler Pierre Cartier in 1917 in return for a 128-pearl necklace, worth a million dollars, for his wife. "For the new moneymakers in America at the beginning of the twentieth century," author and journalist Victoria Finley has noted, "ownership of a strand or two of pearls was like having a house in the Hamptons, a smart yacht, or a few of the new automobiles that everyone was going mad for." An indulgence, in other words, that only a select few could afford.

For F. Scott Fitzgerald, the leading chronicler of a wealth-obsessed decade, jewels were symbols of the era's glamour and decadence. When a teenager in one of his stories boasts to a schoolmate about his family's immense wealth, he makes the outlandish claim that his father owns "a diamond bigger than the Ritz-Carlton Hotel." Fitzgerald's American Dream–chasing millionaire Jay Gatsby indulged in a hobby that reeked of Jazz Age excess. Before settling down in his Long Island mansion, he tells his neighbor-turned-biographer Nick Carraway, he had "lived like a young rajah in all the capitals of Europe—Paris, Venice, Rome—collecting jewels, chiefly rubies." The day before Gatsby's great love, Daisy, marries Tom Buchanan, her husband-to-be gives her a $350,000 string of pearls. A green light at the end of a dock at the Buchanan estate, visible from Gatsby's mansion on the other side of a bay, glows like an emerald that's as distant and unattainable as Daisy.

All that glitter was a lightning rod for Arthur Barry and other thieves. In New York City alone, chief of detectives John Coughlin estimated, detectives investigated the theft of more than $2 million worth of jewelry every year. Too many wealthy women were showing up at theaters and society events "dressed up like a pawnshop window," he complained, and burglars were taking notice. Some rich women locked away their jewelry in safes or safe-deposit boxes and resorted to wearing "paste"—imitation stones made of cut glass—in public. "All this money in jewels that might as well have been paste," a Philadelphia woman lamented after thieves took gems worth $100,000 from her summer home. "I see only the folly in having such valuable jewels."

A Brooklyn newspaper offered jewel buyers some advice in the mid-1920s: "If you must have jewels, don't get expensive ones. If you must have expensive jewels, don't wear them." Luckily for Barry, most members of New York's elite were determined to flaunt the symbols of their wealth and discerning taste.

EIGHT

～～～

CLIENTS

Westchester County, Long Island, and Manhattan • 1923–24

NN FRASER REMOVED the jewelry she had worn that day and placed it on a bedroom dresser before heading downstairs. When she returned after dinner, an assortment of diamond rings and brooches, a necklace, and a bracelet—valued at as much as $25,000—was gone. Her husband, Duncan, the son of a mining and steel magnate, phoned the police on the night of February 28, 1923, to report the theft of his wife's gems. When four officers reached the Ardsley-area home, they spotted familiar clues. A window over a porch roof was open. Footprints in the snow suggested the intruder had used a ladder to reach the second story. "The same methods were pursued by this burglar," the *Yonkers Statesman* reported, as the one who had stolen a fortune in jewels exactly one year earlier from the nearby home of the ill-fated millionaire Henry Graves III.

Westchester County's "ladder burglar" was back in business.

Nineteen twenty-three, noted the *Yonkers Herald*, would prove to be the "biggest year" for the elusive thief. The South Yonkers home of attorney John C. Hoenninger was robbed less than a week after the Fraser break-in. The home of a neighbor, advertising executive James Lackey, was raided in mid-April. There was another spate of burglaries that fall. The North Yonkers home of chemist Orrin Doolittle was robbed in early November. Days later, a ladder was used to enter the home of Franklin Coe, publisher of the must-read magazine of the '20s posh set, *Town & Country.* The break-ins added jewelry worth $7,500 to the burglar's haul.

Yonkers police scrambled to stop the crime wave. More than a dozen off-duty officers volunteered to patrol an enclave of mansions in North Yonkers. Police began to question anyone seen carrying a ladder, and residents were urged to report similar sightings, making life miserable for painters and other workers.

The beefed-up police presence seemed to embolden the burglar. He robbed the home of the city comptroller and several of the man's South Yonkers neighbors in mid-November. On one nighttime foray, he scampered across the grounds of the Yonkers commissioner of public safety, the official who had ordered the interrogation of all ladder carriers. "Traps have been laid for him but he has refused to fall into them," commiserated the *Yonkers Herald.* "Police agree that he is the most elusive criminal in the annals of the Yonkers Police Department."

A mansion in Yonkers, New York, the city where Barry staged many of his early burglaries (Author Collection)

Back in Ardsley, the property owners' association revived the vigilance committee founded in response to the 1922 break-ins. Residents were issued permits to carry guns and, the *Yonkers Statesman* warned would-be thieves, they were "determined to use their weapons unsparingly." One homeowner, John Wheeler, grabbed his army-issue Colt revolver and a flashlight to search his house every time his wife was awakened by a noise, only to have their jewelry swiped on a night they were attending a charity dance. Police whistles were distributed. Searchlights and burglar alarms were installed on some estates. Residents formed nighttime patrols and had the authority to arrest strangers who could not explain why they were in the community. "We had a similar experience last year and we stopped it," a property owners' association official said of the burglaries. "We'll stop it again."

The ladder burglar, however, was still at work in the early months of 1924. Among the victims was vigilance committee member Henry S. Brooks, a telephone company executive, who was at the dinner table with his wife, Clara, on a March evening when jewelry worth $1,000 was stolen from an upstairs bedroom of their Ardsley home.

The property owners' association official who bragged of scaring away the burglar in 1922 had been mistaken. The break-ins had stopped because Arthur Barry was in jail in Connecticut from April to November that year. Westchester police and the county's district attorney's office eventually connected the dots and concluded that Barry had planned and executed most, if not all, of the ladder-burglar heists in Yonkers, Ardsley, and nearby communities during the early 1920s.

The hauls from his Westchester burglaries, however, were often modest. Sometimes he slipped out of a bedroom window with less than a thousand dollars' worth of gems, knowing he would receive only a fraction of their value from a fence. Barry, who was now calling himself Arthur Gibson—or Dr. Arthur J. Gibson, when he needed a full name and respectable title—was in search of richer clients. And his hunting grounds were expanding to the stately mansions scattered along the North Shore of Long Island.

~~~~~~~~~~

BARRY HAD THE choice of four dining rooms at the Central Park Casino, a genteel Gothic-styled retreat with vine-covered stone walls, near the park entrance at Fifth Avenue and Seventy-Second Street: the Café au Lait, offering a slice of Paris; the Blue Room, decorated in ebony, gold, and, of course, blue; the Pergola, where tables were arranged under a tentlike canopy of blue and buff-colored silk and surrounded by latticed walls and potted palms; or "the most elaborate of all," in the opinion of the *New York Times*, the Louis XVI Room, featuring a trio of massive chandeliers, wall panels decorated with Wedgwood reliefs, and doorways framed by Pompeian green drapes.

The Casino—the word referred to pavilion-style structures in parks long before it became synonymous with gambling—was a magnet for New York's socialites. Elegant women in oversized sun hats and frilled well-below-the-knee print dresses converged on the restaurant. They lunched, sipped tea, chatted, and gossiped. An ensemble conducted by a former concertmaster of the Boston Symphony supplied the background music. Some of the diners no doubt noticed the good-looking, well-dressed man in his late twenties sitting alone at a side table. He stood out. Even though the restaurant was no longer a refuge for unescorted women visiting the park—it had opened in the 1860s as the Ladies' Refreshment Salon—few men dropped by on summer afternoons.

Barry noticed them, too. And their jewelry.

"A lot of wealthy women who came into New York shopping used to wind up their afternoons at the casino," he recalled. "So I'd go up there myself to look them over. When I spotted a woman who had plenty of diamonds on her, I'd follow her out to her limousine and take the license number."

He then walked to the nearest public phone and dialed the police department's traffic bureau, a division newly created to bring order to the chaos of Manhattan's automobile-clogged streets. He identified himself as a patrolman—Officer Schultz was one of the names he remembered using—and recited a fake badge number.

"I've got an accident up here," he barked, "and I need the name and address of a Cadillac sedan." The plate number was traced, and moments later he knew who the bejeweled woman was and where she lived— invariably a sumptuous estate in Westchester County or on Long Island.

He employed the ruse many times to identify promising targets—or "clients," as he preferred to call them. "The traffic bureau never took the time to check on Patrolman Schultz," said Barry. "They'd simply give me the name and address." One productive afternoon visit to the Casino yielded a half dozen names and addresses and set in motion a series of break-ins that netted him almost $75,000 in jewelry.

"BURGLARY," BARRY ONCE noted, "is about 80 per cent preparation and 20 per cent luck." He never forgot a lesson he had learned from his mentor, Lowell Jack: "Preparedness and thorough planning are the keystones to successful crime."

Keeping tabs on New York's elite, he discovered, was easy. Barry scoured the society pages of the newspapers for tips and clues, and often found helpful photographs of prominent women flaunting their finest jewelry. "The society columnists of the New York dailies," he confessed, "often were my unwitting accomplices." He learned who had retreated to their summer homes outside the city, who was wintering in Palm Beach, who was traveling in Europe, who was playing host to houseguests. He took note of engagement announcements, wedding dates, notices of upcoming parties, galas, and country club dances. Such tidbits could be invaluable. "I knew that Mrs. So-and-So was going to throw a party on a certain night, and even if her guest list wasn't printed in advance, I knew pretty well who her friends were and who would probably attend." If one of his potential targets was likely to be there—wearing her most expensive pieces—he would reschedule the burglary for a night when both the woman and her gems would be at home. "No use to make a visit," he said, "if the Missus . . . had her load of ice with her."

New York's *Social Register*, an alphabetical guide to the city's millionaires and blue bloods, proved just as indispensable. To one observer, the compendium of famous names and posh addresses conjured up images of "old money, Ivy League, trust funds, privileges of birth, fox hunting, debutante balls, yachting, polo, distinguished forebears, family compounds in the Adirondacks, and a pedigree studded with 19th-century robber barons." The nouveau riche and social climbers eager to join this "roster of fashionables," remarked the sharp-penned critic H. L. Mencken, "make herculean efforts to get their names into it."

For Barry, it conjured up images of diamonds and pearls. He claimed to have memorized large portions of the *Register* as he kept track of the people he was reading about in the newspapers and spotting at the Casino. If so, it was a remarkable feat. A typical edition of the era contained close to twenty thousand entries and ran to a mind-numbing seven hundred–plus pages, from Dr. Robert Abbe and his wife, Catherine, of 11 West Fiftieth Street, to the family of Rufus and Mary Zogbaum, of 125 West Eighty-Seventh Street; the section listing surnames beginning with the letter *W* alone ran to more than fifty pages.

Sometimes he drove to Westchester or Long Island and struck up acquaintances with young women who worked in the grand houses of the wealthy. Maids, governesses, and cooks were flattered to catch the eye of a polite, well-heeled young man—especially one driving a flashy red Cadillac coupe, a $4,000 luxury-class car. "After a few cocktails I was sympathizing with them over the large and small inhumanities inflicted by their employers," he recalled, "and gaining a rather complete picture of the workings of their households." He chatted up one servant in a Westchester home who revealed that her mistress, to thwart burglars, slipped her jewels into a silk stocking at night and covered them with clothing in a laundry hamper. A few nights later, he broke in and retrieved the cache from the unusual hiding place.

For most of his burglaries, however, Barry had to devise his plans without the aid of unwitting informers and inside information. He staked out homes, sometimes for days, to discover the routines of residents and staff. He spent hours hidden in trees or peering over walls at the edges of estates to keep track of arrivals and departures. And he made preliminary forays into some homes at night, to memorize the upstairs layout and to locate likely hiding places in preparation for a follow-up visit and an all-out-assault on the family's jewels. He entered a home in Ardsley four times, he recalled, but could find no trace of the pricey jewels he knew must be on the premises. Unwilling to give up, he spent five more nights perched in a tree and watching the house through binoculars. Finally, he saw some-one in the master bedroom open a dresser drawer, lift a false bottom, and extract a jewel case. Later that night, when everyone was asleep, he broke in and collected his long-sought treasure.

Most homeowners were not as careful with their jewelry. Barry often found expensive pieces left on the tops of dressers and bureaus. If they had been put away, his best bet was to slide open the top right-hand drawer of the dressing table in the master bedroom. "Nine out of ten times." he noted, "that's the spot where I've found the whole haul." His advice to homeowners looking for a safe place to stash their valuables? "Hide your jewels in the kitchen."

Barry had no trouble turning his "swag," as he called it, into cash. "Why," he once remarked, "there were fences in those days who could have got rid of the Statue of Liberty." Hundreds of pawnbrokers, secondhand shops, and jewelry makers bought and sold stolen gems in 1920s New York, he claimed, and he personally dealt with as many as fifty. While some of the larger and finer gems he stole wound up in Europe, to be recut and resold, most of his loot stayed in New York. Bootleggers bought them to launder their enormous profits, stashing loose diamonds and other stones in safe-deposit boxes and converting them to cash as needed.

Most gems and pearls, however, were used to make new necklaces, brooches, and rings, and sold back to wealthy New Yorkers. Some of these well-to-do buyers knew or suspected they had been stolen. "Many individuals who are looking for a bargain in jewels care little as to where the gems come from," a Brooklyn newspaper noted in 1927, "and as long as there are no identifying marks they will take a chance and buy." The recycled gems, in turn, might one day be stolen again. "Jewels," Barry noted, "have strange careers."

He researched jewelry as carefully as he researched the people he robbed. The illustrated weekly magazine the *Jewelers' Circular* taught him how size, color, clarity, and scarcity affected the value of stones. "I never missed an issue," he said. The more he knew, the more money he could demand. Fences, however, were willing to pay only a fraction of the value of stolen gems—somewhere between 10 and 20 percent—so to make more money, Barry went after more jewels. He estimated he was stealing at least a half million dollars' worth of jewels a year in his mid-'20s heyday, netting him as much as $100,000 annually, the equivalent of $1.5 million today. "My difficulty," he complained, was finding fences "with enough ready cash to swing the enormous deals I brought in."

BARRY LEARNED AND refined other tricks of his lucrative trade. Determined never to leave fingerprints, he was obsessive about wearing gloves. He kept them on as he rode the train to and from a job, in case a conductor were to become suspicious and the police were to dust his ticket stub for prints. He never handled a ladder with his bare hands. If an estate had a night watchman, he studied the guard's patrol route to figure out the best time to break in; only once, he claimed, was he forced to flee when a watchman surprised him. Guard dogs were easily calmed and befriended. Barry had a dog of his own, and the scent of his pet often was enough to transform them from fierce to tail-wagging. Sometimes he brought along food or a female dog to distract them long enough to lock them in their kennels. "Nearly everybody keeps male watch dogs," he noted. "That is a mistake."

He devoted time and effort to planning his getaways. "This is only common sense," he pointed out, "but some crooks don't have the wit to do it." Every time he scouted an estate, he took note of the nearest police station and mapped out the route patrol cars were likely to take if they were summoned. If the home was on a patrolman's beat, he broke in when he knew the officer would be as far away as possible. "One can always depend on having five or ten minutes' start on the cops," he noted. "And a good runner, who uses his head, can do a lot in that time."

He spent days exploring the areas around suburban New York's wealthy enclaves. On one excursion, he discovered a woodland path that shadowed a main road for a dozen miles, from Tarrytown to Yonkers, and he was on it after some successful heists, hidden from view as police cars whizzed by in the opposite direction. For most break-ins, however, he relied on the train as his escape route, jumping on at smaller, out-of-the-way station stops. He studied railroad timetables and knew to the minute when the next train would be along to whisk him back to Manhattan. "My jobs," he boasted, "were timed as carefully as a radio program."

For Barry, burglar alarms were little more than an inconvenience. Disabling them, he boasted, "was practically child's work." Pinkerton, Burns, and other security companies often posted signs warning that an alarm system had been installed to protect the premises. The signs were supposed to deter would-be intruders, but Barry was grateful for the heads-up. "These were of enormous help," he noted, confirming that a home he planned to burgle contained valuables worth protecting—and stealing. He ordered official-looking business cards bearing each company's name, donned overalls, picked up a tool kit, and marched to the front door.

"I'm here to service the burglar-alarm system," he announced to the butler or maid who invited him in.

He would be shown to the closet where the system's main panel and alarm bell were installed. A chart usually pinpointed the doors and windows that would trigger the alarm if opened. "It was the work of a moment to cut a few wires," he noted. Sometimes he left the wires intact and bent back the clapper on the bell, ensuring that it would not make a sound when the system was triggered. It was a simple solution, he explained, "like bending the hammer of an alarm clock so it won't go off." When he was done, to complete the charade, he asked a member of the household staff to sign a paper certifying that the system had been checked and was in good working order. The stage was now set for an undisturbed entry within the next few nights.

Posing as a tradesman was only the beginning. Barry soon devised a far more audacious ploy to worm his way into the elegant homes and charmed lives of the people he was about to rob.

NINE

AMERICAN RAFFLES

N ONE OF THE guests recognized the handsome, charming young man, but he seemed to know everyone. He mingled easily. He dropped names, made small talk. He had the grace and bearing of the well-bred. He introduced himself as Arthur Gibson, and he was becoming an expert at crashing Long Island's exclusive parties.

Arthur Barry was a good talker and good company. He could mimic the accents of the Harvard students he had encountered while growing up in Massachusetts. Studying the society pages and the *Social Register* made him a walking encyclopedia of who was who in New York's upper crust. He exuded confidence and class. And he looked dashing in formal wear—more like a Barrymore from Hollywood than a Barry from Worcester.

As the suave, genial Gibson, he hobnobbed with millionaires as he planned how best to relieve them of their elegant and expensive jewelry. Garden parties were the easiest to crash. "There were always so many people at these parties that one didn't know the other," he explained. He would park his Cadillac near an estate, scale the outer wall, and brush off his tuxedo. Once he was on the grounds, he could blend in with the invited guests. "Men and girls came and went like moths among the whisperings and the champagne and the stars," F. Scott Fitzgerald wrote in *The Great Gatsby* of the brilliant garden parties staged at the island's tony estates. All Barry had to do was join the flow.

"Cocktail in hand, I would wander into the house," he recalled, to "commit its geography to memory." He made his way upstairs unnoticed and unchallenged, looking for places jewelry was likely to be stashed. He mapped out the route he would follow when he would return for a later nocturnal visit.

Sometimes he was interested in the guests, not the layout of the home, and was on the lookout for "the most bejewelled feminine necks and fingers." He admired the jewelry on display and began planning how and when he might acquire it. He was said to have donned a butler's uniform to crash some highbrow parties, and on at least one occasion, he put on a clerical collar, passed himself off as a priest, and was invited into a home he was about to burgle.

Barry was "a cerebral crook . . . gentle and urbane," noted his biographer, Neil Hickey. "Thoroughness, cool-headedness, and a chesslike attention to the rules were at the root of his method."

"His manners were impeccable," recalled Robert Wallace, one of the handful of journalists who met and interviewed him. "Barry was a polished individual, a good conversationalist and something of a dandy."

"An elegant devil" was how Barry once described himself. "Cool as a glacier peak."

His crimes were as perfect and flawless as the gems he stole. He invaded homes and lives, but most of his victims never knew he had been there until they discovered their valuables were missing. Sometimes they were downstairs at dinner. Sometimes they were sleeping inches away as he scooped up jewels from nightstands.

"Is that you, Paul?" asked one woman he disturbed as he worked in the darkness.

"Yes," he replied softly, but she was not fooled. She screamed, and Barry made a swift retreat.

On another job, he could not resist leaving a calling card. After discovering jewelry hidden in a hollowed-out book, he left two cigarettes in the once-secure hiding place. One day, when he recognized William J. Burns as he drove past, Barry followed the legendary private detective to his home, broke in "just for the hell of it," and made off with several thousand dollars' worth of jewelry.

After raiding the Westchester County home of Dr. Joseph Blake, who had been a US Army surgeon in France during the war, and his wife, Katherine, the mother-in-law of famed composer Irving Berlin, Barry returned his entire haul—$15,000 in jewelry—by mail. "We don't forget people who do us a favor" was his only explanation for the astonishing and gracious about-face. Press reports on the theft, which cited Blake's war record, had likely tugged at Barry's conscience.

Such misgivings, however, were rare. "Anyone who could afford to wear a $100,000 necklace could afford to lose it," he told one interviewer. John Robie, Cary Grant's jewel thief character in the 1950s Alfred Hitchcock film *To Catch a Thief*, thought along the same lines. "For what it's worth," he notes at one point in the movie, "I never stole from anybody who would go hungry."

"One of my first commandments was calm," Barry revealed. "I never allowed myself to become excited." He claimed he had never injured anyone he robbed. And while he usually carried a revolver, he appeared to have fired it only once, as he fled from the police. Waving around a gun, he noted, ensured that clients would keep quiet; "tact and courtesy" would do the rest. It was also an insurance policy of sorts, a last resort if he was about to be arrested and returned to prison. "I sometimes thought I'd end my own life with it when faced with certain capture," he explained. Most of his burglaries were pulled off without a hitch. He was interrupted and shot at a few times, but never hit. One bullet came so close it grazed his tie pin. "I scrammed," he said, "at the first indication of disturbance."

An unruly teenage delinquent had morphed into a debonair, high-class crook. He was a chameleon, who looked and talked and sounded like he belonged in these rarefied surroundings. He combined the role-playing skills of an accomplished actor with the slickness of a con artist and the devious mind of a master criminal.

Arthur Barry was a gentleman thief. An American Raffles.

RAFFLES WAS THE creation of British author Ernest William Hornung, whose marriage to Constance Doyle, the sister of Arthur Conan Doyle, created an unlikely union of fictional heroes. "The great detective, Sherlock

Holmes, and the great thief, Raffles," the *New York Times* pointed out, "became, in a sense, brothers-in-law."

"Why should I work when I could steal?" the London gentleman and cricket star A. J. Raffles asks his friend, Harry Manders. "Of course, it's very wrong, but we can't all be moralists, and the distribution of wealth is very wrong to begin with." This is how Raffles, the "amateur cracksman," rationalizes his double life—gentleman of leisure by day, safecracking jewel thief by night—and his personal mission to redistribute wealth in the first of twenty-six stories chronicling his adventures.

The Raffles stories—published in major magazines and collected into three volumes between 1898 and 1905—were wildly popular on both sides of the Atlantic. Critic Clive Bloom has called him "the last Victorian hero and the first modern anti-hero." A play based on the stories premiered in New York in 1903 and toured the United States for three years. "This story of the socially irreproachable hero who prefers subtle thieving to cricket," noted the *Times*, "was the talk of the stage." It was also the talk of the movie houses, with John Barrymore among the actors in the leading role in silent film versions. Half a century after the character first appeared, Raffles was, writer George Orwell observed, "still one of the best-known characters in English fiction." In 1905, in the midst of the initial wave of Raffles-mania, French writer Maurice Leblanc produced the first of a series of stories and novels featuring a Raffles and Holmes knockoff, Arsène Lupin, a top-hatted, monocle-wearing thief who solved crimes as well as committed them. The gentleman bandit had become a cultural icon.

Raffles's first name, Arthur, likely paid homage to Conan Doyle. In the stories, the down-and-out Manders (known as Bunny from their days as boys'-school chums) comes to Raffles seeking a loan to stave off financial ruin and, instead, is recruited as a partner in crime. He is shocked to discover his old friend is as hard up for cash as he is, and has resorted to crime to pay the rent on his apartment in fashionable Piccadilly and keep up appearances. "I have nothing but my wits to live on—absolutely nothing else," Raffles says. Manders is mesmerized at the sight of their first haul as a team, from a break-in at a jeweler on Bond Street. Raffles empties his pockets and "the table sparkled with their hoard," which Manders describes as "Rings by the dozen, diamonds by the score . . . flashing bayonets of light, dazzling me—blinding me."

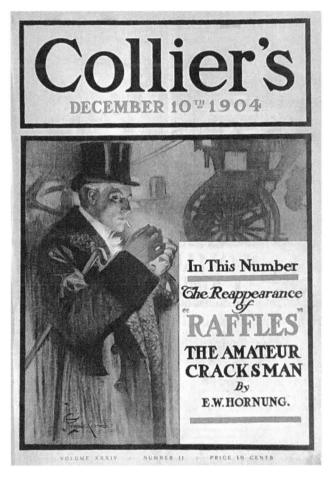

A depiction of Raffles, the fictional gentleman jewel thief (Author Collection)

While Raffles considers himself above the law, he adheres to a personal code of conduct. He is loyal to friends, chivalrous to women, shuns violence, and tends to target the venal, the corrupt, and the obscenely rich— the mining magnate who flaunts his ill-gotten wealth, for example, or the aristocrat who abuses his position and power. What better targets for "the richly immoral" like himself, Raffles reasons in one of the stories, than the jewelry and expensive trinkets of "the immorally rich"? And no gentleman would even think of abusing another man's hospitality. "He will commit a burglary in a house where he is staying as a guest," Orwell noted, "but the victim must be a fellow-guest and not the host." Good sportsmanship and playing a clean game mattered most, even to a gentleman crook; anything else was simply "not cricket."

The character was so popular and so well-known that the word *Raffles* became "a part of headline language," the press critic A. J. Liebling observed. Rendered in large type, it flagged the story beneath as an account of a suave thief who infiltrated high society to prey on the rich. The press began to refer to Barry's crimes as Raffles jobs as early as 1922, when he was pulling some of his first dinnertime burglaries in Westchester County. The references puzzled Barry, who had never heard of the famous character, until he wandered into a public library one day and leafed through one of Hornung's books.

No doubt he was flattered. Bunny described Raffles as a man of "consummate daring and extraordinary nerve." Like Barry, he meticulously planned his heists and staked out shops and houses days in advance of a break-in. Also like Barry, he preferred not to carry a gun, and, when he did, he hoped never to have to use it. "I think it gives one confidence," Raffles tells Bunny after their first burglary. "Yet it would be very awkward if anything went wrong; one might use it, and that's not the game at all." In one story, Raffles swipes an exquisite golden cup from the British Museum, but the patriotic thief promptly returns it to Queen Victoria—"infinitely the finest monarch the world has ever seen"—as a present for her diamond jubilee. Barry's magnanimous gesture of returning the Blake jewels had been just as gracious and unexpected.

~~~~~~~~

IN AN ERA of violent hoodlums and reckless gunplay, Barry's ingenious crimes stood out. Richard and Margaret Whittemore fronted an armed gang that hit at least ten Manhattan jewelry stores in 1925 and early 1926, netting more than a half million dollars in gems. Each time, the robbers burst in with guns drawn, terrorizing and pistol-whipping employees in "an overwhelming show of force," author Glenn Stout pointed out in his chronicle of the gang's crime spree.

Robert LeRoy Parker, better known as Butch Cassidy, was a Wild West incarnation of the Barry-style gentleman bandit. Actor Paul Newman's portrayal of the legendary outlaw as a kindhearted, courteous robber of banks and trains, in the 1969 movie *Butch Cassidy and the Sundance Kid*, was accurate. The charismatic leader of the Wild Bunch gang was polite and well-mannered, rarely fired a gun, and planned his heists with precision. "Pardon us," he told a payroll guard during a holdup, "but we know you have a lot of money, and we have a great need." He was, said one man who knew him, "an exceptionally pleasant and even cultured and charming man." Like Barry, he stole only from those who could afford to absorb the loss—in Cassidy's case, obscenely rich bankers and railroad barons. "Put that away!" he reputedly told bystanders who reached for their cash and valuables as his gang prepared to blow a safe. "We don't want *yours*, we want *theirs*."

Willie Sutton was another crook in the Barry mold. Brooklyn-born, Irish American and five years younger than his jewel-stealing counterpart, he robbed a score of banks, made off with an estimated $2 million in loot, and never fired a single shot. "I had plotted and planned my jobs to make sure that I would not have to hurt anybody," he once explained. He brandished a pistol or a Thompson submachine gun during his heists, but only for show. "You can't rob a bank on charm and personality," he pointed out. The *New York Times* described him as an "urbane scoundrel," and he disguised himself to catch a bank's occupants by surprise—posing as a messenger, a security guard, and even as a police officer—so often that he became known as Willie the Actor. One of the detectives who ended his crime spree in the 1950s considered him the nicest crook he ever locked up. As Sutton fled from one bank, he stopped for a moment to reassure the people cowering inside, with: "Don't worry, the insurance will cover this."

Forrest Tucker, one of Sutton's successors, was a polite stickup man with a penchant for flashy clothes and fast cars. Tucker pulled his first bank heist in 1950, and staged hundreds more, between stints in prison, before his last job in Florida at the age of seventy-eight, when he paused to thank the tellers he had just robbed. "You got to hand it to the guy—he's got style," noted one of the jurors who sent him behind bars. Tucker's heists were meticulously planned—"you need to size it up, know it like your own home" was his advice to would-be bank robbers—and as well rehearsed as stage productions. The guns he toted? "Props," he said. He never intended to fire them. "There is an art to robbing a bank," he told *New Yorker* staff writer David Grann. "Violence is the first sign of an amateur." Arthur Barry would have agreed.

"His stage presence was faultless," journalist Robert Wallace wrote of Barry, "his taste in clothes excellent and his grammar good enough to fool the King of England."

Barry was about to prove it.

3

GENTLEMAN THIEF

TEN

COSDEN AND MOUNTBATTEN

Sands Point, Long Island • 1924

CURTAIN RUSTLED IN the darkness, awakening the man sleeping a few feet away. It sounded like someone had brushed against it, like someone had entered the guest room.

"It was just before daybreak," he recalled. He listened for a moment, then switched on a light. There was no one there. The man had grown up in stately homes, surrounded by butlers, footmen, valets, and maids. He was accustomed to the discreet, almost imperceptible comings and goings of household staff. Perhaps a servant had ducked into the room, he thought. Or maybe a gust of wind from an open window had ruffled the curtain.

Lord Louis Mountbatten—Royal Navy gunnery officer, great-grandson of Queen Victoria, cousin of the Prince of Wales, guest of oil magnate Joshua Cosden—rolled over and went back to sleep.

Mountbatten and his wife, Edwina, had joined the prince's entourage for his holiday on Long Island in September 1924 and were staying at The Cedars, Cosden's estate in Sands Point, on the island's mansion-studded North Shore. The Gold Coast, as it was known, was an architectural mishmash of French châteaux with cone-topped towers, symmetrical Georgian houses, and elegant colonial-style homes perched along the beaches. Each one stood at the heart of a mini kingdom of stables, servants' quarters, and swaths of landscaped grounds and manicured gardens. The Cosdens' neighbors were a roll call of New York's old-money families: Guggenheim,

Astor, Vanderbilt, Whitney. The newly built mansion next door, Cloverly Manor, was the home of Vincent Astor, who was just twenty in 1912 when his father, John Jacob Astor IV, went down with the *Titanic*, leaving him an inheritance of $70 million; today, that would make him a billionaire twice over.

The previous summer, F. Scott Fitzgerald and his wife, Zelda, had rented a house in Great Neck, on the opposite side of Manhasset Bay from Sands Point. And it was there—surrounded, as he put it, by "the consoling proximity of millionaires"—that the writer began formulating the characters and plot for his opus, *The Great Gatsby*. In the novel, Great Neck would be transformed into West Egg, the site of the enigmatic Jay Gatsby's ivy-covered château. Sands Point, at the tip of a peninsula jutting into Long Island Sound, would become the more fashionable and exclusive East Egg, where Daisy Buchanan was ensconced in one of its palatial estates. The Cedars could have been a stand-in for the Buchanan mansion.

Like Fitzgerald and his creation Gatsby, Cosden was an upstart without a blue-blood pedigree. Joshua and his wife, Nellie, had gate-crashed the Long Island social scene from Tulsa, where Cosden & Company operated one of the world's largest refineries. Joshua Seney Cosden had been a clerk at a Baltimore drugstore before he headed west and struck it rich in the Oklahoma oilfields. "Oil gushed up and money showered down," noted one journalist, but this pithy summation ignored years of setbacks and hard work.

His Long Island neighbors may have been born wealthy, but Cosden—a man so determined he became known as Game Josh—had earned his fortune. He was still seen helping out on drilling rigs or behind the wheel of tanker trucks long after his wildcat wells and refinery had made him a multimillionaire. "No story-book hero ever rose to fame and fortune more spectacularly," raved the New York *Daily News*. His Horatio Alger rags-to-riches tale and can-do attitude embodied "the spirit of America," another newspaper suggested. "Without the Cosdens, the men willing to take big risks, ready to fight their way back after every defeat, would not our country become stagnant, backward?" The sixteen-story headquarters he had erected in downtown Tulsa, the city's first skyscraper, was a monument to his ambition and success.

By 1924, at age forty-three, this "small, dapper, energetic man," as one columnist described him, had accumulated the trappings of the ultrarich: an eight-room suite at the Plaza Hotel on Fifth Avenue; a seventy-room Spanish-style mansion in Palm Beach; an estate in Newport, Rhode Island; a hunting lodge in Canada; a private Pullman car christened the *Roamer*. His purchase of The Cedars, the former estate of William Bourke Cockran—the congressman and fiery orator who schooled a young Winston Churchill in the arts of politics and public speaking—planted the Cosdens on the doorstep of New York society. It was one of the finest properties on the North Shore, more than three hundred acres of fields and woodland with three-quarters of a mile of water frontage and views of both Manhasset Bay and Hempstead Harbor. Cosden built a mansion amid the towering trees, added a private nine-hole golf course, and docked his steam-powered yacht, *Crimper*, at the jetty. When he was done, the house and grounds were worth an eye-popping $1.5 million. The New York *Daily News* dubbed it Castle Petroleum.

Money alone could not buy the Cosdens an invitation to mingle with New York's landed gentry. But the interlopers, it turned out, fit in. "Cosden has all the instincts of the good sport," noted journalist and author Winifred Van Duzer, "and Mrs. Cosden has rare beauty and charm." A Virginia stud farm and a stable of more than thirty racehorses were the clinchers. Joshua Cosden's thoroughbreds, including the playfully named Snob II—purchased, it was said, for the outlandish sum of $100,000—competed at Belmont Park, the gathering place for Long Island's equestrian set. "Any millionaire can drive a limousine," Van Duzer explained, "but it takes a thoroughbred to ride a thoroughbred." A cartoon published in 1922 depicted Cosden, clad in a top hat, tails, and woolly chaps, galloping into the midst of a cocktail party, with Nellie riding at his side.

Besides, the Cosdens could play the ultimate social trump card: they hobnobbed with royalty.

MOUNTBATTEN—DICKIE, AS HE was known to family and friends—was as likable and ambitious as Game Josh. He was tall and lanky, with a long, narrow face, a mop of hair, and the wide smile of a man who realized how lucky he was. Born on the grounds of Windsor Castle and on the periphery of the royal family, he had been drawn into the Prince of Wales's orbit in 1920, when he accompanied Edward on a tour of Australia and New Zealand. Official visits to India and Japan followed in 1921 and 1922, cementing their friendship. Mountbatten was six years younger than the prince, but his maturity and inclination to take charge made him a trusted royal chaperone. The prince described him as "a dear boy" and "the closest friend possible," while Mountbatten considered the future king to be "a marvellous person" and "the best friend I've ever had." Edward detested his role as king-in-waiting. "How I loathe my job," he complained to his private secretary before embarking on the globe-circling tours. When his mood turned sullen and he needed to vent about his "rotten" family and his "rotten life," Mountbatten offered a sympathetic ear.

In the midst of the tour of India, the prince's young wingman had become engaged to Edwina Ashley, the daughter of a member of Parliament. She could boast of royal connections of her own. Her grand-father Sir Ernest Cassel, a wealthy banker, had been a financial advisor to Edward VII, and the king had been her godfather. When Cassel died in 1921, she inherited £2 million—just shy of $120 million today—and became, at nineteen, one of the richest women in England. Her hair made a defiant sweep across her forehead and was cropped to fall just short of her dimpled chin. She was smart, elegant, and like her fiancé, astonishingly mature and confident for her age. "She blazed in London society," wrote one of Mountbatten's biographers, "with a fierce brilliance which alarmed some and dazzled almost all." Among the most dazzled was Mountbatten.

The couple were the perfect traveling companions for a royal visitor to America. The Mountbattens, after their marriage in 1922—Edward, natu-rally, had been the best man—had embarked on a ten-week honeymoon tour of the United States. In New York, they were in the stands for baseball games, shook hands with Babe Ruth, and attended the *Ziegfeld Follies* on Broadway. They viewed the Grand Canyon, stayed at the Hollywood home of actor Douglas Fairbanks, and even had cameos in a Charlie Chaplin film. The press had been as fascinated with these near royals—the "close relation of the King of England" and "the richest heiress in the world," the *Washington Herald* called them—as the horde of journalists that was now obsessed with the prince.

"No one living enjoys less privacy," the *New York Times* observed on the eve of the 1924 royal holiday. "The Prince of Wales is as much a topic of conversation at breakfast as is the weather." A boatload of more than seventy journalists was waiting with cameras and questions when his liner steamed into New York Harbor.

One name kept cropping up in the reams of press coverage: Cosden. Edward played an afternoon round of golf on the oilman's private course. He dined with Joshua and Nellie soon after arriving on Long Island. He was spotted boarding *Crimper* for a cruise with the Cosdens' guests, the Mountbattens. "The Cosdens," reported Washington, DC's *Evening Star*, "probably have entertained the prince in a quiet way more than any others." He spent almost as much time at the Cosdens', by one account, as he did at the estate of industrialist James Burden, his temporary home a dozen miles away.

Arthur Barry would have recognized the Cosden name. The couple were listed in the *Social Register*. Their names and doings were a staple of the newspaper society pages he scoured for leads on wealthy potential "clients." The *New-York Tribune* and the *New York Herald* told him when they were at Sands Point, when they held court in their suite at the Plaza Hotel, when they boarded the *Roamer* to spend the winter in Palm Beach. Their expensive jewelry also made the news. Nellie Cosden sported a ring mounted with a large, lustrous black pearl that a newspaper feature on the jewels of the rich and famous described as one of the finest in the world. But even this exquisite piece was no match for the famous Fletcher pearls.

Isaac Dudley Fletcher, a New York manufacturer and art collector who made a fortune from selling coal by-products, spent ten years collecting pearls of identical size and color before presenting the completed strand to his wife. Like the Cosdens' black pearl, it was judged to be among the finest examples of a perfectly matched pearl necklace in the world. The necklace had been sold off as two strands, each fetching $600,000—the equivalent, a century later, of more than $9 million—and Joshua Cosden had bought one for his wife. Photographs of Nellie Cosden wearing the magnificent pearls appeared in the newspapers, making a bold statement of the couple's wealth and status.

Nellie Cosden, left, and Louis and Edwina Mountbatten (Author Collection)

Lady Mountbatten, too, was rarely photographed without at least one strand of expensive pearls dangling from her neck. She insisted on bringing most of her jewelry along when she traveled, even after a burglar swiped some of her collection during a stay at a summer house on the Isle of Wight. Her jewels, noted a biographer, were "a comfort and reassurance." And they made the Cosden estate an even more appealing target for a jewel thief who was adept at mingling in high society. The stage was set for one of the boldest and richest heists of Barry's career.

ARTHUR BARRY PARKED his Cadillac at the edge of the estate's grounds. It was about four o'clock in the morning, but lights still blazed in the Cosden mansion. He would later learn from the newspapers that the couple, along with the Mountbattens and their traveling companion, Jean Norton, had just returned from a dance at an estate on the opposite side of Hempstead Bay. After about an hour, the house went dark.

He retraced his steps of a few nights earlier, stealing across the grounds to the house and climbing a rose trellis to reach a porch roof. It was a warm night, and he quickly found an open window. He knew the upstairs layout from his scouting mission the night he befriended the prince. The Cosdens' five-room bedroom suite was on the west side of the house. Nellie Cosden had taken off the jewelry she had worn to the party before retiring, and had left it on the top of a dressing table. Barry slipped the pieces into his pockets.

He moved next door to the Mountbattens' room and scooped up the jewelry that Lady Mountbatten had tossed onto a tray at her bedside. He spotted a wallet, but before he could grab it Lord Mountbatten stirred. Barry ducked behind a window drape just as the bedroom light was switched on. When the room again went dark, and he was certain the couple was asleep, he crept back to the main hallway.

His foray into the Cosdens' suite had been rewarded with the black pearl ring, diamond pins, and ruby bracelets, worth a total of $130,000. Lady Mountbatten's jewels—three rings glittering with diamonds, rubies, sapphires, and emeralds, plus a platinum bracelet set with more than thirty square-cut rubies—added $42,000 to his haul. The wallet that eluded his grasp, the newspapers later revealed, had been stuffed with $8,000 in banknotes. Barry knew there must be more jewelry in the house, including the priceless Fletcher pearls, but the narrow escape told him it was time to leave.

Within a half hour, he was back in Manhattan. By noon the next day, he had fenced every piece. If he had to settle for 10 percent of the gems' value, his $17,000 cut would have been worth more than a quarter of a million dollars today.

THE COSDENS AND their guests were still asleep at eleven o'clock the next morning, September 9, when Joshua Cosden's valet noticed a pearl shirt stud was missing. A search revealed that other pieces had been stolen. The Cosdens and Mountbattens notified their insurers. Private detectives scoured the estate for clues and questioned the household staff. A watchman who had been stationed downstairs during the night insisted he had not seen or heard anything. The servants, who slept in a separate building, denied any involvement.

The Cosdens, desperate to avoid embarrassment and scandal, tried to keep the theft secret. The news broke the following day, however, sharing the front page on September 10 with reports on the life sentences handed to the infamous Chicago thrill killers Nathan Leopold and Richard Loeb. The heady combination of an enterprising crook, ultrarich victims, and a link to the biggest newsmaker of them all—the Prince of Wales—made the story impossible to resist. The *Daily News* published a photograph of Nellie Cosden posing with her famous pearl necklace in happier times. Baltimore's *Evening Sun* breathlessly reported that the burglar had targeted "two of the wealthiest families of the United States and England." Barry's raid soon made headlines around the world, from Rotterdam to Shanghai. In London, editors of the big Fleet Street dailies offered readers the lowdown on the "Mountbatten Gem Mystery" and "Lady Louis' Loss." Behind the scenes, an outraged British businessman, who lived in the United States, wrote to Downing Street to wag a finger at the prince and his entourage for fraternizing with "social outcasts and parvenus."

The lead investigator, Manhattan private eye Gerard Luisi, tried to downplay the burglary as a minor crime. "There isn't any master criminal mixed up in this," he told the reporters staking out the Cosden estate. "Only a little petty larceny matter, committed by an average crook." The prince's visit, he claimed, had "little or no bearing on the robbery."

No one believed him. There were reports that a gang of international thieves was shadowing the prince on his travels, waiting for a chance to plunder the people he met. The *Brooklyn Daily Eagle* hit the bull's-eye, suggesting the break-in was the work of "a gentleman Raffles . . . a suave, well-dressed individual of insinuating manner" who "circulates among society folk." So did the *New York Times*. "Outsiders are known to have visited social functions held in the Prince's honor," it reported. "An experienced thief familiar with the workings of society would have no difficulty in entering the homes of wealthy persons."

The theft was not reported to the police. Frederick Snow, chief of the force in nearby Port Washington, tried to investigate, but the Cosdens refused to cooperate. So when the couple asked him to send officers to the estate to keep the press at bay, he got even by dispatching a lone patrolman to stand guard.

The Scotland Yard detectives and state troopers surrounding the prince stepped up security. The night after the theft, when race-car and yachting enthusiast William K. Vanderbilt entertained the royal visitor, attendees were screened at the gates to his Long Island estate. "Not a jewel was lost," one newspaper noted wryly. "Not a pearl disappeared from a matronly bosom." Among the guests were Nellie Cosden and the Mountbattens, fresh from a round of golf and, as far as a reporter for the *Daily News* could tell, "apparently unruffled" over the burglary and the lost gems.

Luisi's investigation stalled. He claimed his men had unearthed a "substantial clue," but no suspect was named and no arrest was made. Theories that the crime had been an inside job, with one of the servants guiding the burglar to the gems, were floated and discounted. Reports that the $600,000 Fletcher pearls had been stowed in an unlocked drawer of Nellie Cosden's dresser suggested the thief was an amateur and an opportunist. To other observers, the fact the burglar had taken only gems within easy reach and not rifled through drawers and cabinets—and risked being discovered—seemed like the work of an experienced professional.

A week after the break-in, the Cosdens finally met with the local police. The couple claimed they had seen no need to make an official report, since the jewels were insured and the insurers were investigating, and the burglary faded from the headlines.

In November, Lloyd's of London and another insurance company paid the Cosdens and Mountbattens a total of $125,000, covering the bulk of their losses. "The trackers of criminals on two continents, America and Europe," claimed one news report, "have conducted a fruitless search for the gems."

Posing as the dashing Dr. Gibson to crash one of the Cosdens' parties, taking the heir to the British throne on a tour of Manhattan's nightlife, and the rich haul of jewels, Barry later boasted, marked "the very pinnacle of my success as a gentleman burglar." The truth was, however, that he was just getting started.

ELEVEN

THE PLAZA PEARLS

Manhattan • 1925

H E STEPPED FROM a taxicab where Fifth Avenue met the leafy oasis of Central Park, late in the afternoon on the last day of September. The sun had dipped behind the building that loomed above him, casting a sawtooth shadow over Grand Army Plaza, which gave the hotel its name. The château-inspired roofline—soaring gables, rounded corner turrets, dormer-browed mansards—whispered Paris, but the eighteen-floor elevator ride to get there screamed Manhattan. If Arthur Barry looked up as he walked toward the column-framed main entrance to the Plaza Hotel, his eyes would have been drawn to the windows at the southeast corner of the sixth floor. His destination.

When the Plaza opened almost two decades earlier, it became a magnet for New Yorkers who were accustomed to living in Gilded Age splendor and who appreciated the cachet of a Fifth Avenue address. Heirs to the storied Gould and Vanderbilt fortunes became permanent residents and rubbed shoulders with new-money neighbors, such as Julius Fleischmann, famous for his yeast, and John Warne Gates, whose barbed wire helped to tame the West. Leasing a suite at the Plaza had given the Cosdens a foothold in New York society.

The proprietors had absorbed millions of dollars in cost overruns, the *New York Times* noted, to ensure that patrons experienced a "state of

perfection" unrivaled "by any other hostelry in the world." Their investment in opulence was on display in the more than sixteen hundred twinkling chandeliers suspended from the ceilings and the gold-trimmed
cutlery laid out in the dining rooms. One chronicler of the America's
wealthy described the Plaza's grand ballroom as "New York's best address
for public functions." When F. Scott Fitzgerald was writing *The Great
Gatsby* and needed to pick a swank Manhattan hotel for a confrontation
between Tom Buchanan and Jay Gatsby, the obvious place for two millionaires to square off was in a suite at the Plaza.

New York's Plaza Hotel (Author Collection)

The lobby greeted Barry with old-world elegance—mosaic flooring,
gilt-edged wall panels and coffered ceilings, richly veined white Italian
marble. He was dressed to blend in with the posh surroundings, in a blue
suit, pearl-gray tie, and black homburg. A brown leather briefcase completed the businessman-arriving-home look. He headed for a bank of ele-
vators with decorative bronze doors. Five, he told the attendant. The half
dozen other passengers saw him turn right, away from the stairwell, when
he got off on the fifth floor. The moment the elevator doors closed behind
him, he doubled back and scampered up the stairs to the floor above.

He twisted his hands into a pair of gray silk gloves as he approached a door about twenty paces along the corridor. A passkey opened it, and within seconds he was inside a sitting room. He expected the suite to be empty. But as he closed the door behind him, Barry heard muffled voices in another room.

He froze. He was not alone.

~~~~~~~~~~~~~~

James and Jessie Donahue, the suite's tenants, had spent the summer of 1925 in Europe. Their home on the Upper East Side, just off Fifth Avenue, was being renovated, and the work was still underway when they returned to New York in late September. They could have camped out at their beachfront mansion in Palm Beach, where they entertained lavishly each winter. They could have crashed at Wooldon Manor, their Long Island summer retreat, in Southampton. Instead, they moved into the sumptuous Plaza until the renovation was complete.

James Paul Donahue was a stockbroker with an office on Park Avenue. His family had made a fortune in the unglamorous business of rendering animal fat. They were "well-to-do in a modest way," in the blunt assessment of the New York *Daily News*. He was light-years away from claiming an entry in the *Social Register* until he married Jessie May Woolworth in 1912. She was the youngest daughter of F. W. Woolworth, who founded the chain of more than a thousand five-and-dime stores that bore his name and revolutionized retailing. He turned nickels and dimes into a fortune vast enough to build a sixty-floor New York skyscraper, the Woolworth Building, that reigned as the world's tallest for almost two decades. When her father died in 1919, Jessie Donahue inherited one-third of his $55 million estate—the equivalent, a century later, of roughly $280 million—making her one of the richest women in America. Her tax assessment in 1924 was $1 million, almost as much as Standard Oil's mega-rich founder, John. D. Rockefeller.

The Woolworth millions allowed Donahue to graduate from placing bets on stocks and bonds to trying his luck at roulette tables. He became a regular at a Palm Beach club and reputedly gambled away a jaw-dropping $900,000 over the course of a single winter. In an effort to rein in his losing streaks, his wife worked out an arrangement with the club's management, setting a limit on how much Donahue could lose before being asked to leave.

Jessie Donahue had a passion of her own: jewelry. And like her husband's gambling, it consumed a hefty chunk of her great wealth. She bought and commissioned expensive pieces, and, rather than locking them away in a safe, she flaunted them. She appeared in public "attired like a regal princess," by one account, "dressed in her stunning fashions and opulent jewelry." New York newspapers got plenty of mileage out of a photograph of her at a social event wearing an oversized glittering tiara that would have been at home in the Tower of London. The *New Yorker* cheekily referred to her collection as "the Woolworth family jewels."

Then there was the necklace. "My wife has always been very fond of pearls," Donahue once noted with colossal understatement. The couple had been collecting rose-hued pearls for at least a decade. "Whenever we would see one that matched in with the roseate ones that we started with," he explained, "we'd purchase it." Some were reputed to have once belonged to the royal family of Persia. By 1925, they had assembled a fifty-two-pearl strand that Jessie Donahue wore every day—to lunch, to dinner, even when she climbed into the back of a limousine for her customary afternoon drive around the city. In Paris that summer, they found two pinkish pearls that were a perfect match, and large enough to form the centerpiece of the necklace. The stones were shipped to New York and delivered to the Plaza on September 29. That afternoon, Jessie Donahue took them to Cartier, the Fifth Avenue jeweler, to be added to her cherished strand. They nudged its value to $450,000, putting the Donahues almost in the same league as the Cosdens, with their illustrious Fletcher pearls.

"Well," Donahue remarked to his wife as they admired the new pearls, "I guess that finishes the necklace."

~~~~~~~~~~

A DAY LATER, Barry was inside the Donahue suite with his back to the hallway door, listening to the voices. Two women were talking; sometimes one of them laughed. He could not make out what they were saying.

A former Plaza porter had given him the passkey. He had paid his accomplice to watch the hotel and monitor the comings and goings of the Donahues and their staff. The suite should have been empty at this time of the afternoon.

Should he slip back into the hall and leave empty-handed? Or should he forge ahead and risk being caught? If he were cornered, he could brandish the .32-caliber revolver in his pocket to cover his escape. In a split second, he opted to roll the dice, betting he could find the jewels before someone found him.

Plaza rooms had connecting doors and could be configured into suites of any size, to accommodate short-term guests and longer-term residents. This flexibility, however, meant that every room of a suite had a second door that connected to the main hallway. The Donahues' L-shaped, six-room suite overlooked Fifth Avenue on one side and Fifty-Eighth Street to the south. The sitting room Barry had entered was on the corner of the building, in the middle of the suite. Jessie Donahue's bedroom and bath were on the street side, to his right, while the rooms facing the avenue were her husband's domain.

He crossed the sitting room and opened a door he knew led to the Donahues' bedroom. There was no one there, but the voices were louder and coming from the adjoining bathroom.

Barry rummaged through the drawers of a dressing table but found nothing. He moved on to a bureau, where an unlocked drawer yielded a velvet box laden with jewelry. One stunning piece stood out—a ring with a ten-carat diamond, cut in a slender marquise shape. With it were two guard rings set with diamonds, designed to bookend and enhance the glimmering solitaire. There was a large buckle-shaped pin, covered in diamonds and rubies, another ring, a brooch, and a jeweled vanity case. He stashed the pieces in his briefcase.

He reached farther into the drawer and pulled out six strands of pearls wrapped in tissue paper. Some, he was certain, must be imitation. If all of the strands were real, he was holding millions of dollars' worth of pearls.

"The easy way to tell a real pearl from an imitation," Barry revealed later, "is to rub it gently across your teeth. A real pearl produces a somewhat grating, sandpapery sensation, but a fake is smooth and slippery."

He held one string to his teeth. The pearls were smooth. He discarded that necklace and picked up the rose-tinted, newly completed, fifty-four-pearl strand. It felt rough against his teeth. He dropped it into his briefcase, along with a second necklace of fifty-two pearls that passed the test. It turned out to be valued at $200,000.

He was in the bedroom for no more than three minutes. Any moment, he knew, Donahue or a servant could walk in. Satisfied with his haul, he checked to make sure the sitting room was still empty, then hurried to the hallway door. He could still hear the voices in the bathroom as he closed the door behind him.

He removed his gloves as he took the stairs to the fifth floor and caught an elevator the rest of the way to the lobby. Once outside, he hailed a cab headed east on Fifty-Ninth Street, then got out after a short ride, in case he was being followed. He flagged down a second taxi headed in the opposite direction. The driver dropped him on 115th Street near Morningside Park. He walked the rest of the way to his apartment, on 119th, as the sun was setting. His briefcase was weighed down with almost $700,000 in pearls and gems—the equivalent of $10 million today.

The daring heist had been pulled off in under half an hour.

~~~~~~~~~~

THE COUPLE WAS dressing for dinner that evening when Jessie Donahue slid open the bureau drawer to retrieve her favorite pearls. She had worn the just-completed pink strand earlier in the day when she met her husband for a late lunch at a Park Avenue hotel. Back in the suite about half past four, she had wrapped the necklace in tissue paper to protect the stones, placed it in the drawer, and taken a bath.

Three hours later, the necklace and a second strand of pearls were gone. So were other pieces of jewelry.

"Did you hide my jewels?" she called to her husband, thinking he had moved them as a practical joke.

No, he replied, he had not touched them.

They searched the suite and soon realized they had been robbed. They summoned the hotel detective. The insurers were contacted. A day passed before the theft was reported to the police and word leaked to the newspapers.

The combination of a wealthy victim and a brazen, almost-impossible theft was irresistible to the press. WOOLWORTH HEIRESS ROBBED AT THE PLAZA, the *New York Times* announced on its front page. The *Brooklyn Daily Eagle* proclaimed it "the greatest coup in gem robberies ever reported in the city."

Jessie Donahue, Woolworth department store heiress (Author Collection)

The high-profile crime merited a high-level response. Richard Enright, New York's police commissioner, rushed to the Plaza and spent almost two hours consoling the shaken Donahues. He assigned the case to chief of detectives John Coughlin. Coughlin assembled a team of twenty officers and recruited two of his best men to lead the investigation. Detective Lieutenant Oscar Mayer and Sergeant Grover Brown, one paper noted, had "wide experience in tracing Wall Street bond thieves." The pair was ordered to stay on the case until they had a suspect and the jewels.

Was it the work of professional criminals? Reporters speculated that a band of skilled crooks—"international thieves of high calibre," as they were described in one news report—had followed the Donahues back from Europe. The new pearls had arrived from Paris the day before the theft, and the timing seemed too perfect to be a coincidence.

Or was it an inside job? Jessie Donahue had been in her bedroom all afternoon, stepping out only for the fifteen or twenty minutes she was in the bath. Had someone let the intruder know when the coast would be clear? Coughlin and his men questioned the couple's maid and valet, and a masseuse who was in the bathroom with Jessie Donahue—it was their voices Barry had overheard as he worked—but quickly eliminated all three as suspects. Plaza staff who were working near the suite that afternoon were also questioned and exonerated.

The press soon turned on the couple, accusing them of trying to keep the theft a secret. James Donahue claimed they had feared the publicity would draw attention to their wealth and might embolden other crooks to kidnap and ransom their two school-aged sons. It was a weak excuse; Jessie Donahue's ostentatious displays of her jewels were a constant reminder to everyone that she was filthy rich.

Giving the thief or thieves a head start, Coughlin acknowledged, had hampered his investigation. "We know the jewels are gone, and that is about where we stop," he groused to a reporter. "We lost a day because of the delay in reporting the robbery."

The racy *Daily News*, ever eager to expose the foibles of millionaires and celebrities, chided Jessie Donahue for wearing her expensive pearls every day; many wealthy women, the paper noted, often wore imitation pieces in public and kept the real McCoys locked away.

Columnists at the *New Yorker* mocked her and her loss. While the heiress had been relieved of "several quarts" of jewels worth "ten million nickels," the magazine predicted she would have "little difficulty in replacing the missing real gems with exact replicas from her late father's shops."

Two things were certain. Whoever was responsible had shadowed the Donahues and knew their movements. And the police were looking for someone with an expert's eye for pearls. Six necklaces had been in the drawer—four were imitation strands, purchased in Paris as gifts for friends, James Donahue explained to the police—and only the fakes had been left behind. The culprit was someone with "a shrewd knowledge of pearls," the *New York Times* pointed out, since the imitations "were good enough to have fooled pearl connoisseurs."

Coughlin, however, had an ace to play. He could make it almost impossible for this mysterious pearl-savvy thief to profit from the crime. New York pawnshops and secondhand jewelry stores across the city were warned to be on the lookout for the pearls and other stolen pieces. Cartier, which had assembled the pink-pearl necklace, offered the police photographs and detailed descriptions of each stone. The information had been circulated to police forces across North America and cabled to London, Paris, and other European capitals. The *Daily News* did its civic duty by publishing a photograph of the necklace, so all New York could be on alert. Coughlin issued a warning to the Plaza thief: "It will be almost impossible to get rid of these priceless gems."

Barry may have chuckled when Coughlin, in one of his interviews, described him as "a master criminal." The detective had no inkling that the carefully planned theft, timed to be pulled off when the suite should have been empty, had almost gone awry. And he must have been grateful for Coughlin's warning. If he were to try to fence anything he had lifted from the Donahue suite, he was certain to be caught. He would need to find another way to dispose of his haul, and he knew who to contact.

TWELVE

THE GREAT RETRIEVER

Manhattan • 1925

RTHUR BARRY CLAIMED a chair in the lobby of the Endicott, opened a newspaper, and waited. The hotel was an Upper West Side landmark, seven stories of rust-brown, slender Roman brick on West Eighty-First Street. The marble floor shivered each time a train rumbled by on the elevated line that ran past one side of the building.

A tall, slim man with a neatly trimmed mustache emerged from the revolving door. Barry knew him by sight and by reputation. Noel Scaffa, *Time* magazine once declared, was the "most famed of U.S. private detectives." He had arrived from Sicily with his family when he was nine, and as a teenager had worked as a laborer for his father, a building contractor. His father died young, and he took over the business, but he had failed to keep it afloat. Even with little formal education, noted one account of his career, he was "smart enough to know there was easier money to be made—somewhere—somehow."

A clerical job with the famous Pinkerton detective agency soon led to work on investigations. He discovered he was better at finding clues, solving puzzles, and cultivating sources than he ever was at reading blueprints. He made friends in low places and developed a roster of underworld contacts who could point him in the right direction as he hunted for stolen jewels and other valuables.

By 1920, he had struck out on his own. The Scaffa Detective Agency set up shop at the southern tip of Manhattan, near Wall Street, close to the offices of insurance companies and jewel-owning millionaires. Victims of burglaries hoping to avoid publicity and insurers hoping to cut their losses often called him before they reported the crime to the police. He became known as the Great Retriever, a go-to guy who had recovered millions of dollars' worth of stolen gems. "If Scaffa couldn't get them," in the opinion of the New York *Daily Mirror*, "they were gone for good."

Barry, who had phoned Scaffa at his office to arrange a meeting, rose from his chair and approached.

"I have jewels you might be interested in," he said.

They left the hotel, crossed Columbus Avenue, and walked along the edge of Central Park. Scaffa was the taller of the two—at six feet, he had

Private detective Noel Scaffa (Author Collection)

a few inches on Barry—and a fedora made him look even taller. They stopped at a bench and sat facing the traffic.

"It's possible to retrieve the Donahue gems," Barry said. "How much will the insurance company pay to get them back?"

The Donahues' insurers had not retained Scaffa, but the detective knew from newspaper reports what the missing pearls and other jewelry were worth. He tossed out a figure: $60,000. It was about a tenth of their actual value, and roughly what a fence might pay for them. Barry, who claimed to be acting as a go-between for the Plaza thief, asked for a few thousand more to cover his services.

Scaffa needed a few days to make the arrangements. Then they met again at the Endicott, took a cab across the park, and got out on the Fifth Avenue side. Barry placed his briefcase between them when they sat on a bench. Scaffa pulled out a notebook and made a quick inventory of the necklaces and other pieces inside. But there was a possible deal-breaker. Scaffa produced a certified check for $64,000. Barry had demanded cash.

They devised a plan B worthy of a spy novel: Scaffa would cash the check at a bank, and, in the meantime, Barry would stash the jewels somewhere, to ensure he did not back out and take off with his loot. They took a taxi to Penn Station, on Eighth Avenue, where Barry checked the briefcase at the baggage-check desk and entrusted the claim stub to Scaffa. When Scaffa returned with the money, they retrieved the case and cabbed it back to the same bench in Central Park. Scaffa pocketed the jewels and handed over a thick envelope. Barry opened it and counted sixty-four $1,000 bills, equivalent to almost a million dollars today.

He tucked the envelope into the breast pocket of his suit jacket and shook Scaffa's hand.

"Perhaps," he said, "we'll meet again."

⁓⁓⁓⁓⁓⁓

JOHN COUGHLIN WAS in his office on October 13 when Scaffa walked through the door and placed a package, wrapped in brown paper, on his desk. Inside was the fortune in jewels that New York's chief of detectives had been trying to find for two weeks.

James Donahue was summoned to the police station and confirmed that the package contained all the pieces stolen from the Plaza suite. Scaffa refused, at first, to explain how the pearls and diamonds had come into his possession. His lawyer, he said, advised him to make a statement only to a district attorney.

Late that afternoon, he was taken to the Criminal Courts Building on Centre Street and spent almost two hours fielding questions from Coughlin and Ferdinand Pecora, chief assistant district attorney. Pecora was a rising star among the city's prosecuting attorneys, and a political shape-shifter who had supported Teddy Roosevelt, a Republican, then backed Democrat Woodrow Wilson. Like Scaffa, he had been born in Sicily and his family had moved to New York City when he was a child. A dogged investigator, he earned perhaps the ultimate accolade for a prosecutor: "hard but fair."

Scaffa told them an executive of Chubb & Son, an insurance underwriter, had authorized him to pay $64,000 for their return. The man he had dealt with called himself Sam Layton, he claimed, and he knew nothing more about him. Scaffa did a masterful job of throwing Pecora and the police off the scent. He described Layton as older, heftier, and darker-complected than Barry. The name was Scaffa's invention, not Barry's. And Scaffa said they met only once, at the ritzy Prince George Hotel on East Twenty-Eighth Street, three miles from the Endicott. The exchange of cash for jewels, he said in his statement, had taken place in one of the upstairs rooms.

If the police hoped to find witnesses who had seen the two men together, they would be questioning staff and guests at the wrong hotel and on the wrong side of town. At least one reporter was skeptical enough to check with the hotel, and discovered there was no record of Scaffa booking a room at the Prince George that day.

Dealing with Scaffa face-to-face had been risky for Barry, but he had gambled that the detective would refuse to cooperate with the authorities. Recovering stolen jewels was the Great Retriever's specialty; if he turned in a man who claimed to be acting on behalf of the Donahue thief, no one in the underworld would trust him or deal with him again. "A single double cross," Barry reasoned. "would be the end of it."

Scaffa told one more lie. After he had recovered the jewels, he told

Pecora, Layton had phoned again and offered to turn in the thief if he was paid an additional $5,000. Give me a week, Scaffa pleaded, and he would try to convince Layton to lead him—and the police—to the Plaza thief. Pecora, who did not realize Scaffa was bluffing and buying time, agreed. Facing reporters after the interview, Pecora announced he was giving Scaffa a chance to identify and track down the culprit. In the meantime, he revealed few details of how the gems were recovered, but vowed the "sneak thief" responsible would be found and arrested.

"There will be no compromise with thieves," he declared, "in this or any other case." His boss, district attorney Joab Banton, made the same promise: "No bargains with thieves."

To the press, however, the one-week reprieve granted to Scaffa looked like a deal struck with crooks. Editorials mocked the secrecy surrounding the return of the gems. "The public is entitled to facts," huffed the *Daily News*, attacking Pecora for throwing a "mantle of mystery" over the affair. There were calls for Scaffa's arrest; had he notified the police the moment he was contacted, a trap could have been set and the thief might be behind bars. "What kind of law enforcement is this?" asked the *Brooklyn Daily Eagle*. "This case does not end with the return of the loot. It should begin there." If police and prosecutors turned a blind eye when thieves were rewarded for returning stolen goods, warned a former district attorney, "won't it encourage other thefts in the future?" Legal experts confirmed that Scaffa could be charged with several possible offenses under New York State's criminal law—as an accessory to a crime, for receiving stolen goods, or for "compounding" a felony, a crime committed if a person takes money to conceal a crime or to block or delay the prosecution of a crime.

The one-week deadline passed. Pecora's mood changed from fair-minded to hard-line. With no arrest and no new information on the identity of the thief, he launched a grand jury investigation into Scaffa's actions. Jessie and James Donahue braved a gauntlet of reporters to testify. Coughlin showed up carrying a bag containing their pearls and diamonds, which were being stored in a police vault as evidence. Scaffa's statement was read to the jurors, but Pecora made it clear they should not believe a word of it. Why, he argued, would anyone hand tens of thousands of dollars to a stranger in return for gems that could have been fakes? He was now convinced that Scaffa knew the mysterious Layton and was covering for him. "As to the truth or falsity of the whole story told by Scaffa," he told reporters, "I have a very decided personal opinion."

Scaffa, who had dropped out of sight after returning the jewels, broke his silence on October 22. He conceded he had made "a grave mistake" when he failed to alert the police to his negotiations to recover the jewels. "The underworld knows that I am always on the job when large jewel robberies are reported," he said. "So there is nothing new in having go-betweens get in touch with me relative to the return of stolen gems." He defended his methods and insisted it was not his job to catch those responsible for the heists that kept him in business. "The police," he said, "are paid to see that thieves are caught and punished."

The grand jury disagreed. The day the interview was published, Scaffa was indicted for compounding a felony. If convicted, he faced up to five years in prison.

District Attorney Banton touted the prosecution as the first step in a bid to stamp out the practice of paying thieves and go-betweens to return stolen jewels. Insurance companies cutting deals to save money, Pecora complained, "are issuing an open invitation for widespread thievery." Scaffa, it appeared to the DA's office, was the most high-profile player in a thriving, clandestine trade.

It turned out Scaffa had recovered one of the pieces of jewelry Barry had stolen from the Cosden estate a year earlier and sold to a fence. The piece, a pink-pearl ring worth as much as $40,000, had wound up in the hands of a reputable Manhattan jeweler, who recognized it as one of the missing Cosden gems. The Federal Insurance Company, which insured the Cosdens as well as the Donahues, had authorized Scaffa to pay the jeweler $8,000 to return the ring. The discovery was never reported to the police. When this information was revealed, it prompted the authorities on Long Island to launch a parallel probe into the detective's actions in the Cosden case.

Scaffa's career as the Great Retriever was on the line, but he continued to hunt for stolen jewels as he awaited trial. The New York *Daily Mirror* later published a cartoon depicting him as a top-hatted magician, his arms flailing as he juggled jewels held out by thieves and second-story men and swept them into the hands of the police and insurance companies. "The whole system smells," the paper complained in an accompanying editorial. "A dowager is robbed. Her jewels are insured. Scaffa gets them back. The insurance company is satisfied. The police are relieved of an embarrassing situation, the dowager is happy, the thieves have usually been paid enough to make the operation worth their while, as there is very little profit in selling stolen stuff to a 'fence.' And Mr. Scaffa . . . is happy and well paid for his services to the community."

Barry understood how the system worked and how to turn it to his advantage. The Donahue heist briefly transformed him from a gem thief into a gem kidnapper, who returned what he stole once a ransom was paid. Why risk selling his loot to a fence for a 10 percent cut when an insurance company might be willing to pay that much to recover stolen jewels—and avoid a claim for their full value? "This," he later explained, "was better than a total loss for the company."

And this was why some wealthy victims of burglaries were reluctant to report their losses. If they stayed quiet and played ball with their insurers, Scaffa or another private detective might get their jewels back without alerting the police and a horde of nosy reporters. If a deal was exposed and the police began to ask uncomfortable questions, Scaffa and his ilk, Barry joked, could claim "they had accidentally found the jewels in a hollow tree."

The New York police, meanwhile, continued to search for Sam Layton and the Donahue thief. Coughlin's investigation descended into a farce worthy of a Keystone Cops movie. An ex-con came forward—at Scaffa's urging—to claim that a former cellmate, a thief from England known as English Jimmy Berkley, had tried to recruit him for the Donahue heist. Scotland Yard was asked to help track down the suspect. Detectives reinterviewed the Donahues' maid and valet, to make sure the crime had not been an inside job. Headlines proclaimed arrests were imminent, but no

one was taken into custody. When a man arrested for breaking into a New
Jersey grocery store claimed he was the mysterious Sam Layton, Pecora
dismissed him as a petty crook seeking attention.

Arthur Barry was in the clear. Morris Markey, a writer for the *New
Yorker* imagined the "bold rogue" behind the Donahue heist, his "stirring adventure behind him," catching his breath as the furor in the press
died down and detectives were quietly assigned to other cases. "After all,"
Markey noted, "this is only one crime in a thousand, and the victims have
gotten their stuff back."

Barry had pulled off the biggest heist of his career.

THIRTEEN

ΠIGHTLIFE PLUΠGER

Manhattan • 1920–25

I T WAS ONE of the most infamous addresses in Jazz Age Manhattan—244 West Seventieth Street, an Upper West Side town house just off Broadway, clad in gray stone. On a June morning in 1920, a shocked housekeeper discovered the lone occupant, Joseph Bowne Elwell, slumped in a chair. The forty-seven-year-old, whose reputation as a philanderer almost overshadowed his passion for breeding thoroughbreds and his renown as an expert on bridge, had been shot in the forehead. He was still alive but died within hours.

A slug from a .45-caliber revolver had left a crater in the plastered wall behind him, but the gun was gone. The outer door was locked, and the killer, the police suspected, was someone Elwell had let into the house. Someone he knew so well he did not mind them seeing him in his red silk pajamas, without his false teeth, and with no toupee to cover his bald head. There were plenty of suspects: jilted lovers, gamblers he had fleeced at the card table, rivals on the horse-racing circuit. Detectives probed "old quarrels, old love affairs, turf rows, gambling squabbles and business disagreements," the *New York Times* reported, but every lead and theory hit a dead end. Not even Edgar Allan Poe, the paper was convinced, "could have concocted a murder mystery as clean-cut."

The New York papers feasted on the investigation for weeks. Witnesses tracked Elwell's movements the previous night—dinner with friends at the rooftop restaurant of the Ritz-Carlton Hotel, followed by a showgirl-filled performance of Ziegfeld's *Midnight Frolic*, then home a few hours before dawn. But when no one was arrested, the press gradually lost interest and reporters moved on to new stories of murder and mayhem.

The contents of the home—an impressive collection of mahogany bookcases, leather-bound books, oriental vases, and jade figurines—were auctioned off. The owner, a Manhattan lawyer, eventually rented the town house to Myrtle King, who was acting for a friend who wanted to establish a private club for gamblers. It would be called the Harlequin Club. King's friend, the future proprietor, was a man she knew as Arthur Gibson; she had no idea his real name was Arthur Barry.

"I've been a gambler ever since I can remember," Barry later confessed in a newspaper interview. The few dollars he had earned as a teenager, delivering explosives to safecrackers across New England, were often wagered on rolls of the dice. "I went from town to town, shooting craps and picking up various methods of beating the dice rackets," he recalled. "I can no more resist the sight of the silent anxious huddle around a crap game than a bee can resist the lure of honey. With me, gambling is a greater passion than sex."

Flush with cash after fencing the jewels scooped up in his heists, Barry sought out other high rollers. His gambling strategies were as meticulous as his planning for a break-in. Shooting craps one night with some well-heeled players—including two bootleggers with thick bankrolls and a professional gambler who lost $50,000 without batting an eye—he jealously guarded the paltry $3,000 in his pocket. "I took it easy at first, in the hope of moving ahead slowly," he recalled. "Then I planned to plunge and try for a killing." Barry never revealed if his gambit worked that night, but he left one gambling session with a $35,000 windfall.

He racked up big losses as well, dropping $15,000—a quarter of a million dollars today—in a single disastrous night. His opponents were a motley crew of mobsters, con artists, shady Wall Street brokers, and fellow thieves. "Nobody," Barry recalled, "inquired where another man's bankroll came from."

The venues were secret and changed often, floating to stay a step ahead of police raids on illegal games, and crooks more interested in swiping cash at gunpoint than gambling for it. Barry hopped into the back seat of a limousine in Times Square and wound up tossing dice in a dingy cellar in Greenwich Village, a Midtown loft, the back room of a restaurant, or a swank town house on Riverside Drive. If his bets paid off, the organizers loaned him a bodyguard to ensure that he made it home safely with his winnings. He immersed himself in the Broadway netherworld like a character sprung from a Damon Runyon story, a real-life version of Nathan Detroit, the streetwise craps-game-chasing gambler of the musical and movie *Guys and Dolls.*

Barry opened the Harlequin, his Manhattan gambling club, in the town house on the right, the former home of murder victim Joseph Elwell
(Author Collection)

Establishing the Harlequin Club allowed Barry to indulge his gambling habit while laundering some of the proceeds of his crimes. Craps was the club's mainstay, but patrons also gathered around tables to play stud poker, blackjack, and a high-card-wins game called red dog. He sometimes hosted dice and card games at a venue a few doors down from his apartment. The games attracted Manhattan highfliers and lowlifes. Among them was five-foot-five boxer Abe Goldstein, who was bantamweight champion of the world for much of 1924, and disgraced doctor Robert Thompson, who had served time for the murder of a young woman who died after an abortion he performed in California. William McGee and Edward Fuller, bankrupt stockbrokers who would soon be sent to prison for bilking investors out of an estimated $4 million, rubbed shoulders with a shady character who called himself Dan the Dude. William Fallon often stopped by; known as the Great Mouthpiece, he was a flamboyant, hard-drinking lawyer so renowned for his courtroom theatrics that Broadway stars attended his trials to watch him in action and learn. This "most brazen of attorneys," as journalist Gene Fowler described him, had a crook-laden client list that included reputed World Series fixer Arnold Rothstein and an eyebrow-raising record of more than a hundred acquittals—and not a single conviction—in homicide cases. One tactic that explained his success was exposed in 1924, when he stood trial on a charge of bribing a juror; he was, of course, acquitted.

Perhaps the most infamous figure believed to have gambled under Barry's roof was Joseph Crater, a prominent Manhattan attorney and Democratic Party organizer, who spent his off-hours immersed in the city's nightlife. Good Time Joe, as he became known, was a big spender who frequented Broadway's restaurants and speakeasies with a succession of chorus girls and without his wife. Crater would become the Jimmy Hoffa of his day; in 1930, four months after he was appointed to the New York State Supreme Court, he hopped into a cab on West Forty-Fifth Street and was never seen again.

Barry, for his part, was hesitant to identify his gambling associates, even years later when a nosy reporter was probing his past. "I was too busy dealing the chips and raking in the cash," he claimed, "to pay much attention."

The house was still a magnet for amateur sleuths keen to solve the Elwell mystery long after Barry set up shop. Journalists asked to inspect the bullet hole in the wall or to check the floor plan as they reinvestigated the crime. "Seems the Elwell mystery will never die," he said, shrugging, when he recalled the intrusions. None of the newshounds suspected they were missing a far more sensational story: the man who met them at the door was a gentleman jewel thief turned gambling czar.

Every time Barry climbed onto a porch or placed a ladder under a second-story window, he was taking a gamble. He was not only betting he would not get caught—he was rolling the dice and hoping he would make it out alive.

"My philosophy was to live hard and enjoy the day," he once explained. "The next time I entered a house, there was the chance that a blast of gunfire in the darkness would blow my head off and end the whole adventure. But that's the kind of life I had chosen." He only had to glance at the bullet hole in the wall at the Harlequin Club—a grim memento of the fate of another fast-living gambler, Joseph Elwell—to be reminded of the dangerous world he inhabited.

Live hard and enjoy the day. It could have been the mantra of a generation of hedonistic, rebellious youth. Barry and other young men who had faced death on the battlefield, who had seen comrades horribly maimed or killed, lived for the moment. They wanted it all, and they wanted it now. It was a time that mirrored the early twenty-first century, noted the social historian Lucy Moore, "when youth, wealth and celebrity were venerated, when new technologies seemed set to change almost everything about the way people behaved, and when a sense of living in an ultramodern world, a mood of heady possibility, set the atmosphere alight."

Young people rejected the stifling morality of their parents. "A whole generation had been infected by the eat-drink-and-be-merry-for-tomorrow-we-die spirit," explained a chronicler of the decade, *Harper's Magazine* editor Frederick Lewis Allen. On the home front that tens of thousands of American servicemen never saw again, "there had been a very widespread and very natural breakdown of traditional restraints and reticences and taboos," Allen wrote. Life was lived at full throttle, washed down with bootlegged liquor, and paid for by bets on a booming stock market. "America was going on the grandest, gaudiest spree in history," wrote F. Scott Fitzgerald, who made it his business to understand the forces shaping the era he christened the Jazz Age. "The whole golden boom was in the air—its splendid generosities, its outrageous corruptions and the tortuous death struggle of the old America in prohibition."

Writer Gertrude Stein, an American expat in Paris, gave these disillusioned, rebellious, live-for-the moment young people a name, and her protégé, Ernest Hemingway, made it famous: the Lost Generation. John F. Carter, one of the "wild" youth condemned as selfish and irresponsible in the pages of the *Atlantic*, fired back with a simple explanation for behavior that scandalized parents and grandparents. "We have been forced to live in an atmosphere of 'to-morrow we die,' and so, naturally, we drank and were merry."

A smooth-talking, free-spending man-about-town like Barry moved easily in a world where everyone was rich, spent money as if they were rich, or longed to get rich as soon as possible.

Fads and guilty pleasures abounded, offering antidotes to alarmist headlines of postwar turmoil in Europe and the humdrum of everyday life. Alma Cummings danced for twenty-seven hours at New York's Audubon Ballroom in 1923, outlasting a half dozen partners and inspiring dance marathons across the country. Crossword puzzles and mahjong, a Chinese game played with inscribed tiles, became leisure-time obsessions. The movies beckoned, with promises of drama, excitement, and slapstick comedy. The likes of Mary Pickford, Charlie Chaplin, and Lillian Gish mouthed their lines in new releases flickering in darkened theaters across the country. Magazines and newspaper photo spreads dished the latest gossip to starstruck fans. A celebrity culture was born. After actress Irene Castle appeared on screen with bobbed hair, countless young women cropped theirs, too, giving the era's rebellious flappers their distinctive hairstyle.

America was awash in money. Barry saw the proof every time he broke into a posh mansion and found a cache of jewels. "More people were comfortably well-off, well-to-do, or rich than ever before," the economist John Kenneth Galbraith noted in a study of the money-mad decade. And there were plenty of newfangled must-haves—rumbling Ford Model Ts, crackling radios, scratchy-throated gramophones—to spend it on.

The number of automobiles on US highways and streets quadrupled during the decade, to more than twenty-three million in 1929. Vehicles and other big-ticket items could be purchased on installment plans, putting them within the reach of almost everyone. A housewife living in a rural area was asked why her family owned a car but did not have a bathtub in their home. "Bathtub?" the incredulous woman replied. "You can't go to town in a bathtub."

Radio, a novelty at the dawn of the decade, became the hottest ticket in entertainment. By 1928, there were sets in nine million of the United States' twenty-eight million households, and a nationwide network of radio stations was broadcasting everything from live concerts to presidential election returns. The "nightly miracle," one writer called it, filled even the most remote and humble homes with music and voices. "We are lucky dogs," the novelist Sherwood Anderson remarked in 1926. "We live in the most prosperous country in the world, in what is, perhaps, its most prosperous period."

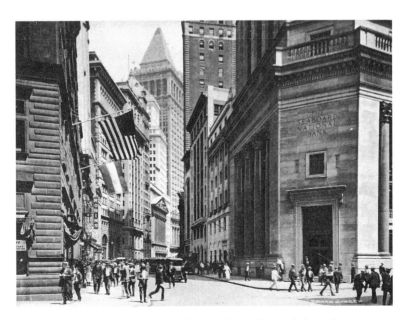

Broad Street in Manhattan's Financial District (Author Collection)

Investing in the stock market—once the domain of the wealthy, the well-connected, and the powerful—became an everyman craze as pervasive as crossword puzzles and nonstop dancing. People now accustomed to buying automobiles on installment plans could buy shares in companies in a similar way, on margin—paying a small percentage of the purchase price up front and covering the rest when the shares were sold, presumably at a profit. As long as shares rose in value, everyone made money. And stock values did rise for most of the decade, as the economy boomed and the influx of first-time investors increased demand for shares and drove up prices.

Barry and his Broadway cronies gambled with dice and cards; almost everyone else seemed to be gambling on Wall Street. Even Calvin Coolidge, perhaps the most cautious and dour US president in history, stopped fretting about the country's moral decay and joined the cheerleaders of speculation and materialism. "The chief business of the American people is business," he conceded in 1925. "They are profoundly concerned with producing, buying, selling, investing and prospering in the world." Like the millions of Americans riding the unprecedented tide of prosperity, he was blind to the financial reckoning and lean years that lay ahead.

"It was that kind of time," noted Barry. "Why not live well?"

THEN, AS NOW, the United States was deeply divided—socially, culturally, geographically, politically—between conservatives and liberals, traditionalists and progressives, small towns and big cities. Religious fundamentalists, who resented and resisted change and fervently believed what the Bible taught, condemned behavior they saw as un-American and un-Christian; God had declared Sunday to be a day of rest, and that was good enough for them, as three men discovered when they were hauled before a judge in rural Maine for flying an airplane on the Sabbath. "I am opposed to bobbed hair," declared one small-town newspaper editor, as if citing a previously unknown eleventh commandment. "The Creator made it long, and I am in favor of leaving it that way." Journalist and commentator H. L. Mencken lashed out at these latter-day "Puritans" and their "almost complete incapacity for innocent joy"—"to be happy," he griped, "takes on the character of the illicit."

One clash of moral codes, above all else, defined the decade: the war on alcohol. As the horrors and sacrifices of the Great War were being swept away by a new era of exuberance, wealth, and social change, Prohibition threatened to spoil the party. The National Prohibition Act—known as the Volstead Act, after the legislation's sponsor, Minnesota congressman Andrew Volstead—took effect in January 1920 and drove the booze business underground. Fast cars and speedboats smuggled rum and whiskey from Canada, where distilleries were still in operation, prompting the *Literary Digest* to publish a cartoon depicting a helpless Uncle Sam looking across the border at a stockpile of bottles and barrels leaking alcohol into his parched country. Bootleggers—named for an old practice of stuffing bottles into boots and hiding them under a pantleg—were easy to find. Countless restaurants and clubs continued to serve alcohol under the table, risking prosecution and closure.

New York became a wet island in a dry country after 1923, when Governor Al Smith repealed the state's Prohibition laws, leaving enforcement of the Volstead Act to federal agents already overwhelmed by a tsunami of illicit alcohol. More than thirty thousand illegal drinking establishments were quenching New Yorkers' thirsts at one point during the 1920s, triple the number of licensed venues operating before Prohibition came into force. One federal agent, Izzy Einstein, kept track of how long it took him to find a booze supplier when he arrived in a new city; in New York, he waited a mere three minutes, ten seconds. And when the mayor of Berlin, Gustav Boess, toured Manhattan in 1929, he was puzzled to see so little evidence that alcohol had been outlawed for almost a decade. "When," he asked innocently, "does the Prohibition law go into effect?" In the speakeasies of "Gotham and Gomorrah," as the *Saturday Evening Post* prudishly described the city, the national ban on booze proved to be exceedingly good for business.

Prohibition had a corrosive, corrupting effect on the society it was supposed to save from the scourge of alcohol. Drinkers paid sky-high prices, and the dizzying profits financed the rise of organized crime and helped create Chicago's Al Capone and other underworld bosses. Gun battles erupted on city streets as mobs defended their turf and seized truckloads of beer and liquor from their rivals. Too many police officers and Prohibition agents pocketed bribes, demanded protection money from bootleggers, or looked the other way when a bartender served booze. The effort to stamp out the liquor trade unleashed "an orgy of graft, perjury, and corruption," as one New York magistrate put it. Some Prohibition agents brazenly flouted the laws they were supposed to enforce. "It was a common sight in certain New York speakeasies," wrote Stanley Walker, a newspaper editor who chronicled the city's Jazz Age nightlife, "to see a group of agents enter a place at noon, remain until almost midnight, eating and drinking, and then leave without paying the bill."

They had plenty of accomplices. Law-abiding citizens who wanted nothing more than a cold beer or a shot of liquor were transformed into lawbreakers. By mid-decade, the *Chicago Tribune* was patting itself on the back for accurately predicting the failure of Prohibition. "We knew of the millions in the great cities," it editorialized, "who would not see any moral wrong in drinking." New Yorkers scrambled for the membership cards needed to enter the best nightclubs, memorized passwords to satisfy wary doormen, ducked through the chaos of restaurant kitchens to get to hidden subterranean barrooms. They might even have run into Jimmy Walker, the staunch opponent of Prohibition they elected mayor in 1925—he became known as the "night mayor," because he was more likely to be found, drink in hand, in a nightclub than in his office at City Hall.

Once immersed in the secretive, enticing world of the speakeasy, New York's great and good drank and chatted with shady characters who robbed and stole, and even killed for a living. "The speakeasies," noted one study of the era, "eroded the boundaries between respectability and criminality," bringing together—as the highbrow magazine *Smart Set* put it in 1927—"the very highest and very lowest of human society." A lyric in the musical *42nd Street*, the 1933 movie that would capture the Broadway zone's Prohibition-era mix of glitz and sleaze, described it as the place "where the underworld can meet the elite."

Some establishments, as a precaution, asked gangsters to check their guns at the door—shoot-outs were bad for business—and mobsters and bootleggers operated some of Manhattan's hottest nightspots. Larry Fay, proprietor of the El Fey Club, where Texas Guinan held court, was a notorious racketeer who controlled milk delivery and the taxi industry with an iron fist, muscling out competitors and prompting the *New York Times* to proclaim him "one of the city's leading public enemies." He dressed like the flashy mobster he was—black, double-breasted suits, indigo shirts, canary-yellow ties—and rumbled around town in an oversized, bullet-proof car.

A jewel thief with class, who could charm the rich and famous over cocktails—then drink and gamble the night away with the denizens of New York's underworld—was in his element.

"I WAS PRETTY much of a night life plunger in those days," Barry admitted. A *plunger*, as newspaper writer Gene Fowler defined the term, lived "high and handsome" when a roll of the dice or other good fortune left him flush with cash. Barry was a regular at the Deauville and Texas Guinan's, the clubs where he had entertained the Prince of Wales on the eve of the Cosden burglary. He often drank with William Fallon at a saloon on Seventh Avenue, perhaps thinking that one day he might need the services of a slick defense lawyer. He became chums with Robert Tourbillon, who specialized in blackmailing wealthy women, had served time in New York and Paris, and was known to everyone as Dapper Don Collins. "One of the busiest swindlers, confidence men and all-around crooks in the city," in the assessment of one private eye, he had also tried his hand at rum-running and drug trafficking. Collins shared Barry's fondness for fine clothes, as well as his choice of victims. Fowler conferred on him an exalted title: the Colossus of Rogues.

Barry thought nothing of blowing $500—more than $7,000 today, enough to buy two new Model Ts back then—on a single night on the town. With Guinan charging ten dollars for a pint of whiskey and twice that for a quart of champagne at her swank club, an enthusiastic plunger like Barry could quickly empty his wallet as he picked up the tab for friends. He was often in the stands for boxing matches at Madison Square Garden. He escorted chorus girls appearing in Broadway musicals on tours of the clubs of the Roaring Forties. He dated several women in the cast of *Blossom Time*, a musical based on the life of composer Franz Schubert—and so popular that two New York productions were staged simultaneously.

At one point, Barry treated himself to a Florida vacation. It was at the height of a land boom, when the wealthy and the gullible alike were snapping up property and claiming a place in the sun. "One had only to announce a new development, be it honest or fraudulent, be it on the Atlantic Ocean or deep in the wasteland of the interior," noted Frederick Lewis Allen, "to set people scrambling for house lots." Barry hung around exclusive hotels, bribed waiters for information about guests, and looked for targets among the wealthy New Yorkers who wintered in Miami and Palm Beach. "You see plenty of jeweled women," he later explained, "and store up much useful information."

He spent many nights staking out a Miami jewelry store where a massive ninety-six-carat yellow-tinted diamond was on display in the window, plotting how to smash the glass and swipe it without being caught by the armed guard on duty. "I wanted it in the worst way," he recalled. The city's electrical grid was prone to blackouts, and he hoped a well-timed power outage would give him the cover he needed, but the lights stayed on.

He spent time in Paris as well, revisiting the city in 1924, for the first time since the war, to sample the nightlife, brush up on his French, and make contact with underworld types who might be in the market for stolen jewels.

Barry's gambling and his plunges into Manhattan's nightlife quickly burned through the proceeds from his burglaries. When the dice went cold and the money ran out, he planned and pulled off more heists, to keep the good times rolling. "Why did I take up stealing?" Cary Grant's classy cat burglar John Robie asks in *To Catch a Thief*. "To live better, to own things I couldn't afford," he explains, and to enjoy a lifestyle "I should be very reluctant to give up."

Barry was not about to give up his expensive tastes and fast-lane life, either. "I never bothered to save any of it," he would one day lament, when asked what had become of the fortune he earned from his thefts.

"It was a gay and hectic life," he had to admit. "I knew how to give money the air."

FOURTEEN

ANNA BLAKE

Manhattan • 1924–25

ARTHUR BARRY KNEW who Jimmy Hines was long before they met in a barbershop on Eighth Avenue. Everyone in his Harlem neighborhood knew Hines, and knew he was the man to go to for favors big and small. Tall and thickset, with a buzz cut and a weathered face, Hines was Democratic Party leader for the Eleventh Assembly District, a fiefdom that stretched northward from the top of Central Park into Harlem, and westward from Eighth Avenue to the Hudson River. The *New Yorker* considered it "a fair microcosm" of the city, "with extremes of wealth and poverty, learning and ignorance, lying side by side." It encompassed the campus of Columbia University, the stately mansions and town houses lining Riverside Drive, and block after block of tenements where Black and Puerto Rican newcomers were transforming neighborhoods that once had been predominantly Irish and Jewish.

Barry's apartment, on West 119th Street, was on the northern edge of the district. Hines would have been pleased to meet a constituent who was either a Democrat or could be persuaded to become one. He would have offered Barry a huge, calloused hand—Hines claimed to have shod forty thousand horses as a blacksmith in his younger days—and a handshake one recipient, journalist Jack Alexander, described as "sudden, firm, and cordial." Hines drew new friends like Barry into his orbit swiftly, confiding and conspiring as if they had known each other for years. Alexander, a writer for the *New Yorker*, marveled at his "knack for making a new acquaintance think himself a great guy," someone "he has taken a special liking to."

As they chatted and compared notes in the barbershop, the pair no doubt discovered that they shared Irish heritage and that their wartime service records overlapped. While Hines was twenty years older than Barry, he had been a lieutenant in the US Army's Motor Transport Corps and had "hauled both bullets and bacon," as New York's *Evening World* put it, to supply the Allied Army of Occupation as it kept watch on the Rhine.

They met again a couple of days later at the Monongahela Club, housed

Tammany Hall boss Jimmy Hines with his family outside the
Monongahela Club (Author Collection)

in a brownstone near the corner of Manhattan Avenue and West 112th Street. This was Hines's headquarters, one of a network of clubhouses that acted as district outposts for the city's powerful Democratic Party organization, Tammany Hall. The name Tammany had become synonymous with municipal corruption, thanks to notorious nineteenth-century bosses William Tweed and Richard Croker, who had amassed fortunes as they collected kickbacks and stacked City Hall, the district attorney's office, the judiciary, and the state legislature with their hand-picked loyalists. Even New York's governor was either a Tammany man or an ally.

Civic reformers and press exposés had weakened the Hall's grip on government by the 1920s, but Hines, whose father and grandfather had been Tammany officials, was determined to take charge and restore it to its corrupt glory days. He had risen to prominence in 1921, when he openly attacked Tammany boss Charles Francis Murphy, the successor to Croker and Tweed, as an arrogant, bullying "Czar," who abused his "one-man power to make and break" public officials. Hines only sounded like a civic-minded reformer—he did not object to such dictatorial power; he simply wanted to be the one to wield it.

After Murphy died in 1924, Hines's influence began to spread from the Monongahela Club to the whole of Manhattan and into the surrounding boroughs. He had friends in low places as well as high ones. He was linked to some of New York's most infamous crooks—nightclub owner Larry Fay, mobster Owney Madden, bootlegger William "Big Bill" Dwyer, racketeer Dutch Schultz. "The name of Hines," the *New York Post* would one day claim, "has been a thing with which to work miracles in the corridors of public buildings and in the darkest poolrooms."

The Monongahela had been founded in 1910 to "promulgate and promote" the Democratic Party's "principles and ideals" and to further "the intellectual, moral, economic and social interests" of voters. Within a decade, it boasted a membership of four thousand men and women. But the club's real function, everyone knew, was to build Tammany Hall's political power base and to dispense everything from scuttles of coal and Christmas turkeys to jobs on the city payroll to residents, and government contracts and concessions to business owners. "The district leader is a Santa Claus on duty twenty-four hours a day all year round," observed the *New Yorker.* The recipients of this largesse were expected to return the favor at election time. "The payoff came when voters went to the polls," notes a history of Tammany Hall, "where they cast their ballots not so much on the merits of individual candidates but in gratitude for the services provided by their local district leader or one of his subordinates."

Barry had a connection to the party—Joseph Crater, who gambled at the Harlequin Club, was an organizer for the Cayuga Club in the neighboring Nineteenth Assembly District—but was more interested in socializing than politics. The clubhouse's main floor assembly room could host meetings and dances for up to six hundred people, there was an upstairs dining hall, and there were allegations that gambling, one of Barry's favorite pastimes, was tolerated on the premises. It was there he met the boxer Abe Goldstein and the wily lawyer William Fallon, who sometimes represented Hines in court battles. Everyone at the club knew Barry as Arthur Gibson, a salesman who seemed to make a good living from hawking office supplies.

Another regular he met was Val O'Farrell, a former New York cop turned private detective. While journalist Gene Fowler considered him "the town's foremost Sherlock," O'Farrell, too, was fooled by Barry—he pegged the "intelligent, courteous and well-mannered" Gibson as an articulate and educated scion of a well-to-do family. Within a few years, once the truth was known, the hoodwinked sleuth with a score to settle would become Barry's most formidable adversary.

Hines became fond of his fellow Irishman and war veteran. Barry, for his part, would have understood the value of befriending a powerful political fixer. Hines was known to intervene with Tammany-friendly prosecutors and judges when a constituent or friend ran into legal trouble; his minions could fix a parking ticket or fire-code violation, dispatch lawyers to get bail for offenders under arrest, arrange for early parole, and even have serious criminal charges delayed, dropped, or dismissed. "The district leader, aided by the rest of the Tammany organization," noted the *New Yorker's* Jack Alexander, "is able frequently to make the machinery of justice stand still, like the sun at the bidding of Joshua." If Barry were picked up in a raid on a gambling den or a speakeasy—or, worse, was caught in the midst of a burglary—his affable, well-connected friend might be able to help.

Sometime in 1924, Hines introduced Barry to one of the political workers who kept his constituents happy—and voting Democrat. She was a petite, blue-eyed blond woman in her midthirties, with a wide, dimpled smile and a confident air.

"Art," Hines said, "I want you to meet one of the best damned captains in my district."

"This is Arthur Gibson," he continued, turning to Anna Blake. "He votes, so be nice to him."

~~~~~~~~~~

SHE WAS A survivor who had overcome sudden tragedies and unimaginable losses. Born in 1889, Blake was the seventh child of Lawrence and Rosanna Farrell. Like Barry's parents, the Farrells were first-generation Irish Americans. Her parents had married in 1878 in Providence, Rhode Island, where Lawrence was a switchman on the New York & New England Railroad. The family had moved to the New York area, and Lawrence was working as a laborer, by the time Anna was born. A double tragedy shattered her childhood. She had just turned three when her father died. Then, a month shy of her fifth birthday, her mother passed away in 1894.

Anna and one of her sisters were dispatched to Manhattan to live with her uncle, James Farrell, a teamster, and his wife, Delia. Despite the humble occupations of the Farrell brothers, money does not appear to have been a problem for either her birth family or her adopted one. Her uncle "was comfortably fixed financially," she recalled, "and, as my parents also had been quite well-off, we were well provided for." She grew up on West Forty-Ninth Street and attended Holy Cross Academy on West Forty-Third Street, a girls' school run by the Sisters of Charity of Saint Vincent de Paul since 1858. The towering stone-trimmed brick academy building was barely a block from the bustle of Longacre Square, recently renamed Times Square.

Anna wore the school's blue-and-gold colors until she was fifteen, when she dropped out after completing grade eight. "My uncle had great plans for me, wanted to send me to college," she explained. She had other plans. A year later, she married Frank Blake, a cabdriver who was eight years her senior. He was soon operating his own fleet of taxis, and they could afford a six-room flat at 204 West 114th Street. Their only child, Francis, was born in 1907.

The Blakes summered at Lake Ronkonkoma, a popular resort area at the midway point of Long Island. On an August afternoon in 1912, not far from the lake, Anna was involved in a horrific car crash. She was riding with local businessman Frank Avery, a family friend, when their automobile skidded off the road, slid down an embankment, and overturned. She was thrown clear and unhurt, but Avery, the driver, was pinned under the car. The gas tank exploded, engulfing the car in flames. Blake struggled to pull him free. She strained to lift the car. She tried to douse the fire, likely

Anna Blake (Author Collection)

using sand from the embankment. Nothing worked. "It's no use," Avery told her. "I've got to perish here. You go away." She flagged down a woman passing by in a horse-drawn wagon, but help arrived too late to save Avery. She had to relive the horrible experience when she testified at a coroner's inquest the following day.

While Blake insisted that she was happy in her marriage, she had married young and become a mother when she was still a teenager. She wanted to be more than Francis's mother, more than Frank's wife. "We never 'settled down' in the usual sense," she once explained. "I used to go off on trips by myself if Frank was too busy to take me." Then, at the Monongahela Club, a seven-minute walk from her flat, she found the perfect outlet for her organizational skills and her pent-up energy: politics.

Blake joined millions of American women who were defying convention and challenging stereotypes. Women voted for the first time in a presidential election in 1920, after a decades-long fight for suffrage. An unprecedented number of women had jobs or careers. Three million women would join the eight million already in the workforce before the decade ended, although most were paid less than men doing comparable work. Better educated and less restrained by custom and convention, women were breaking free of their traditional roles as schoolteachers, nurses, secretaries, waitresses, and department-store clerks. They opened their own restaurants and shops, were welcomed into publishing houses and advertising agencies, wrote Hollywood screenplays, and sold everything from real estate to coal. They were breaching the male bastions of law, medicine, science, academia, and politics. A growing number were continuing to work after they married, even those who were comfortably middle-class and did not need the money. The trend was novel enough to attract the attention of the *New York Times*, which ran a full-page feature from a female contributor that explored "the working wives' problem."

In the nation's newsrooms, women were no longer confined to writing society and fashion news or editing the women's page. They covered crimes, disasters, business, and politics, enduring the ridicule of male colleagues who resented the intrusion of "girl reporters" and "sob sisters" into their world. One of these pioneering journalists, a young woman from

Atlanta who would become one of America's most accomplished foreign correspondents, remembered the exact date she received her first pay envelope: Tuesday, September 30, 1924. It contained twenty dollars, her week's wages as an office clerk. "No childish excitement can compare with the feeling that came over me," Mary Knight recalled. "No woman in our family had ever worked before."

Women were even challenging men in the skies, dispelling a widespread assumption that they lacked the physical strength and mental toughness needed to fly an airplane. French pilot Adrienne Bolland set a record in the fall of 1923, executing ninety-eight aerial loops in under an hour. "A wonderful feat," *Time* magazine reported, before noting—in an aside that revealed the casual, ingrained sexism of the times—that "the loop is by no means a difficult stunt" and "men have done better." Amelia Earhart, one of the most famous aviators of the era, bristled at "this first-woman business," as she put it. "It's time biology and sex were squeezed out of accomplishment." She rejected the notion that men were better suited to be pilots—or anything else. Women, she insisted, were the equals of men, and not just in aviation. "In everything."

Anna Blake was determined to prove that women were the equals of men in the world of politics. Both Hines and Tammany Hall recognized that female voters and political leaders could make or break their hold on power. In 1917, New York had become one of the first states to allow women to vote in local and state elections, largely due to strong support in Tammany-controlled districts when the issue was put to a referendum. By 1922, more women than men were registered to vote in Hines's Eleventh Assembly District, and some took on leadership roles. Hines named Ernestine Stewart, a formidable political organizer—she was sometimes called the Lady Astor of Harlem in the press, after the trailblazing British member of Parliament—as the district's coleader. And more than a thousand women backed his battle against Charles Murphy, launching a door-to-door campaign across the city to urge Democrats to repudiate the Tammany boss—a "public-spirited" display of political clout that impressed editorial writers at the *New York Times*. Blake may have been among the canvassers.

As one of fifty-three captains in the Eleventh District, she played a key role in Hines's Democratic organization. The district captains were go-betweens who connected constituents in need of help with the man who had the power to grant favors. Most held a Tammany-supplied job on the public payroll—court clerk, sanitation inspector, assistant district attorney—but for Blake, it appears the captain job was full-time, not a sideline. Each captain was assigned a section of the district—as little as a block or two in densely populated areas—and was expected to know everyone living there "by their first names," noted journalist Jack Alexander, as well as "their ailments, their family tribulations, and their children's progress in school." Blake comforted the destitute, battled red tape, and helped immigrants adjust to their new country. A social worker and a political foot soldier rolled into one, she gathered with her fellow captains at the Monongahela Club to update Hines on the needs of his flock—"my people," as he called them. Eviction notice? Hines could make it go away. Unemployed? Hines could pull strings and come up with a government job. Homeless after a fire? Go to Hines for clothing and temporary shelter. A death in the family? Count on Hines to cover the funeral expenses.

And every year, the club staged an event known as the June Walk, a picnic outing in Central Park. Thousands of children, some dressed as miniature Miss Libertys and Uncle Sams, were treated to free ice cream and hot dogs. Blake was among the club workers who herded the excited kids to the park and dispensed the goodies. Hines, with a marching band at his heels, led a parade of future voters from the club to the park. Newspaper photographers were invited along to get shots of the man who made it all possible as Hines mingled with his people. "Two, four, six, eight. Who do we appreciate?" the kids chanted. "Jimmy Hines! Jimmy Hines! Jimmy Hines!"

On election days, Blake performed her most important duty: getting out the vote. District captains were on hand at polling stations to check off the names of party supporters as they cast their ballots. An hour or two before the polls closed, assisted by a team of helpers hired for the day, they fanned out to round up stragglers. They drove them to the polling station in their own cars or dispatched them in taxis. An offer of a few dollar bills was usually enough to lure the reluctant from their homes in time to vote.

Blake's hard work and growing stature in the Monongahela organization were recognized in September 1924, when she was sent to Syracuse to attend the Democratic State Convention. She was there when Al Smith, a Tammany Hall man who would be the Democratic candidate for president in 1928, was nominated to run for a third term as governor, sparking a boisterous parade through the convention hall. Delegates endorsed a campaign platform that promised to legalize the sale of beer and light wines, reaffirmed "the constitutional liberties of all citizens, races, and religions," and condemned the resurgent Ku Klux Klan.

Blake returned home to discover her husband, who had recovered from a serious illness earlier in the year, had relapsed. Frank Blake died on October 2, barely a week after the convention ended. At age thirty-five, she was a widow and a single mother to a seventeen-year-old son.

HINES HAD INTRODUCED Blake to Barry sometime in the summer of 1924. Thinking back, he was certain they'd met at the Monongahela Club, but she remembered chatting with him for the first time at a house party, held to celebrate her husband's recovery from an initial bout of his illness. Everyone called him Dr. Gibson. "For all I knew he might be a society doctor," she recalled thinking, and it was some time before she realized the title was only a nickname.

After her husband's death, she needed time off from her district captain's duties and spent two months in Florida. When she returned to Manhattan, one of the first people she met on the street was Barry. They discovered they had both been in Florida at the same time—Barry had been in Miami, scouting out wealthy, bejeweled women escaping the New York winter and coveting that big yellow diamond on display in the store window.

"It almost seems like Fate," she said later.

They arranged to meet, and were soon an item. He began spending weekends with Blake at a bungalow she rented in Lake Ronkonkoma, just ninety minutes from Manhattan on the Long Island Rail Road. It was on Woodlawn Avenue, a few minutes' walk from the lake and its beaches, with a screened-in veranda at the gabled entrance that faced the street. They spent their days there swimming, reading, and playing bridge. Barry was a hit with Blake's Long Island friends, and he was soon recruited to join a local lodge of the Benevolent and Protective Order of Elks.

Back in Manhattan, when Blake did the rounds of her district on behalf of Jimmy Hines, he tagged along and swapped stories with her neighbors around a succession of kitchen tables. He joined her for the Monongahela Club's outings to Central Park and helped her to ply the kids with ice cream and hot dogs.

Their social circle included the celebrated escape artist and illusionist Harry Houdini, one of the most famous people on the planet. Blake was friends with Houdini and his wife, Bess, who lived in an ornate four-story terraced brownstone on West 113th Street, around the corner from Blake's apartment—"the finest private house that any magician has ever had the great fortune to possess," he called it, with an oversized tub installed in one of the bathrooms, where he practiced his underwater escapes. Barry and Blake dined at the Houdini home on at least one occasion, and often socialized with the couple.

"When I was with Arthur I was so happy nothing else mattered," Blake gushed years later. "I was crazy about him." She was almost eight years older than Barry and more mature and far more intriguing than the chorus girls who had been turning his head. He called her "my darling" and "sweet." Blake, widowed for only a few months, was swept off her feet. He was kind and considerate, with a "happy-go-lucky" attitude, she later explained, and was "always romantic." He said little about his past and came up with a cover story to explain why he was always flush with cash—and where he spent the days and nights he was planning and pulling his heists. "I have a little money of my own," he told her. "Mostly, I just sell things—office furniture and supplies. It keeps me out on the road sometimes, travelling around to different cities."

On one of their dates, not long after the Prince of Wales's visit to Long

Island and the Cosden heist, Barry took her to the Deauville Club. To her surprise, one of the managers approached them and bowed.

"Have you heard from the Prince lately?" he asked. Barry smiled and simply said that, no, he hadn't.

After they were seated at their table, Blake noticed they were the center of attention. "All the waiters kept watching him and making a big fuss over him," she recalled, "while diners at various tables were eyeing him as though he were some tremendously important individual."

"What did the manager mean by 'the prince'?" she asked.

"During the Prince of Wales' visit to America, we had a little party together here," he replied. "And ever since they treat me as if I were the Prince himself."

She was desperate to hear the details, but Barry downplayed his brush with royalty and would say no more about it.

"Don't you worry about such matters, my dear."

Barry was not about to tell her the whole story of how he came to be at a nightclub with the heir to the British throne. And it was some time before he revealed his real surname. As he remembered it, one night they encountered someone from Worcester who called him Arthur Barry, and he had to admit the ruse.

Why, she asked, did he use an alias? They had differing recollections of his explanation.

When Blake told her story to the press in the early 1930s, she said he confessed that he made his money from gambling and had once run his own club. By the time Barry told the story decades later, however, he was sure he told her he was a bootlegger. "I deal in it a bit. It's where part of my money comes from."

That admission would not have shocked Blake or anyone else Barry knew—most New Yorkers considered Prohibition an annoyance, and considered the bootleggers who kept the booze flowing heroes, not criminals. Even the Great Gatsby of fiction, after all, was assumed to have made his pile from bootlegging.

Blake admitted she did not care if Barry was involved in shady dealings or how he made his money. "He was handsome, gay and kind—that was enough for me."

In December 1925, they slipped out of town and were married in Baltimore on the tenth, Barry's twenty-ninth birthday. His real name appeared on the marriage certificate, but Blake's friends back in New York assumed she was now Mrs. Gibson.

One friend, however, was wary of her personable, well-heeled new husband. Rudy Ganter, who had boarded with the Blakes for years, was a hotel detective, a job that had made him a professional skeptic and a keen judge of character.

Barry was "popular with Harlem's fashionable going-about-carousing set," he said. "He always had plenty of money, and he spent it like so much water.

"I told her to watch out for him."

4

PRINCE OF THIEVES

FIFTEEN

A SCHOLARLY COP

Long Island • 1923–25

A HUDSON TOURING CAR careened through the Long Island village of Hempstead in the spring of 1923, forcing another automobile to skid off the road and slam into a tree. The driver then veered toward an oncoming police paddy wagon with a motorcycle escort. As the Hudson rumbled past, the officer on the motorbike turned and roared off in pursuit. The chase continued for three miles through the village and reached speeds of up to forty-five miles an hour. The patrolman drew his revolver as he steered with one hand and fired three or four shots at the Hudson's tires. Then he gunned his machine, pulled alongside, and took aim at the driver.

"Pull over," he shouted, "or I'll shoot."

The driver hit the brakes.

By the time the chief of police caught up in the paddy wagon, the patrolman was taking down the driver's name in his notebook. The man, to no one's surprise, was drunk. The Brooklyn papers took note of the "spectacular arrest" in their Long Island backyard and identified the take-charge motorcycle cop: Patrolman Harold King.

King had been with the police force in Hempstead, at almost the dead center of Nassau County, for three years before his wild ride. Born in 1894, the youngest of three sons of a Brooklyn doctor, he had served overseas as a motorcycle courier in a reconnaissance unit in the final months of the war. Most days, policing a community of less than ten thousand meant dealing with a parade of petty criminals and minor crimes: stolen cars, thefts, joy-riding teenagers. When a down-on-his-luck war veteran broke a window next door to the police station so he could spend Christmas in a warm cell, King stepped outside and made the arrest. The monotonous routine was punctuated by the sudden adrenaline rush of chasing down a drunk driver, aiding the victim of a mugging, or rounding up a murder suspect.

Newcomers and money, however, were rapidly transforming a county that was within twenty miles of America's largest city. Upgraded highways and Henry Ford's cheap cars encouraged New Yorkers to escape into the countryside for vacations or to make year-round homes. The Long Island Rail Road whisked commuters to Penn Station, in the heart of Manhattan, and back home by dinnertime. Nassau County's population grew fourfold between 1900 and the mid-1920s, to just over two hundred thousand. And some of the newcomers were incredibly wealthy, making it one of the richest counties in the country. "A suburb of Wall Street," the globe-trotting journalist John Gunther called it; a bastion of "entrenched privilege and luxury."

Then, in April 1924, a deadly shoot-out during a bank robbery shocked residents and shattered complacency. An armed gang based in New York City robbed a bank in the hamlet of Bellmore, and shot and killed a customer—a well-known local businessman—as they fled. King was among the officers and sheriff's deputies who fanned out in search of the bandits, but the manhunt was delayed and disorganized. The incident exposed the need for a police agency with countywide jurisdiction and a system to communicate with officers in the field. A patchwork of dozens of village police forces was no longer suited to the task of patrolling and pro-tecting an area that was more than twelve times the size of Manhattan and becoming a magnet for big-city crooks. What was needed, the *Brooklyn Daily Eagle* advised county officials in the wake of the Bellmore robbery, was "a police system in good working order."

King, too, was ready for bigger things. He quit the Hempstead force that spring and joined the Nassau County sheriff's office, where he specialized in hunting down car thieves and recovering stolen automobiles. He was soon investigating everything from illegal clam digging to a train robbery. In one case, he identified a murder victim by patiently tracing the man's scarf, gloves, and shoes to the New York stores where they were purchased.

King's timing was perfect. Within a year, he was one of fifty-five deputies transferred to the newly formed Nassau County Police Department, based in Mineola, the county seat. He was promoted to sergeant. King and the other recruits were required to pass a civil service examination to keep their new jobs. Eight of the fifty-five former deputies failed the test; King placed second, with a score of 92.69 out of 100. Within days, he was put in charge of the detective division.

Nassau County chief of detectives Harold King (Author Collection)

A brief press announcement of the appointment credited "sheer ability and hard work" for his meteoric rise to top detective and described him as one of the most popular officers on the force. And he was newly married to Marion Smith, a widow with a ten-year-old son and the daughter of a former Nassau County sheriff. She also was a victim of one of the most sensational crimes of the era—her first husband, a bond salesman, had been one of thirty-eight people killed in the terrorist bombing of Wall Street in 1920. The couple made their home in Hempstead. Headline writers were already calling him the Nassau Sleuth. He intended to stay on Long Island.

King's first major test came that summer, when the body of a taxi driver was found buried under the rubble of a demolished building. Louis Panella had been shot in the head. For King, the execution-style killing hit home: the father of two had lived a few blocks away from him in Hempstead. Panella's Buick sedan and one hundred dollars he was carrying had been stolen. King traced the car to a dealer's lot in Manhattan, where it had been put up for sale by a man posing as Panella. The car had been washed and cleaned, removing any bloodstains or fingerprints, but the discovery secured the lead needed to crack the case. The seller matched the description of Philip K. Knapp, an airman stationed at Mitchel Field, who had been absent without leave for days. King headed for Knapp's hometown, Syracuse, to find out everything he could about the fugitive's background. He pieced together a troubling portrait of a promising university-educated young man from a wealthy family who had become reckless and unstable after suffering head injuries—and seemed capable of murder.

The headline-grabbing case made King the public face of the fledgling Nassau County force. He looked older than his thirty-one years, and his receding black hair, square chin, and somber, studious expression gave him gravitas. He was well-spoken and confident, traits that became assets when dealing with the county's wealthy and powerful residents. "King would have been at home in any drawing room," as one journalist put it. He was affable and close-mouthed at the same time. "He'd talk to you all day," a colleague recalled, "but tell you practically nothing." He let his work do the talking. He was so good at digging up clues and carefully assembling evidence that he became known as the "scholarly cop."

The police dragnet failed to catch Knapp, who was believed to have escaped across the border into Canada. King refused to give up and would devote years to making inquiries and following up leads. But in the fall of 1925, as Knapp's trail went cold, his attention turned to a new adversary—a clever, brazen jewel thief who was operating on his turf.

SIXTEEN

THE PHANTOM

Long Island • 1925

A MAID SENT UPSTAIRS on an errand was startled to find a stranger in one of the bedrooms of the Long Island home of Dr. Mozart Monaelesser, the medical director for the American Tobacco Company. The man was bending over a dresser but turned to face her as she let out a gasp. He was neatly dressed in a dark suit, and clean-shaven except for a small mustache. The dashing young man had taken off his gray felt hat and placed it on the dresser. A newly arrived guest of the doctor and his wife, she assumed, and she muttered an apology and began to back out the door. Then she looked down. He was holding Isabelle Monaelesser's jewelry box.

The man smiled, put down the box, coolly pressed his hat onto his head, and bolted for the bathroom, slamming the door behind him. The maid screamed, and reinforcements converged on the bedroom from downstairs. As Dr. Monaelesser stood to one side holding a loaded revolver, the door was flung open. The bathroom was empty. The man had escaped through the window, onto a porch roof, and dropped down to the lawn. His escape route appeared to have been planned in advance.

The foiled burglary on the night of October 5, 1925, at the Monaelesser home in Roslyn, four miles due north of Mineola, was one of a string of jewel thefts in Nassau County that fall. Real estate broker Harvey Shaffer and his wife, Eva, lost diamond and emerald jewelry worth almost $12,000 when someone entered Boxwood Manor, their mansion near Great Neck. The next victim, two weeks later, was former polo champion Thomas Hitchcock, whose son Thomas Jr. was a star player on the American team that had competed during the Prince of Wales's visit to Long Island the previous year ("the Galloping Hitchcocks," the *New Yorker* called them). Hitchcock, who was credited with introducing both polo and the steeplechase to wealthy, equestrian-minded Americans, had left jeweled pins, a pair of cuff links, and a watch on the bedroom dresser of his Westbury home before dinner; when he returned, the items were gone.

Thomas Hitchcock Sr. and Eva Shaffer (Author Collection)

King and his detectives were convinced the crimes were the work of the same man. They were right. Arthur Barry became a suspect in each burglary and later admitted to raiding Hitchcock's home. And there seemed to be a connection between the Long Island break-ins and the theft of Jessie Woolworth Donahue's pearls from her Plaza Hotel suite on September 30:

When Manhattan and Nassau County detectives met to compare notes on their investigations, they realized the Donahues and the Shaffers knew each other. "They belong to the same clubs, play on the same golf course," the *Daily News* reported. "Any one familiar with the habits of the Donahue family would know much about the movements of the Shaffers." The couples, it turned out, had attended the theater together on October 2. The Shaffers had commiserated with Jessie Donahue in the wake of her loss, only to be burgled themselves the following night.

~~~~~~~~~~

A WARM SPELL had thawed the ground on the night of November 7, 1925, revealing how Barry entered the mansion of Brooklyn lawyer August C. Flamman in Kensington, a village just south of Great Neck. Traces of mud from his boots were found on the sill of a ground-floor window, where he had stood, grasped the top of a shutter with his fingertips, and lifted himself to the second story. More mud was smeared on the top of the shutter, which had served as a precarious foothold as he pried open a bedroom window.

Flamman, a former assistant district attorney who was in the running for an appointment as a federal court judge, and his wife, Margaret, had been entertaining guests while Barry extracted $13,000 in jewelry from the upstairs bedrooms. A noise had been heard, but when someone at the dinner table joked it was either a rat or a maid making a bed, no one bothered to investigate. It was after nine o'clock by the time the break-in was discovered and the police were called.

The crime made headlines in newspapers as far away as Miami. It was not what was taken that had caught the attention of editors, however, or the victim's prominence in New York legal circles—it was how the burglar did it. The "elusive and daring" thief had displayed "the agility of a human fly," the *Atlanta Constitution* told its readers. A New Jersey paper was impressed with the athleticism of a man able to enter homes "by climbing up ledges, sills and shutters." The *Brooklyn Daily Eagle* suggested that anyone who could scale a building's facade with such ease "would make some of the stunt artists of the movies envious."

Barry eventually confessed to the burglary. In the meantime, King and his detectives gave the punctual, agile burglar a nickname—the Dinner Thief. "In every instance the thief entered the victims' houses while the owners were dining," one journalist pointed out, "making his way to the principal bedrooms by climbing up porches." The Flamman heist brought his haul of jewels for a few nights' work to $54,000—$900,000 today. When the crimes and methods were dissected at the dining tables and in the drawing rooms of the Gold Coast's gilded mansions, he earned another name: the Phantom.

The police toyed with the idea of posting officers to stand guard at as many estates as possible on Long Island's North Shore, but even the hundred-man force would have been stretched thin. Instead, squad cars and patrolmen on motorcycles cruised the highways and roads from sunset to early morning, stopping and questioning drivers.

One reporter covering the story sought out the officer in charge of the investigation, Nassau County's chief of detectives Harold King.

"He believes the thief is a man who studies carefully for several days the house he intends to rob," readers were told, "and then when the time is ripe walks straight to the room where he has learned the valuable jewels of the household are kept."

King was soon proven right. Someone, it was discovered, had broken into the home next to the Flamman estate while the owner was on vacation. Nothing had been taken, but police were convinced the thief had camped out in the vacant house and spied on the Flammans as he planned the burglary.

King was beginning to understand how his quarry pulled off his amazing heists. Now all he had to do was catch him.

~~~~~~~~~~~~

THE BURGLAR STRUCK again in late November, at the palatial home of one of the richest families—on one of the finest estates—in Nassau County. Lawyer and businessman John S. Phipps, heir to the fortune amassed by his father, a partner of the steel magnate Andrew Carnegie, reported the theft of at least $12,500 in jewels and valuables. King and a squad of detectives raced to Westbury House, a magnificent sixty-six-room Georgian mansion that commanded 160 acres of manicured grounds and formal English gardens. The thief had waited until Phipps and his wife, Margarita, were away in New York City, climbed onto a porch roof, and entered through a second-floor window. His search of the bedrooms had yielded pearl studs and other small pieces, including a miniature painting of Margarita in a small gold frame. The wire fence and thick hedge surrounding the estate had not kept the burglar out. And the trio of police dogs that patrolled the grounds had not made a sound.

The Phipps mansion in Westbury, Long Island (Author Collection)

His next stop, a week later, was at Greentree, an estate that covered more than a square mile of Manhasset and boasted a stand-alone building housing an indoor tennis court and pool. It was the home of Payne Whitney, one of the richest men in America, a blue blood the *New York Times* recognized as "a power in financial circles," thanks to investments in banks, railroads, and mines. The intruder, spotted by a maid, escaped through a ground-floor window and outran two servants who chased him across the grounds. Whitney's wife, Helen Hay Whitney, the daughter of a former US secretary of state, thought she knew what the burglar was looking for—her prized pearl necklace, worth $100,000. Informed of the break-in at the dinner table, her first thought was to send someone upstairs to make sure it was still there. She was assured it had not been touched. "Thank God for that," she said.

Barry was a suspect in the Phipps and Whitney burglaries as well. But these would be his last on Long Island for many months. With King and his detectives on high alert, Nassau County was becoming a risky place to do business. There was another county where he knew he could find plenty of mansions—and plenty of safer targets.

SEVENTEEN

"WELL-MANNERED BANDITS"

Westchester County and New Jersey • 1926

NOISE AWAKENED MABEL Stilwell at four o'clock in the morning. She squinted into the beam of a flashlight as two men climbed through the bedroom window of her Yonkers home. She woke up her husband, but before she could scream, one of them spoke.

"Were you at the opera?" Arthur Barry asked nonchalantly. He had been watching the house and knew the couple had been out for the evening, until after midnight. He had a revolver in his hand.

"Don't get excited, now, no one is going to be hurt."

He sat at the edge of the bed in the darkness as the other man scooped up jewelry left on a dressing table and rifled bureau drawers. He chatted with the couple and said he was sorry for intruding. He asked to see Mabel's hands, in case she had worn her rings to bed, but it was too dark to see them, and he apologized for touching her fingers to make sure they were bare. "Politeness," noted one newspaper account, "marked every accent of the burglar."

"Don't be alarmed and whatever you do keep quiet," Barry said at one point. "All you've got to do is lie still. We're after a few trinkets."

When the other man was satisfied with their haul, they climbed out the window. Barry turned to the couple and smiled. "Don't move," he said before he disappeared down the ladder, "and you will be all right."

John Stilwell, who had served as an army officer during the war, sprang out of bed, grabbed his revolver, and fired several times from the window as the men roared away in a car. His wife tried to phone the police, but the line was dead. The intruders, it was later discovered, had cut the phone and electrical wires before they entered. They escaped with diamond rings, watches, and other valuables.

The robbery on the first day of August 1926 at Ardenwold, the Stilwells' grand home, was one of a series of attacks on the wealthy residents of Westchester County that year. Stilwell, an executive with a utility company and known as Colonel Stilwell, told police that both men were dressed in dark suits and looked like businessmen. "Gentlemen crooks," the *Yonkers Statesman* called them. Its rival, the *Yonkers Herald*, preferred "the polite gunmen."

Something else made this Westchester robbery stand out to the press. The county's "famous 'ladder burglar,'" one news report observed, was "operating with a companion."

The second man was James Monahan. Barry was no longer a lone wolf.

FOURTEEN PRISONERS IN handcuffs stepped from a bus at the Worcester County Jail on a freezing January day in 1921. They were headed back to their cells after appearing in court to answer to an array of charges, from burglary to forgery and theft. Monahan, the third man from the end of the line, had just been sentenced to a term of eight to ten years in the Massachusetts State Prison, after pleading guilty to a break-in at a Cadillac dealership. After cracking open the safe and swiping thirty-eight dollars, he and another man had picked out one of the vehicles on display—a high-powered touring car—and parked it on the street. As Monahan had walked back to close the garage door, he had been spotted by a patrolman and chased for several blocks before he was tackled and arrested.

When all the inmates were off the bus, Monahan twisted free of his handcuffs, outran two deputy sheriffs, and vaulted over the iron fence that surrounded the jail yard. More deputies and a police posse joined the search, but it was already dark, and the search was soon called off. Years later, Monahan would make his Houdini-like escape sound easy. "I just gave a tug on the handcuffs and to my surprise they came off," he claimed. "Then I sprinted for freedom and I could run a lot faster than those deputy sheriffs." The handcuffs told a different story: smears of blood and torn patches of skin showed how desperate he had been to wrench them from his wrists. "I was prepared to take any chance," he confessed, "rather than go to jail for that amount of time."

News of the daring escape made the front page of the *Boston Globe*. Monahan's mug shots, fingerprints, and description—five foot eight, medium-stout build, black hair, dark complexion, scar over the left eye— were distributed to police forces across the country, and a $200 reward was offered for his capture. Monahan wound up in New York City, where he used a slew of aliases to hide his identity. He had the cheek to pass himself off as James Thayer, son of the Massachusetts judge who had sentenced him to prison just before his bold escape. "I thought it would be a good joke on the judge to use his name," he later explained. His underworld friends called him Boston Billy Williams.

Worcester police received reports that he had been sighted in New York, but detectives dispatched to the city were unable to find him. There were rumors he had returned to Worcester several times to visit relatives, dressing as a woman to avoid being recognized. Now and then, Monahan mailed a greeting card to Worcester's police chief or superintendent of detectives, just to taunt them. The messages scribbled inside, the *Worcester Telegram* noted dryly, "were not entirely complimentary to the police department."

Not long after the escape, he reconnected with a childhood friend who had also fled Worcester for New York: Arthur Barry. Monahan, the son of a foundry worker, had grown up in a neighborhood a mile and a half from Barry's three-decker in Vernon Hill. He was a year younger than Barry, they were both from large Irish American families, they were both Catholics, and they were both in trouble with the law at an early age. At fourteen, Monahan was arrested for "gambling on the Lord's Day," and he soon racked up a string of convictions for burglary and theft. He earned the nickname Duck Monahan and a reputation around Worcester as "a street corner 'tough boy.'" Probation orders and a stint in reform school had no effect.

In January 1917, he was sent to the Massachusetts Reformatory at Concord and briefly reunited with Barry, who was incarcerated there for part of the year before he was released and joined the army. While Barry was overseas saving lives and keeping the peace, Monahan was back in Worcester and working at the Union Water Meter Company's factory when he was not pulling thefts and burglaries. By the time he registered for the draft in September 1918 at age twenty, the war was almost over. He was never called up for service.

Monahan, like Barry, was a nightlife plunger, who frequented speakeasies and sought out craps games. "We palled around together at times in many of New York's gambling houses," Monahan recalled. They were regulars on the dance floor of the Grand Central Palace, adjacent to the railroad terminal, billed as "the one place in the city to have a real enjoyable evening." They frequented the prizefights at the St. Nicholas Rink on West Sixty-Sixth Street, a skating arena that had been converted into a boxing venue. And in April 1922, they had ventured out of the city to dance

Barry's accomplice James Monahan, alias Boston Billy Williams (New York State Archives)

at Schwaben Hall in Bridgeport, Connecticut, where Monahan insulted a woman and killed a man in the confrontation that followed.

Second-story work was a risky business. Barry had already had close calls with maids and other occupants of homes who had interrupted his work. And each heist he pulled ratcheted up the risk. The police became more vigilant. Homeowners who worried they could be next bought guns or hired watchmen to patrol their estates. By 1925, Barry was convinced that two jewel thieves might be better than one. He approached Monahan with an offer.

"If you're willing," he said over drinks at a speakeasy on Eighty-First Street, "we might find it profitable to get together on a few projects."

Break into mansions and steal jewels? Yes, Monahan was willing. His birthday, he later joked, was in April, after all. "That means my birthstone is a diamond."

Monahan could take on some of the grunt work—identifying "clients," staking out mansions, planning heists. One of them could act as a lookout and watch for the cops while the other was inside. A lone burglar sneaking into an empty bedroom at dinnertime, however, could only scoop up what was within easy reach. When Barry picked up newspapers to read accounts of his heists, he often discovered he had left behind jewels worth thousands of dollars, either because he had overlooked them or they were locked in a safe. If they both went inside, they could confront homeowners and order them at gunpoint to open safes or produce hidden gems. Each man would have his own role: Barry could sweet-talk the couple, to keep them from trying to flee or shouting for help, while Monahan gathered up the loot. "If you spoke quietly and reassured them," Barry noted, "they'd relax." The Stilwell robbery was one of their first working as a team.

It was a partnership of convenience. Sometimes they teamed up. Sometimes they planned a burglary together but only one of them followed through. And there were times they acted alone, pulling their own jobs without having to split the takings. Monahan proved to be as adept as Barry at worming his way into high society. He was a dapper dresser and despite a grade nine education he could slick-talk others into believing he had made his money in real estate. "He had polished himself at night clubs, gambling houses, prize fights and race tracks," the *New York Times* would note, "and was able to play the part of a well-to-do man of sporting tastes." A good golfer, he wrangled passes to play on courses at exclusive Long Island and Westchester country clubs; while Barry leafed through the *Social Register* in search of possible targets, he was picking up information on wealthy jewel owners as he chatted with members and fellow players.

Barry rarely introduced Anna Blake to his "business associates," as she called them, but she did meet Monahan. She was told they were partners in a venture of some type. "I supposed it was in a gambling-house," she recalled.

They made an unlikely pair. Barry was refined and confident. Monahan was edgy and cocky, with a perpetual smirk on his face and a chip on his shoulder. A reporter for a Brooklyn newspaper who observed both men found Barry was cheerful and talkative, like the salesman he pretended to be. While Monahan could turn on the charm, he was "moody and haughty" and he bragged boorishly about his conquests. "With a golf bag and a ritzy looking car I can get any woman," he once claimed. "Women of the upper classes have a very low standard of morality."

The night of the fatal shooting in Bridgeport, Barry saw firsthand how

Colonel John Stilwell, left, and Donaldson Brown (Author Collection)

impulsive and hot-headed Monahan could be, how quickly he could turn violent. He must have believed he needed an intimidating accomplice who was good with a gun as he fought an escalating war against the police and well-armed homeowners. Recruiting Monahan, however, was a decision he would come to regret.

~~~~~~~~~~~

BARRY HAD BEEN returning to Westchester County to pull occasional heists as he expanded his operations on Long Island. In November 1924, he slipped into the mansion of bank president Marselis Parsons in Rye, near the border with Connecticut. A few weeks later, he broke into the home of Donaldson and Greta Brown in Irvington, on the Hudson River side of the county. Brown, a vice president of General Motors, was also a director of the chemical giant DuPont. Barry's loot from the two burglaries topped $16,000. In January 1926, he burgled the Port Chester home of Roy Allen, an executive of the company that made Life Savers candies, and returned to Rye in May to rob Frederick Wheeler, president of the American Can Company and past president of the US Golf Association.

That June, Barry and Monahan were exploring a bedroom in the Tarrytown home of Alfred Berolzheimer, who headed the Eagle Pencil Company, when one of them brushed against a table and awakened his wife, Madeleine.

"Don't wake your husband and you won't be harmed," said one of the burglars, likely Barry. "We've cut the wires, and we want all your jewelry and money." As Berolzheimer slept and the second man searched the room, Barry sat at the bedside and "discussed topics of the day" to distract and calm Madeleine, according to a newspaper account. She later told police the man "appeared to be cultured" and had spoken to her in a low, soothing voice. She did as she was told and did not wake up her husband until they had left—with about $10,000 in gems and valuables. A headline in a Westchester newspaper called them "well-mannered bandits."

That September, a little more than a month after the Stilwell robbery, Barry and Monahan ventured deep into New Jersey to attack the mansion of Matthias Plum, vice president of the International Paper Company, in the coastal township of Rumson. It was a hundred-mile round trip by car from Midtown Manhattan. At three o'clock on a moonless morning they grabbed an iron ladder from a greenhouse on the grounds and climbed onto a porch.

Barry prided himself on knowing the layout of the houses he robbed, but this heist was poorly planned. The pair blundered into a bedroom and woke up Plum's two adult sons. They locked them in a closet and moved on to their parents' room. Mary Plum, who claimed she was the only one who knew the combination to their safe, refused to open it. The men threatened her sons, then threatened to shoot her. She relented.

As one man cleaned it out, the other stood guard with a pistol. Barry and Monahan hit the jackpot, carrying off at least $50,000 in jewelry. As they sped away, one of them—no doubt the trigger-happy Monahan—took a potshot at the couple as they stood at the back door of their mansion; the bullet narrowly missed Matthias Plum.

New Jersey police investigated, but no one suspected the culprits were Westchester County's ladder burglars. One of the men had worn a mask, and the threats and gunplay suggested the job was the work of hardened and dangerous crooks, not the polite, never-masked gentleman bandits.

Like their counterparts on Long Island, Westchester County's police forces were under pressure to catch the thieves and end the crime spree. "It is of grave importance to the peace, the prosperity and the very lives of ourselves that every effort be made to bring to justice the marauders now in our midst," an editorial writer for the *Yonkers Statesman* harrumphed in August 1926. While the Westchester thieves had pointed guns and made vague threats, none of their victims had been physically harmed. "It is to be hoped," the writer added, "that capture will be made before these 'Raffles' lose their peaceful dispositions."

EIGHTEEN

THE ROCKEFELLER GEMS

Greenwich, Connecticut • 1926

IAMONDS SPARKLED IN the beam of Arthur Barry's flashlight. Four pieces of exquisite jewelry had been left on top of a dresser at Owenoke Farm, the hotel-sized summer home of Percy and Isabel Rockefeller. As he scooped them into his silk-gloved hands, a woman screamed—the Rockefellers' twenty-two-year-old daughter, Winifred, had passed the bedroom and spotted him. He ducked through the window. Servants and the night watchman rushed outside in time to see him drop to the ground and run toward the edge of the estate. Barry was soon in his car and speeding away.

The bold theft from the nephew of Standard Oil founder John D. Rockefeller made headlines across North America in October 1926. Percy had inherited his fortune from his father, Rockefeller's brother William, a cofounder of the petroleum giant and a leading New York banker. At forty-eight, Percy was one of the world's richest men, with a net worth estimated at $100 million. A major Wall Street player, he was a director of dozens of corporations, invested in banks, railroads, utilities, and copper mines, and grew richer as stocks soared skyward. "A capitalist of first magnitude" and "a shrewd and highly versatile financier," the newspapers said.

His wife, Isabel, was the daughter of James Stillman, the former president and chairman of New York's National City Bank and William

Rockefeller's closest friend and business ally. Stillman had been a multimillionaire in his own right, and, after he died in 1918, so was Isabel. The marriage in 1901 of these "Scions of Millions," as the *Baltimore Sun* described the couple, was the second to unite two of the wealthiest and most powerful families of the Gilded Age; Percy's brother was married to Isabel's sister.

Barry's quick foray into the bedroom netted him four items worth $25,000: a gold wristwatch, a gold bracelet, a pendant, and a ring, all set with diamonds.

Isabel Rockefeller had no idea what they were worth. "I didn't buy any of them. They were all given to me by my father," she told the New York *Daily News*. She had received the watch when one of her daughters was born, and the rest were presents to mark other special occasions. "For that reason they are worth more to me than all the other jewelry I own."

The police suspected the crime was the work of the burglar who had swiped $30,000 in jewels a month earlier from Freestone Castle, a Tudor-style mansion surrounded by nine acres of grounds only three miles from Owenoke Farm, home to a retired shoe manufacturer Duane Armstrong and his wife, Jane. It was. Barry's haul that night had included a finger-width ten-carat diamond ring.

For Percy Rockefeller, who avoided the spotlight, the break-in and the press attention were a nightmare. Owenoke Farm—the *New York Times* later called it "one of the outstanding country residences of Southern Connecticut"—was his refuge. He had joined the exodus of New York's superrich to Greenwich, transforming a rural hamlet into an estate-studded community that was said to boast the highest per capita income in the United States. The vast grounds kept the world away. The imposing mansion oozed grandeur and sophistication, with sixty-four rooms spread over three floors. It was a showcase for the couple's extensive collection of museum-quality fine art and antiques, including eighteenth-century Flemish tapestries, oriental silk rugs, Chinese porcelain, statuettes, paintings, and carved walnut furniture dating to the Renaissance.

It was also Rockefeller's bunker. The Wall Street tycoon "lived in mortal dread of earthquakes," a Greenwich-area newspaper later revealed.

Even though it had been more than a century since a major quake rattled Connecticut, he took out a million-dollar insurance policy to cover earthquake damage and instructed his builders to encase the mansion in three-foot-thick walls of reinforced concrete.

A skilled second-story man, it turned out, posed a greater threat than earthquakes to Rockefeller's sanctuary and his family's privacy. Newspapers made light of the burglar's hasty exit, publishing a photograph of Winifred Rockefeller alongside a cartoon of a bob-haired flapper wielding an umbrella and chasing a shabby-looking masked man. Rockefeller hired the renowned William J. Burns International Detective Agency to try to hunt down the man who had invaded his fortresslike home.

Financier Percy Rockefeller, nephew of oil magnate John D. Rockefeller
(Author Collection)

Owenoke Farm, Rockefeller's estate in Greenwich, Connecticut (Author Collection)

The break-in, Barry later revealed, was an "impromptu venture." Working alone, he had set out to rob another estate in the area, but it was swarming with visitors. On the drive back to New York, he spotted Owenoke Farm. Only later, it appears, did he discover that it was Percy Rockefeller's estate. His plan, he explained, had been "to touch nothing." He would slip inside, explore the layout, and return another night for the valuables, as he had done many times before. When he spotted the jewelry, however, it was too tempting to resist. His payoff for a few minutes' work was a haul worth more than $400,000 today.

NINETEEN

"THAT SLENDER RIOTOUS ISLAND"

Long Island • 1926–27

AROLD KING AND two patrolmen were passing through Great Neck, near Nassau County's western boundary with the borough of Queens, when they stopped at a call box. The detective wanted to check in with headquarters in Mineola. A Great Neck resident, the dispatcher reported, had just contacted the police after spotting two prowlers on the lawn of a neighboring estate. The location? The home across the street from the call box.

King and his officers drew their revolvers and rushed toward the house. A man was emerging from an upstairs window as another man held a ladder in place.

"Stop there, or I'll shoot!" King yelled.

Arthur Barry slid down the ladder and took cover as the officers opened fire. He and James Monahan disappeared into a clump of shrubbery. Monahan fired back, forcing King and his men to duck behind parked cars, then dashed across the lawn—firing as he ran—and took cover behind a garage. When a patrolman moved toward the house, Barry fired a single shot from his own revolver to pin him down. The muzzle flash, he then realized, had exposed his hiding place. He retreated until he reached a fence, jumped over, and ran through backyards until the gunfire stopped and he was sure there was no one chasing him. Monahan had run off in the opposite direction.

The gun battle was over in a couple of minutes. No one was hit. King had been handed his best chance to finally catch the Dinner Thief but had blown it. The encounter, however, confirmed something Nassau County detectives had suspected for months. The elusive burglar sometimes worked with an accomplice.

~~~~~~~~~~~

LONG ISLAND'S ELITE were under siege in the summer of 1926. Break-ins in three North Shore communities netted more than $13,000 in jewels. Then, the home of Standard Oil executive Benjamin Brewster Jennings and his wife, Kate, in the village of Glen Head, was burgled at the end of July. Someone climbed onto a porch roof and pried open a window screen. One piece alone—Jennings's pearl tie pin—was valued at $10,000. Barry and Monahan were later identified as suspects in this and the other three burglaries.

Every unsolved jewel heist made the police look powerless—even foolish. The Nassau County force had almost quadrupled in size by 1926, to just shy of two hundred sergeants and patrolmen. The detective division, "one of the most important units of the reorganized force," in the opinion of the New York *Daily News*, had a roster of at least fourteen. A network of call boxes like the one King used on the night of his shootout with Barry and Monahan had been installed countywide, allowing headquarters to send information and alerts to officers in the field. "The sweeping reorganization of the county police force," boasted a feature in the *Daily News*, had delivered on the promise of reducing the local crime rate. Officers on motorcycles or in cars—two-seater Model Ts with the letters *P.D.* painted on the sides—patrolled "the far-flung stretches of Nassau."

The jewel thieves, however, were making a mockery of the beefed-up enforcement efforts and the new detective squad. Harold King and his men scoured mansions and estate grounds for clues but came up empty. Details of the stolen gems were circulated to pawnshops and secondhand stores, but no one reported seeing them or being asked to buy them.

The unsolved thefts were piling up just as King's career was taking off. He passed his captain's exam with top marks and was promoted, boosting his salary to $3,500—a drop in the bucket in Barry's world of easy money and Broadway high rollers. A newspaper photographer was on hand when Nassau County's chief of police, Abram Skidmore, pinned the captain's badge on King's lapel. "Proud Moment," read the caption when the photo appeared in print.

Margaret Thayer Talbott and Harold Talbott (Author Collection)

The following month, there was another major burglary in Manhasset, just five miles from police headquarters. On the evening of September 29, Barry and Monahan broke into the summer home of newspaper magnate Ralph Pulitzer—publisher of the New York *World* and son of the famous purveyor of yellow journalism Joseph Pulitzer—and stole a case containing $23,000 in jewelry. The victims were Harold Talbott and his wife, Margaret, who were renting the forty-room mansion. Talbott, a businessman from Dayton, Ohio, had come to New York to join the board of Chrysler Corporation and to Long Island for the polo. His wife of barely a year, Margaret Thayer, was from a prominent Philadelphia family. Her parents had the misfortune of booking first-class tickets on the *Titanic*; her father, a vice president of the Pennsylvania Railroad, went down with the ship, but her mother and an older brother survived. Peggy to her friends, the wealthy heiress had made headlines in 1924, when she went big-game hunting in East Africa and donated the heads and skins of her kills to a museum in her hometown.

King's investigation was hobbled from the start. The Talbotts reported the theft to their insurers, who called in private detective Noel Scaffa to investigate. Scaffa, still facing trial on a charge of compounding a felony for his role in recovering the Donahue pearls from Barry, interviewed the staff but found no evidence of an inside job. More than a week passed before the burglary was reported to King.

It had all the hallmarks of a Dinner Thief heist. The Talbotts had dined at home and passed the evening in front of a fireplace. Their dog had snarled and barked at one point, but no sounds were heard and the couple and their servants were not alarmed. The theft was not discovered until the following morning. The burglar—Barry later claimed he acted as lookout and Monahan went inside—had climbed onto a porch, entered through a bedroom window, and taken the jewelry case from a highboy. Peggy Talbott's offer of a reward for the return of the seventeen pieces of jewelry inside went unclaimed.

The next target was the North Hempstead home of Nathan Jonas, a Brooklyn banker and philanthropist. Monahan, acting alone, used a ladder to enter a second-floor bedroom on an evening in late November. Lacking Barry's well-honed skills, he made so much noise that Jonas went upstairs to investigate. As Jonas entered his bedroom, Monahan stepped out of the adjoining library, pointing a revolver. He held his other hand over his nose and mouth, in an effort to conceal his identity.

"Back into that room!" he barked.

The distinguished, goateed Jonas was accustomed to issuing orders, not obeying them.

"What for?"

"If you make another noise, I'll plug you."

"We have no valuables here," said Jonas. "We don't keep them in the house."

Brooklyn banker Nathan Jonas (Author Collection)

Monahan lost his nerve. He bolted down the stairs and out the back door of the house.

Jonas, a man who worked with bottom lines, offered one to reporters who interviewed him after the encounter.

"He got nothing."

~~~~~~~~~~

ANNA BLAKE'S BUNGALOW in Lake Ronkonkoma, thirty miles east of Mineola, in neighboring Suffolk County, became Arthur Barry's base on Long Island. It was close enough to make it easy to locate and stake out promising Gold Coast mansions, and far enough away to give Harold King and his men the slip if a heist went awry. Selling office supplies kept Barry on the road, and he was often out of town on business—at least, that was how he explained his frequent absences. Blake never questioned where he was going or what he was doing. She knew he gambled, and sometimes, she recalled, he claimed to be meeting up with other gamblers. "It was his business," she later explained. "I never quarreled with him."

The Long Island burglaries continued in the spring of 1927. The first target was the colonial-style brick home of William Couchman, a broker with a seat on the New York Stock Exchange, in Plandome, across Manhasset Bay from Great Neck. Couchman's wife, Adelaide, and their two sons spotted a ladder propped against the house. As they checked the upstairs rooms, a man armed with a revolver confronted them. It was Monahan. He backed into a bedroom and escaped down the ladder, dropping a jewelry case as he fled. Monahan tried to cover his face, but Couchman got a good look at him. Barry later admitted he had helped to plan the attempted robbery.

In early April, a diamond-studded platinum wristwatch was among the jewelry taken from the home of banker Robert Sealy and his wife, Amelia, in Hewlett Bay Park, on the county's Atlantic coast. The heist joined the long list attributed to Barry and Monahan. Days later, the home of E. M. Richardson, a director of the Sherwin-Williams paint company, was hit. Barry and his partner had planned the crime, but only Monahan had gone inside.

That same month, the pair broke into a twenty-five-room mansion in Hewlett Bay Park and hauled out a seventy-pound safe containing almost $10,000 in jewelry. They lugged it a short distance to a vacant lot, broke it open, and discarded some of the less valuable pieces. Weeks passed before the homeowners, architect John Cameron Greenleaf and his wife, Marion, discovered the safe was missing. King's detectives scratched their heads as they tried to reconstruct how the burglars had managed to get the heavy safe out of the house without leaving any marks on the floors or windowsills.

Nassau County detectives were "up against a blank wall," King admitted. "They had checked up on possible suspects but had learned nothing of value." His men had amassed enough witness statements and reports on unsolved jewel thefts to fill several file-cabinet drawers but had yet to find a single fingerprint. "The man is always careful to wear gloves," he lamented. "Detectives have scrutinized the surfaces of ladders used, and have gone carefully over porch columns, but they have found nothing."

King huddled with Nassau County district attorney Elvin Edwards and chief of police Abram Skidmore and announced the formation of special squads to patrol the besieged county. Detectives and uniformed men in more than a dozen cars would fan out in search of the burglars, along with officers armed with machine guns, automatic rifles, and revolvers. And King offered some blunt words of advice to homeowners who had guns of their own and spotted a prowler on their property: "shoot him on sight."

The well-publicized patrols seemed to work. There were no burglaries for several weeks. Then, one day in early May, at about seven o'clock in the morning, realtor William Tregoe and his wife, Ada, awoke to discover there was a man in the bedroom of their Great Neck home. He was stuffing his pockets with jewelry from a bureau. When he heard them stir, he stopped, moved his hand toward his hip pocket as if to signal that he was carrying a weapon, and fled through a window. The gems stolen were worth more than $4,000. Reporters were certain it was the Dinner Thief, working a morning shift to outfox King's nighttime patrols. One newspaper gave him a new name to suit his new office hours: the Breakfast Burglar.

The intruder was undoubtedly Barry or Monahan. And despite the risk of running into a heavily armed police patrol or a trigger-happy home-owner, they were only days away from pulling the riskiest and most auda-cious of their Long Island crimes.

TWENTY

THE MASTERPIECE

Kings Point, Long Island • 1927

TWO GHOSTLIKE FIGURES approached a mansion in Kings Point, overlooking Long Island Sound. It was just after sunset on one of the last days of May, and their gray suits blended into the deepening twilight. The men had driven around Jesse Livermore's estate days earlier and had a good idea which window would be the best entry point. A quick peek through the ground-floor windows confirmed the mansion's owners were dining with guests, and their servants were either with them or having dinner in their quarters.

Barry, with a boost from Monahan, grasped the rungs of a trellis and climbed to the second floor. As Monahan acted as lookout, Barry opened the window, crossed through a maid's room, and slipped into the hallway. Thick carpeting muffled his footsteps as he entered a large bedroom across the hall, which he suspected was the master suite. He spotted some jewelry but nothing worth taking—Dorothea Livermore, he thought, must be wearing her best pieces; they would have to be patient. He retraced his steps to the window, then climbed down the trellis. He and Monahan took cover in the shrubbery.

The Livermores and another millionaire couple, the Aronsohns, left the mansion after dinner and drove away in their cars. They were dressed for a night out, and it would likely be hours before they returned. Barry and Monahan fetched chicken sandwiches from a nearby diner, returned to their posts, and waited.

Evermore, the mansion they were staking out, was a palace-sized confection of brick, limestone, and slate, with a two-story main structure and identical wings on either side, to maintain its Georgian symmetry. It was a showpiece fit for a Wall Street tycoon. "There has been no expense spared in creating here an estate of surpassing beauty," noted one description of the property, calling the period-inspired flourishes "architectural triumphs." There were twenty-nine rooms, which was why Barry wanted a look inside to get his bearings. On the water side, a stretch of lawn cascaded down a slope to a private beach. There was also a jetty for *Athero II*, the $3 million private yacht—one of the largest and most expensive afloat—that had ferried Livermore and his guests from Manhattan that afternoon. The Olmsted Brothers, the landscape design firm run by the sons of Frederick Law Olmsted, designer of Central Park, had been hired to sculpt the estate's eleven acres, never suspecting that the shrubbery they planted could provide a perfect hiding place for burglars.

Earlier that day, the king of Belgium had awarded the Order of Leopold, his country's highest honor, to a gangly young American airman as European leaders feted the first pilot to fly solo from New York to Paris. Charles Lindbergh's courageous thirty-three-hour flight had begun the week before and just ten miles from the Livermore estate, when the *Spirit of St. Louis* roared down a muddy runway at Long Island's Roosevelt Field. Another victory over time and space had been declared in Manhattan the previous month, when the bluish-tinted face of Secretary of Commerce Herbert Hoover appeared on a screen as he spoke over the phone from Washington; it was the first public demonstration of a new technology *Time* magazine called "sight at a distance"—television. "It was as if a photograph had suddenly come to life," exclaimed the *New York Times.* Babe Ruth of the New York Yankees hit his twelfth home run that day and was on his way to becoming the first major leaguer to slug sixty in a season. And a seven-year legal battle to spare the lives of Nicola Sacco and Bartolomeo Vanzetti, Italian immigrants convicted of robbery and murder in Massachusetts despite compelling evidence of their innocence, was almost over. The previous month, Judge Webster Thayer—the judge who had tried to send Monahan to prison in 1921, inspiring one of the burglar's many aliases—had sentenced them to die in the electric chair.

It was after midnight when the cars returned. Barry and Monahan were close enough to hear the couples chatting as they went inside. Hours passed before the last bedroom light switched off.

They made their move at twenty minutes to four. Leftover chicken from the sandwiches placated the guard dogs. A ladder, liberated from the garage on a neighboring estate, was planted under what Barry assumed was the window of the Livermores' bedroom. He was surprised when he climbed in and came face-to-face with their guests.

Harry Aronsohn, fifty and German-born, had come to America as a child, made his first million while still in his thirties, and operated silk weaving mills that employed hundreds. He had helped to establish Paterson, New Jersey, as America's Silk City, and that city's grateful newspaper believed that "no finer, charitable and congenial a gentleman . . . ever lived." Regina Aronsohn, twenty years younger than her husband, was the daughter of a Brooklyn jewelry salesman and had worked as a stenographer before their marriage in 1917.

"Good evening," Barry announced, his voice gentle and almost a whisper. "We have only come to take the jewelry, and not to hurt anyone. Please don't be upset." Barry and Monahan were carrying revolvers. "We'll leave quietly when we've collected it."

A search of the room by the beam of a flashlight turned up $9,000 in jewelry—including a ring with a six-carat diamond and a pearl scarf pin. A platinum wristwatch, Barry estimated, was worth another $1,500.

"Don't take that, please. It's a keepsake from my mother," Harry Aronsohn pleaded, hoping to convince them the watch was of little value. "It's only nickel plated."

One of the intruders—likely Barry—retrieved $200 from Aronsohn's wallet, peeled off two one-dollar bills, and handed them to the millionaire before pocketing the rest.

"You may need this," he joked. "I wouldn't like to see you broke."

"I feel ill," Regina Aronsohn piped up. "I think I'm going to faint."

"Oh, don't do that, for heaven's sake," Barry pleaded. "Would you like an aspirin?"

As Monahan stood guard over her husband, Barry helped her out of bed, escorted her to the bathroom, found the tablets, and handed her a glass of water. "This will help. Now just relax."

After cutting the wire to a bedside phone, Barry told the couple to stay quiet. If they tried "any monkey business," he warned, they had accomplices waiting in the wings. "We are sorry, indeed, to have disturbed your rest." After locking the bedroom door and pocketing the key, he and Monahan climbed out the window and down the ladder.

Their flashlights awakened their next victims.

"Don't make any outcry," Barry warned as they entered the Livermores' bedroom through the window. "We've just come to collect jewels. You'll

Dorothea Livermore (Author Collection)

Jesse Livermore (Smith Archive/Alamy)

never miss them." Jesse Livermore reached for his bedside phone. "Naughty, naughty," Barry scolded. The revolver Barry was holding in the same hand as his flashlight convinced Livermore to drop the receiver.

"Well," Livermore said, "take them and get out!"

The intruders collected an $80,000 strand of matching pearls and a diamond ring worth another $20,000. Barry tossed aside Livermore's gold cuff links but picked up a matching pair of expensive diamond-and-sapphire rings.

They ordered Livermore to open a wall safe, even though he assured them there were no jewels inside. After Livermore fumbled with the combination lock without success, Monahan went down the ladder to fetch tools from the estate's garage. As they waited, Barry realized Dorothea Livermore was still in her nightgown. He retrieved her robe and draped it over her shoulders.

"You'll catch cold," he said.

She accepted Barry's offer of a cigarette, hoping she might get a look at his face when he struck a match. He shielded his face, however, with his other arm, then asked her husband if he wanted one.

"I smoke cigars," Livermore growled.

Barry was one of Broadway's nightlife plungers, but there was only one Boy Plunger of Wall Street. Jesse Lauriston Livermore—who, by chance, had grown up on a farm near Worcester—earned the nickname as an aggressive young investor who struck it rich in 1907, the year he turned thirty, when almost everyone else lost money in a stock market meltdown. A "magician of finance," one newspaper called him.

Barry gambled on rolls of the dice; Livermore, haughty and stern-faced, a man who found it hard to smile even when posing for a photograph, was a short seller, who placed big bets that a stock would fall in value. He cashed in when the share price tanked, and suffered staggering losses if he was wrong. Every time he was wiped out, he rebounded to build a new fortune. "The first requisite to success is confidence in one's self," he told a reporter. "I never lost my nerve." When he bought and sold, other investors and brokers took notice and followed suit. "If ever there was a stock market god," a biographer observed, "then Jesse Livermore was it." Just weeks before he awoke to find two armed robbers in his bedroom, he had reportedly made a $4 million killing in a Texas oil stock.

Livermore was struck by the burglars' coolness and confidence. "They seemed not only without fear, but without hurry," he said later. In their gray suits and matching gray fedoras, he thought, they looked like the young businessmen and clerks he dealt with on Wall Street. And they called him Jesse so often, as if he was an old friend, that he began to wonder if it was possible he had met them before.

Monahan climbed back into the bedroom with a sledgehammer. Barry used it to break open the safe with a couple of well-aimed blows. There were no jewels, only papers.

"You're a man of your word," he told Livermore. "My apologies for not believing you."

Barry's gallantry and politeness gave Dorothea Livermore an idea. She would test his good nature.

"Please don't take my little pinky ring," she pleaded. "Pops gave it to me." She appears to have made up the nickname on the spot—she never called her husband Pops, even though he was old enough to be her father. A petite brunette woman, she was a chorus girl in the *Ziegfeld Follies*—and "a Broadway beauty," in the estimation of the New York *Evening World*—when Livermore caught the show and she caught his eye. Now twenty-seven, she was from a wealthy family and had slipped easily into the role of Long Island and Palm Beach socialite. She had "a way with words and a turn of phrase," by one account, and she was about to prove it.

The ring was the smaller of the matching diamond-and-sapphire bands. Barry dutifully fished it out of his pocket at her command and bowed as he handed it to her.

"I hope it brings you luck," he said.

"And please don't take Pops's little pinky ring. I gave it to him."

Barry rummaged in his pocket. "He can have that back, too."

"Oh, you're a devil," she said.

Monahan had seen enough of Barry's generosity. His partner had just given back loot worth at least $60,000. "My God," he said. "Let's quit while we're winning."

They headed for the window.

"Good-by!" Barry announced. "You have been such good sports that we are sorry we had to do this. But it is our business. Don't make any noise for at least half an hour, and you'll be all right."

Just before he followed Monahan down the ladder, Barry returned one more item—the watch Harry Aronsohn claimed had only sentimental value. "Give this to your house guest," he said, "and tell him it's time he learned the difference between nickel-plate and platinum."

Then he handed Jesse Livermore a key. "Would you be good enough to free your guests?" he said, flashing a smile. "I'm afraid they're locked in their room."

~~~~~~~~~~~~

HAROLD KING'S PHONE jangled. "The Livermore place was burglarized this morning," one of his officers reported from headquarters. The robbery had been reported at half past five, and an estimated $100,000 in jewelry had been taken. King left his breakfast on the table and rushed to his car. He was waved though the estate's imposing entrance gates and spotted the Livermores' yacht, riding at anchor just offshore, as he drove through the grounds. He made a mental note to question the crew members, in case they had seen something. A butler directed him to the library, where the Livermores and the Aronsohns were waiting to be interviewed.

Dorothea Livermore and Regina Aronsohn did most of the talking. They recounted the back-and-forth with the burglars, the return of the rings and watch, the cheery goodbyes, how the politest of the two intruders apologized for robbing them. "He said that in such a soothing, chummy sort of way," Dorothea Livermore told King, "that I felt as if he were doing us a favor."

King found their stories hard to believe. "There was something fishy about this burlesque burglary," he remembered thinking. "Facetious burglars have been known to 'kid' their victims, but I had never read or heard of one who gave back thousands of dollars' worth of jewels voluntarily." He wondered if the couples were the victims of a practical joke, engineered by a friend with a twisted sense of humor. He was about to raise this possibility when the owner of the estate next door dropped by and revealed that his canary-yellow Chrysler roadster had been stolen during the night. For King, this was no coincidence—it must have been the burglars' getaway car.

When news of the robbery broke the following day, the *Brooklyn Daily Eagle* declared it "one of the most sensational thefts Long Island has ever known." The *New York Times* ran the story at the top of its front page, giving it a berth alongside coverage of the worldwide celebrations of Lindbergh's triumph. The "quiet but firm politeness" of the gun-toting burglars and their return of expensive jewelry in the midst of the robbery, the paper noted, made this crime stand out. The intruders were "dainty in their methods," wrote *Daily News* crime reporter Grace Robinson, "cooing protestations of friendliness into their victims' ears while they menaced them with revolvers."

From Lansing, Michigan, to Spokane, Washington, from Fort Worth to San Francisco, editors snapped up the offbeat story from their wire services and gave it prominent play. Some press accounts put a more sinister spin on the story. A gun was held to Regina Aronsohn's head to stop her from screaming, the *Daily News* claimed. One of the robbers threatened to shoot Dorothea Livermore, the *Times* and other papers reported, unless she held and steadied the ladder as the men descended and escaped.

Every detective on the Nassau County police force was combing the mansion and grounds for clues. "The robbers without doubt were experts in their line," King told the *Times*. Investigators were said to be impressed with the burglars' audacity—they were in the house for at least an hour and went about their work without waking a half dozen servants, another houseguest, and the Livermores' young children. "Even bold robbers hardly ever linger more than ten minutes on a job," noted Robinson.

While a ladder had been used to enter the house, detectives doubted it was the work of the "ladder burglars" who had been targeting Long Island estates while homeowners and their guests were at the dinner table. "Police do not recognize the handiwork of the thieves as similar to that of any other jewel robbery in their experience," noted Edward Riis, a reporter for the Brooklyn *Times Union*.

Livermore had showered his wife with gifts of expensive jewelry, and her engagement ring alone, a massive emerald in a platinum setting, was worth $150,000. One of Robinson's reports revealed that gems worth tens of thousands of dollars had been transferred to a vault in Manhattan days before the robbery. The trouble the robbers took to crack open the safe suggested they knew there could be more jewelry in the house. Was it an inside job? Detectives spent more than a day questioning the estate's servants, the yacht's crew, and other employees before eliminating them as suspects.

King had little to go on. Neither man wore a mask, but the glare of the flashlights had prevented the victims from getting a good look at their faces. The burglars ditched the flashy Chrysler stolen from the neighbor near the railway station in Manhasset, about a twenty-minute drive away. Then they stole a taxi and drove east, toward New York, before abandoning it as well. King suspected a third man was involved and had acted as lookout. A witness in Manhasset, however, claimed to have seen five people—four men and a bob-haired woman in her late teens—get out of the Chrysler. Did the robbers tell the truth when they warned the Aronsohns they had accomplices outside? Were the police looking for two thieves or five?

When Riis interviewed King a few days after the break-in, Nassau

County's chief of detectives was dejected and surprisingly candid. "He did not know just what to make of it," the *Times Union* reported, and "he did not have much hope of getting hold of any clue of real value." His comments appeared under the headline LIVERMORE THEFT RIDDLE TO POLICE.

King, however, was telling Riis and other reporters what he wanted the robbers to hear. He knew precisely who he was looking for. "There were so many similarities in the technique, actions, and warnings," he noted later, "that I was thoroughly convinced it was the work of our friend, the 'dinner-time Raffles.'"

The sensational robbery would cement Barry's reputation as a Jazz Age gentleman thief, a genteel, courteous, smooth-talking rogue with an eye for diamonds and a heart of gold. The men who robbed the Evermore estate, the *New York Times* noted, "acted much like the 'gentleman burglars' of fiction." How many criminals had displayed such chivalry, returning jewelry worth tens of thousands of dollars to its owners, simply because it had sentimental value?

"I am kind-hearted," Barry explained a few years later. "I dare say most fellows in my business would have thought this a bit thick." He called the heist "my masterpiece and my most interesting job."

It would also be his undoing.

5

~~~

THE RECKONING

TWENTY-ONE

THE TRAP

Long Island • 1927

T HE COMMUTE FROM Manhattan to Lake Ronkonkoma should have taken an hour and a half. But the Long Island Rail Road train Arthur Barry and Anna Blake boarded on the first Sunday in June often slowed to a crawl. Sometimes the cars lurched to a halt between stations long enough for passengers to step off and stretch their legs. Barry, fed up with their slow progress, considered abandoning the train during one stop between towns. They could cut across a farmer's field, he suggested, and find a taxi to take them to the bungalow. The weather, however, was iffy. The sun was playing hide-and-seek with dark, menacing clouds. And Blake, who was wearing a black silk coat over a long dress and a black hat embroidered with gold thread, was not dressed for a hike in the country. They decided to climb back on board.

James Monahan and his girlfriend had seen them off at Penn Station. A week had passed since the Livermore robbery. Monahan, they agreed, would find a buyer for the pearl necklace—he had already fenced the other loot collected that night—and they would split the proceeds fifty-fifty. Monahan handed over a small gray cardboard box containing unsold jewelry worth about $15,000, left over from previous jobs—a jumble of diamond rings, watches, and other pieces, some loose stones, pearl shirt studs, and a few trinkets and heirlooms of little value. Barry gave it to Blake to carry on the train.

The two of them planned to spend a few days at the lake, then load up the red Cadillac and head west for a vacation. After seven years of keeping tabs on socialites, staking out estates, posing as a party guest, and climbing through bedroom windows, Barry was ready to make a fresh start. He had decided the Livermore job would be his last. Days earlier, he had gathered up the tools of his trade—flashlights, revolvers, ammunition—and pitched them into Lake Ronkonkoma.

Barry had bought a newspaper before boarding, and he would have been following the daily reports on the Livermore investigation. He must have smiled when he read that Noel Scaffa and his operatives had joined the hunt, leading to an awkward encounter with a *Daily News* reporter.

"My first job is to find the thieves and see they are convicted. Recovery of the jewels is secondary," the Great Retriever claimed. "That always has been our policy." Scaffa paused, then added: "With one exception."

"The one exception was the Donahue jewelry?" he was asked.

"Yes."

A letter, bearing a Brooklyn postmark, had arrived at the Livermore estate after the robbery. "We are coming to see you again tonight and we are coming to see you on business," it said. Written in pencil, it was signed "The Gentlemen Robbers." Then a man phoned and asked a maid to pass along a message to Jesse Livermore: "Tell him it will be a serious matter if he does not heed the warning." The threats kept the story in the headlines, but King dismissed them as the work of cranks.

An anonymous call to the Nassau County Police Department, however, seemed to offer tantalizing leads. It was traced to a pay phone in Harlem, and the caller knew details of the robbery that had not been made public. King, however, refused to reveal what the man had to say.

The newspapers, handed a new mystery to solve, ran with every scrap of information they could dig up. A Harlem-based gang had pulled the Livermore job, it was claimed, and the jewels were supposedly stashed in a safe-deposit box at a local bank. There had been a falling-out—some reports said it was over a woman; others claimed there was a dispute over how to divide he proceeds. A member of the gang had been beaten up. "He talked out of his turn and was hit on the head with an iron rod," was all reporter Grace Robinson managed to wring from her police sources.

Barry might have found the rumors amusing if Robinson had not revealed something that hit home. The gang's headquarters, according to the tipster, was on West 116th Street, near the intersection of Lenox Avenue. That was only a few blocks from Blake's apartment. King and some of his detectives had teamed up with the New York police to nose around the neighborhood. "One suspect was being closely watched," King assured the *New York Times*.

Monahan could be careless and mouthy, Barry knew. Had he been bragging about the heist? Were the police closing in? Were he and Blake being tailed?

The anonymous call, King told another newspaper, was "the most important clew to date, and it is on this phone call that we base our hope to make an arrest."

As the train crawled toward Lake Ronkonkoma, Barry had no idea that the Nassau County Police had just fielded another, more urgent call from New York.

SCAFFA HAD A rival as he hunted for the Livermore robbers and the stolen jewels. The Federal Insurance Company had offered private eye Val O'Farrell a $5,000 reward if he could solve the case. New York's "super-sleuth," as the *Daily News* called him, was a former police detective with a talent for self-promotion. He was fifty-one, tall and fit, with a thicket of curly white hair and a ready smile; one journalist he charmed thought he could pass himself off as "the vicar of a smart suburban parish." A voracious reader, he could quote classic works of literature, and kept an unlikely reference work on his office desk: *The Oxford Book of English Prose*.

Born in Boston, Valerian Joseph O'Farrell grew up on the tough streets of Manhattan's Lower East Side. One of his childhood buddies was Al Smith, now New York's governor. He joined the New York Police Department as a patrolman in 1900 but seemed ill-suited for the job. He faced disciplinary action for allowing a prisoner to escape, using "vile and threatening language" on the job, and loitering on the beat. After his promotion to detective in 1907, he earned a commendation for "excellent police duty." O'Farrell and two colleagues assigned to the Broadway district were lauded in the press as "first class thief catchers." William Pinkerton, who headed the famous private investigation agency, had considered him "one of the best detectives in the United States."

Then, in 1911, his career imploded. Suspected of leaking information to investigators who were probing police misconduct, he was demoted from lieutenant to patrolman, banished to walking a beat in the Bronx, and his salary was slashed in half. Within months, he was accused of taking a $1,000 bribe and lying to his superiors about the source of the money. He was docked a month's pay and allowed to retire from the force in 1912, ostensibly due to ill health.

He reinvented himself as a private eye. "There was more money in getting people out of trouble," he reckoned, "than getting them into it," according to one account of his career. He obtained a license within weeks of leaving the police department, established the Val O'Farrell Detective Agency in 1915, and soon opened a branch office in Philadelphia. Recovering $25,000 in jewelry stolen from the home of a New Jersey state senator was an early headline-grabbing coup. Clothing manufacturers retained him to catch pilfering employees and to handle security during strikes.

His methods, however, attracted unwelcome attention. A union accused O'Farrell's men of beating and intimidating picketers and tried to have his license revoked. One of his detectives was arrested for impersonating a federal agent; another was accused of complicity in a kidnapping. In 1919, after a client absconded and left him to make good on a bail bond, O'Farrell was forced to declare personal bankruptcy.

He rebounded. He opened an office at Fifth Avenue and Forty-Second Street, next door to the main branch of the New York Public Library, and soon had more than twenty investigators and support staff on the payroll. One of his specialties was rounding up the wayward sons of millionaires who had fallen under the spell of Broadway nightclubs and into the clutches of thieves and blackmailers. Divorce work was lucrative—the

New Yorker called it "the Klondike" for private detectives—and became a mainstay. Nine out of ten of his clients were women, and most wanted cheating husbands shadowed and caught with their mistresses. O'Farrell soon enjoyed a lifestyle on par with some of his well-heeled clients, complete with a twelve-room home in Jackson Heights, a staff of servants, and a chauffeur behind the wheel of his expensive Packard.

His methods, however, again came under fire. Detectives he sent to raid a young woman's apartment in search of a client's husband were accused of stealing a diamond bracelet. When the woman and her supposed lover confronted O'Farrell's agents at his offices, a scuffle broke out. Doors and glass partitions were smashed, and the dustup rated almost a column of embarrassing coverage in the *New York Times*. O'Farrell earned more unwanted publicity when a woman sued him for perjury and fraud, claiming one of his employees had lured her to a hotel and posed as her lover in a plot to furnish her husband with grounds for divorce. His methods were "pretty shady," conceded the man in charge of New York's Bureau of

Barry and Blake were taken into custody at the Ronkonkoma railroad station
(Lake Ronkonkoma Historical Society)

Licenses. A Federal Bureau of Investigation dossier on the agency's check-ered history, compiled in the 1930s, described its reputation as "unsavory."

O'Farrell craved attention, good or bad. He had a "passion for seeing his name in print," noted one press profile, and he would have known that cracking the Livermore robbery would put him in the headlines for the right reasons. His investigators fanned out to work their underworld con-tacts. They were on the lookout for anyone, he later noted, who was "flush and spending money." They shadowed known and suspected jewel thieves, hoping for a break. "Bit by bit," O'Farrell added, "information seeped into the office." He worked his contacts in Harlem and paid a source to cough up the name of a possible suspect: Arthur Gibson, someone O'Farrell knew from the Monongahela Club.

On the afternoon of June 5, a woman phoned his office with a tip that Gibson was on a train to Lake Ronkonkoma and traveling with a blond woman. O'Farrell hung up and called the Nassau County Police. It was a thirty-mile drive to Lake Ronkonkoma from Mineola. With the train run-ning late, Harold King had time to assemble a few detectives and alert the authorities in neighboring Suffolk County before he raced to intercept the suspects.

THE TRAIN REACHED the station more than two hours behind sched-ule. It was just after seven o'clock. Barry's red Cadillac was parked in the hedge-bordered parking lot with Otto Becker—a local garage employee who sometimes chauffeured for the couple—at the wheel. Barry and Blake were climbing in when three men in suits and fedoras confronted them.

"Are you Arthur Gibson?" asked the man who seemed to be in charge. The others drew revolvers and pinned Barry against the car.

"Look, if this is a holdup, go ahead and take my money. But I'm going to yell for the police the minute you're gone."

"Are you Arthur Gibson or aren't you?" the man demanded as more officers in plainclothes converged on the car.

"Who are you?"

"Captain King, Nassau County police. The stationmaster says you're Arthur Gibson."

Hunter and hunted had finally come face-to-face.

"I am."

Barry was holding the cardboard box. King snatched it from his hand, saw the jewelry inside, and stuffed it into his pocket.

"You're under arrest."

TWENTY-TWO

OWNING UP

Mineola, New York • 1927

H IS NAME, THE Livermore robbery suspect insisted, was Arthur
Gibson. He was a salesman, not a jewel thief.

Harold King and his detectives took turns questioning Arthur
Barry at police headquarters in Mineola. "He sneeringly and sullenly
refused to answer," King recalled, adopting an "attitude of assured
defiance."

Eventually, Barry admitted he had served time in the Massachusetts
Reformatory for theft and three months in a Connecticut jail for assault.

How did he acquire the jewelry he was carrying? King and his detectives estimated the box contained $15,000 worth, equivalent to almost a
quarter million dollars today. All of it was his, Barry claimed, purchased
from "a man on the Bowery" he refused to identify.

Hour after hour, he stuck to his story. "He was nonchalant and at ease
most of the time during his questioning," one reporter was told by someone in the room, "using English that would be a credit to a college graduate." King and his detectives prided themselves on not resorting to "third
degree" methods common at the time—intimidation, threats, beatings—to
extract confessions. Barry, a member of the district attorney's staff later
insisted, was questioned "without any rough treatment being given or even
threatened." The interrogation continued all night. By daybreak, however,
Barry "was as wide awake and watchful as he had been the minute when

he had jauntily stepped off the train at Ronkonkoma," King recalled. And he had revealed nothing about the Livermore robbery.

The Nassau County Courthouse in Mineola (Library of Congress Prints and Photographs Division)

The next morning, he and Anna Blake were taken to Nassau County's dome-topped, porticoed courthouse and led up a circular staircase to an office on the top floor. Craggy-faced, forty-five-year-old district attorney Elvin Edwards, his graying brown hair swept to one side as if he had just escaped a windstorm, led the interrogation. As a kid, he had wanted to be a cop; when his parents steered him into a legal career, Edwards had gravitated toward criminal law. Joining the DA's office soon after he graduated from law school had offered the chance to track down bad guys alongside King and his men. "He arrived at the scene of violent crimes," a magazine profile noted, "neck and neck with the detectives." His tactics for wringing the truth out of suspects, the profile added, were "tremendously effective." He lobbed softball questions, gauged reactions, and looked for weaknesses to exploit. Then he moved in for the kill. "I seldom use bulldog tactics," he explained.

Edwards was about to face one of his toughest challenges as the county's top prosecutor. King and his detectives had nothing to show for their many hours of questioning. Despite years of investigation, Long Island's string of headline-grabbing jewel thefts was shrouded, as Edwards later put it, in "an impenetrable fog of mystery." Only one thing seemed certain: "the whole series of burglaries," he was convinced, had been "committed by one man, or a gang controlled by a master mind."

Was this the man?

The DA questioned the couple together. He faced them across his desk, sizing them up. Blake readily handed King the jewelry she was wearing, including an expensive-looking ring set in sapphires and diamonds that sparkled on her finger. Edwards was satisfied she had no idea it might have been stolen. Barry slumped in his chair, with his hands deep in his pockets. "His lips," Edwards noticed, "were tightly compressed into a sneering smile." It was the look of a man with something to hide. Edwards engaged them in small talk, inquiring about their relationship and how long they had been together. Blake was chatty and assured the district attorney her "sweet and beautiful" man could not be guilty of a crime.

Edwards's phone rang. King was on the line. Blake's ring matched the description of a $5,000 sapphire-and diamond ring stolen from the home of New Jersey business executive Matthias Plum in 1926. It was the leverage the district attorney needed. King entered and handed the ring to Edwards, who dropped the bombshell news that it had been stolen.

Blake never forgot that moment, when she realized the allegations were true: her husband was a jewel thief. "I reeled back and almost fainted from this blow. I couldn't believe it." Barry's gambling windfalls. His frequent absences. The expensive ring. All of it suddenly made perfect, horrible sense.

"Oh Art, how *could* you do this to me?" she cried out. "Will—will—they put *me* in jail?"

"No! God, no, Babe," Barry sputtered as he put his arm around her. "You know I wouldn't hurt you for the world."

"Arrest this woman," Edwards barked, "for being in the possession of stolen property." A pair of handcuffs clinked, but before King could put them on Blake's wrists, Barry told him to stop.

"I'll tell you everything!" he shouted. "She's innocent."

On the afternoon of Monday, June 6, after holding out for fifteen hours, Barry said he was ready to cut a deal. He would confess if the district attorney released Blake and agreed not to prosecute her.

Edwards pressed a buzzer to summon a stenographer to join them.

"Tell me the whole story," he said, "and I'll see that she goes free."

<hr />

BARRY ADMITTED HE had broken into the Livermore home, smashed open the safe, and robbed the couple and their guests. He described the "very touching way" Dorothea Livermore had asked him to return her pinky ring and how he had turned it over, saying "I hope it brings you luck." He had taken her pearl necklace, a diamond ring, and other pieces of jewelry.

"I make this statement with the full realization that I entered into this scheme to rob this place, and I know it was contrary to law," he said, "although I was sincerely sorry after I found out that Mr. and Mrs. Livermore were such good sports under the stress of the circumstances."

Blake, he continued, "did not know anything about the robbery, or that I was engaged in this work in any way." The district attorney, he noted, had assured him that "if I told the whole truth about the matter, he would release her and let her go back to her home. As that is the only fair thing to do, I have unqualifiedly owned up to my connection with this robbery."

Despite his promise to tell "the whole truth," Arthur Gibson's signature appeared at the bottom of the document. It would be several hours before a check of his fingerprints revealed his real name. And he managed to withhold something else to protect Blake—neither the police nor the press realized they were married.

Blake was still in the office and had heard every word of Barry's damning confession. Edwards glanced in her direction just before she was led away. She was "as still and white," he noted, "as if carved in stone."

Victims of Long Island burglaries were invited to police headquarters to see if they could identify any of the pieces in the couple's possession. Robert Sealy confirmed that an $800 diamond-studded platinum wristwatch in the box had been stolen two months earlier from his home in Hewlett Bay Park. One of his neighbors, Marion Greenleaf, picked out an emerald ring and family heirlooms that had been in the safe taken from her home in April. The authorities could tie Barry to two more burglaries.

The Livermores and Aronsohns had also made the pilgrimage to Mineola to take a look at the jewelry seized from Barry and Blake. None of it, however, had been stolen by the gentlemen bandits. The Livermores were ushered into Edwards's office to see if they could identify Barry as one of the men who had invaded their home. Neither of them was sure; the bedroom had been too dark to see their faces clearly.

Barry, eager to help, tried to jog their memories. He reminded Dorothea Livermore that he had lit her cigarette and had gallantly returned her pinky ring.

"I see that little ring brought you luck after all," he quipped when he noticed it was back on her finger. "I hope I didn't frighten you too much."

That evening, Blake was brought to the jail. Guards allowed them to kiss. They were both in tears.

"I'm sorry that I got you into this. Now I'm trying to fix it up as best I can," he told her. "I am going to confess everything. They are trying to hold you for something you knew nothing about."

Edwards kept his end of the bargain. Blake spent the night at a hotel with police officers standing guard—she remained a key prosecution witness—but she was soon released on bail. "I believe she is clean as a whistle as far as the robberies are concerned," the district attorney told reporters. "Her story that she believed Barry to be a successful gambler I believe to be the truth."

The New York *Evening Post* congratulated the Nassau County force on cracking the Livermore case so quickly, praising the "notable piece of police work." King was confident that Barry's confession was only the beginning, that files on dozens of Long Island's unsolved jewel thefts might soon be closed. Barry "did not want a lawyer," he noted in a press briefing. "He seems to want to come clean."

~~~~~~~~~~

ONLY TWO OTHER people had known that Barry and Blake would be on the train to Lake Ronkonkoma. Barry was convinced James Monahan or his girlfriend was the source of the anonymous tips phoned in to Val

O'Farrell and Harold King. And by handing over the box of stolen jewelry as they left Manhattan, he had ensured that the police would catch them with incriminating evidence.

Barry had a score to settle. His confession named "Bill Williams" as his accomplice in the Livermore robbery. That was the only lead King's detectives needed. They checked criminal records and soon realized they were looking for Boston Billy Williams, the alias of the fugitive burglar from Worcester. Barry kindly provided a list of Manhattan haunts where they might find him.

A detective dispatched to the Times Square Hotel, at Eighth Avenue and Forty-Third Street, arrived just minutes after Monahan had checked

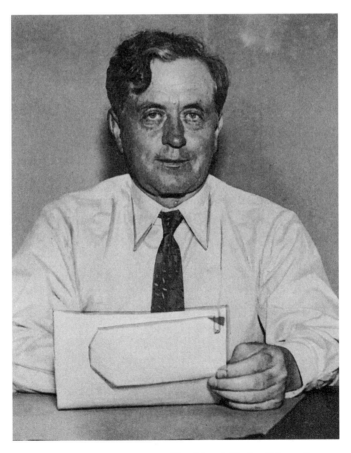

Nassau County district attorney Elvin Edwards (Author Collection)

out. Police forces across New York and in neighboring states were alerted, in case he tried to flee the city.

The Livermore heist, Barry told Edwards, had been Monahan's idea. He was "the real brains of our team," he claimed. "I usually acted as lookout." When the newspapers picked up the reference to Monahan as the brains behind the Long Island burglaries, the notion took hold that the likable Barry had been an underling and Monahan had called the shots. Blake backed him up. "My boy," she assured reporters, had been a tool in his devious partner's hands. A *New York Times* headline referred to the pair as the "BOSTON BILLY" GANG. The *Daily News* considered Monahan a "master-mind," and Brooklyn's *Daily Eagle* called him the "jewel bandit leader."

There was, the *Daily Eagle* acknowledged, another possibility: Barry could be trying to minimize his role in the crimes. "Barry's confession lays the whole robbery plot on 'Boston Billy.' The leader either confided very little in his confederate, or Barry has told only a portion of what he knows."

The district attorney agreed. "He told the truth—but not the whole truth," Edwards said later, and had "offered only enough to fulfil his bargain." He also suspected that Barry, who was willing to go to prison to protect Blake, was not ruthless enough to have engineered scores of jewel heists. "The ingenuity with which the robberies had been planned and executed, signified a warped, but extraordinarily keen, vicious intelligence, and this, the debonair, sentimental Barry did not possess," Edwards reasoned. "I was convinced that Barry was merely the tool—and that his elusive partner was the real master-mind."

The district attorney had been hoodwinked.

A HANDSOME, GENTLEMANLY jewel thief; a mystery woman; a falling-out among thieves; and a supporting cast of wealthy, socially prominent victims—it was, as reporters and editors liked to say, a story with legs. Accounts of Barry's arrest and confession and the hunt for Boston Billy sometimes upstaged the biggest news story of the week, Charles Lindbergh's imminent return to America and the hero's welcome that awaited him. The *New York Times* published daily updates on Barry's case despite the Lindbergh mania sweeping the country. The Associated Press and other wire services flashed details of his capture to newspapers across the country, making him front-page news from Kansas to Kentucky, from Utah to Florida, from Lincoln, Nebraska to Joplin, Missouri.

The New York *Daily News* led the charge, attacking the story with a barrage of headlines, a splash of photographs, and articles revised and updated on the fly, to jam in the latest details for its late editions. America's first Fleet Street–style tabloid, the *Daily News* boasted the highest circulation of any paper in the United States; more than a million copies rolled off its presses every day, and almost a million and a half on Sundays. The tabloid format, partway between a magazine and an unwieldy broadsheet, was perfect for reading on New York's crowded subways. But it was content, not just size, that induced so many people to shell out two cents for a copy and a nickel for the beefy Sunday edition. The paper courted middle- and working-class readers with short, punchy stories, breathless writing, and a front page devoted to photographs of the day's top newsmakers and events.

"Nothing that is not interesting is news," the paper declared in its debut editorial in 1919, and publisher Joseph Medill Patterson, the grandson of the founder of the *Chicago Tribune*, knew what his readers wanted. "Lay emphasis on romantic happenings," he instructed his editors and reporters, and ensure that each issue featured photographs documenting "a crime committed the previous day" in New York. "The things people were most interested in," he told his staff, "were, and in order, (1) Love or Sex, (2) Money, (3) Murder."

Barry's exploits ticked the first two boxes, guaranteeing the *Daily News* would assign one of its star police reporters to the story. John O'Donnell, a thirty-year-old who had served as an infantry officer in the war and studied literature at Harvard, had just joined the paper after stints in the newsrooms of the *Boston Record* and the *New York American*. "He was tireless in the pursuit of elusive news," noted a colleague, who remembered him as a gifted storyteller on the page and "a delightful raconteur" after hours.

O'Donnell sought out Val O'Farrell, who eagerly claimed most of the credit for nabbing one of "the outstanding jewel thieves of the decade."

The *Daily News* coverage played up the wealth and social standing of those targeted in the burglaries. A note to readers urged them to pick up the next day's issue "for further developments in this startling story of upper stratum crime." Lists of prominent Long Island residents who were suspected to be among Barry's victims appeared under the headlines BARRY GANG GOT GEMS OF SOCIETY FOLK and JUST SOME OF GEM THIEF'S VICTIMS!

And O'Donnell portrayed Barry and Blake as star-crossed lovers, their romance as doomed as Romeo and Juliet's. "The robber who stole suavely and confessed chivalrously," he wrote, was taking the rap to ensure that his "blonde inamorata" would be set free.

Blake forced a brave, dimpled smile as she posed for photographers with Barry's favorite dog, an Airedale named Jerry, but it was clear that the arrest and learning the shocking truth about her husband had shattered her world.

"I love him and will keep on doing so," she told O'Donnell, her eyes welling with tears. "It makes no difference to me that he is guilty of those robberies. It was because he loved me, and to get me clear of it, that he told the whole story to the district attorney."

With Barry behind bars, she became fair game in the press. The age difference between them was noted, to Blake's detriment. O'Donnell described her as "matronly" and noted how she looked at Barry with "almost maternal affection." Another, crueler reporter referred to her as Barry's "elderly sweetheart." King revealed Blake's ties to the Monongahela Club, adding a whiff of political scandal to the story. WOMAN ARRESTED IN CASE REVEALED AS A TAMMANY "WORKER," trumpeted a headline in the *New York Times*. Jimmy Hines, scurrying for cover, distanced himself from his district leader. While he told the *Times* he had known Blake for at least fifteen years, he claimed it had been a half dozen years since he had seen her last. "She had never been an active worker in his club," he lied. No one appears to have asked Hines if he knew Barry as well. Blake brushed aside a reporter's questions about her role in the club: "I would rather say nothing about that."

Reporters who showed up at the Barry home in Worcester, however, got an earful from his mother. She said she could do nothing for him.

"I've struggled to keep this home together, and I have had a hard enough time to meet the needs of life without helping Arthur," sobbed Bridget Barry, who was now in her midsixties and caring for Barry's disabled father. "Whatever he has done was against my heart and soul, and all that he ever learned from his father or me." It turned out he was not Bridget Barry's only wayward son—Barry's older brother Frank was doing time in a Connecticut prison for safecracking.

No detail was too trivial for the papers to overlook. There were reports the gentleman thief broke a finger in an ungentlemanly scuffle with an unruly drunk who had been tossed into his holding cell.

When news became elusive, the *Daily News* and other papers peppered their reports on the Long Island Raffles with distortions and fabrications. O'Donnell's imagination transformed the Lake Ronkonkoma bungalow into a "sumptuous mansion," where Barry and Blake "posed as persons of wealth and leisure" as they lavishly entertained Long Island's elite. There were equally far-fetched reports the couple had a winter home in Palm Beach. Otto Becker, the garageman who sometimes drove Barry's Cadillac and was briefly detained, became the couple's "liveried chauffeur" in O'Donnell's coverage. Barry's younger brother William had been staying at the bungalow when Barry was arrested, and when he was taken into custody for questioning, there were enough suspects in the mix for the *New York Times* to credit the police with smashing a "New England mob" of jewel thieves. O'Donnell's boldest foray into fiction, however, was a dubious report that Barry had booked passage for Europe shortly before his arrest and had almost escaped with his loot to live "a life of gentlemanly ease" on the Riviera.

"If everything had gone right," Barry had supposedly lamented as he sat in his cell, "I would have passed Lindbergh on the ocean by today and been safe in London by the end of the week."

TWENTY-THREE

ONLY HIGH-CLASS WORK

Long Island and Westchester County • 1927

F OUR DAYS AFTER his arrest, Arthur Barry emerged from the Nassau County Courthouse and stepped into the midday sunshine. The building's twenty-four-foot-high white dome, towering above a facade of reinforced concrete that had been tinted and formed to resemble blocks of granite, gleamed like a giant pearl. The temperature topped eighty degrees, and a brisk southwest wind was whipping clouds into ominous thunderheads. It was so hot that a man collapsed on a Manhattan street corner that afternoon and had to be revived by passersby. The *Daily News* declared June 9 the "first day of real summer."

Barry, however, looked cool and confident as he marched toward a line of parked automobiles. The double-breasted jacket of his gray pencil-striped suit was buttoned up in defiance of the heat. A white hand- kerchief peeked out of his breast pocket, and a matching wide-brimmed hat, turned up slightly on one side at a rakish angle, shielded his eyes. News photographers had been waiting for hours to capture this moment, and he obliged them by flashing a smile. "He walked out with the air of a man going for a casual stroll," noted a reporter for the *Brooklyn Daily Eagle*. He seemed oblivious to the detective walking beside him and the handcuffs that linked their wrists.

Barry and his guard settled into the back seat of the second car in the convoy. Anna Blake, who was allowed to accompany them, sat at his right side. Harold King was in the front seat beside the driver. The lead car, filled with detectives, pulled away from the curb, Barry's car followed, and a motorcycle cop swung into line behind them. Reporters and photographers, crammed into five more vehicles, brought up the rear.

Barry handcuffed to a guard after his arrest (Author Collection)

Their destination was Boxwood Manor, near Great Neck, the home of real estate broker Harvey Shaffer. The mansion was one of eighteen properties on a list of unsolved burglaries King had compiled. Barry had agreed to take a look and would confirm which ones he and James Monahan had looted in the fall of 1925. Reporters billed it as the "tour of the lost diamonds" and a trip "along a path of plunder." The outing, Barry promised them, "will look like a visit to the *Social Register*."

During the nine-mile drive, his right arm, the one free of handcuffs, was around Blake's waist. The reporters traveling behind could see them kissing. "He might have been a student out on a necking party," John O'Donnell told *Daily News* readers, "instead of a dangerous criminal enjoying what will probably prove to be his last journey in the open air until he rides to prison."

Barry's cuffs were removed when they arrived at the Shaffer estate, and he accompanied King on a walk around the house. A detective armed with a Thompson submachine gun was close behind.

"Stand back," the guard warned the reporters who were gathering to watch. "If this fellow makes a break I want a clean sweep at him."

Barry recognized the house and stopped beneath a pillar supporting a porch roof.

"Williams and I slipped in here late that night, and I boosted him up the pole," he said. As he acted as lookout, Monahan entered through a second-story window, Barry told King. Then, he stopped midstory. He seemed surprised to see a stenographer from the district attorney's office standing nearby, scribbling in shorthand.

"Are you taking notes?" he asked King.

"Yes, of course."

"I won't go further and I won't do anything else until I talk to the District Attorney."

The convoy returned to Mineola. Barry had admitted robbing the Livermores. He had pleaded guilty the previous day to counts of first-degree burglary and first-degree grand larceny and faced a long prison term. He was cooperating with the authorities. But with no defense lawyer to advise him—surprisingly, he never had one—he had started out on the tour before he realized he risked being charged with every burglary he confessed to committing. After meeting with Edwards to confirm he would be prosecuted only for the Livermore robbery, he agreed to visit more estates.

Barry had one more duty to perform that day. He testified before a grand jury investigating Monahan's role in the Livermore robbery. The Livermores also testified, and reporters were waiting for the couple when they arrived at the courthouse. One asked what they thought of the man who had confessed to invading their home, holding them hostage, and stealing their jewelry.

"I know he's terrible," said Dorothea Livermore, "but isn't he charming?"

KING ORGANIZED A new round of crime scene visits on the following day. Police relied on these outings to gauge whether a suspect recognized the location and was telling the truth. One of the first stops was the Evermore estate, where Dorothea Livermore invited them inside. Barry, who was handcuffed to a detective, was familiar with the rooms and recounted his conversations with the couple on the night of the robbery. At one point, as a test, King asked if he knew what was behind a pair of hand-carved wooden doors in a hallway.

"Certainly," Barry replied. "Ladies' hats."

Dorothea Livermore opened the doors to reveal her hat collection.

There were stops at a half dozen other homes. The gentleman burglar, noted John O'Donnell of the *Daily News*, seemed as comfortable and carefree as "a week-end guest visiting a hostess whom he has met but once before." Monahan, Barry said, had broken into four of the homes while he acted as lookout and had done one of the jobs on his own.

Barry scoffed when they stopped at a Long Island home where someone had clumsily used a crowbar to pry open a window.

"No," he replied when asked if it was one of his heists, "we only did high class work."

A GOLD BADGE and a string of rosary beads, found among the odds and ends of jewelry seized from Barry at the Ronkonkoma station, exposed him as Westchester County's infamous ladder burglar. Wall Street broker

Coster Steers identified the rosary as part of the $10,000 in jewels that two intruders had carried off from his Port Chester home the previous June—it was in a gold box engraved with his wife's initials. The honorary sheriff's deputy badge belonged to Alfred Berolzheimer and had been taken from his Tarrytown home in 1926.

Frank Coyne, an assistant district attorney, was dispatched to Mineola from White Plains to question Barry, who admitted he had operated in the county. He "confessed to having committed so many robberies in Westchester," Coyne announced after the interview, that "he could not remember the number."

Then Barry made a shocking allegation: Monahan, he told Coyne, had killed a policeman. He and Monahan had stolen a car in Westchester County four years earlier, in the summer of 1923, and were stopped by Sergeant Jack Harrison of the Scarsdale police force. Barry said he fled into the woods, and claimed he was a half mile away when he heard two gunshots. The next day, back in New York, Monahan told him he'd had to "shoot a cop who stuck his nose in my business." He had grabbed Harrison's revolver during a scuffle, Monahan said, and had shot the thirty-six-year-old father of three in the arm and chest. He was still carrying the officer's gun and had shown it to Barry.

Coyne was inclined to believe the story. Barry had mentioned losing his cap that night as he escaped, and a discarded dark-brown cap was one of the few scraps of evidence investigators had found at the murder scene. The assistant DA, however, doubted that Barry's allegations alone were enough to charge Monahan with murder. "We have very little evidence to get an indictment," he acknowledged, "and if we did go to trial, it would be one man's word against another." Monahan, however, still faced a long prison sentence for robbery if he was caught.

"He'll be a hard man to take alive," warned Barry, as if he were inviting the police to shoot first and ask questions later. Monahan wore a bulletproof vest, he said, and carried two revolvers, concealing the weapons under his jacket. "He's a desperate man, and if he's cornered, he'd rather try to shoot his way out or die in the attempt than submit to arrest."

Monahan fired back in a letter mailed to the *New York Times* that branded Barry a liar and fingered him as Harrison's killer. "You've got to be careful of Barry because he's a natural-born thief and a natural-born bum," who "would send his own brother to the chair," claimed the missive, written in pencil and posted in Rhode Island. "He killed Harrison. I will prove that when I am caught." Police compared the letter and Monahan's signature to samples of the fugitive's handwriting and concluded the note was genuine.

When an anonymous caller to the Nassau County Police threatened retribution for Barry's "squealing," Barry was transferred from the police lockup to a more secure cell at the county jail, at the rear of the courthouse. Officers armed with machine guns were dispatched to stand guard and prevent a possible attack.

Edwards agreed to send Barry to Westchester County to identify homes he had robbed. King and a pair of armed sheriff's deputies drove Barry there in mid-June for a marathon one-day tour. The route was kept secret, to ensure that no one tried to stage an ambush. They crisscrossed the county, viewing homes in Ardsley, Yonkers, and other communities where Barry had operated for years. He identified at least fourteen dwellings he said he had robbed with Monahan and accused him of breaking into many others on his own.

When they stopped at a home in Rye, owner Robert Mallory came outside to meet them.

"I want to thank you, Barry, for the gentlemanly way in which you robbed me," said Mallory, a forty-year-old partner in the New York investment firm Spencer Trask & Company. He was a graduate of Yale, where he had been a member of the exclusive Scroll and Key Society, and he had a request. "Do you remember what you did with the college pins that were in the loot?"

Barry said nothing but pointed to a wall that ran alongside the house, indicating where he had tossed them. Mallory was on his hands and knees in the grass, searching for the missing pins as the group drove away.

As Barry confessed to break-ins and police added new ones they suspected were his work, estimates of the value of the jewelry he had stolen ballooned into the millions of dollars. It was more than enough for the

Daily News to declare him "the most successful robber of the decade." The Brooklyn *Times Union* added to the hype, crediting Barry with "a string of robberies that overshadows the adventures of any crook of fact or fiction." These estimates, however, did not include his most spectacular and lucrative crimes—stealing the Cosden and Mountbatten jewels in 1924 and swiping the Donahue pearls the following year. When questioned about those thefts, Barry denied any involvement. Since Barry had "admitted other robberies so readily," the *New York Times* reported, Edwards "did not see any reason to doubt his denials."

While Barry would be sentenced in Nassau County only for the Livermore robbery, the scale of his crimes and the value of his suspected loot could prompt a judge to add years to his prison term. He tried, belatedly, to tone down the sensation he had created. His bravado and swagger faded. He accused his victims of inflating their losses to flaunt their wealth and impress their "society friends." A New York City–based mob was also preying on Long Island homes, he claimed at one point, and these rivals often swept in and robbed estates before he and Monahan had a chance. His share of the take from the Westchester County thefts, he claimed, was a paltry $20,000. "I could have made a better living as a salesman," he told Edwards.

At the end of June, when King took him on a final tour of fifteen Nassau County homes that had been burglarized since 1925, Barry admitted to three of the break-ins and said Monahan had done a few more on his own. As for the rest, one reporter noted, Barry conceded "he might have participated in some of those robberies and forgotten the layout of the houses."

~~~~~~~~~~~~

NASSAU COUNTY DEPUTY sheriff Frank Davis collected Barry from his steel-cage cell on the first day of July. Davis handcuffed their wrists together, and they walked sixty paces through a dimly lit underground tunnel that linked the county's jail and courthouse. Passing through a pair of heavy steel doors, they entered the courthouse basement and ascended a staircase that took them directly into the courtroom on the second floor. The courtroom was about the size of a tennis court, but an eighteen-foot-high vaulted ceiling made it feel larger. Snow-white wall paint offset the dark warmth of the quarter-sawn oak trim. As they entered, Barry was smiling.

His fate was in the hands of county judge Lewis Jerome Smith, a stout fifty-one-year-old with a deep part that sliced like a furrow through the middle of his brown hair. He was a close friend of Edwards, who had succeeded him as district attorney, and together they were leading a crackdown on bootleggers and other Prohibition violators in the county. Smith's habit of imposing the maximum penalty for liquor violations had earned him the nickname "the dry judge."

The hearing was over in minutes.

Under New York law, the offense of first-degree burglary carried a minimum sentence of fifteen years. The judge asked Barry if he had anything to say before his sentence was imposed. Barry shook his head.

"The Court then imposes sentence of 25 years at hard labor."

Reporters who scanned his face, hoping to gauge his reaction, drew a blank. "Barry took his sentence with the same unconcern which has characterized his demeanor since the 'gentleman burglar' was first arrested," one noted.

He turned to face Nassau County's sheriff, William Strohson. Part of the sentence did not sit well with him. "I don't like that hard labor stuff," he said as he was led back to his cell.

The district attorney and the jewel thief, the *Daily News* revealed, had struck a deal soon after his arrest. In return for Barry's confession, cooperation, and the guilty pleas that would make a trial unnecessary, Edwards agreed not only to release Blake but to seek a sentence of no more than thirty years in prison on the Livermore charges. "Barry," Edwards pointed out, "helped us in our investigation of the various robberies in which he was concerned." King likely had hoped for a longer prison term. "Severity of punishment," the detective noted later, "is the only way to keep a check on the present-day criminal."

Despite Barry's confessions to a raft of break-ins in Westchester County, he was never prosecuted as the ladder burglar who had been targeting homes there since the early '20s. His confessions had closed the books on many of the county's unsolved burglaries, and assistant district attorney Frank Coyne announced that his office was content to let Nassau County punish him. "Barry has charges enough against him," he explained "to keep him in jail for the rest of his life." That decision remained unchanged even after Barry received a lighter-than-expected sentence. The Connecticut authorities, too, let Edwards take the lead. The break-in at Percy Rockefeller's Owenoke estate in 1926 was among the thefts Barry admitted after his arrest, but there was no attempt to prosecute him for that crime or for his escape from the Bridgeport jail in 1922.

A conviction for a single offense after he had confessed to dozens must have looked like a victory to Barry, even if it meant he might spend the next quarter century behind bars. His efforts to shift the spotlight onto Monahan and to reinvent himself as a junior partner in the burglaries had paid off. Edwards and King were now focused on catching and prosecuting Monahan as the mastermind behind the Livermore robbery and other heists—and as the suspected killer of a policeman. "We are still looking for his confederate, 'Boston Billy' Williams," the DA reminded reporters as Barry was taken from the courtroom to begin serving his sentence.

On the way back to his cell, Barry and his guards stopped partway through the tunnel so he could light a cigarette. Anna Blake ran up to them, and the couple were granted a few moments together. Then Barry turned, waved goodbye, and continued down the corridor to the jail.

Blake had been a rock in the weeks since Barry's arrest. "I am usually very calm when things happen," she later noted, "although I collapse when they are over." She had recovered from the shock of learning the truth about her husband, endured the humiliation of the press attacks, and rebounded from the destruction of her world. But with Barry ripped from her life and on his way to prison, she said, "I went to pieces." It would be two weeks before she pulled herself together and felt able to visit him in prison.

If Barry were to serve his full sentence, he would not be released until 1952. "I'll be an old man when I get out," he said as he waited to be taken to prison. "By that time," he added, "there will be airplanes all over" and "everybody will be using them instead of automobiles."

TWENTY-FOUR

UP THE RIVER

Ossining, New York, and Long Island • 1927

T HE LADDER BURGLAR was back in Westchester County within hours of being sentenced, handcuffed and jammed into a car between two other prisoners. As they passed Yonkers, Ardsley, and other towns, Arthur Barry likely caught glimpses of a few stately mansions he recognized or had burglarized. Three Nassau County sheriff's deputies, one armed with a sawed-off shotgun, escorted them on the sixty-mile drive from Mineola to the Hudson River village of Ossining, home to Sing Sing Prison. Their destination was almost due north of Manhattan and so infamous that "up the river"—a phrase, the New York *Daily News* noted, "sure to strike terror into the heart of the criminal"—had become synonymous with serving time.

The car parked at the prison's south entrance. A metal door groaned open, and Barry and the other prisoners were handed over to the guards inside. Walls studded with cone-roofed watchtowers loomed above their heads and a long, rectangular cellblock—a forbidding building worthy of the name "big house"—rose to their right like a massive stone coffin. New arrivals stood "limp and dejected, like cowed and beaten dogs," noted Lewis Lawes, Sing Sing's warden. The metal portal to the outside world snapped shut behind them "like the murderous jaws of a hungry shark."

"This way," a guard ordered after Barry's handcuffs were removed. He was led to a low yellow-brick building. The former "death house," where more than two hundred men had died in the electric chair, was now an administration center.

A clerk asked him dozens of questions for the prison's receiving blotter. His name and aliases—Arthur Gibson, Arthur Williams, Arthur Cummings—were recorded. He was thirty but claimed he was six years older. His confession to burglary and larceny, the three weeks he had served in jail in Mineola, and his military service were noted. He said "no" when asked if he used drugs, "yes" when asked if he smoked. His education? He was a high school graduate, he said, making no mention of his many scrapes with the law as a juvenile. He continued to claim he was single, to protect Anna. He attended church regularly, he said, even though his preferred places of worship had been speakeasies and craps games. He was a salesman earning thirty-five dollars a week when arrested, he insisted, and the clerk—who was clearly not a newspaper reader—recorded this as if it were true. One of the last questions was why he had broken the law. Many men blamed booze or gambling, and Lawes reckoned that one out of seven claimed they were innocent. Barry attributed his crimes to "Evil Associates."

The man who had stolen jewelry worth millions of dollars handed over his meager possessions: a pair of cuff links, a shirt collar stud, and $105.35 in cash. The clerks preferred to deal with men serving life sentences, since there was no need to figure out the inmate's possible release date on parole. Barry's was penciled in later. Inmate 80071 would be eligible for parole in just under twenty-one years, on April 12, 1948. He would be in prison until he was at least fifty-one.

The next step was "dressing in." He was ordered to strip and shower, and searched for drugs and other contraband. Then he traded in his street clothes for his prison uniform: gray coat, gray trousers, and pin-striped work shirt. A doctor assessed his health. He collected an iron bucket from a rack in the prison yard before being taken to his cell.

New inmates spent their first few weeks locked up in Gallery Thirteen, one of the tiers of cells stacked six stories high inside the cellblock. Built a

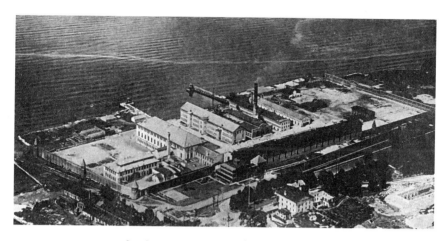

Sing Sing Prison in the 1920s (Author Collection)

century earlier, the building was cold, dark, damp, and poorly ventilated, a throwback to a time when prisons were designed to punish, not reform. "There is only harshness that seems to reach out and grip one with ghastly hands," Lawes said of the sensation of stepping inside, "a heaviness that presses down upon the spirit like a huge millstone."

A lattice-topped steel door clanged shut, and Barry was locked in a dungeon-like cell. Six and a half feet high and seven deep, it was a yard and a few inches across, barely wide enough to accommodate a narrow cot and straw mattress. A lightbulb in a fixture of emerald-green glass cast an eerie glow. There was no running water, only a tin cup to be filled when a guard did the rounds with a jug of water. And there was no toilet, which was why Barry had been issued a bucket. The hinged lid that covered this portable toilet did little to suppress the nauseating stench.

The large gray blocks used to fashion the walls, ceiling, and floor made it feel like a cavern hewn from solid rock. "Little cubbyholes of cold stone," Lawes called them. One inmate described the cells as "no bigger than a dead man's grave," while another said they were hellholes "you wouldn't put your worst enemy in," the work of "the devil himself." Actor Charlie Chaplin, one of many curious celebrities who toured the prison, stepped inside one of the claustrophobic cells and quickly retreated. "My God!" he exclaimed. "It's inhuman!" Most men, noted Lawes, "no matter how hardened and stolid," succumbed to despair after the lights went out on their first night entombed in Sing Sing. They wept.

Sing Sing's new inmates remained in isolation as they settled in. They left their cells only for meals, medical and psychological examinations, and tests to determine whether they needed remedial education. Once the assessments were complete, prison officials decided whether an inmate would be assigned to a cushy job in the prison library, would toil in one of the in-house factories that produced shoes, clothing, furniture, and other goods, or would be condemned to the backbreaking work of quarrying stone or hauling and shoveling coal to feed the prison's steam boilers. Barry's mug shots were snapped, and the fingerprints he had never left at a crime scene were inked onto paper. Barry's stint in Gallery Thirteen, however, was cut short. Inmate 80071 was soon needed back in Mineola.

GORDON HURLEY, A thin-faced, black-haired Nassau County detective in his early thirties, was chatting with the owner of a garage in Sound View, Connecticut, a seaside hamlet a dozen miles west of New London. Had the mechanic seen or worked on a Nash coupe? he asked. A two-seater hardtop with a long snout, and room for a rumble seat at the back. Green paint. Newly purchased. As Hurley spoke, he glimpsed a flash of green as a car sped past. He ran to the garage window in time to see the Nash he had just described pull in behind a cottage. He called to his companion, a private eye named Charles Sheraton, and they raced to their car. They pulled up in front of the cottage, drew their revolvers, and jumped out.

"You take the back door," Hurley commanded, "and I'll cover the front."

The driver of the Nash, who was inside, spotted Sheraton as he ran toward the rear of the cottage. The man burst through the front door, grabbed a porch column, swung around it to the ground, and ran.

"He came through the door like a thunderbolt," Hurley recalled. "I never saw a man his age travel as fast as he did."

Hurley fired two quick shots. The second bullet hit the man in the left leg. He collapsed face-down on the grass. The detective jumped on his back, pinning him on the ground.

"One move out of you," he growled, "and I'll kill you."

The wounded man put his hands above his head. Hurley, still clutching his revolver, frisked him with his free hand. His quarry, he had been warned, usually carried two handguns and was unlikely to surrender without a fight. The man, however, was unarmed.

It was the morning of July 7, six days after Arthur Barry was sent to Sing Sing. The elusive Boston Billy Williams was finally in custody.

Hurley, considered "an ace detective" on the Nassau force, and one of the officers who arrested Barry, had been hunting for James Monahan for weeks. Sheraton had been on his trail much longer—since the fall of 1926, when Percy Rockefeller hired his employer, the Burns Detective Agency, to find the second-story man who had broken into the fortress-like Owenoke estate. While Barry had pulled that job alone and remained the chief suspect, Sheraton was convinced that Monahan either had helped him or had swiped the Rockefeller jewels on his own. With the blessing of chief of detectives Harold King, Hurley and Sheraton had teamed up a few days earlier, compared notes, and traced Monahan from Worcester to Connecticut and, eventually, to Sound View. Identifying his new car had been the breakthrough they needed.

They drove Monahan to a nearby hospital to be patched up. The wound was minor—Hurley's well-aimed bullet had entered just below the knee and made a clean exit. "I'd be better off, I guess, if the bullet had hit me in the head," Monahan joked to a reporter who turned up at the hospital. The detectives caught a ferry to Long Island and were back in Mineola with their prisoner before the end of the day.

District attorney Elvin Edwards questioned him for five hours. While Barry had been tight-lipped in the interrogation room, Edwards noted, Monahan was "facetious and scornful." He denied any involvement in the Livermore heist and scoffed at the suggestion that he had been the leader of their two-man gang. He had been a petty thief, he claimed, until Barry recruited him to join his raids on suburban estates—the "society racket," Monahan called it. "Barry is a rat," he snarled to Edwards. Fingering him for the Livermore job "was grudge work on his part," he said. "We had a row and this is the way he has taken to work his spite against me."

He was confronted with Barry's allegation that he had killed Jack Harrison, the Scarsdale police officer. Monahan "is obviously scared of being charged with murder," King told reporters. Edwards did not mince words: "He's afraid of 'burning' in the electric chair."

He was arraigned on the Livermore charges before Judge Lewis Smith in the courtroom where Barry had been sentenced only days earlier. The "cold, debonair, wise-cracking master criminal," as *Daily News* crime reporter John O'Donnell described him, walked with a slight limp from his wound. "If I had a little hacksaw in my shoe last night I would not be here today," he told his guards. It was not clear whether he was joking or putting them on notice.

As a four-count indictment was read, accusing him of burglary, theft, and receiving stolen goods, Monahan smiled and appeared slightly bored. He absent-mindedly rubbed a bald spot on the back of his head. "Not guilty," he replied, when asked to enter a plea. He was dispatched to the county jail to await a trial later in the month.

Judge Smith signed an order to return Barry to Mineola to testify against his former partner.

"If I put those two men in one room," Edwards joked after the hearing, "I would not account for what might happen."

~~~~~~~~~

THE STATE'S STAR witness against Monahan arrived at the Nassau County jail from Sing Sing just after ten o'clock on the morning of July 11. Barry's drab prison grays were gone, replaced with a suit and tie, a handkerchief in his breast pocket, and a newsboy cap that stood out among the fedoras and boaters that surrounded him. Long Island's "Dapper Gem Thief," as a headline called him, was back.

Barry spent most of the next two weeks shuttling between the jail—he was put in a cell as far as possible from Monahan's—and the grand jury room in the courthouse. Anna Blake had been ordered to appear before the grand jury as well and, like her husband, was eager to get even with Monahan for betraying them. One reporter was curious how she reacted to the news of Monahan's arrest. "I'm tickled to death about it," she said.

Monahan spent his time devouring pints of ice cream—he had them delivered to his cell to stave off a summer heat wave—and dispensing advice to fellow inmates. "It doesn't pay to try to beat the law" was among his nuggets of wisdom. "Don't get mixed up with women," he griped after learning that a former girlfriend was cooperating with the police. "You have a mighty good time while you are having it," he told a reporter for the *Brooklyn Daily Eagle* who visited his cell, "but you end up in the 'hoosegow,' so what's the use?"

Jesse and Dorothea Livermore came to the Mineola jail to take a look at Monahan, but they did not recognize him. Adelaide Couchman and her two sons and Nathan Jonas, however, identified him as the armed man they had confronted after he broke into their homes. It was no longer the word of one crook against another. Barry's allegations "would have been worthless without corroboration," noted the *Daily Eagle*. With the testimony of four reputable eyewitnesses to bolster his story, his former partner seemed certain to be convicted of at least two burglaries.

Monahan's legal woes were multiplying. In mid-July, the grand jury indicted him for break-ins at the homes of businessman Harold Talbott, polo pioneer Thomas Hitchcock, and architect John Greenleaf, as well as the confrontations with the Couchmans and Jonas. He was about to be put on trial on charges of burglary, larceny, and receiving stolen goods for his role in the Livermore heist. Edwards announced he would seek to have Monahan imprisoned for life under New York State's Baumes Laws, introduced the previous year to mete out harsher sentences to repeat offenders. Authorities in Westchester County could also charge him with the burglaries he and Barry had committed in their jurisdiction. Police were reviewing fingerprints and ballistics tests and threatening to indict him for the murder of the Scarsdale policeman. And if New York did not put him in the electric chair, Connecticut might hang him for another murder. After Monahan's arrest put his photograph on the front pages, three witnesses identified him as the gunman who shot Peter Wagner outside a Bridgeport dance Hall in 1922, finally freeing Barry from suspicion that he had been the shooter. An indictment and extradition order were being considered.

The district attorney told Monahan to make a choice: risk a death sentence or admit to his role in the Long Island burglaries and face a long prison term—a sentence "so long," Edwards told him in one of their meetings, "that other prosecuting authorities won't be interested in you."

There was another option. Monahan had already served notice that he would try to escape. "This can," he had boasted the night he arrived at the jail, "will be easy to get out of." A spoon, which he had hidden after a meal and scraped against his cell wall until it was shaped like a crude key, was found in his cell a couple of days after the grand jury indictments. Monahan kicked and screamed as guards dragged him to a solitary confinement cell as punishment.

"I'll go crazy here," he yelled from inside the sparsely furnished cell. "Let me out of this dump." He cursed the guards and banged the cell bars, creating a din loud enough for Barry and the rest of the inmates to hear. He refused a meal of bread and water, and set fire to his mattress, apparently with matches he had managed to conceal. Guards smelled smoke and removed the damaged mattress, leaving him to try to sleep on the cot's metal rungs.

He appeared in court in a rumpled suit, a reporter observed, "glassy eyed and shaking like a leaf."

Edwards, convinced that Monahan's erratic behavior was a ploy to support a possible plea of insanity, arranged for psychiatrists to examine him. They concluded he was sane.

Before the month was out, he pleaded guilty to counts of first-degree burglary and grand larceny for swiping jewels from Harry and Regina Aronsohn during the Livermore robbery. Grim headlines predicted he would be clobbered with a prison term of up to eighty years. Offered a chance to shave time off his sentence if he coughed up any hidden loot, Monahan sparked a brief treasure hunt near the Connecticut town of Darien. Shortly before his arrest, he claimed, a state trooper had stopped him for speeding, then sent him on his way. Dorothea Livermore's expensive pearls were in his car, and Monahan, spooked by the encounter, said he had dumped the necklace in bushes at the roadside, hoping to come back for them. Detective Gordon Hurley was sent to Connecticut to lead a search, but the piece was never found.

Monahan, cleaned up and clad in a new gray suit, shook his head when Judge Smith asked if he had anything to say before he was sentenced. Fifty years at hard labor, the judge announced, double the prison term he had imposed on Barry weeks earlier and, as the press noted, "tantamount to life in prison." Monahan would be pushing seventy-three by the time he was eligible to apply for early release in 1969. As Edwards had predicted, the harsh sentence prompted other jurisdictions to abandon bids to put him on trial for murder.

As guards led him from the courthouse to a car, he raised a handcuffed wrist and blew kisses to a couple of young women who were leaning out windows to catch a final glimpse of a man the *Daily News* had dubbed the "Beau Brummel of house breakers." On an earlier trip to the courtroom, Monahan had passed a scrap of paper to a spectator. It was a childish poem he had written for Barry, the "dirty rat" who had put him behind bars. "I squealed on a pal / To save my old gal," read one stanza.

Barry, who was no longer needed as a witness, was already locked up in Sing Sing. Monahan was on his way to join him.

TWENTY-FIVE

SING SING

Ossining, New York, and Long Island • 1927–29

SQUEALER IN PERIL BY SING SING CODE warned an ominous head-line in the New York *Daily News* on July 28, the day James Monahan arrived at the prison. Arthur Barry was in solitary confinement, to protect him not only from his mouthy, volatile accomplice, but from other inmates who might take exception to having a "rat" in their midst. "Prisoners at Sing Sing are incensed at Barry's action in turning on his pal," the paper claimed, "and might do him bodily harm."

Monahan was kept under close watch. "I won't be here long," he vowed. "I'll beat this place the first chance I get." The number of guards on his tier of cells was doubled.

Sing Sing officials considered transferring Barry to another prison, then decided to rid themselves of the troublesome Monahan. On August 4, a week after his arrival, he was dispatched to Clinton state prison in the village of Dannemora, close to the Canadian border. It was reserved for convicts deemed dangerous, incorrigible, or likely to try to escape. "There are herded the state's ugliest criminals," *Time* magazine noted, a "vicious, degenerate brotherhood." Manhattan crooks who dreaded being exiled there had a nickname for the remote penitentiary in the Adirondacks: Siberia.

With Monahan gone, fears for Barry's safety subsided. There were no news reports of other inmates threatening him, and none seemed interested in taking sides in the feud. Less than three weeks after the transfer, Lewis Lawes ordered that Barry be released from his solitary cell. "Few men's minds," the warden noted, "could stand the strain of such confinement for more than a short time."

BARRY'S OFFHAND COMPLAINT at his sentencing hearing—"I don't like that hard labor stuff"—irked the editor of a small-town newspaper in Westchester County. "Most labor is hard whether it is done in the factory or in the office," scoffed an editorial in the Port Chester *Daily Item*, which had followed Barry's exploits. Barry, who had chosen "what appeared to him to be an easier life—a life that would bring him 'easy money' . . . must now do the hard labor that was repellant to him."

Barry had seen his future workplace, it turned out, on the day he arrived at Sing Sing. The prison yard he crossed on his way to the intake office was as meticulously landscaped as the grounds of any Long Island estate he had robbed. Gravel walkways framed manicured lawns, flower beds, and clumps of rosebushes and shrubs. Blue spruces and other trees offered shade. The centerpiece was a circular fountain, complete with water lilies and goldfish. The gardens, "an inspiration to dark and troubled souls," in the words of the state's prison commission, were the creation of Charles Chapin, a former editor of the New York *World*, who was serving twenty years to life for murder. Chapin had been facing financial ruin in 1918 when he shot his wife in her sleep—"to keep her from starvation and want," he claimed—and said he had intended to kill himself, but instead he had surrendered to the police. With the support of the warden and donors who supplied seeds, bulbs, and plants, the Rose Man of Sing Sing, as he came to be known, had turned the dusty, rock-strewn prison yard into an oasis of life and color.

Barry was among the three dozen inmates who tended the gardens under Chapin's supervision. Most, like him, were newcomers who had been cooped up in the old cellblock, awaiting their first work assignments. "You can imagine what cheerful helpers they make when they are brought into the open and permitted to exercise for several hours with shovels, spades, and hoes," Chapin told the editor of House & Garden magazine.

While the work was easier than breaking rock or shoveling coal, the Rose Man was a demanding boss who had ruled his New York newsroom like a tyrant. "When he gave me an order," Barry recalled, "I knew there was to be no dispute about it."

Chapin was incensed to discover that some inmates stopped working the moment he left the grounds. "Shirking," he complained in a letter to the warden, "will not be tolerated."

The former jewel thief and the former newsman hit it off. Chapin had known Harry Houdini—they had met when he performed for Sing Sing inmates, a captive audience that was no doubt eager to see the world's greatest escape artist in action. After Houdini died in 1926, his widow, Bess, befriended and often visited the prison's celebrity gardener. When Chapin discovered that Arthur Barry and Anna Blake had been neighbors and friends of the Houdinis, he convinced the warden to make the jewel thief a permanent member of his gardening staff. Barry was given the title of superintendent of the greenhouse, where Chapin nurtured his roses and helped to build the garden's most elaborate feature—a round, domed aviary that housed the prison's collection of parrots and other exotic birds. Chapin, who had no children, called Barry "son."

The gardens were the most visible evidence of Lawes's efforts to transform Sing Sing from one of the nation's most dreaded prisons into one of its most progressive. A baby-faced former prison guard with a reformer's zeal and empathy to spare, he studied social work and was only thirty-six when he was handed the keys to Sing Sing in 1920. His goal as warden was to turn lawbreakers into law-abiding citizens. He disarmed guards who circulated among the inmates, building trust and defusing tensions. Recreation and sports were encouraged, and inmates filled the bleachers when the prison baseball and football teams hosted squads from nearby communities. When critics accused Lawes of coddling prisoners and running a "country club for criminals," the warden invited them to spend twenty-four hours inside the prison walls; no one took him up on the offer.

"Treat a man like a dog, and you will make a dog of him," he declared. "Brute force never reformed any man."

Every inmate was classified as a Grade A man upon arrival and permitted to have visitors on four weekdays and one Sunday every month. If an inmate violated prison rules—something as minor as smoking on the job was an offense—he could be downgraded, ordered to serve additional prison time, and limited to two visits a month. It was, Lawes put it, "a powerful incentive to good behaviour."

Lawes knew Barry. They had met at a Manhattan restaurant only months before his arrest. When they came face-to-face at Sing Sing, the warden offered a few words of advice.

"Stay out of trouble," he said, "and you'll get along fine here."

That was Barry's plan. "I was determined to be a model prisoner," he later explained, "and apply for parole as early as possible."

Blake visited every week, sometimes making the trip with Bess Houdini when she drove to the prison to see Chapin. Visitors and inmates sat on wooden stools, and with no barriers or screens to separate them, couples were allowed to kiss and embrace. "I just lived for the day when he would return to me," Blake said, hoping that a combination of good behavior and early parole might shorten his quarter-century sentence. "I knew it would be a long time, but I was willing to wait." Blake considered moving to Ossining to be closer to Barry, and told the *New York Times* she would devote her life to "trying to obtain his freedom." She would soon demonstrate the lengths she would go to get her husband back.

That summer, the New York Giants came to Sing Sing to play an exhibition baseball game against the inmate team, "the prison nine." The big leaguers won handily, 12 to 4, and the sixteen hundred prisoners in the stands "gazed with envious eyes," one newspaper claimed, as a Giants slugger's home-run ball disappeared over the wall. When Gene Tunney outfought former champ Jack Dempsey in September to retain the world heavyweight title, everyone in the prison—even the residents of death row—was allowed to listen to the live radio broadcast from Chicago. Barry may have spotted Dempsey, Babe Ruth, or actors Jimmy Durante and Edward G. Robinson in the steady stream of celebrities, justice officials, and university students who toured the prison; the highlight, for many, was a chance to sit in the electric chair. On Christmas Day, Barry and every other inmate received a gift package that included cigarettes, candy, apples, a half pound of coffee, a cake, a pie, and a bleak reminder that his life was slowly slipping away: a 1928 calendar.

Barry spent his free time reading—striving, he later explained, to "fill the great gaps" that stints in reformatories had left in his education. The prison library offered fifteen thousand books, a collection that ranged from the novels of Louisa May Alcott to the obscure military memoir *Wild Sports in Zulu Land*. He had his pick of more than thirty volumes on American history, multiple biographies of Cromwell, Jefferson, Napoleon, and Washington, and his mind could escape into more than four hundred accounts of travel and adventure. One title found in the reference section, *The Gold-Seeker's Manual*, could have been his life story. Back issues of *Harper's* and other popular magazines were available, and Lawes allowed inmates to read the New York dailies, rejecting the popular notion that sensationalized accounts of crimes in newspapers could be "a bad influence" on prisoners. "If they are good enough to be received into homes where they are read by everyone, from the schoolgirl to grandpa," he argued, "I fail to see why they should be excluded."

Barry settled into the prison routine. A bell jolted him awake each morning at six o'clock. Inmates dressed, grabbed the lidded buckets that served as toilets, and filed out of their cells—"the malodorous march," Lawes called it—to dump them into an open sewer. They worked a seven-hour day and ate their meals at long tables in the cavernous dining hall. After the workday ended, prisoners chatted, smoked, or played catch in Chapin's gardens. Movies were shown in the prison chapel every evening, to reduce the number of hours the men were locked away for the night in their cramped, dank cells—"the smallest area," one journalist asserted, "in which men have ever been kenneled in this country."

The nightmarish cells were about to be abandoned. New cellblocks being built on a hillside overlooking the prison grounds would soon make Sing Sing one of the most modern and progressive prisons in the United States. The heated, well-lit cells were the size of a small bedroom, and each one had a toilet and sink. Inmates would be permitted to hang pictures on the walls, cover the barred window with a curtain, even listen to the radio. Cells on the west side of the new buildings offered views of sunsets over the Hudson River valley. Hundreds of trusted prisoners and inmates serving short sentences were relocated during 1928, and Barry would have expected he would soon join them.

One of Sing Sing's dungeon-like cells (New York State Archives)

THE AUTHORITIES IN Nassau County had long suspected the Livermore heist was an inside job. So did Charles Sheraton, the Burns detective who had hunted down James Monahan. And they agreed on the possible culprit: Edgar Kane, thirty-two, who had been a chauffeur for Dorothea Livermore's mother for six years. The Livermores let him go a year before they were robbed, so he may have held a grudge. Kane knew the layout of the Kings Point mansion. He also knew Barry and Monahan, who were regulars at a Harlem speakeasy he opened in 1926. District attorney Elvin Edwards, who had labeled the establishment "a dive for criminals," was convinced that Kane had tipped off the robbers and acted as lookout while they were inside.

Kane had disappeared in May 1927, about the time of the robbery, abandoning his wife and ten-year-old daughter. To Edwards, this was proof of his guilt. Sheraton tracked him through upstate New York to Montreal before the trail went cold.

Just before Christmas 1928, a tip led the detective to Kenosha, Wisconsin, south of Milwaukee, where Kane was working in a mattress factory. Kane insisted he was innocent as he was extradited to Mineola to face charges of burglary and larceny. "I'm going to fight," he vowed. "They've got nothing on me." He was wrong. At some point, he discovered, Monahan had given a statement to the police implicating him in the heist.

Barry was on his way to Mineola as well. Weeks earlier, the state's court of appeals had decreed that grand jury investigations were mandatory in felony cases. The ruling created chaos in the justice system—"a most ridiculous mess," fumed one newspaper editorial. Barry was one of an estimated nine thousand inmates who had pleaded guilty without the formality of facing a grand jury, and who could now challenge their convictions. Edwards devised a simple solution to keep Barry behind bars—he would ask Nassau County's grand jury to indict Barry as well as Kane for the Livermore robbery.

Barry arrived at the Mineola courthouse from Sing Sing on December 28, shackled and casually puffing a cigarette as armed guards escorted him inside. Offered a chance to testify against Kane before the grand jury, he refused. There was, Barry insisted later, nothing to tell. Kane's only crime had been to mention his wealthy former employer in passing one night at the speakeasy; Barry and Monahan had run with the tip, and Kane had not known their plans. Four indictments of burglary, larceny, and receiving stolen goods were returned against each man—two for robbing the Livermores and two for the jewelry taken from their guests, the Aronsohns.

Barry was arraigned the following month and again pleaded guilty, just as he had in 1927. Judge Lewis Smith sentenced him to twenty-five years in prison, just as he had in 1927, and gave Barry credit for the eighteen months he had already served. When court officials recorded his personal details, he acknowledged for the first time that he and Blake were married.

Kane stood trial within days. A phalanx of armed guards ushered Monahan into the courtroom. He testified with his wrists in handcuffs and took a sledgehammer to the state's case. Kane had not "located" the Livermore mansion, Monahan insisted—he had. And Kane had not been with them the night he and Barry pulled off the robbery.

Edwards, desperate to salvage his case, confronted his star witness.

"Didn't you tell me that Kane came out with you to the Livermore place?" he demanded, "and that you paid Kane $300?"

No. Monahan said, he had not.

Dorothea Livermore's testimony was the final blow. She vouched for Kane as an honest and reliable employee, so trustworthy that she had sent him on errands to Cartier and other Manhattan stores to pick up jewelry for her. After three hours of deliberation, the jury acquitted him. The remaining charges were dropped.

On his way back to Clinton Prison by train, during a stop in Albany, Monahan scuffled with one of his guards, slipped off his handcuffs, and crashed through the window of a Pullman car. Another guard fired two warning shots over his head before he was recaptured, dazed and bleeding from cuts to his head. Monahan's offer to testify against Barry and Kane, Edwards acknowledged when reporters confronted him with the news, had been nothing more than a ruse to get him out of prison so he could try to escape.

Barry, meanwhile, was locked up more than 250 miles from New York City. On December 30, 1928, after the grand jury issued its indictments, he had been shipped from Sing Sing to Auburn, the state's oldest prison, thirty miles west of Syracuse, in the Finger Lakes region. The sudden transfer, possibly to relieve overcrowding at Sing Sing, was a blow to Barry and to Blake, who would face a long journey each time she visited. She wrangled a meeting with Warden Lawes and pleaded with him to reconsider, but the transfer stood.

When he was sentenced a second time, Barry asked Edwards and Judge Smith to recommend that he serve his time in Sing Sing. The request was ignored, and he was returned to Auburn. He would not be there for long.

6

THE FUGITIVE

TWENTY-SIX

BREAKOUT

Auburn, New York • 1929

T HREE Auburn Prison inmates crouched in a stairwell, a cool oasis on a sweltering July afternoon. George Small, a red-haired former medical student in his early thirties, who looked more like a clerk than a crook, was doing twelve years for the armed robbery of a Manhattan jeweler. Joe Caprico, a tough, steely-eyed young hoodlum from Rochester who was also in for robbery, had served six months of a twenty-year term. The third man was Arthur Barry.

Small banged on the door to a guardroom. He was an orderly in the prison hospital and a trusty—an inmate considered reliable enough to move freely within the prison and to run errands for the staff. A voice asked who was there. Small identified himself and said he was delivering a lunch box for one of the guards.

When Merle Osborne opened the door, Small sprayed him in the face with ammonia. Temporarily blinded by the caustic compound, the guard fumbled for his handgun and fired a volley of shots that went wild.

"I'll kill you for that," Small snarled as he struck him on the head and knocked him unconscious.

Barry and Caprico rushed in after Small and tackled Tom Wallace, the other guard inside, before he could draw his pistol. Wallace was beaten and stripped of his keys, including one that opened the prison arsenal. Within seconds, the convicts were grabbing pistols, riot guns—short-barreled shotguns that scattered pellets and were designed to wound rather than kill—and rounds of ammunition. At least one of the men scored a prized submachine gun.

Most of Auburn's inmates were in the exercise yard that afternoon. Small, one of the guards later claimed, stood on a balcony and shouted to other convicts, inciting one of the worst prison riots in the history of New York State.

"Come on, you fellows," he yelled, "now's your chance."

As dozens of convicts stormed the arsenal and helped themselves to weapons, Barry, Small, and Caprico sprinted toward the outer wall and the main gate. Framed by twin crenellated towers, the iron-barred gate was the last barrier between them and freedom. A slightly built inmate from Buffalo with sandy hair, Steve Pawlak, caught up to them as they ran. Not yet thirty, he was serving a life sentence after a string of convictions for robbery and burglary.

Milton Ryther, the lone guard stationed at the gate, saw the four convicts rushing toward him and tossed the oversized key through the bars and onto State Street, which ran along the front side of the prison. He drew his revolver but was shot and wounded before he could fire. Ryther retreated into one of the towers and backed a few steps up a spiral staircase that led to the top of the outer wall. Pawlak, his gun leveled, followed him, with Barry and the others at his back.

"Open that gate," Pawlak growled, "or I'll blow out your brains." When they discovered the guard had thrown the key beyond their reach, Barry took over.

"We'll have to go over the wall!" he shouted.

They climbed the staircase to a walkway along the top of the wall. Clutching Ryther as a human shield, they fired volleys to pin down guards gathering on the prison's inner wall and manning nearby watchtowers. There was only scattered return fire; one inmate was wearing a guard's cap, another a guard's coat, making it difficult for the defenders to tell friend from foe.

A guard's bullet grazed Barry's right shinbone. Another slammed into his back and lodged near his left shoulder. He was still clutching a riot gun as he leapt over a metal railing running along the top of the wall and dropped twenty feet to the ground.

Barry was shot twice before he jumped from the wall at Auburn Prison's front gate
(Author Collection)

AUBURN WAS THE oldest prison in the state's corrections system. When it opened in 1818, a few years before Sing Sing, the United States' fifth president, James Monroe, occupied the White House. An eleven-foot-high metal statue of a Revolution-era solder—nicknamed Copper John by inmates— stood at attention atop the bell tower of the main administration building, a nod to the facility's long history. It was the birthplace of the Auburn system, a strict disciplinary regime that brutally punished prisoners for merely speaking to one another in their workshops or cells. Adopted in many other states, some of the system's trappings—striped uniforms and inmates marching in lockstep—survived into the early twentieth century.

Auburn was just as infamous as the site of the first execution of a convicted killer using the electric chair, in 1890, a procedure so badly botched that the New York *World* described it, with unintentional irony, as "very cruel and very shocking."

Barry had settled into a familiar routine there. Out of bed shortly after seven o'clock, hands on the bars of his cell door as guards conducted their count, a march into the yard to dump his bucket, a workday punctuated by lunch and a couple of ten-minute smoke breaks. Auburn prisoners were treated to one movie a week and spent other evenings in their cells, reading or listening to a prison-wide radio broadcast. Barry was entitled to one bath a week. He wrote scores of letters, most to Anna Blake, but he also kept in touch with his mother and his sisters Lucy Manning and Rita Estabrook back in Worcester. He was assigned to the cabinetmaking shop, where he worked alongside Joe Caprico. His old Sing Sing number was discarded; he became Inmate 43077, and good behavior had earned him the right to wear a white disk on his uniform, identifying him under Auburn's classification system as a first-grade inmate.

Auburn's cells, like most of Sing Sing's, were throwbacks to the nineteenth century—stone caverns seven feet long and three feet, eight inches across, with no toilets or running water. "In these pigeonholes," one journalist noted after an inspection tour, "the dust gathers on a man's soul and the spiders of gloom weave webs on his mind." While Sing Sing was moving inmates into larger, more comfortable cells, state officials had only begun planning a new, modern cellblock for Auburn. More than 1,750 prisoners were crowded into a facility that had fewer than 1,300 cells. Hundreds, spared from being locked in the claustrophobic cells at night, slept on bunk beds lining the corridors.

Grievances festered. Lice and bedbugs tortured the men at night. They grumbled about the bad food; the state of New York spent the same amount to feed inmates—a measly seven cents per man per meal—as it had in the Civil War era. The only ventilation was air that seeped through the barred windows of the cell doors, leaving men to gag on the stench of their own excrement. "All about me was living death . . . starved souls, hatred and misery," lamented one inmate, "a world of suffering men." Auburn was a living hell, a powder keg ready to explode.

Overcrowding made it impossible to separate and segregate prisoners. Close to three hundred men serving time for homicide or rape were
cooped up with burglars and thieves. "The good mixed with the bad," warden Edgar Jennings admitted, and "the more desperate characters influ-
enced the others."

There were two other classes of desperate prisoners. A growing number were repeat offenders who had been sentenced, under the draconian
Baumes Laws, to long stretches inside with little hope of early release. Men
who had not hurt or killed anyone were serving the same life terms meted
out to brutal murderers. And many were tough-guy gangsters or professional criminals like Barry who were behind bars for the first time. "These
men have been used to no little luxury, a free and restless existence. They
are appalled by the prospect of what seems endless punishment," John
Kennedy, vice chairman of the New York State Commission of Correction,
told the *New York Times* in the summer of 1929. "It is this type of men," he
warned, "who organize and try to carry out desperate efforts to escape."

When Blake visited her husband at Auburn for the first time, she was
shocked. A floor-to-ceiling wire screen kept them apart. "We could not
kiss," she lamented, and Barry looked depressed and defeated—"broken in
spirit," she thought, "like a lost soul." She came to see her husband twice
a month, staying overnight each time at a hotel so she could visit on back-
to-back days before she returned to the city. Twice a month, Barry could
forget about the bedbugs and the food and the foul air.

Soon after Barry's transfer from Sing Sing, Blake complained of pain
in her chest. She brushed it off as bruising from a minor traffic accident,
when she had struck the steering wheel. Barry was alarmed; she was losing
weight, and her face looked thin. He urged her to see a doctor. She finally
did, and the diagnosis was frightening. Cancer. She was not yet sure how
far the disease had progressed, but she would likely need surgery.

Barry could not embrace her and console her. Her would not be there
to support her and care for her as she went through the ordeal. She could
die without him by her side. "I felt the overpowering desire—now that she
needed me—to be with her there on the outside, if only for a few days, a few
weeks," he recalled. Barry, a born gambler, was willing to risk anything,
even his life, to be with her.

The man who spent years devising ways to break into houses had a new mission: finding a way to break out of prison. "I picked out a couple of the most intelligent fellows who wanted to break," he recalled. He huddled with Small and Caprico in the bleachers at the prison's baseball diamond to hammer out a plan to steal weapons and rush the main gate. "We decided that what the prison authorities considered their strongest point was really our easiest—the arsenal." Small stole a pint of ammonia from the hospital. Barry scrounged a tennis ball. They cut a small hole in the ball and filled it with the liquid; when Small squeezed it, ammonia would squirt into the guard's face. They would break out on July 28, a Sunday, when the workshops were idle, inmates were free to roam the exercise yard, and many of the guards had a day off.

If Barry made it out of Auburn alive, he would need a place to hide until the police gave up looking for him. Blake made the arrangements. They pretended, in case a guard overheard them discussing the details, that one of Barry's friends needed a place to crash. She rented a furnished two-room apartment in the Yorkville neighborhood on the Upper East Side and left the key above the doorframe. She traveled to Auburn to visit him on July 16 and stayed overnight for a second visit on July 17. Then she returned to New York and waited.

JACOB REESE WAS driving past the prison that Sunday afternoon in a Packard sedan with his wife, Sarah, and their four-year-old, Carl. The forty-six-year-old truck driver heard muffled bangs—gunshots fired from inside the walls—and thought he had blown a tire. When he parked to take a look, Arthur Barry and Steve Pawlak sprang from the base of the wall and jumped into the rear seat.

"Step on the gas," Pawlak barked.

Reese, who could feel the barrel of a riot gun pressed against his back, sped away from the prison. George Small and Joe Caprico, who had made it over the wall as well, stole a parked car and fled.

"Don't you think it's a terrible thing to take a child on a ride like this?"

Sarah Reese pleaded as they roared through Auburn. "Didn't you ever have a mother?"

"We're desperate," Pawlak blurted out. He thought for a moment. "I'll take a chance," he said, then ordered Reese to stop just long enough for his wife and son to get out of the car.

Pawlak seemed to be in charge as his companion recovered from the shock of being shot twice before he leapt over the wall.

"Barry," Sarah Reese noted when a reporter caught up to her, "never said a word."

Reese drove at top speed for twenty-five miles, until they reached Solvay, a village of eight thousand on the outskirts of Syracuse.

Barry recognized the entrance to the local fairgrounds—he had delivered explosives to a client there years before, when he was a courier for safecracker Lowell Jack—and he told Reese to turn in. There was no one around.

"I knew then they intended putting me out of the way," Reese recalled.

When one of the inmates got out of the car, Reese bolted from the driver's seat, punched the man in the face, and ran. One of the escapees fired a volley of shots at him. A bullet grazed Reese's pants and pierced a wad of banknotes in his back pocket, but he was uninjured. He did not see who took the shots; by the time he dared to look back, the men were driving away. Barry would later deny he was the shooter.

The pair ditched the car and broke into an empty house in search of clothes to replace their prison grays. Pawlak found a suit that fit, but Barry was only able to cobble together some odds and ends—a sweater, cap, and checkered golf socks. "I figured I would last about two minutes in public in that getup," he recalled, "but what else could I do? I put it on." They discarded their prison uniforms, stuffing one of them under the cushions of a sofa. Barry, who had broken two toes when he jumped over the wall, winced as he jammed his swollen left foot back into his boot. Unable to find a first-aid kit, he taped a washcloth over his shoulder wound to stop the bleeding.

Thunderstorms rumbled through the area overnight. "The worst deluge

I ever saw," Barry later lamented. They dumped the car in the woods and slogged through heavy rain and mud as they searched for a replacement. They spotted a car in an open garage at a hilltop home and reckoned they could push it down the incline and start it far enough from the house to avoid being heard. Barry climbed in, and Pawlak pushed.

As the car rolled out of the garage, the homeowner leaned out an upstairs window and fired a shotgun blast. The windshield imploded, peppering Barry's face with razor-sharp fragments. He screamed and covered his face.

"Both my eyes were filled with splinters of broken glass. I was blind."

"Don't move or I'll fire again!" the car's owner shouted.

Barry dove from the car and took cover behind the garage. He called out to Pawlak, but there was no answer—he had fled and left Barry behind. Barry slipped down the muddy hillside, colliding with trees and bushes as he scrambled to get away. "I couldn't see an inch in front of me," he recalled.

He stumbled into a knee-deep pond and sat on the bank, hoping he was far enough away. His right eye was swollen shut, but when he pried open the left one with his thumb and forefinger, he could see again. He was soaked and miserable, and in excruciating pain. He had two bullet wounds, could barely walk on his swollen foot, and had thought he was blinded for life.

"Right then and there," he confessed later, "I finally realized what a damned fool I had been all my life. I was cured. If I lived . . . I'd never steal anything again."

He heard police sirens in the distance and limped off. A line of headlights confirmed he had reached the main road to the state capital, Albany. He surveyed the scattered homes for another car to steal—one final theft, to ensure his getaway—and spotted a sharp-looking car with a tan body, black roof, and wood-spoke wheels. It was a 1926 Franklin, built in Syracuse and advertised as "the fastest car over the road . . . by an appreciable margin." The keys were inside. The gasoline gauge read full.

He sped along the Mohawk River Valley through the darkness and the downpours, holding his good eye open with one hand and steering and shifting gears with the other. By morning, he was a hundred miles east of Syracuse. He stopped near the train station in the village of Fonda, named for an ancestor of a young actor named Henry, who would make his Broadway debut that year.

He found a cloth in the car, wiped the blood from his face and the mud from his clothes, then grabbed a felt hat from the back seat to shield his wounded eyes. He had $125 in his pocket and bought a ticket to Albany, still forty miles away.

A few state troopers were watching the station, but no one seemed to suspect that an escapee could have made it so far from Auburn so quickly. He encountered several more troopers on the train, he later claimed, but none of them noticed his injuries or questioned him. "I suppose I looked like a crazy drunk, staggering around after an all-night bender, and nobody wanted to get near me," he said in retrospect.

He looked up someone he knew in Albany, who gave him a change of clothes. "A bottle of home brew exploded on me," he explained to a doctor he found, who was willing to remove the slivers of glass, bandage his right eye, and tape open the other one. "You're lucky to have any sight at all," he was told.

One of the buildings torched during the July 1929 Auburn riot (Author Collection)

Black Sunday or Terror Sunday, as it became known, was the biggest news story of the day, diverting attention from ominous reports of falling stock prices on Wall Street. After the four escapees went over the wall, armed prisoners and guards exchanged gunfire for hours. Inmates set fires, and smoke billowed over the walls. Newspapers hired aircraft to fly overhead and bring back photos of the battle unfolding below. State troopers and National Guard units joined forces with the outnumbered prison guards to disarm the mutineers and regain control.

Two inmates died, and at least fifteen more were shot or injured. Five guards, along with four Auburn firemen who ventured inside the walls to fight the fires, were wounded. Five massive workshop buildings were gutted, leaving sections of blackened brick wall that would have reminded Barry of the ruined villages of wartime France. Governor Franklin Roosevelt ordered "a sweeping and thorough investigation" of prison conditions and the causes of the riot.

Guard Milton Ryther was hailed as a hero for his split-second decision to toss his key through the gate and prevent more convicts from breaking free. It was midnight before the last of the prisoners were herded into cellblocks and a head count revealed who had escaped from what *Time* magazine later described as an arena of "revolt, sabotage, death."

Barry needed to disappear. His photograph was already on the front page of the Brooklyn papers; his name seemed to be in print everywhere, from the *New York Times* to the *Poughkeepsie Eagle-News*. He was being described in the press as a ringleader behind the prison break and the "most notorious" of the escapees.

Anna Blake was stunned when she saw the headlines. "I stood for a moment just staring at the paper," she recalled. Her heart was pounding. Her mind raced, careening between hope and fear. "Where was he, had they captured him, how soon would I see him, had he been hurt or killed?" she recalled thinking. "I knew he would give me the word as soon as he felt it was safe."

Barry paid the doctor, promised to return the following day to have the dressing on his right eye changed, and caught the next train to New York City.

TWENTY-SEVEN

REFUGE

Manhattan • 1929

BUREAU DRAWER SCRAPED as it slid open. The sound woke up Edith Hutchinson, whose bed was only a few feet away. A man holding a flashlight was rummaging through the drawer. She could not see his face—it was four o'clock in the morning, and the room was too dark. She froze for a moment, then screamed. The man bolted, disappearing with an exquisite strand of matching pearls and other jewelry, a haul valued at a quarter of a million dollars.

Detectives scoured the colonial-style, seaside mansion in Beverly, Massachusetts, just north of Salem, for clues on the morning of August 10, 1929. The burglar appeared to have climbed onto a porch and through an open window to enter the summer home of Philadelphia broker Sydney Hutchinson. He wore cotton gloves, ensuring that he left no fingerprints, and took only the most valuable pieces. Almost two weeks had passed since the spectacular escape from Auburn Prison, and investigators had a suspect in mind.

"The robbery was perpetrated by one man, obviously a professional and a connoisseur of gems," the *New York Times* reported. "The police believe it was the work of Arthur Barry."

An intense manhunt was already under way. Telegrams describing the escapees had been circulated to police forces and sheriffs' offices across upstate New York. Authorities in Texas had been notified, in case the men were headed for Mexico.

Warden Edgar Jennings's offer of a fifty-dollar reward for each man captured—an attractive sum as the Depression took hold—caught the attention of a couple of amateur sleuths. A man in Sunbury, Pennsylvania, two hundred miles south of Auburn, reported a suspicious newcomer who resembled Barry. Once he saw a recent mug shot, however, he realized he was mistaken—the man he was watching was "a criminal of some kind," he was certain, but he was not the famous thief. An Ohio man named John Cornell contacted the prison after meeting a man on a train who introduced himself as C. C. Barry. It was not only the name that Cornell thought was suspicious; at a time when work was scarce, the stranger had offered to help him find a job.

Writers for the New York *Daily News* assumed Barry would be desperate for money and saw his handiwork everywhere. The "bold marauder" who robbed the Hutchinson estate in Massachusetts, the paper declared, was undoubtedly the "super desperado and notorious jewel thief." When four men robbed a payroll courier in Westchester County soon after the escape, witnesses shown a photograph of Barry said he looked like one of the assailants. The newspaper named him as a suspect in the theft of gems worth more than $80,000 from two Long Island homes that August.

Another man, meanwhile, had confessed to the Hutchinson theft, but the idea that the master jewel thief was once more lurking in the shadows, ready to strike, took hold. Wealthy residents of Long Island were said to be canceling parties and hiring night watchmen as they braced for the return of "a terror phantom" who was "striking dire fear into the hearts of the rich."

The man haunting the high and mighty, however, was in no condition to steal jewels. Barry was holed up in the Upper East Side apartment Blake had rented, nursing his wounds. He picked up bandages and other first-aid supplies at a drugstore and put his training as a battlefield medic to work. "I know about cauterizing wounds and how to prevent infection," he explained, and used silver nitrate to clean the entry wound to his shoulder, wincing as the solution burned his skin. Cleaning and draining the wound was a painful daily routine. He eventually found a doctor who was willing to remove the bullet without reporting the injury to the police.

In mid-August, he felt well enough to send for Blake. She received a message through friends, asking her to meet him in Times Square. She took a taxi to Broadway and was swallowed up in a tide of people pouring out of theater matinees. Barry approached her as she stood near a newsstand, the agreed-upon rendezvous.

"Hold me," she whispered. "I am afraid I am going to faint."

"Don't break," he said as he embraced her. He led her away from the crowds.

Where would he go? she asked.

"You mean where are *we* going?" he replied with a smile. "You're coming with me."

These were words she had longed to hear. "I loved him," she confessed, "more than anything in the world." She was scared of what lay ahead, but more afraid of not being with him.

"We would always be hunted beings from that time on," she noted later, "always moving from place to place in order to keep a step ahead of the law."

There was no telling when the police might catch up with them. "If we get three years of it," Barry admitted, "we will be lucky."

To Blake, only two things mattered: "He was safe—for the moment at least." And for the moment, they were together.

They would have to be careful. Police in New York City were confident Barry would return to his old haunts, and were on the lookout for both him and Blake. "The air was full of tips to Barry's whereabouts," noted Theodore Prager, a police reporter for the *Daily News*, who tagged along as detectives checked out an uptown apartment rumored to be his hideaway.

When the police finally caught up with Blake, she claimed she had no idea where Barry was and denied knowing of his plan to break out. Her apartment was searched. She was kept under surveillance but managed to steer the plainclothes officers tailing her away from Barry's refuge. She became adept at ducking into subway stations and switching taxis to shake off her pursuers as she traveled from her apartment to Barry's and back.

"Every time I went anywhere," she recalled, "it was necessary to keep doubling on my tracks."

As Barry's wounds healed, Blake's health worsened. "I was so ill at one time," she acknowledged a few years later, "that I was afraid I was going to die." While she did not use the word *cancer* or describe how her illness was being treated, for weeks she was confined to bed and unable to walk. "Arthur was my comforter, my nurse, my cook and general 'housemaid,'" she said. Their devotion to each other grew deeper.

They discussed what they would do if her condition worsened and she had to be taken to the hospital—a nightmare scenario for them both. To ensure that Barry would not be exposed and arrested, they agreed that he would put her in a taxi, send her to her doctor's office, and disappear. The doctor could admit her to the hospital.

Barry, however, was not sure he could go through with the plan. "If anything happened to you, sweet," he told her, "all this freedom would mean nothing to me." Blake recovered, sparing him from having to make such an agonizing choice.

One by one, Barry's fellow escapees were rounded up. George Small tried to rob a garage that September and was shot five times during a wild chase through the streets of Brooklyn; he almost died, and a bystander caught in the cross fire—a young mother pushing her child in a carriage—was killed. Police in Los Angeles picked up Joe Caprico for car theft and shipped him back to Auburn. Steve Pawlak was wounded in a gun battle with police in Buffalo and was returned to the prison to continue serving his life sentence.

When Auburn inmates staged a second, even bloodier riot in December, taking the warden hostage and brandishing guns hidden in the chaos of the July uprising, Pawlak was one of eight convicts who died. Ordered to surrender, his last words before state troopers stormed the prison and shot him were "Go to hell." An editorial writer for one upstate New York newspaper hoped the captures would convince other inmates of the folly of trying to escape for the sake of a "few weeks of brief and precarious liberty." Barry, the writer said, "if he is still alive and remains uncaptured, has simply exchanged a new set of dangers and worries for the old."

Barry took comfort in being in a city he knew so well, where his was just one face among millions. "There's no safer place in the world to hide," he said, "than in the heart of New York City." But he still carried a revolver—possibly one grabbed from the prison arsenal during the escape—when he ventured outside for a nighttime walk on Third Avenue, slipped into a darkened movie theater, or risked a trip to a store.

"I do not intend to let them take me alive," he told Blake ominously. "I'll blow out my brains first."

BARRY DYED HIS hair a lighter shade to make it harder for someone to recognize him from a newspaper photograph. A pair of round-lensed glasses gave him a studious air. As a finishing touch, he grew a toothbrush mustache, the nose-wide style that became a trademark of movie comics Charlie Chaplin and Oliver Hardy, and was popular before Adolf Hitler made it synonymous with evil.

As his looks changed, so did his public image. Shooting his way out of prison and igniting a deadly riot transformed the suave gentleman jewel thief of the Roaring Twenties into a ruthless, desperate thug. His "dapper appearance and quiet manner, suggesting a broker's clerk," the *New York Times* warned shortly after the escape, "belie his dangerous nature." The *Daily News* submitted the "murderous break for liberty" at Auburn as proof he would "stop at nothing to hold his freedom."

There were comparisons to Gerald Chapman, nicknamed the Gentleman Bandit, and the first 1920s crook to be declared public enemy number one in the press. Chapman had posed as a member of New York's elite while leading a gang of armed robbers and, like Barry, had broken out of prison. With Chapman dead—hanged in 1926 for killing a Connecticut police officer in a shoot-out—the *Daily News* declared Barry the new "super-criminal—a prince of thieves who makes honest men gasp at his imagination and daring."

Burns detective Charles Sheraton went public with his account of the 1927 capture of Boston Billy, describing the "cold and calculating" Arthur Barry as "a real killer" and the "more cruel of the two," even though James

Monahan was the prime suspect in two murders. Barry's Long Island nemesis, Harold King, weighed in with an equally damning assessment. "Barry was one of the most dangerous, if not *the* most dangerous, criminal we ever handled," he told a writer researching a feature on the fugitive burglar. "When we had him here in Mineola, the whole jail staff kept watch over him, for we knew he would try to make a break if the slimmest sort of opportunity were given him." Barry, King claimed, made the Old West outlaw Jesse James and John "Bum" Rogers—a slippery escape artist and leader of a vicious gang of stickup men, convicted of pulling a 1925 payroll robbery on King's Nassau County turf—"look like Sunday-school kids."

When he was alone in the apartment, Barry listened to the radio, played solitaire, and read the newspapers to pass the time. He would have been bemused to see reports of jewels he had supposedly stolen and the futile search for his hideaway. That fall, the new US president, Herbert Hoover, marked the fiftieth anniversary of the invention of the incandescent lightbulb by thanking Thomas Edison for introducing "an element of surprise in dealing with burglars" and banishing "the goblins that lived in dark corners and under the bed."

There were plenty of bogeymen stalking Wall Street, however, as stock values tanked in late October. A massive sell-off ruined countless investors, from savvy brokers to average Joes who had "saved money and borrowed money and borrowed on their borrowings," *Time* magazine lamented, to buy "little pieces of paper" that were suddenly worthless. A warped joke made the rounds saying that hotel clerks were asking arriving guests whether they wanted an upper-floor room for sleeping or jumping. Hoover, however, decried the mood of "over-pessimism" pervading the nation in the wake of the stock market crash. "Any lack of confidence in the economic future of the U.S.," he said, as oblivious as anyone to the chaos ahead, "is foolish."

As the glitter of the Jazz Age faded and a grim, hungry decade dawned, New York's newly crowned supercriminal decided it was time to move on.

TWENTY-EIGHT

MR. AND MRS. TONER

Newark and Andover, New Jersey • 1930–32

OST DAYS, A man with a toothbrush mustache strolled through Branch Brook Park, a four-mile-long strip of meadow and forest on the north side of Newark. He fed peanuts to the squirrels and pigeons, and he always had a treat for a stray dog or cat. Often a petite woman joined him. They took long walks on the park's trails and along the shore of its serpentine lake. One day, they stopped to watch some kids playing baseball. A police officer, who was among the spectators, approached them.

"Believe me," the woman admitted later, "my heart was in my mouth."

The officer had a question for the man who liked to feed the squirrels and pigeons: Would he be kind enough to umpire the game?

Arthur Barry had abandoned his Manhattan hideout early in 1930 and rented an apartment a half hour's drive away, in New Jersey's largest city. Newark was a success story—"a city teeming with activity," one local booster noted. Prudential and other major insurance firms were headquartered there, and factories produced everything from carriages to dentures. It also had a booming underworld. The city center was the fiefdom of Jewish mob boss Abner "Longy" Zwillman, who cashed in on Prohibition and built a gambling, racketeering, and bootlegging empire.

Crooks gravitated to Newark because the local police could be bought. A deputy chief was removed from office in 1927 after being accused of accepting a diamond ring from grateful bootleggers and underworld figures. Two years later, a prosecutor investigating "instances of improper reception of money" made waves when he tried to seize the bank records of every man on the force as well as the accounts of some of the officers' wives. The judge who rejected the request defended the force—"as a body they are honorable, straightforward, and their duty is well done"—but conceded there were undoubtedly some "who do not measure up to the required standard." It was an understatement. The city had the dubious distinction in those days, noted one chronicler of New Jersey's underworld, of being home to "the most corrupt police, prosecutors, and courts in the country."

Barry's new bolt-hole was an apartment on Summer Avenue in Newark's Forest Hill neighborhood, a twenty-minute walk from Branch Brook Park. The six-story brick building boasted a name fit for a president: the Hoover Apartments. Anna Blake spent as much time with him as she could but returned to her apartment for a week or more each month to pay her bills and reconnect with friends. If she suddenly vanished from New York, they realized, the police would suspect they were together and hunt for her as well.

They went by the names James and Anne Toner. Blake was careful to call him Jim even when they were alone, to make sure she did not slip up when she might be overheard. Barry kept up the pretense even when he bought her valentines and Christmas cards, signing them "Love, Jim." It was "a rather quiet, unexciting life," Blake recalled, until they ventured out to the park or to take in a movie. Every time Barry left the apartment, it was possible someone—an old friend, a sharp-eyed police officer, someone who remembered seeing his photograph in the newspapers—would recognize him. Two of the tenants in their building, they discovered—men they greeted in the hallway and chatted with about the weather—were members of the Newark police force.

"We never knew at what moment Arthur might be taken," Blake recalled. "We lived in constant fear, day and night, and yet we learned to put that fear away. We learned to be happy, to get the most out of life."

Barry tried to reassure her. "These cops couldn't catch a cold," he was fond of saying. But he pocketed a loaded revolver when he left the apartment, just in case. "If they ever get me in a tight spot," he told her, "I'll shoot my way out." And if he could not escape, he reminded her, he would rather turn the gun on himself than go back to prison.

His bravado and resolve only added to Blake's fears. "The strain was telling on me day by day," she confessed. "Every policeman I passed made me shiver."

Money was tight. Rent was fifty dollars a month. While journalists and detectives were convinced Barry had a stash of jewels or cash left over from his heists—and repeatedly said so in print—Blake scoffed at the idea. "The truth is," she said, "he didn't have a cent to his name." There was no hidden fortune; he had spent it all, she insisted, or gambled it away before his arrest.

Since Barry could not risk looking for work, they lived on her savings until they lucked into a windfall. His wartime service made him eligible for a government bonus, and he applied using his real name. None of the bureaucrats who processed the claim connected him to his crimes. Blake traveled to Worcester to pick up the check for $785, the equivalent of about $14,000 today.

Barry also worked out a cover story in case a nosy neighbor or police officer asked what Jim Toner did for a living. He answered a classified advertisement from a firm seeking representatives to sell window cleaners. A package soon arrived with the samples and promotional literature he needed to pass himself off as a squeegee salesman.

One afternoon, they decided to risk a trip to Manhattan. "We were hungry for the old scenes," Blake explained. As they left the subway station, someone tapped Barry on the shoulder.

"Don't you remember me, Art?"

He wheeled around. He recognized the man; he was a former police officer. "I thought it was curtains," Barry later admitted.

They stared at one another for a few moments.

"How much do you want?" Barry asked.

"How much you got on you?"

The man took the money and walked away.

⁓⁓⁓⁓⁓⁓

"WHERE IS BARRY?" asked one journalist as reports trickled in that he had boarded a ship bound for Hawaii, had been seen relaxing on the Riviera, or could be hiding out in Canada or Argentina or the Philippines. Some moviegoers might have wondered if he had escaped to Hollywood. In the summer of 1930, actor Ronald Colman—a dead ringer for Barry—starred in *Raffles*, an adaptation of the E. W. Hornung stories that had burned the image of the dashing gentleman burglar into the popular imagination. "He keeps his bland air of unconcern equally through cricket games, crime and love scenes," the *New York Times* said in appreciation of Colman's performance. On screen, one of the detectives pursuing the high-class bandit confesses his admiration for his quarry: "You can't help liking him."

Hollywood came back for more in 1932, with *Jewel Robbery*, casting the debonair William Powell in the role of a gallant Raffles-like thief; he could loot a jewelry shop "with the delicate touch of a surgeon," one reviewer noted, and "kiss a woman's hand—while relieving it of a diamond bracelet." At one point in the film, Powell's character claims he swiped one woman's jewels in the midst of a ritzy soirée. "The lady stood beside me. The Prince of Wales was announced. I could have removed her dress."

The real-life Raffles, it turned out, never strayed far from New York. "I figured it was safer to stay around where they didn't expect to find me," Barry explained. "He felt it didn't matter where he went," added Blake. "He would always be sought."

Barry may have stuck close to the city to spare her from being branded a fugitive as well. Later, when they talked about their time in New Jersey, neither of them mentioned her health, but Barry may have also feared she was not well enough to follow him to another state or country.

Barry moved again, in 1931, but stayed in Newark. A couple he knew—they were identified in the press only as the Smiths—ran a restaurant downtown. Barry took a room on the third floor of the restaurant's building, a Gothic Revival–style mansion that was once the home of a millionaire leather manufacturer and was still furnished with a smattering of antiques and suits of armor. Newark's police commissioner and other senior officers frequently dined at the restaurant and gathered for a weekly dinner in one of the mansion's large rooms. The genial Jim Toner "hob-nobbed with the police," Barry later boasted, and even played cards and checkers with the unsuspecting officers.

Newark, New Jersey, in 1930 (Author Collection)

There were other humorous moments during their "exile," as Blake called their years in hiding. When a census taker knocked on the door of their Summer Avenue apartment in the spring of 1930, Barry coolly identified himself as James J. Toner, a thirty-year-old electrician from

Oklahoma; Blake gave her birthplace as Ohio and must have been delighted to shave almost a decade off her real age.

Jim Toner was twice summoned for jury duty, but Blake and Barry convinced Newark court officials the man they were seeking was visiting relatives back home in Oklahoma. Barry was a fan of detective magazines—a copy of the January 1932 issue of *True Detective Mysteries*, with a cover story called "Rochester's Shocking Torture Atrocity," would be found in his possession—and he later claimed he wrote and submitted stories that were published under a pseudonym.

He ran into an army buddy on a trip to the grocery store and was relieved to discover the man had no interest in turning him in; Barry wound up inviting him back to the apartment for dinner.

Once, as Blake walked through Times Square, she realized two men—she assumed they were private detectives—were following her. Thinking fast, she walked up to a police officer. "There are two mashers following me," she told him. "They're trying to steal my purse." The officer intercepted and questioned the detectives. By the time he was satisfied with their explanation of who they were and what they were doing, Blake had disappeared.

By 1932, Barry was ready to move on again. His new hideout, he decided, would be more secluded. An advertisement in a Newark newspaper, offering a room in a farmhouse fifty miles away, in the lake-dotted mountains of northwestern New Jersey, caught his eye. The rent was two dollars a week. Barry took a bus from Newark to Sussex County to check out the red gabled house with wrap-around veranda. It fronted on a dirt road that ran north through Andover Township and was within thirty miles of the Pennsylvania and New York state lines. It would be, he decided, "a good place to live."

Barry hit it off with the owner, Otto Reuter, who had emigrated from Germany before the war and had worked as a toolmaker and carpenter before buying the remote hundred-plus acre farm as a summer home. The dour fifty-six-year-old lived there alone—his wife and two daughters were in Linden, New Jersey—and was as grateful for the company as he was for the extra cash. Reuter took an instant liking to Jim Toner. "A splendid young fellow," he said later. "A perfect gentleman and a fine friend." Barry told him he was a disabled war vet—he walked with a slight limp, from the gunshot wound he'd suffered during the prison break—and claimed he had studied to be a doctor, but he said little else about his background.

A woman soon joined them. "A small, thin blonde," as Reuter later described her, "with nice eyes and teeth." Barry introduced her as Anne, his wife. Blake stayed for weeks at a time and returned periodically to New York, as she had before, to ensure that she was not missed.

Reuter was so delighted he did not charge the couple extra rent. "She was so handy around the house," he recalled, "washing, cleaning and cooking, and doing things to make us all comfortable."

The farmhouse was cold and rustic—they drew water from an outside well, using a wooden bucket—but Blake enjoyed her time at "the camp," as she called it. On summer afternoons, they took long walks through the boulder-strewn woods and swam in nearby lakes. During these strolls, Barry recalled, "I disclosed to her all the details of my nefarious career."

Back in Newark, when they had kissed goodbye as Barry left the apartment on an errand, Blake recalled, "we never knew when such a kiss would be the last." She felt safer in the country. "Everything was peaceful."

Barry helped out around the farm, pruning apple and peach trees in the orchard, repairing farm machinery, and helping Reuter erect an outbuilding. He was not much of a carpenter or mechanic, Reuter discovered, but he dug a cellar and washed the dishes without complaint. To earn a few bucks, he knocked on doors and sold some of the squeegees he had ordered on consignment. He picked up shifts as a laborer for construction companies, repairing local roads and erecting a small hydroelectric plant on nearby Lake Mohawk. "I'm an empire builder," he joked to Blake. He handed over his first paycheck to her, along with a note: "The hardest money I ever earned, to the Sweetest Gal in the world." Anna wept when she read it, and kept it for the rest of her life.

As he made his sales pitch for the window-cleaning wands, Barry got to know his neighbors. "He was the life of every party," neighbors told one reporter. "He drank little, never used profanity, and would play checkers or bridge, but never for money."

Barry, like Blake, felt comfortable and safe. "I enjoyed my stay there," he later said of Reuter's farm, "more than all the other years of my life put together."

Barry began sitting in on local government meetings and sometimes spoke up when issues were discussed. He planned to register to vote in the upcoming fall elections and toyed with the idea of running for office after local power brokers suggested he join the Democratic Party ticket as a candidate for township clerk; the post would be a steppingstone to a future run for the office of tax collector. "He had a great political future in Andover," said Ernest McMickle, a local assessor. "We thought he was as honest as the day was long." Barry was flattered, but he declined. Campaigning for election as Jim Toner was too risky—"skirting too near the danger line," as Blake put it.

Among the local worthies he befriended was George Losey, mayor of Andover Township—population 479 in 1930—and the local news agent. Barry put in a standing order for a stack of New York City papers, to be delivered daily to the farmhouse.

There was plenty of news to keep up on in 1932. New York governor Franklin Roosevelt and his New Deal for a Depression-weary country were steamrolling incumbent president Herbert Hoover in the race for the White House. A man with a mustache like Barry's, who claimed that only his Nazi Party could save war-ravaged Germany from Communism and chaos, was clawing his way to power. And Britain and its worldwide empire were still fixated on finding a mate for Barry's old drinking buddy, the Prince of Wales; among the candidates that year was Sweden's Princess Ingrid, sixteen years his junior.

Toner's interest in the news of the day struck Losey as odd. Why, he wondered, was a door-to-door salesman living on an isolated New Jersey farm reading so many New York papers?

WHEN SOMEONE PULLED a slick jewel heist in the New York area, Barry discovered, as he perused the day's news, that his name and photograph often surfaced. BARRY'S BACK, PROBABLY, a *Daily News* headline proclaimed when gems worth $20,000 were stolen from a Long Island estate in the summer of 1930. The "cat-footed thief," the *New York Times* agreed, "worked with the same cunning that was characteristic of the operations of Arthur Barry." There was another coincidence—the couple robbed were attending a costume ball at the home of Harold Talbott, one of Barry's many victims, when the jewels were stolen. Harold King, however, dismissed the idea that his old adversary was back on his turf. "Barry is too clever a thief to return to Nassau County, where he and his methods are so well known," he assured a reporter.

As Barry was settling in at Reuter's farm, jewel thieves began to target the Park Avenue homes of some of New York's wealthiest and most influential citizens. Amid the crime wave, Muriel Vanderbilt Church Phelps reported the loss of a family heirloom, a shimmering bracelet set with 240 diamonds. While it was not clear whether the piece had been stolen or simply fallen out of her handbag—Phelps noticed it was missing while she was on a shopping excursion—the Vanderbilt name attracted plenty of press attention. "You'd think Arthur Barry and his mob were back on the job," an unnamed police official told more than a million and a half *Daily News* readers in January 1932. When $30,000 in gems were stolen from the wife of a New York stockbroker weeks later, the New York *Daily Mirror*—a racier rival tabloid—was sure that Barry had come back "for a second helping."

Barry was still in the news. And he was about to be accused of a far more shocking and odious crime.

TWENTY-NINE

THE EAGLET

Hopewell, New Jersey • 1932

EADLIGHT BEAMS SLICED through the darkness as a car pulled up in front of the farmhouse. It was Otto Reuter's nephew, John Koenig, and his girlfriend, Barry realized, out for a late-night drive. He went out to say hello and climbed into the car to join them. A biting north wind had kicked up ahead of an approaching storm, pushing the temperature below freezing. It was the first of March, an hour or so before midnight, and the crescent moon would not rise above the horizon until almost dawn. The perfect conditions, Arthur Barry might have thought, for pulling a burglary.

The radio was playing, and an announcer interrupted the program. The Associated Press had issued a bulletin at 11:03 p.m.: Charles Augustus Lindbergh Jr., the twenty-month-old son of the transatlantic flier and his wife, Anne Morrow Lindbergh, a diplomat's daughter, had been kidnapped that evening from the couple's estate near Hopewell, New Jersey, about fifty miles away.

"We were all startled," Barry recalled. Whoever did it, exclaimed one of the visitors, "ought to be strung up to the nearest tree when captured."

The next morning, Barry retrieved his daily armload of New York papers from the farm's roadside mailbox. LINDBERGH BABY KIDNAPPED FROM HOME was the headline in the *New York Times*. TAKEN FROM HIS CRIB; WIDE

SEARCH ON. The *Daily News* ran a full-page photograph of the child asleep in his crib below a black banner that screamed LINDY'S BABY KIDNAPED.

Reuter, who had apparently slept through his nephew's visit, had yet to hear the shocking news.

Barry held up one of the papers, displaying its large-type headline, and shouted to his landlord as he rushed up the walkway. "Somebody's kidnapped the Lindbergh baby!"

THE ABDUCTION WOULD become known as "the crime of the century," even though two-thirds of the twentieth century—and a long list of sordid, sensational crimes—still lay ahead. From the moment the baby was taken, the Lindbergh case commanded the world's attention like few other crimes. Lindbergh was the most celebrated and admired man on the planet. His daring solo flight across the Atlantic in May 1927, a landmark in the history of aviation, transformed a young barnstormer and airmail flier into an American icon. An estimated 350 million people worldwide had grabbed a newspaper or had listened to radio broadcasts to follow his progress on the long, perilous flight to Paris. The humble, determined man who had conquered an ocean and the sky, in the opinion of *Time* magazine, was "the nation's No. 1 hero." The press gave him a folksy nickname, Lindy, but he also became known as the Lone Eagle. And when his son and namesake was born in 1930, the blue-eyed child with the golden curls became known as the Eaglet. The *Daily News* did not exaggerate when it declared the boy "the most famous baby in the world."

Within hours of the kidnapping, before Barry had the chance to shout the news to Reuter, an army of police officers, state troopers, and volunteers was on the lookout for the child and his captor. The Coast Guard and federal investigators joined a manhunt that stretched from Boston to Baltimore and grew into the largest search, *Time* noted, "since Booth shot Lincoln." A helpless infant snatched on a cold winter night, at the mercy of someone cruel and callous enough to plan and execute the heinous crime—this was every parent's nightmare.

The Lindberghs were wealthy and privileged, a celebrity couple who

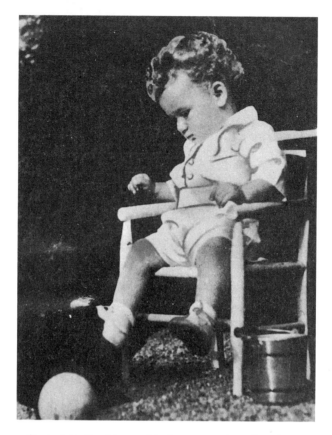

Charles A. Lindbergh Jr., son of the famous transatlantic flier, who was
kidnapped in 1932 (Author Collection)

lived in a newly built, sprawling mansion and employed a squad of servants. But none of that mattered, not even to the millions of Americans
who were desperate to find work or lining up at soup kitchens. Al Capone,
locked up in Chicago after being convicted of tax evasion, offered to join
the search for the child. "It's the most outrageous thing I ever heard of!"
exclaimed the ruthless mob boss who had done his share of outrageous
things.

By noon the day after the kidnapping, four hundred reporters and photographers had gathered at the Lindbergh home, ten miles north of the
state capital, Trenton, looking for a scoop or a glimpse of the stricken family. Even the most cynical denizens of the nation's newsrooms, however,

lost their icy seen-it-all detachment. "This was a story," noted the *New-York Tribune*'s Ishbel Ross, "that penetrated the thickest skin." All America seemed to be hoping and praying for the child's safe return. "The great nation of more than sixscore millions," the *New York Times* was certain, "thought of little else."

The kidnapper left behind few clues. A twenty-foot homemade ladder, built in three sections so it could be taken apart and transported by car, had been discarded near the house. It was long enough to reach an unlocked window of the child's nursery on the second floor, but one of the side rails was broken. A nine-inch chisel, likely brought along in case the window had to be pried open, was found on the grounds. Footprints left in the red clay near the house had a woven surface, suggesting that socks or a cloth covering had been slipped over the intruder's boots or shoes, possibly to muffle the sound of footsteps when the room was entered. The wind was howling that night, drowning out any sound the intruder may have made, and not even the Lindbergh's black terrier, Wahgoosh, had detected someone's presence in the house. The footprints and a second, smaller set—possibly made by the daintier foot of a woman—led to the main road, where it appeared a car had been parked for a swift getaway. A ransom note, demanding $50,000 and including the Germanic-sounding assurance that "the child is in gut care," was found on a radiator cover under one of the nursery windows. Two interlocking circles appeared at the end of the note, a symbol the kidnapper would append to follow-up messages to prove they were genuine.

The kidnapping was the most high-profile of a rash of abductions across the United States at the outset of the 1930s. KIDNAPPING WAVE SWEEPS THE NATION warned one headline in the wake of the Lindbergh baby-snatching. St. Louis chief of police Joseph Gerk, who kept track of kidnappings for ransom across the country, claimed the 208 he counted in 1931 were the tip of an iceberg—ten times that number, he estimated, had not been reported to police. "There were so many kidnappings in Depression-era America," author David Stout would later note, "that newspapers listed the less sensational cases in small type, the way real estate transactions or baseball trades were rendered."

Organized crime was behind the epidemic. For the gangs that controlled bootlegging, gambling, and vice, the economic shock of the
Depression had been bad for business; the looming end to Prohibition—it
would be repealed in late 1933—threatened to draw off even more illicit revenue. The "snatch racket," as it became known, was a lucrative alternative.
A "centuries old" crime is "being organized on an unprecedented scale
and with unheard-of extremes of cruelty and audacity," warned a writer
for the *New York Times*. In Washington, lawmakers fast-tracked legislation
already before Congress that would make kidnapping a federal crime and a
capital offense in cases where victims were taken across state lines.

In the meantime, editorial writers struggled to capture the nation's outrage. The New York *Evening Journal* denounced the "atrocious and shameful crime," and the city's *Evening Post* predicted "the beasts" responsible
would be "torn limb from limb by the people of the United States" if the
baby was mistreated or harmed. "Even murder," the *Brooklyn Daily Eagle*
observed, "is not more dastardly than robbing a mother and father of their
helpless offspring." In Washington, DC, the *Evening Star* hoped that indig-
nation over the kidnapping would spark a "rebellion against the ruthless
rule of crime."

The Hearst media empire's racy New York *Daily Mirror*—a paper that
freely admitted its contents were "90 percent entertainment, 10 percent
information"—considered the cowardly crime nothing less than "a final
affront to American civilization." Its tabloid rival, New York's *Daily News*,
still the largest-circulation newspaper in the country, denounced the thugs
who preyed on "legitimate society" and singled out victims "for their
wealth, prominence and high standing." And both papers were prepared
to name two possible culprits.

~~~~~~~~~~

RAFFLES AND GIRL HUNTED IN KIDNAPPING cried a *Daily Mirror* headline soon after the baby was snatched. "Into the baffling case were injected
the names of Arthur 'Raffles' Barry, the notorious ladder burglar" and
"Anna Blake, his girlfriend," the paper revealed. "The phantom burglar . . .
is the one man, say the army of detectives working on the Lindbergh case,

who could have conceived the daring plot and carried it through to frui-tion." The kidnapping, according to the *Mirror*'s unnamed police source, had "all the earmarks of a Barry job."

The *Daily News* ran with the allegations on March 3, less than two days after the abduction. "Veteran detectives," it reported, believed the kidnapping "was stamped with the technique of the society gem thief." Detectives in Newark, the *Daily News* claimed, were searching for Barry—"the shrewdest criminal at large"—and Blake, "his plump sweetheart." A request had been sent to Auburn Prison for a sample of Barry's handwrit-ing, so it could be compared to the ransom note.

At first glance, there were parallels between Barry's break-ins and the Lindbergh crime. The kidnapper, like Barry in his gem-stealing heyday, used a ladder to access an upper floor and entered and fled without being seen or heard. Barry always wore gloves, and so did the kidnapper; the only fingerprint police recovered was an unidentifiable smudge on the envelope that contained the ransom note. Both newspapers and their police sources, however, ignored a glaring inconsistency: Barry swiped jewels, not chil-dren. And there was nothing, other than similar methods and plenty of conjecture, to link him to the crime, let alone any evidence to suggest he had ever been on the grounds of the Lindbergh estate.

Blake was mortified. The tabloids' allegations and the police comments accusing them of snatching the child, she recalled, "nearly broke my heart."

There was worse to come. On March 5, the *Daily News* launched a guest column bearing the byline of "crack man-hunter" and "former ace police detective" Val O'Farrell. The private eye who had helped to put Barry in prison back in 1927 had been retained to review the evidence and offer his take on the kidnapping and who might be responsible. The abduction, he wrote in his first installment, was likely the work of "skilled, painstaking professionals" and an inside job—someone in the Lindbergh household, he alleged, had conspired with the perpetrators and possibly had passed the child through the nursery window. The kidnappers must have watched the home for weeks, possibly months, before taking the child. The economic meltdown had been as tough on second-story men and jewel thieves as everyone else, he noted, and crooks were finding it tough to fence their loot. Kidnapping had become a lucrative alternative. "Life is now worth more than jewelry," they had decided, according to O'Farrell. "Let's steal living things."

Blake had picked up the paper the day it appeared and could scarcely believe what she was reading: "The ideal type of criminal to fit the Lindbergh job," in O'Farrell's opinion, "would be Arthur Barry and his female accomplice, Anna Blake." The detective boasted of his role in their arrest at Lake Ronkonkoma and reminded the Lindbergh investigators that pieces of jewelry found in their possession had been taken from a home in Rumson, New Jersey, just fifty miles from the Lindbergh estate. Blake, he added, may have been a key player in the kidnap plot. A man and woman traveling with a stolen baby "can pose as a happy family," he said, and "male crooks, like all men, dislike the idea of caring for a baby over any length of time. Anna Blake would have filled the bill perfectly." Barry's photograph accompanied the column, and the paper ran a four-panel comic-style artist's depiction of the crime, which showed a man clutching the baby as he fled from the house and a woman running to catch up. O'Farrell even accused "the Blake woman," as he called her, of smuggling guns into Auburn to help Barry break out. His sources, he added, confirmed she "has taken up again with this desperate fugitive" since his escape.

Blake was stunned. "It made me ill," she said. She marched into the *Daily News* newsroom—on the seventh floor of a newly built $10 million art deco tower on East Forty-Second Street—and demanded a retraction. "Arthur Barry might have been guilty of many crimes, he might have been a robber," she insisted to the reporter assigned to hear her out, "but he was not the type of man who could do this inhuman deed."

The paper backed its star detective. Blake's comments were published the following day alongside a new column from O'Farrell, who doubled down on his allegations against the couple. "I am more and more inclined to stress the belief that either Arthur Barry or some brilliant and daring criminal of his type conceived the crime," he said, "and was the man who brought the Lindbergh baby down the ladder from the nursery to the Lindbergh lawn." The evidence he marshaled to support his case, however, was circumstantial and weak: There was no moonlight the night of the kidnapping, and Barry had timed many of his jewel thefts for moonless nights. Barry employed ladders to reach second-story windows (although O'Farrell failed to mention that Barry did not bring his own, preferring to use ones found near the homes he burgled or borrowed from a neighboring estate). Barry walked with a slight limp, and O'Farrell claimed the footprints in the mud suggested that the kidnapper, too, put more weight on one foot than the other. And the silence of the Lindbergh's terrier, the columnist contended, also pointed to "our old friend Barry." The jewel thief had pulled off many jobs without disturbing guard dogs "and managed to cultivate the friendship of the animals." Once again, a photograph of Barry accompanied O'Farrell's musings.

Barry was being tried and convicted in the press for a crime that had enraged the entire country. His photo was back in the widely read *Daily News*, increasing the risk that Otto Reuter or someone else he knew in the Andover area might recognize him.

The Lindberghs' ordeal dragged on for weeks. Thousands of homes were searched. Suspects across the country were detained, questioned, and released. One man who was driving home to Trenton from a vacation in the western United States complained of being stopped more than one hundred times because his car had New Jersey plates. "No story was too fantastic for investigation," noted the *New York Times*.

Dr. John F. Condon, a retired school principal, became a go-between, using advertisements in his local newspaper, the *Bronx Home News*, and the pseudonym Jafsie (a mashup of his initials, J. F. C.) to send messages to the kidnapper. A man who called himself John responded and met Condon at a park to discuss how to exchange the baby for the money. While the man claimed to be acting for the kidnapper, Condon and the police assumed he had snatched the baby. He spoke with a German accent—"Have you gottit the money with you?" he asked at one point—and even though it was dark, Condon was able to get a good look at the man's features. After Lindbergh agreed to pay the $50,000 ransom, Condon arranged to meet "John" again on the night of April 2 and handed over a box containing the money. The man left with the cash and was not heard from again.

More than a month later, and just days after Charles Lindbergh Jr.'s chubby face appeared on the cover of *Time* magazine, the child's body was found in a wooded area within five miles of his home. A blow to the head suffered on the night of the abduction, seventy-two days earlier—possibly when the ladder broke and the kidnapper and baby fell to the ground—had fractured his skull. The *Daily News* broke the terrible news in a two-word headline—BABY DEAD—set in a thick font and large enough to fill its front page. WHO KILLED LINDY'S BABY? asked the New York *Evening Journal*. WHO COULD HAVE? WHO WOULD? The police were no longer looking for a kidnapper; the hunt was on for a cruel, cold-blooded child killer. And Arthur Barry, fugitive jewel thief, was a prime suspect.

7

A MOST DANGEROUS CRIMINAL

THIRTY

LINDBERGH SUSPECT

Andover and Newark, New Jersey • 1932

V AL O'FARRELL WAS not the only one who believed Arthur Barry could be the Lindbergh kidnapper. Reports and tips implicating him had been trickling in to investigators working on the case for months. A civic-minded New Jersey man named George Schneck contacted the superintendent of the New Jersey State Police, Colonel H. Norman Schwarzkopf in May 1932, insisting the fugitive was "the actual kidnapper of the baby." A police informer claimed Barry had been overheard discussing plans to snatch the Lindbergh baby as part of a series of child kidnappings. The targets included the infant son of former world heavyweight boxing champion Gene Tunney, and Julia Hodgson, the adopted teenage daughter of Babe Ruth.

"Lindbergh took me off the front page," Barry was said to have complained, when the flier's return to America after his transatlantic flight had upstaged the Livermore robbery. "It would be a good joke if he put me back again."

Newark police had received a more credible tip—the *New York Times* attributed it to "an underworld source"—that Barry was hiding in rugged, sparsely populated Sussex County. It was enough to justify sending someone to nose around. "We are like men adrift in mid-ocean as far as the case is concerned," confessed Newark's deputy chief of police Frank

Brex, who was in charge of the detective division. "We are ready to follow the faintest clue."

The detective sent to the area stopped in Andover in mid-October and showed Barry's photograph to George Losey, the news agent who doubled as the township's mayor.

"That's the man," Losey exclaimed, "who owes me for two weeks' papers!"

~~~~~~~~~~~~

GEORGE LOSEY PARKED his car in front of Otto Reuter's farmhouse at about half past eight on the evening of October 22, a Saturday. Clouds scudded and danced in a chilly west wind, exposing patches of stars in the moonless sky. Inside the house, the man considered the greatest jewel thief of his time, the bold escapee who had evaded capture for more than three years, was in the middle of a mundane chore: he was giving Reuter's dog, a white miniature poodle, a bath.

Losey was nervous. After he identified Arthur Barry, Newark detectives and state troopers had asked him to help set a trap. At first, he refused. He was afraid of being used as bait to catch a dangerous fugitive. His wife had died a couple of years earlier, and he was raising their five daughters—the youngest was only seven—on his own. But he found it hard to believe that the man he knew as Jim Toner and considered a friend was, as he put it, "a hard character." He had agreed to try to lure Barry into the open.

He blew the car's horn and waited.

The unknown visitor put Barry on edge. When he recognized the man at the wheel, he relaxed.

Losey called out, saying he wanted to collect the three dollars he was owed for delivering papers. Barry still had soapsuds on his hands as he stepped outside and walked toward the car. Newark detectives Howard Fallon and Frank Carr sprang from bushes near the house and seized him. As many as a half dozen state troopers and local constables quickly joined them. Barry did not struggle as he was handcuffed.

"I felt the guns against my side," he recalled. He had been caught off guard. His loaded revolver was upstairs, in his room.

"America's most notorious jewel thief," the *Daily News* was pleased to report, was back in custody. *Time* magazine applauded the capture of "the slickest second-story man in the East." The *New York Times* devoted a full column on its front page to the arrest of the "suave robber" and noted with amusement that Barry's newspaper-reading habit—"he was unable to restrain his curiosity in the doings of the world at large"—had been his undoing.

A headline in the *Daily News* asked a question on many people's minds: DOES BARRY ARREST SOLVE KIDNAPING?

ANNA BLAKE WAS in New York when she spotted a newspaper report announcing her husband's arrest as a suspect in the Lindbergh murder. "I couldn't believe it," she said. "It was too fantastic." She headed underground and sought solace amid the crowds and clacking wheels of the subway, riding aimlessly for hours as she read every press account of his arrest she could find.

She soon proclaimed his innocence in an interview with the *Daily News*, going head-to-head with O'Farrell. "It makes me sick—sick all over—to have any suspicion cast on Arthur in connection with the horrible crime," she sobbed. "He's the most tender-hearted man alive."

At police headquarters in Newark, Barry denied any involvement in the abduction and murder. The Lindbergh kidnapping "was a terrible thing, I felt it as much as anybody," he said when he was given the chance to speak to reporters. "I can account for every minute of my time for ten days before the baby was stolen and for several days after it."

He scoffed at O'Farrell's suggestion that the kidnapper's custom-built ladder linked him to the crime. "I never brought a ladder to any job I ever pulled," he said. "If I didn't find a ladder on the place, I got in without one." He seemed to resent the attack on his reputation as a skilled second-story man as much as the allegation that he was a child murderer. He had devoured press coverage of the kidnapping and had studied published photographs of the Lindbergh home and grounds, and had reached his own conclusions. "I'll lay a bet I could have gotten into that house with my

Barry after he was recaptured, handcuffed to a chair at Newark police
headquarters (Author Collection)

hands and feet tied," he boasted. "Some bungling amateur grabbed that
Lindbergh baby, and you can take my word for it."

Barry insisted he had not pulled a single jewel theft in the more than
three years he had been on the lam. "I haven't had my fingers in anything
since I've been out." He was confronted with the informer's tip that he had
been overheard discussing plans for a series of kidnappings of children.
Nonsense, he said. "I've never done anything worse than steal from the
rich," he protested. Why would he resort to kidnapping?

Then, a woman who called herself Daisy Brown came forward to take
credit for the tip that led to Barry's capture. "I am convinced he kidnaped
the Lindbergh baby," the woman, who refused to reveal her real name,
told *Daily News* reporter Alfred Albelli, who had been investigating the

kidnapping for months. "He's just a no-good rat." She claimed to have known Barry for years—they had met when he was pulling his Long Island jobs and "spending money like nobody's business"—and said he was "cruel enough and clever enough" to have snatched the child.

Reuter, however, gave Barry a solid alibi. He remembered the moment Barry shouted the news to him as he fetched the papers the next morning. While Barry sometimes borrowed Reuter's car—he did not have one of his own—"he did not take it" the night of the kidnapping, Reuter assured the Newark police, "and I'm certain he stayed around that night."

"We questioned Barry about the Lindbergh case," Newark's chief of police, James McRell, reported to the *New York Times*. "But he denied all knowledge of it, and we are convinced he is telling the truth." Asked about O'Farrell's claims that there was evidence that pointed to Barry's involvement—the ladder, a limping man's footprints, the silent dog—McRell dismissed the detective's allegations as "rot."

With the reputation of its in-house detective under attack, the *Daily News* scrambled to find more links between Barry and the crime. O'Farrell produced three more columns, published on successive days and accompanying news coverage of Barry's capture, each one peppered with what-if speculations, factual errors, wishful thinking, and sometimes laughable leaps of logic. Barry's prowess at silencing watchdogs? He must drug them, O'Farrell believed, and this explained why the Lindbergh terrier did not bark. The symbol of interlocking circles that the kidnapper used in the ransom note and follow-up messages to the Lindberghs? "A distinctly Barryesque touch," the sleuth claimed, "the kind of imagery in which his criminally warped mind would delight." He scolded and lectured the Newark police, accusing them of failing to undertake "elementary police work" and, what was worse, ignoring his advice. The man they had in custody, he warned, was "the most desperate criminal in America . . . gifted with the cunning of the devil, who would stop at nothing." In his October 27 column, O'Farrell issued another directive to the police: Dr. John Condon should be brought face-to-face with Barry, to see if he could identify him as the man who had disappeared with the ransom.

The New Jersey State Police were several steps ahead of O'Farrell. Two officers had already visited Condon at his Bronx home. Condon, a bear of a man who reveled in his sudden fame as a key figure in the Lindbergh story, had been following the press coverage of the jewel thief's arrest. "Barry had no connection whatsoever with his negotiations," Condon had told them, and "nothing to do with the receiving of the Ransom money." Another officer had collected a pair of Barry's shoes from the farmhouse to compare to a plaster cast of footprints found outside the Lindbergh home, apparently without making a match. Olly and Elsie Whateley, the Lindberghs' butler and housekeeper, arrived at police headquarters and confirmed they had never met Barry or seen him lurking around the estate.

Condon was also brought to Newark to see Barry in person. Fourteen detectives and reporters were asked to stand with Barry in a lineup. Condon recognized Barry from his photographs. "A dapper, intelligent-looking young chap, he was obviously worried as I came into the room," he later recalled. "The slender, adept fingers that had caressed so many fine jewels, tugged nervously at his moustache." After scrutinizing each man and confirming none of them looked like the mysterious man he'd met in the park, Condon took Barry aside and asked him a few questions. At his request, Barry repeated words and phrases the man who took the ransom had used. Then Condon inspected his hands. He had shaken hands with John at one of their meetings and noted a lump at the base of the man's thumb—the calling card of a skilled worker who had held the same tool for many years.

"The man I gave the money to was much taller," Condon announced, and "those are not his hands."

"Thank you, Doctor Condon," Barry said. One of the reporters present could see the look of relief on his face. "I've done a lot of things in my time. But I never would get mixed up in anything as rotten as the murder of the Lindbergh baby. You've done me a good turn."

"I've done nothing but tell the truth," Condon assured him. "I'd never mistake the man I gave the money to in a million years."

They shook hands, posed for news photographers, and chatted for a few minutes about their shared Irish heritage. They discovered they had both been altar boys. At Condon's urging, and as detectives stood by in astonished silence, Barry joined him in reciting the Lord's Prayer in Latin.

Barry with Dr. John F. Condon, who confirmed the jewel thief was not the
Lindbergh kidnapper (Author Collection)

The Newark police agreed to return Barry to Auburn Prison.
Superintendent Schwarzkopf of the New Jersey State Police was also satisfied there was no evidence to link him to the kidnapping. While the
Lindbergh case remained unsolved—the man eventually executed for the
child's murder would not be arrested until 1934—the Newark force had
scored a major coup. Detectives Fallon and Carr, the *Brooklyn Daily Eagle*
pointed out, had collared "the prize police catch of 1932."

After being fixated on Barry for almost a week, the press was ready to
move on. The *Daily News*, however, was about to get a lot more mileage out
of the exploits of Arthur Barry.

THIRTY-ONE

CELEBRITY CROOK

Newark, New Jersey • 1932

GRACE ROBINSON, HER fashionably short, dirty-blond hair tucked under a dark beret, struck a match and held it at arm's length. Arthur Barry leaned forward until the tip of the long, thin cigar in his lips touched the flame. A couple of rings were scattered on the table in front of them, and he was presenting a master class in how to tell real gems from fakes. The jewel expert could not light a smoke on his own—his wrists were handcuffed to his chair.

"Police and newspapers have called me the most dangerous criminal in America. They have tried to make me out a killer—a heartless, bloodthirsty fellow, who with a gentlemanly, Barrymore-ish exterior, masked the heart and soul of Satan himself," he told Robinson, star crime reporter for the *Daily News*.

"To the charge of being a thief, I plead guilty," he said. "But as a killer— never! Neither could I ever find it in my heart to kidnap a helpless, innocent child. I feel sickish—almost weak—when the authorities question me about the Lindbergh baby horror."

With those words, the *Daily News* launched "the intimate life story of Arthur Barry, prince of jewel thieves," an eight-part series of illustrated features billed as a complete first-person account of the "reckless career" of "the arch thief of this decade." To trumpet this journalistic coup, the first

Crime reporter Grace Robinson interviewing Barry before his return to prison (New York *Daily News*)

article included an image of a handwritten note from Barry: "This is the only story I have ever given to any publication," he confirmed. His signature appeared as the byline, hammering home the notion that America's Raffles was speaking directly to *Daily News* readers. The series debuted on October 30, in a Sunday edition that reached more than 1.6 million readers. One- or two-page installments appeared every day until the following Sunday.

Robinson was one of the highest-paid female journalists in the country. She had covered the biggest cases of the '20s, including the double murder of Rev. Edward Hall and one of his parishioners, Eleanor Mills, in New Brunswick, New Jersey, and the trial of Ruth Snyder and her lover, Judd Gray, for the murder of Snyder's husband in Queens. "She is small, slim, frail in build," noted fellow journalist Ishbel Ross, "but tenacious of purpose, sturdy of will." She was an accidental journalist—her father's death in 1917, when she was in her junior year of college, forced her to quit school and find a job. She did a stint at the *Omaha Bee* in her native Nebraska and was women's page editor for a New York paper before joining the upstart *Daily News* in 1922, first as a society columnist and then on the crime beat. Lightning-fast shorthand made her a natural for delivering verbatim accounts of trial testimony. A calm, reserved demeanor—one colleague described her as "an iron-willed wisp"—masked her determination and courage. Crooks, politicians, and celebrities alike underestimated her razor-sharp interviewing skills. Bootlegger Jack "Legs" Diamond, who had been shot almost a dozen times in gunfights and assassination attempts, once invited Robinson to his hotel room, hoping to convince her he was being wrongly portrayed as a thug in the press. He dismissed his bodyguards, leaving them alone in the room, and locked the door, but she refused to be intimidated.

"I'm not a bad fellow," he told her.

"Mr. Diamond, you say you are not a gangster," she shot back. "Just what do you do for a living?"

Robinson was thirty-eight when she interviewed Barry, and about to embark on a swing through Europe. She would watch Hitler's brown-shirted thugs march through the streets of Berlin, pursue the reclusive actress Greta Garbo, and score a scoop with a report that New York City's disgraced mayor Jimmy Walker, who had fled to Italy, was retiring from public life. Within a few months, she would cover Franklin Roosevelt's inauguration, when the new president assured his beleaguered nation that "the only thing we have to fear is fear itself."

She was more than a match for a suave gentleman burglar. Robinson met with Barry several times for the series. He was escorted from a cell to an office at the Newark police headquarters for each session. A half dozen detectives were present, and, as they spoke, he was either handcuffed to a chair or to one of the officers. Barry was a chain-smoker, every detective was puffing a cigarette or cigar, and with the windows closed—a precaution to ensure that Barry did not try to escape—the air became a gray fog. "I lost my voice for a few days," Robinson later complained about the sessions, "due to smoke."

She had covered the Livermore jewel robbery and was surprised to see how much Barry had aged in five years. His thick, combed-back hair was streaked with gray, and his face was thinner and hardened. "Barry's good looks & finesse were over-estimated," she recalled, looking back on their encounter decades later. Serving time in prison was "not conducive to beauty."

Barry described to her his "masterpiece," the Livermore heist, and how he had graciously returned expensive rings at Dorothea Livermore's request. He thought back to the first time he broke into a home and stole jewelry. He spoke of slipping into parties in evening wear and hobnobbing with the rich and famous so he could get a look inside the mansions he was about to rob. He relived his escapes from Auburn and from the Bridgeport jail and recalled his time in Sing Sing as one of Charles Chapin's gardeners. When he revealed a fascination with astrology—"I always consulted the stars before an important undertaking"—the paper rolled out an advertisement to promote the series. "He stole by the stars—and with their aid!" it proclaimed. News photographs, pictures of him in uniform during the war, and family snapshots taken with Anna Blake at Lake Ronkonkoma and while he was hiding out in New Jersey illustrated the series.

Asked to divulge the tricks of his trade, Barry described how he had cased estates, disabled alarms, and befriended watchdogs. He had worn gloves, he said, even when handling ladders and climbing through windows, to ensure that he left no fingerprints. "That's why Barry was such an enigma to the police," Robinson noted. "He followed the first commandment of burglary—he covered his traces." At one point, Barry said he felt sheepish about revealing his methods. "They are so simple anybody with a head could pull them. In fact I worry, telling them, for fear some imbecile will read them, start out doing the same smart things I did, and find himself ultimately in the far-from-smart plight I'm in now."

Barry was reluctant to discuss his encounter with the Prince of Wales. "It sounds like bragging," he explained. He only relented after Robinson revealed she had pieced together "the whole amazing story" from people who had seen him with the prince in Manhattan nightclubs back in 1924. Barry marveled at how easy it had been to meet and entertain the future king. "It merely shows how far a gentleman burglar can get," he said, "if he brings looks and manners to his profession of collecting jewels." Robinson, who had covered the visit for the *Daily News*—she had donned an evening gown and crashed one of the Long Island galas, in search of a scoop—remembered the night the prince disappeared until five in the morning. The mystery of where he went and who he was with "has never been cleared up until now," she reported. "He was seeing Broadway in the company of Arthur Barry."

As she prodded him for details, Barry made a startling admission: "It was I who pulled off the Joshua S. Cosden robbery." He had attended a party at the Cosden mansion—entering "through a bedroom window," he said—but he declined to reveal more about the theft of jewels belonging to Nellie Cosden and Lady Mountbatten during the Prince of Wales's Long Island holiday. "I may have to stand trial for it some day," Barry said.

When he tried to be evasive, Robinson went on the offensive and confronted him with the facts. She reproduced his long list of crimes as a juvenile, even though he insisted it "must be the record of another Barry." He declined to identify the "pal" who had been his accomplice, but Robinson named James Monahan in her published report and reminded readers how Barry had turned on him to save Blake from facing charges. She made inquiries to confirm his war record and his claim that he was recommended for a medal for bravery. When he described how fond he was of Cuddles, the poodle he had been bathing just before he was captured, and how he had mended the dog's broken hip after it was hit by a car, she asked Newark deputy police chief Frank Brex what he thought of Barry's apparent kindheartedness. "Barry is the type of criminal that combines extreme cruelty and extreme tenderness," he said. "It's completely in accord with his character . . . that he should be tenderness itself to a helpless dog, and yet have no scruples about terrifying innocent women by breaking into their homes at night."

As Barry reflected on his crimes, he became wistful. And he sounded remorseful. "The career of the great Barry doesn't seem so hot when I try to hold my wife, Anna Blake, in my arms, and the handcuffs prevent me," he told Robinson.

While he could face "the book"—a life sentence—as punishment for his escape, there remained a chance he could earn his freedom with an early release.

"Ahead of me, at Auburn, lies a hell on earth. But I still cherish some little hope of beating life-long imprisonment," he said. "I have a right to some such hope—that is, if incarceration of a criminal really is intended only to confine him until he's proved he can earn a living in a decent way. I've proved that in these precious three and a half years of freedom since the Auburn break."

BARRY WAS A press sensation across America and beyond. The mere mention of a possible link to the Lindbergh kidnapping, a story that had eclipsed all others, had transformed the captured jewel thief into an international criminal superstar. The Associated Press and other wire services flashed news of his arrest and updates on Barry's interrogation at the dizzying speed of a word every second. Editors from Fort Worth, Texas, to Wausau, Wisconsin, typesetters from Klamath Falls, Oregon, to Elizabethton, a city of just eight thousand in northeastern Tennessee, gave him page-one treatment. So did their colleagues across the border in the Canadian cities of Winnipeg and Vancouver. A Reuters wire service report on his arrest was picked up by a paper in Liverpool, England. "Barry admits that he is a thief," noted a correspondent for London's *Daily Telegraph*, "but stoutly denies that he would stoop to kidnapping." American expats who had followed Hemingway, Fitzgerald, and the rest of the Lost Generation to Paris learned of his capture from a report sent via wireless and published in the European edition of the *New York Herald Tribune*. L'ÉTONNANTE CAR-RIÈRE D'ARTHUR BARRY marveled a headline in one French newspaper, over a story that offered an outline of his astonishing career. In the pages of Vienna's *Die Stunde*, he was touted as a *Gangsterführer*—gangster leader—almost on par with Al Capone.

Letters poured into Newark police headquarters from people begging for Barry's autograph. Newspaper photographers clicked away as he posed for staged shots; one widely published picture showed him admiring the ring on a detective's finger. He slicked back his hair, combed his tiny mustache, donned his horn-rimmed glasses, and stepped in front of a trio of newsreel cameras. He had squandered his chance for a law-abiding life of "success and glory," he lamented, and "chosen the other road," one that led to "nothing but heartache and headaches." With a performer's sense of timing, he held up his manacled hands. "Let this be a lesson to the youth of the land," he declared as the cameras whirred. "Crime doesn't pay."

Crime, in fact, could pay. Newsreel producers ponied up $75 for a few minutes' work, about $1,500 today. Barry had asked for $300. "I'm a born actor and the highest-paid crook in the world," he was heard to complain afterward, perhaps in jest, "and the movies only pay me chicken feed." The *Daily News* likely paid him for the tell-all series as well. While there is no record of a payment, it probably would have taken a handsome offer to convince him to cooperate with the paper that had published Val O'Farrell's damning theories and allegations and had dragged his name—and Blake's—through the mud.

Paying for exclusive first-person crime stories was a common press practice in the Jazz Age. Jane Gibson, a key figure in 1922's Hall-Mills double murder, was suspected of selling her life story and an eyewitness account of the crime to the press. She was "a few hundred dollars richer," the *New York Herald* noted, after inviting reporters into her home for interviews and posing for photographs. Crooks, too, cashed in on the public's hunger for first-person accounts of their exploits. "Serialized memoirs," crime writer Ellen Poulsen has noted, "helped to pay legal fees and keep the rent paid for a while."

The Lindbergh case provides one of the most infamous examples of the ethically dubious practice that became known as "checkbook journalism." The *New York Journal*, one of William Randolph Hearst's flagship newspapers, covered the legal fees of the attorney who defended Bruno Richard Hauptmann, the German-born carpenter living in the Bronx who was convicted in 1935 of murdering the baby, in exchange for exclusive rights to interview Hauptmann's wife. Even the associates of the bad guys could make crime pay, though sometimes for only a modest fee. Mary Kinder, whose boyfriend was a member of John Dillinger's bank-robbing gang, revealed that she sold her story to the press for "$25.00 and a couple of gowns."

It was an era of hype and ballyhoo. Big stories built journalists' careers, attracted radio listeners, lured people into theaters to watch newsreels, and made rich press barons even richer. And then, as now, crime stories were big stories. "The fact about crime news," journalist Silas Bent noted in a 1920s exposé of his profession's addiction to sensationalism, "is that it builds circulation." Between 1899 and 1923, the space allotted to news about crimes and criminals in US newspapers, according to a survey Bent cited, jumped by an astounding 58 percent; political news, in contrast, barely moved the needle, with a 1 percent increase in column inches.

The spotlight on Barry and his crimes fueled a debate in the Letters to the Editor section of the *New York Times*. Gordon Knox Bell, who was in charge of the New York House of Refuge on Randall's Island—America's first reformatory for juvenile offenders—chastised the *Times* and other newspapers for giving Barry "any prominence, or indeed any notice." Criminals, he fumed, were "among the most self-opinionated and conceited people in the world" and "love to see their names and pictures in the papers." The press were enablers, encouraging the crooks they glamorized to break the law and enticing young boys "to follow their example and get themselves before the public."

Another reader, identified only as A.W., responded with a call for better coverage of the causes of crime and the efforts of the police to put offenders behind bars. "The capture of a man like Barry, an enemy of society, is reassuring news," argued the reader, who scoffed at the notion that press coverage created criminals. "I doubt whether lads of impressionable age do much newspaper reading, especially boys in the poor neighborhoods that produce most of the criminals."

Press accounts of crimes, a New Jersey reader chimed in, encouraged business owners to invest in alarm systems, helping to cut down on thefts and burglaries. "Those of us like furriers, jewelers, banks, &c., who have something worth stealing are forewarned," noted John T. Quigley. "We can thank the newspapers for keeping us from having losses."

Editors and reporters were giving people what they wanted. The deepening Depression had whetted the public's appetite for escapism, and crime news delivered. "The world was really sitting pretty" in 1932, humorist Will

Rogers deadpanned, "outside of everybody not working, and nobody buying anything and nobody knowing what the morrow might bring forth." But anyone who could scrape together a few Buffalo nickels or a couple of thin Mercury dimes could buy a stack of newspapers and follow the exploits of clever, larger-than-life crooks who were beating the system and fleecing the rich.

"In the early 1930s a new kind of criminal appeared in this country," noted Lew Louderback, an author who chronicled the rise of this new generation of public enemies. "They used cars instead of horses, Thompson submachine guns rather than Colt .44s—but these were simply new wrappings on what was essentially an old American package—the frontier badman."

Nineteen thirty-two was the year Bonnie Parker and Clyde Barrow launched their infamous spree of robbery and murder across Texas and a half dozen other states. Pretty Boy Floyd, who boasted he "robbed no one but the monied men," was knocking over banks across Oklahoma. John Dillinger was about to be released from an Indiana prison and would soon assemble a gang and raid more than ten banks. All of them would become folk heroes and household names, despite the body counts they left in their wake. "Banks, after all," Louderback pointed out, were "hardly the most popular institutions in the country."

Barry was a different breed from the reckless, ruthless outlaws of the Dirty Thirties. He was a throwback to a time of glitz and excess that now seemed as remote and distant as the Middle Ages. He had stolen by stealth, not with guns blazing. His weapons had been smarts and charm, not Tommy guns. "I suppose the fact that I don't look like a thug helped me a lot," he told Robinson. "Good manners," he added, sounding more like a disciple of self-improvement guru Dale Carnegie than a felon, "inspire confidence in any line of business."

He had avoided violence, at least until he fled from Auburn Prison in a hail of bullets. But his victims, like those of the public enemies, were not the people standing in breadlines or living in squalid shantytowns, the people who had lost everything—jobs, homes, businesses, farms, even hope.

One New Jersey newspaper called him a "Modern Robin Hood," even though he had given none of his crime earnings to the poor. "I only robbed the rich," he wanted everyone to remember in the days after his capture. "If a woman can carry around a necklace worth $750,000, she knows where her next meal is coming from."

THIRTY-TWO

A FAIR TRIAL

Auburn, New York • 1932–33

A LINE OF SIX automobiles filled with police officers emerged from the Manhattan end of the Holland Tunnel and snaked toward Midtown. A squad of New York City cops on motorcycles led the way, clearing a route through streets clogged with Saturday afternoon traffic. A gray November sky added a touch of foreboding as the motorcade neared Grand Central Terminal with its cargo, a passenger with a one-way ticket to Cayuga County, home to the state prison at Auburn.

Once Arthur Barry had been eliminated as a suspect in the Lindbergh kidnapping and murder, warden Joseph Brophy moved swiftly to get him back behind Auburn Prison's walls. New York governor Franklin Roosevelt, days away from being elected the thirty-second president of the United States, signed the extradition order to bring him back from New Jersey. On November 5, Barry put on a dark pin-striped suit, knotted a necktie at the collar of a white shirt, tucked a handkerchief into his breast pocket, and donned a newsboy cap. The mustache that had outlived its days as a disguise had been shaved off, but he still wore the glasses that made him look more like a scholar than a master thief. Before leaving Newark, he was granted a few moments to say goodbye to Anna Blake.

"Be brave," he told her.

He was handcuffed to two Auburn guards who had come to collect him.

Leg irons slowed his gait to a shuffle. Four Newark detectives piled into one of the cars with them, and armed officers manned the other vehicles. At Grand Central Terminal, more police officers stood at street corners and near the entrance. Barry and his guards were the first to board the train.

As he settled into a private car with a guard at his side, he leaned back and put up his feet, exposing the leg shackles. A camera clicked and the *Daily News* ran the photograph the next day under the headline PRINCE ARTHUR OFF TO HIS IRON PALACE. A reporter along for the ride passed the time by counting how many packs of cigarettes (three) and how many cigars (two) Barry smoked on the journey.

The prisoner and his entourage changed trains in Albany, and Warden Brophy was waiting at the station in Syracuse to accompany him on the drive to Auburn. As he was led through the main gate and under the wall he had jumped from almost three and a half years earlier, noted another reporter, he did not look up.

Auburn had been transformed since the 1929 riots. Many of the burned-out buildings had been replaced, and new cellblocks and workshops were under construction. Governor Roosevelt had set up a commission to investigate the riot, and its recommendations for modernizing Auburn and other state prisons were being implemented. There were more guards, fewer inmates, and bigger cells. The arsenal Barry and his confederates had so easily raided was more secure and considered riot-proof. Prisoners played basketball and checkers in the exercise yard that had once been a battlefield, squared off against visiting baseball teams, and tapped putters on a thirteen-hole miniature golf course. Even the food was better, with fresh fruit and vegetables showing up on mess hall plates.

Barry was given back his old number—43077—and lodged in the prison's newly built, 190-cell segregation unit. His cell was larger and better equipped than the one he had fled, with a toilet and sink and room for a table and chair as well as a bed. "No longer is he housed with the hated 'bucket,'" the *Syracuse Herald* noted, in case Barry was looking for a blessing to count.

He had been back in Auburn for three weeks before Blake was able to visit. Security was heavier than before the riot, to ensure that visitors did not smuggle in drugs or weapons. They sat on either side of a metal screen, four feet apart, with a guard watching them. "I was astonished to see how well he looked," she recalled. The shabby prison garb he had worn before the riot was gone, replaced with a military-style gray uniform, complete with vest and flat-top kepi cap. "The atmosphere no longer was depressing," she was pleased to discover. "Arthur no longer seemed broken in spirit."

The way the prison system handled and classified prisoners also changed in the aftermath of the riots. The goal, noted the report of Roosevelt's investigative commission, was to prepare inmates for their eventual release with a program tailored to each man's abilities and needs—"fitting a square peg into a square hole," as the commissioners put it. Barry was subjected to a battery of interviews and examinations to assess his background and his mental and physical health, and administrators would use the results to decide what work he would do as he served his time and any treatment, training, or education he needed.

Asked about his medical history, he accounted for his bullet and shrapnel wounds and revealed that he had contracted gonorrhea in 1920, soon after his discharge from the army. Questioned for a psychiatric and sociological report, he lied yet again about his age—he claimed he was about to turn forty-two, when he was a month shy of his thirty-sixth birthday. He talked about growing up in Worcester and associating, when he was young, with persons "of an undesirable type." He confessed once again to the Livermore robbery and recounted the details of how his most famous heist was planned and executed.

He also met with the prison's Catholic chaplain and reckoned he had not attended a church service in at least two decades. Another prison official, tasked with matching Barry's skills to a job in one of the prison's workshops, summed up his employment record in a single sentence: "This man claims he never worked for a living."

For the time being, he remained in the segregation block, a prison within a prison where men were locked up for much of the day and cut off from the rest of the inmates. It was a form of solitary confinement and reserved for the most violent and dangerous inmates. "The worst of Auburn prison's collection of bad men," one newspaper called them—thugs who had attacked other inmates, refused to follow prison rules, or had a reputation for stirring up trouble. The isolation cells also were used to keep gang members from reuniting and to protect convicts who had made enemies or helped to put an accomplice behind bars. Barry was there to make sure he did not try to escape again and for his own protection.

There were reports in the press that his life could be in danger— inmates punished for taking part in the July 1929 riot, it was said, were furious that he had escaped during the chaos and were out for revenge. "Barry made tools of them all," the *Daily News* claimed. He was also being punished. Auburn officials were convinced he had instigated the riot to cover his escape. A blue paper index card, bearing his mug shot and used to record inmate disciplinary infractions, included an entry that accused him of "Assaulting and shooting officer, causing riot." A Cayuga County jury would soon decide whether he was guilty as charged.

<hr>

BARRY HAD BEEN indicted, while on the lam, for planning and inciting the deadly riot. And he had already been convicted in the local press as the "leader" of the riot and the "brains" behind the uprising. Blake pleaded her husband's case in the press as his trial approached. "He is absolutely innocent of riot. Because he escaped during a riot is no proof that he had anything to do with the uprising," she argued in the pages of the *Daily News*. "If his trial is fair," she assured a *Syracuse Herald* reporter who tracked her down at an Auburn hotel, "he will be acquitted."

Privately, Barry held out little hope of beating the rap. The jury could be stacked with friends of guards or prison employees, or businessmen who supplied goods or services to the facility. And the trial would begin on December 12, a day after Auburn marked the third anniversary of the second riot, which had left eight convicts and a guard dead. The milestone would revive memories, one newspaper noted, of how inmates had "run wild with gun, knife and torch" during the earlier melee. Barry had applied for a change of venue, claiming he could not get a fair trial in Cayuga County, but the gambit failed. "I can expect a hometown verdict," he told Blake as the day of reckoning approached, "but whatever it may be, it can never dampen the happiness that I enjoyed the last three years."

He had a court-appointed defender, a local lawyer named Max Goldman. Barry's fellow escapee George Small, who still walked on

Arthur Barry and George Small on trial in 1932 for inciting a riot during
their escape from Auburn Prison (Author Collection)

crutches three years after he almost died in a shoot-out with police in
Brooklyn, was put on trial at the same time. Small opted to defend himself.
Each day, guards escorted them the half mile from their cells in segregation to the Cayuga County Courthouse, an imposing citadel of gray-tinted
stone and soaring Greek columns, where justice had been dispensed for
almost a century. Security was tight. State troopers guarded every entrance
to the building. Only spectators who could produce a pass issued by the
sheriff or the district attorney were admitted inside the courtroom. The
defendants wore their gray prison uniforms to court for the first few days,
until Barry appealed to Auburn's warden and won them the right to show
up in suits.

It took almost three days to choose the jury. More than one hundred men were summoned for duty—it would be another five years before New York State allowed women to serve on juries—and Small and Goldman questioned and rejected most of them. As the Depression deepened, odds were that many of the prospective jurors were out of work.

"How's your business going to get on while you are here?" Small asked one candidate.

"There isn't any," replied the man, and laughter rippled through the courtroom.

Barry took notes, and, as the process dragged on, Blake was allowed to huddle with him and Goldman at the defense counsel's table so they could discuss candidates—taking advantage, as one reporter put it, of "the proverbial intuition of a woman." They ended up with a jury made up mostly of men who lived outside the city and were less likely to have ties to the prison: eight farmers, a barber, a shoemaker, and two mechanics.

Small turned the trial into a circus. Balancing on his crutches, he grilled witnesses, quoted Shakespeare, and cited principles of physics. He mocked and goaded district attorney Theodore Coburn, telling him to "pay attention to the testimony." He sparred with Judge Kennard Underwood, lecturing him as if he were a child. "You were not there, Your Honor, and of course you don't understand," he said at one point. Whenever the judge tried to rein in his wide-ranging questions, Small demanded a mistrial. Goldman was content to take a back seat and allow Small's antics to deflect attention from Barry.

Guards took the witness stand and described the escape. Merle Osborne said Small was the inmate who attacked him with ammonia and knocked him out during the storming of the guardroom. Milton Ryther, who had stopped a full-scale breakout by tossing away the front-gate key, identified Small as one of the armed men who used him as a human shield, but not Barry. Another guard, Robert Tincknell, swore he had exchanged gunfire with Barry during the breakout. Goldman, however, chipped away at his story during a withering three-hour cross-examination: Tincknell had not recognized Barry as his assailant until he saw his photograph after the riot. He had reviewed the district attorney's notes on testimony at an earlier riot trial, he admitted, to refresh his memory. Had he once said "I hate all convicts—I have no use for them"? Goldman asked. Tincknell denied making the statement, but the idea had been planted in the jurors' minds. The most damning evidence against Small came from guard Edwin C. Walter, who claimed to have seen him brandishing a submachine gun as he yelled "Come on, you fellows, now's your chance" to other prisoners. Small fought back, accusing Walter of cowering behind a building during the firefight and seeing and hearing nothing.

The trial dragged on for more than a week. In his summation, Small dismissed the prosecution's evidence as "incompetent, irrelevant and immaterial," and he was right: they were charged with inciting a riot, not escaping. Goldman echoed Franklin Roosevelt, who had launched his bid for the White House that April with a promise to help the struggling "forgotten man at the bottom of the economic pyramid," and urged the jury not to saddle Barry with a longer prison term and make him the "original forgotten man." He pointed to Blake and pleaded with them to think of "that little woman who sits in the courtroom and who is willing to wait for him."

Judge Underwood delivered his instructions to the jurors on the morning of December 23. "I've tried to give these men a fair trial," he said. He urged them not to allow sympathy for the disabled Small or Barry's faithful wife to affect their "common sense consideration." While the defendants had the right not to testify, the judge ignored the law and suggested they should have. "I think you must consider here the failure on the part of the defendant, Arthur Barry, to show he was in some other part of the prison," Judge Underwood told the jurors, "and the failure of Barry to show where he was during the riot."

The jury returned to the courtroom at one point to review what the foreman described as conflicting testimony from the guards, then deliberated through the night. At six o'clock on the morning of Christmas Eve, an hour before dawn, they filed into the courtroom, bleary-eyed from lack of sleep. Blake had held vigil in the courtroom all night. Her face was the color of chalk as she gripped the arms of her chair and braced for the verdict.

Not guilty.

Blake exchanged a smile with Barry, who was nodding his head, and blew him a kiss. There were cheers in the courtroom, and someone reached out to shake Blake's hand. "Those two words," she noted later, "meant the difference between a life sentence for Arthur and of keeping up hope for an early release from prison."

The judge was stunned. His voice trembled as he lashed out at the jurors, saying that their verdict was "the height of error." The district attorney had presented "a clear, clean-cut picture" that proved "these two defendants were present, armed, and taking part beyond any reasonable doubt," he growled. "I do not begrudge Arthur Barry or that poor cripple Small one single hour of any freedom which may ultimately be theirs, thanks to your action. I do begrudge the granting of mercy to them at the expense of simple justice to the people of the State of New York."

Guards surrounded Barry and Small and led them from the courtroom. Barry shook them off long enough to turn to the chastened jurors.

"The verdict is O.K. by me," he assured them. "You did your duty."

The *New York Times*, as outraged as the judge, decried the verdict as a "perversion of justice." Edward Mulrooney, New York City's police commissioner, weighed in and blamed the verdict on tabloid newspapers and newsreels that "glorified" the exploits of criminals like Barry. "You can't blame the juryman," Mulrooney said in a speech a few days later. "You can't expect him to read about a 'hero' on Tuesday and convict him on Wednesday."

Blake was able to visit her husband soon after the verdict. "We both were so happy we could hardly talk," she said. The acquittal was "the grandest Christmas present in the world."

The celebration, however, was premature. Barry was still under indictment for escaping custody, and he pleaded guilty to that charge in February 1933. "Since his escape and until the time of his capture," his lawyer argued, "he lived as a good citizen, despite economic conditions." Judge Underwood ignored the plea for leniency and imposed the maximum sentence, tacking an additional seven years onto his existing prison term.

Back at Auburn, a clerk in the prison's records department pulled Barry's inmate card and penciled in a new release date. If he was denied parole and served his full sentence, he would be behind bars for almost three more decades, until September 19, 1962. He would be two months shy of his sixty-sixth birthday. Blake would be seventy-three.

THIRTY-THREE

"MY LIFE OF LOVE AND FEAR"

New York City • 1933

I T WAS BILLED as "the first enthralling account" of a "strange courtship and marriage"—a series of weekend newspaper features written by the wife of "celebrated international, big-time jewel-thief" Arthur Barry. "Behind this daring figure," promised an editor's note atop the first install-ment, "stands a woman—petite, blue-eyed, blonde-haired, loyal, candid and courageous." Anna Blake's story was one "of romance, hectic fear, gay adventure, brief happiness, mental torture—a picture of life that rarely has found its way so vividly into published fact—or fiction."

The seven-part series ran on consecutive Sundays beginning in mid-Jan-uary 1933, just after Barry's surprise acquittal on the charge of inciting the Auburn riot. Each two-page feature carried the same attention-grabbing headline: MY LIFE OF LOVE AND FEAR AS THE SWEETHEART AND WIFE OF ARTHUR BARRY, THE WORLD'S MOST FAMOUS JEWEL-THIEF. The distrib-utor was King Features Syndicate, the Hearst media empire's syndication service, which supplied illustrated weekend features and the iconic comic strips *Popeye*, *Krazy Kat*, and *Blondie* to hundreds of papers nationwide.

Blake joined an impressive list of Jazz Age luminaries—heartthrob actor Rudolph Valentino, boxing champ Jack Dempsey, and slugger Ty Cobb among them—who sold their life stories to King Features. She likely received a fraction of the fees paid to those household names, and she commanded a smaller audience than Barry had reached through the pages of the *Daily News*. The *Atlanta Constitution* and the *Minneapolis Tribune*, with a combined circulation of about a quarter of a million, appear to have been the only major papers to pick up the series.

Anna Blake in 1932 (New York *Daily News*)

Blake supplied photographs from their past lives and their time together to illustrate the articles. She posed for pictures at her New York apartment and at Reuter's farm. As a camera shutter clicked, she stared glumly at Barry's empty chair at the dinner table, played solitaire, held Cuddles the poodle, and pretended to tap out her story on a typewriter. Artists' depictions captured the highlights of Barry's career—watching chorus girls with the Prince of Wales, returning rings to Dorothea Livermore, surrounded by armed detectives at the Ronkonkoma railroad station.

Blake used the series to settle scores with Val O'Farrell and other "slanderers" who had portrayed her in the press as a gangster's moll or as Barry's accomplice. She denied knowing anything about her husband's double life as a jewel thief before his arrest in 1927 and swore he had been "straight as a die" since his escape from Auburn. She also took a swipe at James Monahan, accusing Boston Billy of hounding Barry until he agreed to pull the ill-fated Livermore job. With the Livermores unable to identify him, she wondered aloud whether Barry had acted rashly when he admitted to being the courteous burglar who stole their jewels. "If Arthur had not signed his own confession, in order to exonerate me," she wrote, "he might not be where he is today."

Barry was grateful, she revealed, for the time they had together while he was a fugitive. "That happiness we enjoyed," he told her in one of his letters, "nothing can ever take away from my memory. And when things seem a little dark, I will look back . . . and smile and say it was worth it a thousand times!"

She felt the same. "We knew it could not last, but oh how we cherished those precious three years." And she declared that she would never give up hope that, someday, they would be together again.

"The gray future will find him changed and me changed," Blake wrote as she concluded the series, "but when the prison gates finally open for him I shall—God helping me—be waiting there."

8

~~~~~

REDEMPTION

THIRTY-FOUR

HARD TIME

Auburn, New York • 1933–37

AFTER HIS RETURN to Auburn, Arthur Barry was locked up for twenty-three hours a day, every day. He ate his meals alone in his cell. The segregation unit's cells were stacked five tiers high, so enemies could be kept apart and friends could not communicate with each other. Once a day, guards opened the door, snapped on handcuffs, and escorted Barry to a rooftop exercise yard. He had an hour to walk around an enclosure of blank walls, with a barred roof that opened to the sky, as armed guards stood by. It was "tantamount to being outdoors," claimed one New York prison warden of the time. If Barry looked up, he could watch clouds drift past; if he was lucky, he might catch a glimpse of an airplane buzzing overhead. He was allotted two books a week from the prison library. He could read magazines or listen to selected radio programs on a headset, but he never saw a newspaper. He showered once a week, had his hair cut once a month. Anna Blake visited him, but it is not clear how many visits were allowed and how often she made the journey from New York.

The catastrophic physical and mental damage inflicted on many prisoners locked away in solitary confinement was well-known in the 1930s. While visiting a prison during his 1842 tour of North America, Charles Dickens encountered inmates subjected to "rigid, strict and hopeless

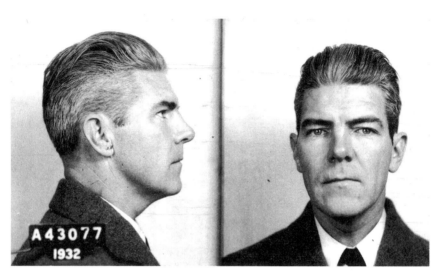

Barry's prison mug shot, taken at Auburn in 1932 (New York State Archives)

solitary confinement" who had been reduced to a catatonic state, "dead to everything" and barely able to speak. "I hold this slow and daily tampering with the mysteries of the brain, to be immeasurably worse than any torture of the body," he wrote afterward. The US Supreme Court noted the "serious objections" to the widespread practice in an 1890 ruling on prisoners' rights. Many inmates held in isolation, even for short periods, became suicidal or insane, the court found, and "those who stood the ordeal better were not generally reformed, and in most cases did not recover sufficient mental activity to be of any subsequent service to the community."

One man who spent a decade in solitary confinement likened it to being "buried alive." Others, cut off from everyday life and human contact, hallucinate or hear voices, as minds starved of stimulation struggle to fill the void. Their sense of time and their grip on reality can slip away as the world moves on without them. Prisoners have fought back by developing routines to manage the tedium—with everything from doing hundreds of push-ups a day to looking for tiny holes between the bricks of a cell wall and drawing imaginary lines to connect them. "It's an awful thing, solitary," said former United States senator John McCain, who spent more than two years in isolation as a prisoner of war after his plane was shot down in Vietnam. "It crushes your spirit and weakens your resistance more effectively than any other form of mistreatment."

Inmates in segregation at Auburn cracked under the mental and physical strain. One woman went public with the plight of her nineteen-year-old son, who was a year into a twenty-five-year term for robbery and, like Barry, was confined to his cell for twenty-three hours a day. "He has nothing to do but sit and brood over his troubles," her lawyer told the *Buffalo News* in 1931. "This is bound to drive him mad in time." Another Auburn inmate was so desperate to escape the unit that he confessed to a murder he did not commit; he preferred a quick death in the electric chair, he explained when his story was proven false, to languishing in an isolation cell. A former Auburn inmate who took part in one of the 1929 riots and spent five years in segregation recalled the fate of twenty-two others subjected to the same punishment: "Five killed themselves," he claimed when he was arrested for bank robbery in 1935, "and 17 went crazy."

———

BARRY HAD BEEN in solitary confinement before, but only for a short time, after he arrived at Sing Sing. He now faced months, or even years, locked away and almost forgotten, as punishment for escaping. "I wonder if I can go through with that," he had told reporter Grace Robinson just before his return to Auburn. "Some men, I hear, have lived in solitary several years." To keep in shape, he paced back and forth in his cell each day until he was satisfied he had walked about three miles.

He wrote to Blake often, to fill the empty hours. "Am feeling O.K. under the circumstances," he assured her in one letter. "As long as I know you are alright nothing else matters."

He composed a poem to express his love for her, but the schmaltzy result proved he was better at stealing jewels than writing:

> *I have tried my darndest, to write a poem of cheer*
> *To the finest and sweetest little girl, my own dear;*
> *But words seem to fail me when I try to impart*
> *The true feeling I have for you deep in my heart.*

Weeks became months became years. Nineteen thirty-three drifted toward 1934. Nineteen thirty-five blurred into 1936, then faded into 1937. Hitler seized power in Germany. Prohibition was repealed. Police and federal agents ambushed and killed John Dillinger and Bonnie and Clyde. Bruno Richard Hauptmann was convicted of killing the Lindbergh baby after Dr. John Condon picked him out of a police lineup and identified him as "John," the man he had met to deliver the ransom. Amelia Earhart's plane vanished over the Pacific. The first vehicle crossed the Golden Gate Bridge. The airship *Hindenburg* crashed in flames.

Barry later recalled hearing prisoners who had reached the breaking point scream and shout as guards dragged them out of their cells and hauled them away to the prison hospital. In July 1933, an inmate named Diaz, who was lodged in a cell next to Barry's, flew into nighttime rages. He yelled, spewed threats, kicked walls. Guards ignored the racket, and Barry, unable to sleep, took matters into his own hands. As he passed Diaz in a corridor on the way to the exercise area, he punched him with his uncuffed fist and kicked him as he hit the floor before guards pulled him away. The nightly tantrums ceased.

Barry's punishment was a dozen days in a wing of dungeon-like cells that were even bleaker and more isolated from the world. The cells, separated from the rest of the segregation unit, were cold, bare concrete-walled closets—"ice boxes," inmates called them, since the men inside had been put "on ice." A bucket served as a toilet, and their occupants subsisted on a couple of slices of bread and a quart of water per day. It was the only disciplinary infraction, besides the escape, on Barry's Auburn record.

In 1937, Barry appealed to the state's commissioner of corrections to intervene and order Auburn's warden to end his time in segregation. He assured officials he was too old to try to escape again. On November 15, the request was granted. Barry survived the ordeal and later claimed he could have endured another five years in isolation. He could once again work and socialize with other inmates as he served his sentence. His time at Auburn, however, was over.

THIRTY-FIVE

"nO DICE"

Long Island and Attica, New York • 1937–49

A COLD RAIN WAS flecked with snowflakes on the day Arthur Barry got his first glimpse of Attica. The prison's thirty-foot reinforced concrete wall dwarfed the one he had jumped from at Auburn. It formed a cordon more than a mile long to enclose the prison grounds. A string of cupola-topped watchtowers poked skyward from the ramparts like the turrets of a storybook castle. One loomed above a main entrance framed by a gothic arch, as if it were the portal to a church instead of purgatory. The weather vane at its apex quivered in the brisk wind blowing in from Buffalo and Lake Erie, thirty-five miles to the west.

New York's newest state prison had opened in August 1931, in the wake of the Auburn riots, to relieve overcrowding in the prison system. "Nothing has been spared to assure decent living conditions for its inmates," noted a writer for the *New York Times*. Each forty-eight-square-foot cell had a toilet, a porcelain sink, electric lights, and its own radio. Light and fresh air flooded into the cells. The interiors of the cathedral-sized dining halls were decorated with arcades of limestone columns and featured forty-foot floor-to-ceiling windows. The kitchens were equipped with the latest appliances, including an electric potato peeler. There was grumbling in the press about prisoners enjoying the comforts of a modern hotel and living in a "convicts' paradise."

Critics decried the money spent on modern conveniences and architectural flourishes but not on Attica's state-of-the-art security measures. An automated system allowed guards to close rows of cellblocks with the turn of a crank. Inmates pushed a button to confirm they were in their cells when head counts were taken. The bars of each cell's door and window were made with hardened steel that would shatter a hacksaw blade. Tiers of cells, which faced open galleries in older prisons, were separated by concrete floors to make it tougher for inmates to communicate and incite disturbances or riots. The watchtowers were equipped with machine guns and searchlights.

Residents of Attica, a town of a few thousand, welcomed the influx of murderers, gangsters, bank robbers, and thieves that doubled the population—the prison was almost escape-proof (only seven inmates tried to flee during Attica's first fifteen years of operation, all while working outside the walls), and the new jobs and government money lifted the Depression's gloom. "Attica takes as much pride in it as Niagara Falls does in its cataract, and Gettysburg its battlefield," the *New York Times* claimed. On Barry's first Christmas Eve in Attica, carolers from local churches gathered in front of the prison to serenade the men inside.

The front gate at Attica, and one of the prison's cellblocks (Author Collection)

Conditions were light-years ahead of the state's older prisons, even better than in the rebuilt Auburn, leading one journalist to suggest that convicts regarded a transfer to Attica "more or less as a privilege." For Barry, after years in solitary confinement, it was a fresh start.

Attica's comforts and modern facilities, however, came with drawbacks. New York's prison system was struggling to cope with a surge of new inmates, and Attica was already overcrowded. "We frequently have trouble in finding room for newcomers," one guard admitted in 1937. A fourth cellblock, able to hold almost five hundred more inmates, was under construction but would not be ready for two years. "We may have to start putting them in tents," warden William Hunt complained. Barry would have been among the November arrivals who slept on cots in corridors until a cell became available, but it was better than being cooped up for twenty-three-hours a day.

Attica officials could do nothing to alleviate a more serious problem: the prison's remote location. To get there, visitors from New York City traveled 350 miles by car or bus across New Jersey and the northeast corner of Pennsylvania, or took more roundabout routes by highway or train. Soon after the prison opened, tear gas was used to quell small riots staged by inmates from the city who were upset at being cut off from family and friends. New York, journalist Tom Wicker would later note, banished its criminals to faraway prisons where "most were as effectively removed from their communities and families and jobs—if any—as if they had been swallowed by the sea." Attica was the most distant of these outposts.

Anna Blake's poor health and the cost of travel and hotels made the long journey especially difficult for her. She had moved in with her former boarder, Rudy Ganter, who had a home in Hempstead, on Long Island. Her son, Francis, now in his thirties and a boatswain's mate in the US Navy, lived with them. She underwent surgery at some point after Barry's transfer, but the operation failed to stop the spread of her cancer. She was admitted to a charity ward in Long Island's Meadowbrook Hospital on December 30, 1939.

As the end neared, Nassau County chief of detectives Harold King posted an officer at her bedside, hoping she might clear her conscience and reveal where Barry might have hidden any of the loot from his burglaries. Most of the stolen jewels had never been recovered, and a chance discovery,

six years earlier, had revived speculation that Barry had a fortune waiting for him when he was released from prison. In the spring of 1933, four
men digging a shallow trench for a sidewalk in Lake Ronkonkoma had
unearthed a gold mesh bag from under a tree root. Inside were thirty-three
pieces of jewelry, including a few pairs of cuff links, some shirt studs and
stick pins, and three gold rings. There were brooches and larger pieces as
well, but most of the gemstones had been removed, leaving only the gold
settings. The men tried to sell some of the pieces, but jewelers and pawnbrokers had no interest in the odds and ends. One of the workers gave his
share of the find to his children as playthings, and someone notified the
police. "Lake Ronkonkoma's treasure trove," as the *Daily News* called it,
was discovered only a few blocks from the bungalow the couple had shared.

Press reports claimed the cache was worth as much as $50,000, but
police soon downplayed the find. King consulted Fifth Avenue jewelers
and announced the items were castoffs worth no more than $3,000 as scrap
gold. It was still a significant amount, almost $63,000 today, and the police
had little difficulty linking the items to Arthur Barry and James Monahan.
A cigarette holder had been stolen during their raid on the Livermore
estate. They had liberated one of the brooches, which was now missing a
large central diamond, from the home of architect John Greenleaf in April
1927. State troopers had to seal off the area to hold back residents who
showed up armed with shovels, hoping to strike it rich. The authorities
hired laborers to dig up the area near the find but turned up nothing.

Was there more buried loot? King visited Blake in her hospital room a
couple of times. An insurance company, he told her, was offering a $24,000
reward for the recovery of jewelry taken in a burglary that was suspected to
be one of Barry's Long Island jobs. She could collect the money and leave
it to her son in her will, the detective noted.

Blake's reply was curt.

"No dice."

~~~~~~~~~~

A GUARD APPROACHED Barry as he played chess in the exercise yard. It
was April 29, 1940. Blake, he was told, had died at 2:35 that morning. She
was fifty-one. The woman he loved, the woman he had gone to prison to

protect, and broken out of prison to be with, the woman who had remained loyal to him until the end, was gone. He was almost the last to know—the news was already appearing in the evening papers.

Grace Robinson, who had interviewed Barry when he told his life story back in 1932, broke the news of the death of "the trusted wife of Arthur Barry" to readers of the *Daily News*. If there was a cache of stolen gems, she noted, it was now "as irretrievably lost as Capt. Kidd's treasure."

A telegram arrived from King, who feared an escape attempt—and new attacks on the homes of Nassau County's wealthy residents—if Barry were to be allowed to attend her funeral. Prison officials brushed aside his opposition, and two guards accompanied him to the funeral home in Queens. He was allowed to view her body, and his handcuffs were removed so he could kneel beside her casket.

She was buried alongside her first husband, Frank Blake, in Gate of Heaven Cemetery in Hawthorne, Westchester County, within a half dozen miles of some of the homes and estates Barry had burgled years before in Ardsley and Irvington. She had so little money that Nassau County covered the funeral expenses.

Police officers rummaging through her effects later found one of Barry's letters to her from prison. "All my heart's love to you," he had written, "the sweetest and truest pal in the world."

MANY OF ATTICA's inmates, like Barry, were veterans of the Great War. With the world engulfed in a new war, they were eager to pitch in. Men who earned as little as five cents a day in the prison shops raised more than $800 for a war relief fund in 1940. After the attack on Pearl Harbor plunged the United States into the fight, convicts gave up cigarettes and candy and set aside enough pocket change to buy $1,000 worth of war bonds. Barry was later identified as a leader of the fundraising efforts. Attica's convicts worked double shifts in the prison's textile shops to produce cotton material for the armed forces, earning praise and a certificate from the War Production Board. "The only regret we have is that we cannot serve personally in the armed forces and help get this thing over quickly," George Mason said when he accepted the honor on behalf of his fellow inmates in 1943. That year, prisoners purchased more than $6,000 in war bonds, raising the bulk of the money in just forty-eight hours.

PRISON IS THEIR STOPPING PLACE...BUT THEY'RE IN RED CROSS GALLON CLUB

Posing here for the first newspaper picture ever taken of convicts in Attica Prison are the seven members of the Regional Blood Center's "Gallon Club" from that institution. The prison, according to the Red Cross, has a blood-giving record in war and peace unmatched by any other similar place. From left here are Howard Nigley, Ernest Hobbs, Arthur T. Barry, Joseph Baumann, Richard Walters, Peter Martin, Everett Joseph, studying Attica's donation records.

Barry and other Attica inmates receiving recognition for their generous blood donations
(*Democrat and Chronicle*, Rochester—USA Today Network)

They also rolled up their sleeves to save lives on the battlefield. In 1942, inmates asked a blood bank in Rochester to send its mobile collection unit to the prison. It was soon making regular visits, and by March 1945 had collected almost fifty-five hundred pints for the Red Cross. "While the inmates themselves are deprived of liberty, they have not lost the inherent American love for liberty and the American way of life," Warden Hunt told the press.

Barry was a regular donor and became a member of the prison's Gallon Club, a group of inmates who had given at least eight pints. After the war, when seven members of the club posed for a photograph published on the front page of the Rochester *Democrat and Chronicle*, Barry stood in the center of the group, his thick hair now snow-white. A reporter asked the men why they were so generous. "Well, let's just say that we're trying to make up for our previous bad habits," one joked. "I gave a pint of blood to a buddy once, in the first World War," said another, "when I had to lie down beside him in the battlefield to do it, and I know how much it means."

Barry was a model prisoner. He served more than a decade in Attica without a single disciplinary infraction. *Exemplary* was the word a judge would later use to describe his conduct. Prison officials considered him a good influence on the younger inmates he took under his wing. He was put in charge of the prison laundry, where one of his duties was to issue uniforms to new inmates as they arrived.

In February 1948, Attica reached a milestone. Barry handed a uniform to the ten thousandth inmate to pass through the main gate. That month, he launched a bid to win his freedom.

THIRTY-SIX

"EASY COME, EASY GO"

Mineola, New York • 1949

THE GATE AT the base of Attica's main tower swung open. Arthur Barry stepped into a tense Cold War world on the cusp of the 1950s, where sobering news of atom bombs and missile tests hogged the front pages. A tweed suit and heavy overcoat shielded him from the chill of a stiff late-fall breeze. The no-longer-fashionable newsboy cap covering his snow-capped head marked him as a man out of his time. It was November 15, 1949. He had been paroled after nineteen years behind bars, only to find his past was waiting for him.

Three Nassau County detectives took him into custody. Captain Howard DeMott produced a half dozen arrest warrants based on long-forgotten twenty-two-year-old indictments still on file at the courthouse in Mineola. While Barry had been serving time for robbing the Livermores, charges of burglary and theft from other homes had been lying in wait like paper time bombs, ready to detonate the moment he was released. That moment had come.

Barry's right wrist was handcuffed to one of the cops who would escort him back to the county where he committed so many of his crimes. As the group walked to a car, reporters who had turned up to record the event lobbed questions at America's most famous jewel thief.

"There's nothing much I can say," was his polite reply. "I'd just like to forget the whole thing."

The sun blinked through gaps in the cloud cover as they drove toward Long Island. Barry looked out the window at a world that was both familiar and as futuristic as science fiction. The cars and trucks whizzing past and the airplanes droning overhead were sleeker and faster than the ones he remembered. Earlier that year, the crew of a Boeing B-50 bomber named *Lucky Lady II* completed the first nonstop flight around the world, returning to a Texas air base after ninety-four hours in the air. The first passenger jet, the de Havilland Comet, completed test flights that summer as a new age of commercial air travel dawned. Barry's prediction when he was first sent to prison, however, had not come to pass. Airplanes had not replaced the automobile.

He had a request. The driver pulled over at a roadside bar. There was something Barry wanted to see, a technological wonder that had been introduced to the public just before the Livermore heist ended his high-flying career. This device now could be found in almost one out of ten American homes. His escorts took him inside to watch television.

~~~~~~~~~~~~~~

BARRY HAD BEEN fighting to get out of prison for almost two years. He filed a court action in 1948 that challenged the state's byzantine sentencing rules and claimed he had the right to apply for early release. A judge of the New York Supreme Court agreed, and ruled he had been entitled to apply for parole "for some time." When parole was granted in November 1949, the authorities in Nassau County dug out the old indictments in a last-ditch bid to put him back in prison. Barry, the *Daily News* noted, would have to confront "the evil ghosts of his wild old days."

Barry mailed a letter to the county's district attorney, Frank Gulotta, pleading for the revived charges to be withdrawn. "God knows I have paid a penalty for my wrongs. That the parole people have released me is proof enough of this," he wrote. He begged to be allowed to return home to Worcester "for what little peace I can find. I am grateful to God for sparing me to see the hour of my freedom. I am depending upon your fairness and mercy to make it a sure and quick reality."

Gulotta, the forty-two-year-old son of Italian immigrants, was in the early years of a legal career that would take him to the Court of Appeals, the state's highest court. A fellow judge later summed him up in three words: "hardworking, gregarious and meticulous." While Barry fought the Second World War with blood donations and war bonds, Gulotta was a major in the US Army and took part in the invasions that drove the Nazis out of North Africa and his parents' homeland; at one point, he served as military governor of a large swath of Italy. Facing prejudice and stigma for much of his life—when he was being vetted for a judgeship, he was asked point-blank if he was a member of the Mafia—he had honed his sense of

Barry, back in Mineola to face decades-old theft indictments after he was paroled in 1949 (Bettmann Archive via Getty Images)

right and wrong. As a prosecutor, he had a reputation, the *Daily News* noted, as "hard-driving and gutsy, but always remaining a gentleman." An assistant district attorney for eleven years, he had taken over the top job only a few months before he was called on to decide Barry's fate.

The indictments accused Barry of larceny, burglary, and receiving stolen goods in connection with three heists between 1925 and 1927, from the homes of polo legend Thomas Hitchcock, architect John Greenleaf, and Harold Talbott, an aviation industry leader who would be appointed secretary of the air force in 1953. There were, as well, leftover allegations of theft and burglary arising from the Livermore break-in. "I don't know what I can do with them," Gulotta admitted in the press.

If Barry pleaded not guilty and stood trial, it would be difficult to convict him after so much time had passed. The lead investigator, Harold King, had resigned in disgrace in 1945 after he was indicted on charges of conspiracy and attempted bribery; he was accused of offering fifty dollars to a subordinate to protect an illegal gambling joint. King was acquitted at trial, but his career was over. Elvin Edwards, who had prosecuted Barry in 1927—and acted as defense counsel for his former "right hand man," King, when the bribery allegation surfaced—passed away in 1946. Private detective Val O'Farrell, who had been instrumental in Barry's arrest at Lake Ronkonkoma, died of a stroke in 1934, at fifty-eight, while interviewing one of his wealthy clients. Other detectives who had investigated the Long Island jewel theft cases were retired or dead, and robbery victims and witnesses had moved or died. Stock market wizard Jesse Livermore, who was forced into bankruptcy during the Depression, shot himself in the cloakroom of a Manhattan hotel in 1940. "My life has been a failure," said a note he left behind, and he was "tired of fighting."

Barry spent the night of his arrest in the Nassau County jail. The next day, Gulotta and King's replacement as chief of detectives, Stuyvesant Pinnell, questioned him for six hours. They wanted to know if there were hidden jewels he had waited all these years to recover. "If there was so much as a cuff link," he assured them, "I would tell you to try to prove that I have learned my lesson and that I am willing to cooperate." He had fenced all his loot, he said, and the money was long gone. "It was easy come, easy go in those days. We sold the stuff as fast as we got it and then gambled away the money," he told Gulotta. "Honestly, I'm surprised to know now what some of it was worth, especially when I think back on the little bit we got for it." After some jobs, he recalled, he blew $15,000 or more in a single night and had to bum a few dollars for cab fare to get home. "If you laugh when you win, you can't cry when you lose."

"Barry is a changed man," Gulotta told reporters after the session. He had agreed to plead guilty to every charge in all six indictments. In return, the district attorney would recommend that the judge impose a suspended sentence. "I feel that if the man hasn't learned his lesson by now he never will. I feel the humane thing to do is to give him an opportunity to live right."

A week later, when he stood before Judge Henry Collins, Barry was as dapper as he had been when he had appeared in the same courtroom twenty-two years earlier, in 1927. In his gray pin-striped suit, blue shirt, and diagonal-striped necktie, "Barry easily could double for a bank president or a steamship magnate," noted one of the reporters on hand. Another journalist said he could have been "a respected citizen, a leader, had it not been for his passion for wealth that was waiting to be taken."

Judge Collins—lauded as "conscientious, honest, and fair," someone "who loved God and his fellow man"—accepted Gulotta's recommendation, imposed a suspended sentence, and set Barry free. He would be under the supervision of parole officers until 1962, the judge reminded him, and if he broke the law again, he would be thrown back in prison. "Though you may have spent about one-third of your life in custody, and though you may have some sorrows secret to yourself, society demands that your behavior be acceptable for you to continue your liberty."

Barry walked out of the courtroom and into the autumn sunshine with about sixty dollars in his pocket and a small bundle of belongings under one arm. A car with two women inside—one of them was likely his younger sister, Lucy Manning, who had agreed to take him in—was waiting outside the courthouse. He jumped into the back seat and waved to reporters as the car pulled away.

It was a long drive to Worcester, 180 miles away, but they made a detour to Gate of Heaven Cemetery before leaving the state. In his first hours of freedom, Barry visited his wife's grave.

THIRTY-SEVEN

AN HONEST MAN

Worcester, Massachusetts • 1949–61

THE JOB PAID fifty dollars a week, and Arthur Barry could usually count on fifteen-cent tips from customers. He made sandwiches, waited on tables, and manned the cash register at the Montrose Dairy, a busy roadside restaurant in Worcester. Few patrons realized the avuncular man in the checked shirt, necktie, and apron, peering at them through thick-lensed half-frame glasses, was a legendary criminal.

After his release, Barry moved in with his sister Lucy and her husband, Thomas Manning, a Worcester firefighter, and their two children. Lucy Manning was about three years younger than Barry, and they had stayed in touch; she visited him during his years in Attica, sometimes bringing along her young son. He moved into the Mannings' large apartment on Park Avenue on Worcester's west side, on the top floor of a wood-framed three-story building with shops on the ground floor. It was about two miles across town from the Perry Avenue three-decker where he grew up. His parents had died while he was in prison—his father in 1932, the year of his capture in New Jersey, and his mother in 1941.

There was a chain of four Montrose restaurants in the area and one of the owners, a friend of Barry's from childhood, took a chance and offered him a job. Soon, he was entrusted with tallying up the day's proceeds, bundling banknotes and rolls of coins into a leather briefcase, and taking the money to the bank for deposit. "The townspeople began to accept me

Front Street, Worcester, in the 1950s (Worcester Historical Museum Collection)

as a completely reformed man," he noted. "Arthur Barry, the daring jewel thief, was now Arthur Barry the aging ex-convict."

Worcester police officers who knew all about his checkered past were surprised, but relieved that he was causing them no further headaches. "I never thought I would live to see the day but I have seen it, and there's no doubt of it," one told a visiting journalist. "He's an honest man."

~~~~~~~~~

FEATURE STORIES ON Barry's stranger-than-fiction past continued to surface in newspapers and magazines. COUNTRY'S SUPER THIEF READY TO GO STRAIGHT was the headline on a full-page article published in a Tennessee paper soon after his release. The *World's News*, published in Sydney, Australia, included him—along with bank robber Willie Sutton and 1920s bandit Gerald Chapman—on a short list of American crooks "as notorious for their charm . . . as for their daring robberies." There were predictions that Hollywood would soon come calling. "Wonder how many film companies are fighting for the right to film the story of the life of Arthur Barry, the fabulous crook?" mused a columnist for Long Island's *Newsday*. Memories of the Roaring Twenties and the Great Depression were fading; America had just emerged from the horrors of the Second

World War and was waging a new, cold one against the Soviet Union. Barry's crimes were a throwback to what seemed like a more glamorous, more innocent time.

Coronet magazine, a *Reader's Digest*–style monthly published by the founders of *Esquire*, weighed in with the story of "the No. 1 criminal of the age" in 1952. It ran alongside illustrated features on Pope Pius XII and a new postwar phenomenon, flying saucers. "From now on," Barry was quoted as saying, "I want to live a life as far removed as possible from my old one." Writer Henry Lee, drawing on press reports, recounted Barry's jewel-stealing exploits for the magazine's half million readers and wondered aloud if the "arch-crook" was harboring a secret—"the location of a long-hunted cache of stolen jewels." Long Island authorities had mounted a recent search, he revealed, using metal detectors to scour Barry's old Lake Ronkonkoma neighborhood; it appeared nothing had been found.

In 1956, *Life* magazine staff writer Robert Wallace convinced him to open up about his past. The magazine, one of the most popular and influential in America, had almost six million subscribers that year and an estimated readership of more than seventy-five million. "Getting on the cover of *Life*," noted one study of the magazine's impact, "was considered the pinnacle of postwar success." A headline for the feature on Barry—A THIEF WHO STOLE $10 MILLION IN JEWELS TELLS HOW HE DID IT— appeared on the cover, alongside a photograph of President Dwight D. Eisenhower, who had just announced he would run for a second term.

"The greatest jewel thief who ever lived," Wallace revealed, was now "a reputable and popular citizen" in his hometown. He was no longer on parole—supervision to ensure that he was living up to the terms of his release had ended early, in recognition of his good behavior—and he was free to talk about his career as "an incomparable second story man." Wallace explained the term for readers more familiar with the single-floor suburban homes of the '50s than the mansions of the Jazz Age. "There was a time," he noted, when second-story men "were aristocrats among thieves, and Barry himself was a king."

Barry described his methods and told of crashing Long Island parties in a tuxedo so he could memorize the layouts of the mansions and grounds in advance of future nocturnal visits. "Wealthy matrons, awakening at night to find him puttering about their bedrooms," Wallace claimed, "often failed to scream" when they saw the handsome intruder.

Barry gave a blow-by-blow description of the Livermore robbery, but he would only discuss how he "thought" the Rockefeller mansion had been burgled. The article described the theft of the Donahue pearls from a Plaza Hotel suite and the jewelry taken from the Cosdens and the Mountbattens during the Prince of Wales's visit in 1924, but there was no admission that Barry was the culprit.

Surprisingly, then, he cast himself in a starring role in the Auburn escape. He had sprayed a guard in the face with ammonia and fired a gun in the air to incite the riot, he claimed, even though numerous witnesses had confirmed these were the actions of his fellow escapee George Small.

Barry working the cash register at a Worcester diner after his release (Author Collection)

The article featured then-and-now photographs of a dapper Barry handcuffed to a detective in 1927 and an older, stouter, and bespectacled Barry carrying the restaurant's daily deposit to the bank in a briefcase.

Two years later, Barry's tales of high-class larceny caught the eye of Neil Hickey, a twenty-seven-year-old New York-based writer for the *American Weekly*, a Hearst Corporation magazine distributed in the Sunday editions of newspapers nationwide. His story was a good fit for a magazine that offered a mix of celebrity profiles, self-help advice, and what a Hearst biographer termed "pseudo-scientific pieces" on subjects ranging from child rearing to how to "dream your way" through college.

In January 1959, the magazine ran Hickey's two-part feature, presented in Barry's own words. He again stopped short of confessing to the Cosden, Mountbatten, Rockefeller, and Donahue thefts. "Those felonies stand on the books today as unsolved and naturally I deny all knowledge of them," he teased. He presented himself, in his heyday, as a polite, businesslike, and gracious criminal. "The bandits of the Old West were colorful, to be sure, but—by my own standards—a distasteful lot, singularly uninventive and almost wholly disorganized."

He spoke candidly of how easy money and fast living had lured him into a life of crime. "My tastes were expensive and I was forced to carry on a heavy volume of thefts to pay for them," he explained. One day, he'd known, he was bound to be caught. "But my successes emboldened me," he said. "Soon there was no turning back. I was, to paraphrase the ancient Chinese proverb, on the tiger's back and unable to get off." His crimes had cost him his freedom and destroyed his chance for a life with Anna Blake. Looking back, he said, "I've wished a thousand times that someone had punished me severely the first time I ever broke the law."

The features became the basis for a book-length biography. Holt, Rinehart & Winston released Hickey's *The Gentleman Was a Thief: The Colorful Story of Arthur Barry, a 1920's Rogue* in the summer of 1961. "Arthur Barry was the most successful jewel thief in U.S. criminal history," the first-time author declared at the outset of the book. Hickey, who had broken into journalism while in college, had already profiled such luminaries as author Vladimir Nabokov and actor Paul Newman.

He researched news reports of Barry's crimes, and they met for follow-up interviews. Hickey had served in the navy during the Korean War, and the veterans of different conflicts seemed to hit it off.

He coaxed Barry into confessing to the Cosden, Mountbatten, Donahue, and Rockefeller thefts and describing how he pulled off each of these brazen heists. The book captured Barry's audacity and daring. "Only a criminal with a sense of irony could have imagined the plans for some of these crimes, many of which bear the mark of bizarre practical jokes rather than the felonies they are," Hickey wrote. Yes, the author conceded, his deeds were "lawless and indefensible." Yes, he had carried a gun and he had been ready to use it. And, yes, he had broken out of prison under cover of a bloody riot. But "in an age of rascals," Hickey argued, a clever, debonair thief who preyed only on the rich "stood out."

Both Barry and Hickey downplayed James Monahan's role in his crimes. Barry had been careful never to name him while he was in prison, for fear Monahan's friends or other convicts would target him as a rat. Even though the *American Weekly* articles appeared long after Barry's release, he insisted on referring to his Livermore accomplice by a made-up name, Ryan.

After Monahan's death in 1960, he finally felt free to identify him. But Boston Billy plays a minor role in the book. There is no mention of the fatal shooting at a Connecticut dance hall in 1922, when Barry went to jail to protect Monahan from a murder charge. And while the pair had known each other for years and had joined forces to burgle dozens of homes before 1927, Barry is portrayed as a "lone wolf" in the book. He refused to share the spotlight with his former friend turned bitter enemy.

The Gentleman Was a Thief earned mostly positive reviews, and a hardcover edition was published in Britain the following year. "Smooth thieves like Arthur Barry" and the "fantastically daring" burglaries he pulled off, a *New York Times* review noted, were "a rarity in this era of organized crime." The *Nashville Banner*'s reviewer found himself rooting for the villain and predicted readers would be "extremely happy that Barry is successful against the odds." An Iowa paper was amazed the book was a work of nonfiction: "This true story reads like fiction."

A few reviewers, however, griped that Hickey's sympathetic portrayal glorified crime. One felt the gentleman thief had not expressed sufficient "remorse or repentance," while another complained that "Barry appears almost heroic or, at worst, an old rogue or rascal." *New York Times* crime reporter Emanuel Perlmutter, who wrote the paper's review, was the most critical. "There is no censure for Barry's many crimes, but evident admiration for his skill as a thief and his intelligence and personal charm. Many readers may not share this appraisal of the life of a criminal."

Then, Mike Wallace's people called. Wallace, already a veteran TV announcer and game show host, fronted a late-night ABC interview program, *PM East*, that went head-to-head each weeknight with NBC's popular *Jack Paar Show*. "It's TV that's fresh and new and worth looking into" promised an advertisement when the show debuted in 1961. Barbra Streisand, an early guest, became a regular, and the exposure helped to launch her career. The July 24 episode, "The Criminal," featured Wallace's interview with Arthur Barry, along with Frank O'Leary, another New York jewel thief. O'Leary had been sent to Sing Sing in the 1930s for robbing an actress; paroled in 1948, he reinvented himself as a freelance writer and the compiler of a dictionary of underworld slang. Barry was promoting Hickey's book, which had been released a couple of weeks earlier.

The former thieves swapped stories of their exploits, their long terms in prison, and their transitions to life on the outside. It turned out they had known each other in Prohibition-era Manhattan but neither had suspected they were both in the jewel-stealing business. O'Leary and an accomplice had posed as messengers delivering flowers to get inside the actress's home, tied her up, and made off with $13,000 in jewelry. Barry told Wallace about his night on the town with the Prince of Wales and his cloak-and-dagger dealings with private detective Noel Scaffa after he swiped the Donahue pearls. He explained how he had brought a female dog to one estate to distract the watchdogs patrolling the grounds. A television broadcast was the first thing Barry had wanted to see the day he was released from Attica; a dozen years later, he was on the screen.

"It was evident that the two men took quiet satisfaction in some of their deeds, relishing the details," the *Boston's Globe*'s television critic,

Percy Shain, wrote of the segment. The banter between the "two paunchy gentlemen—not at all the Cary Grant type," he said, was proof there was little glamour in stealing jewels. "They appeared more like retired bartenders or perhaps storekeepers than ex-aces of the light fingered gentry."

"What did it get them?" Shain asked. "A few years of high living," followed by many more in prison. "Today," he said, "they're reformed . . . glad to be out of the racket, scratching out a living but undeniably in their declining years."

Barry took a final bow in the celebrity spotlight on November 16, 1964, when he appeared on *The Tonight Show* with Johnny Carson, alongside singer and actress Rosemary Clooney and stand-up comic Milt Kamen. Carson put him on the spot; like the journalists, detectives, and district attorneys who had followed Barry's career, he was curious to know what had happened to all that money and all those jewels. He had received "only about 10 percent of the value of everything" he stole, Barry insisted. And the small fortune he did reap from his burglaries, he assured Carson and his viewers, was long gone.

UNCLE ARTIE

Worcester, Massachusetts • 1962–81

I T WAS THE late 1960s, and Sean Galliher was just a kid, but he remembers the day he was caught in a downpour with his great-uncle, Arthur Barry. They ducked into a grocery store to get empty boxes to use as makeshift umbrellas as they hurried home. Sean's father had recently died, and his mother, Mary, often invited Barry—her godfather as well as her uncle—to visit them in Buffalo. When the rain-soaked duo reached the house, there was no one home and neither of them had a key.

Barry went out back, fetched a stepladder, and put it under a locked window. As Galliher looked on, he fished a quarter from his pocket, angled it toward the latch, and in a flash the window was open. "I don't know what he did or how he did it, but it worked," Galliher recalled in 2023. "Every time I saw him, I wondered how he got in that damn window."

Years later, while rummaging through a closet in search of a book to read, he found his mother's copy of *The Gentleman Was a Thief.* As he flipped the pages, he was astonished to see his great-uncle's photograph—and to learn, for the first time, about his incredible career as a jewel thief.

"That's how he did it," he said. "He was a professional." Galliher, a lawyer in Los Angeles, who's now in his early sixties, may be the last person to have seen Arthur Barry at work. "I actually saw him break into a place."

~~~~~~~~~

BARRY'S GRANDNEPHEWS AND grandnieces adored him. With no children of his own, Barry doted on the younger members of his extended family. "He was a great guy," said Galliher—smart and kind, chatty, fun to be with. "He was one of those interesting Irish guys who could tell a bunch of stories." At family weddings and gatherings at Christmas and Thanksgiving, he would be the one with an audience gathered around him, laughing and hanging on his words.

"We loved him. He was great," Galliher's cousin Mary Schumacher, Lucy Manning's granddaughter, said over the telephone from her home in Denver. Her family visited Worcester often when she was growing up, and she remembers the man she called Uncle Artie settling disputes as she played with her sister or surprising them with a magic trick. Thomas Manning had died shortly after Schumacher was born, she added, and "he was the closest thing to a grandfather that I had."

Galliher's cousins often remark on how much he looks like his famous great-uncle. He has the same thick silver-tinged hair, square jaw, and easy smile. His sense of humor is just as dry, and his rich, husky voice, they say, sounds like Barry's. They even had similar military careers—Galliher served as a medic in the US Navy for eight years before embarking on a legal career that has taken him to courtrooms and boardrooms in New York and California. "Obviously," he joked, "we took different vocational paths."

Barry told stories about the "chaos and hell" of the Great War, Galliher recalls, describing how he dragged wounded men off the battlefield and was burned by mustard gas. "He was lucky he was alive," Galliher said. But he brushed aside questions that might expose his life of crime. He mentioned he had spent time in "a government hotel" or "away at school," but the meaning eluded his young listeners. Galliher once asked him about a strange scar on his shoulder. "I just hurt it when I was younger," was all Barry would tell him. It was a gunshot wound, a souvenir of his escape from Auburn.

Even when Galliher was older and knew about Barry's exploits, he was told never to ask him about them. After the magazine articles and Hickey's book appeared and Barry was once again a celebrity criminal, Galliher remembers, his past remained a taboo subject at home. One of Barry's sisters was married to a prominent Worcester attorney and another was a high school principal in the city, and Schumacher says neither wanted to hear about his lawless previous life. "They were trying to live respectable lives," Schumacher noted.

Barry knew he had hurt and embarrassed those closest to him. "As you can see," he had said when he was released from prison in 1949, "I'm the black sheep."

When Schumacher was about eleven, she realized she had no idea what her favorite uncle had done for a living. "He's a retired what?" she asked her parents. They filled her in but told her not to mention his past to anyone in the family, not even Barry. It was "a sore subject," she remembers being told. "Don't bring it up."

Over the years, other jewel thieves adopted Barry's methods and claimed them as innovations of their own. They too scanned the press for news of the rich and photographs of women flaunting their jewels. "To a thief," said one of his disciples, who targeted Hollywood stars and other notables from the 1960s to the 1980s, the society pages "read like advertising brochures." Some, like Barry, crashed high-society parties or followed women decked out in jewels back to their mansions or penthouse apartments as they planned break-ins. Gerard Graham Dennis cruised Westchester County in the 1940s on the lookout for homes with "big lawns and Cadillacs parked in the driveway."

Today, Barry's successors monitor the social media posts of celebrities to find out who has jewels worth taking. In 2016, Kim Kardashian flooded her Instagram account with images of her bling in the weeks before two armed men broke into her Paris hotel room and robbed her of jewelry worth $10 million.

As the years passed—and to the relief of some members of his family—Barry's fame receded. A 1964 *New York Times* feature on jewel thieves, the "aristocrats of crime," was one of the few times his name resurfaced in the press. Schumacher became the Manning clan's genealogist, and as she assembled her family tree, she learned more about his life. "I always told people my uncle was a really cool jewel thief," she says. "And nobody'd ever heard of him."

~~~~~~~~~~

As BARRY SETTLED into his life in Worcester, he sought out the company of fellow veterans. His battlefield wounds in France made him eligible to join the Military Order of the Purple Heart, which supported disabled vets and their families and helped them to file compensation and pension claims. President John F. Kennedy was a member. When a Worcester chapter was formed in 1963, Barry served on the executive committee. Each November 11, he marched in the Veterans Day parade to the war memorial in Lincoln Square. In 1975, during a postparade dinner in the Grand Army of the Republic Hall—located, appropriately, on Pearl Street—the Worcester Veteran's Council named him the city's veteran of the year, in recognition of "his work for and with veterans."

The dapper thief who had once donned evening wear so he could crash parties and case mansions, Schumacher recalls, often lounged in the Park Avenue apartment in slacks and a tank-top undershirt. "We called it an Artie vest," she chuckles. The reformed gambler who had blown thousands of dollars in a single night of shooting craps preferred a friendly game of cards at the local Veterans of Foreign Wars post. When her family was staying over, Schumacher said, the Broadway plunger who had been a fixture in Manhattan nightclubs and speakeasies during the Roaring Twenties often picked up a box of doughnuts on his way home from a card game, to be shared over a pot of tea.

Barry outlived not only Val O'Farrell but most of the other detectives who were once on his trail. His most relentless pursuer, Harold King, died of a stroke in 1956, on Barry's sixtieth birthday. A week later, Gordon Hurley, the Nassau County detective who took part in his arrest at Lake Ronkonkoma and later captured James Monahan, killed himself with his .38-caliber police revolver; he had been in poor health for a year. Noel Scaffa stood trial for the offense of compounding a felony—a result of the handsome fee he had paid Barry to recover the pearls stolen from James and Jessie Donahue's Plaza Hotel suite—and was acquitted in 1928. Seven years later, he was accused of collusion with Florida jewel thieves, jailed for six months for perjury, and stripped of his private detective's license. The Great Retriever was fifty-three when he died of a heart attack in 1941.

And Barry was still standing after many of the famous people he had known or robbed were gone. The Prince of Wales, proclaimed King Edward VIII in 1936, abdicated within a year so he could marry American divorcée Wallis Simpson, proving that he—like Barry, his onetime guide to Manhattan's nightlife—was willing to sacrifice everything for the woman he loved. Reinvented as the Duke of Windsor, the former monarch served as governor of the Bahamas during World War II and died in 1972. Lady Edwina Mountbatten passed away in 1960, and Irish Republican Army bombers assassinated her husband in 1979. Tulsa oilman and social climber Joshua Cosden, who entertained the prince at his Long Island mansion in 1924, was wiped out in the Depression and died of a heart attack in 1940. James Donahue died by suicide in 1931 at age forty-four. "Society's greatest gambler," as the *Daily News* called him, swallowed poison after locking himself in a bathroom. His widow, Jessie Donahue, heiress to the Woolworth fortune, outlived him by four decades; she died in 1971 at her Fifth Avenue home, a half dozen blocks from the Plaza Hotel. Percy Rockefeller lost millions in the stock market crash—a pittance, given his vast fortune—and was just fifty-six when he died in 1934, after a long illness. Jimmy Hines, the Tammany chieftain who befriended Barry and Blake at the Monongahela Club, was convicted in 1939 of using his political clout to protect Dutch Schultz and other racketeers, served five years in Sing Sing, and died in 1957 at the age of eighty.

James Monahan spent almost three decades in Clinton Prison, and was in and out of solitary confinement for an array of offenses, from minor infractions such as stealing ice cream to defying guards and fighting with other inmates. Press reports over the years claimed, erroneously, that he was insane or had died. He was paroled in 1956, only to be scooped up and imprisoned in Massachusetts to serve time for the auto theft conviction that had been hanging over his head since his escape in 1921. He was released in 1958 at age sixty and returned to Worcester "an old, embittered, befogged man," by one account, and unable to find a job. If all the treasure in the world was piled on the Worcester Common, "just ready for the taking," he told a reporter after his release, "I wouldn't cross the street to look at it." When he died in 1960, he was a resident of the Belmont Home for the Indigent, a refuge for the destitute. The *New York Times* and *Time* magazine took note of Monahan's death, but the obituary writers confused him with Barry. The thuggish, defiant Monahan was transformed into a charming gentleman jewel thief known for his "flawless attire and courtly manner," who had "mingled gracefully" with New York's elite. While he and Barry had lived in the same city for two years, it appears they never met again.

Barry had at least one unexpected encounter with a person from his past. He was concerned about "the problem of wayward youth," he noted in a magazine interview, and wanted to warn teenagers about how easily they could be seduced, as he had been, into a life of crime. He spoke to church groups about juvenile delinquency, and when a parent-teacher association on Long Island invited him to speak about the hard lessons he had learned, he accepted. He was standing outside the venue, smoking a cigarette as people filed in, when a woman approached. She knew his name, but he did not recognize her. When she mentioned a long-ago robbery and "a rather gallant burglar," he realized who it was.

Dorothea Livermore, he likely knew from the papers, had faced demons of her own. After divorcing Jesse Livermore in 1932, she had moved to California with their sons. Three years later, during an argument with her oldest boy, Jesse Livermore Jr., she shot and nearly killed the sixteen-year-old. She was drunk, and he began downing liquor as an act of defiance—"to get sodden drunk," he explained later, "so Mother will know how it looks and will stop her drinking." She screamed, "I'd rather see you dead than drinking!" before finding a rifle and almost making good on her threat. She was prosecuted for assault with intent to kill, but a court eventually dismissed the charge.

That night on Long Island, as she listened to the former thief who had treated her with kindness and had returned the rings she cherished, Dorothea Livermore blew him a kiss.

―――――――――

IN THE MID-1970S, when Lucy Manning relocated to California, Barry moved in with his sister Rita, who lived in a small house on Mill Street that overlooked a lake. Her husband had died in 1924, and she never remarried. Now retired from her post as a school principal, she was no longer as concerned about the stigma of her older brother's past. "They reconciled," noted Mary Schumacher.

On July 15, 1981, after spending a hot, sunny afternoon puttering in the yard, Arthur Barry retreated to his room at about five o'clock for a nap before dinner. When his sister went in an hour later to awaken him, he was dead. Barry, who had survived being gassed in the Great War, being shot while escaping prison, and years in solitary confinement, was in good health until he died. The funeral was held at Worcester's St. Charles Borromeo Church, and he was buried in the Manning family plot at nearby St. John Cemetery, 150 miles from the grave of his wife, Anna Blake. He was eighty-four.

"I am not good at drawing morals," Barry told *Life* magazine in 1956, "but I would like to say this. When I was a young man I had many assets. I was not only intelligent, I was clever. I got along well with people on any level and, if I do say so, I had guts. I could have gone anywhere—to Wall Street, maybe—and made an honest fortune."

He wanted the magazine's readers to understand how much he regretted the choices he had made. The allure of jewels and easy money and living at the speed of the Jazz Age had exacted a terrible toll: Nineteen years of his life wasted in prison, five of them in the hell of solitary confinement. More than three years on the run, knowing he could be caught at any minute. The years of separation from Anna Blake. The heartbreak of being unable to care for or comfort her in her final years.

"When you put down all those burglaries," he told interviewer Robert Wallace, "be sure you put the big one at the top. Not Arthur Barry robbed Jesse Livermore, or Arthur Barry robbed the cousin of the King of England, but just Arthur Barry robbed Arthur Barry."

ACKNOWLEDGMENTS

WHILE ARTHUR BARRY preferred to work alone, even a master jewel thief needed an accomplice now and then. Authors, too, tend to be loners, but they rely on the kindness and patience of others, especially when researching and writing during a pandemic. I'm grateful to everyone who helped to put this book into your hands.

In Nassau County, court assistant Sue Chung of the Tenth Judicial District, and Cheryl A. Max, in the Office of the Nassau County Clerk in Mineola, tracked down records of burglary charges filed against Barry and James Monahan. Kevin C. King searched for Nassau County District Attorney's Office records of these prosecutions. Kim Jeffrey of the Westchester County District Attorney's Office, Jackie Graziano of the Westchester County Archives, and Nick Brilis of the Yonkers Police Historical Society fielded my requests for information about Barry's thefts in that county.

Eirini Melena Karoutsos of the New York City Municipal Archives located records of Noel Scaffa's prosecution for helping Barry to unload his loot from the Plaza Hotel heist. Susan Bigelow of the Connecticut State Library in Hartford found files that revealed Barry's role in a 1922 shooting outside a Bridgeport dance hall. In Pittsfield, Massachusetts, court clerk John D. Lizzo and Erin Hunt, curator of the Berkshire County Historical Society, fielded my requests for information about Barry's theft conviction there in 1914. Wendy Essery of the Worcester Historical Museum helped me to access local press coverage of Barry and his crimes, as did Claire Drone-Silvers and Amber De Angelis at the Boston Public Library.

I researched Barry's 1929 escape from Auburn Prison and the riot that followed with the assistance of Nicole Westerdahl and Madelaine

Thomas of the Special Collections Research Center at Syracuse University Libraries, Karyn Radcliffe at the Cayuga Museum of History and Art in Auburn, and Lin Sullivan at Seymour Library, also in Auburn. Amy Cooper Cary of the Raynor Memorial Libraries at Marquette University in Milwaukee provided Val O'Farrell's FBI file, while Haley Antell at Kent State University Libraries supplied the FBI file on the Lindbergh kidnapping, which includes a discussion of Barry as a suspect. Gregory Ferrara, archivist at the New Jersey State Police Museum and Learning Center in West Trenton, tracked down records of Barry's capture in New Jersey and the state police investigation that exonerated him.

Vicki Lynne Glantz of the American Heritage Center at the University of Wyoming sent me New York *Daily News* journalist Grace Robinson's recollections of her 1932 interview with Barry. Sarah Maspero, Emily Rawlings, and Sabrina Harder of the Archives, Manuscripts and Special Collections section of the Hartley Library at the University of Southampton provided copies of press clippings on the theft of Edwina Mountbatten's jewels. David Sager, Courtney Matthews, DeCarlos Boyd, Kelly Dyson, Tomeka Myers, and Chamisa Redmond provided access to records and photographs held by the Library of Congress. Evelyn Vollgraff of the Lake Ronkonkoma Historical Society, Charmain Dunn and Michel Brideau of Library and Archives Canada in Ottawa, and Patricia Chalmers of the University of King's College Library in Halifax, Nova Scotia, also helped to locate information or photographs. Michael Dabin of NYDailyNewsPix (the photo archive of the New York *Daily News*), Drew Cuthbertson of the USA Today Network, and Tamra Coles of the Rochester *Democrat and Chronicle* helped me to source images.

Mary Weber, Clare Flemming, and other staff members of the New York State Archives spent countless hours combing through the records of Sing Sing, Auburn, and Attica prisons to help me reconstruct the nineteen years Barry spent behind bars. Among their finds were reports with new insights into Barry's family and upbringing in Worcester and a never-before-published mug shot, taken after his capture and return to Auburn in 1932.

Mary Schumacher and Sean Galliher shared memories of their Uncle

Artie and his life after his release from prison. Emma Glassman-Hughes scoured the Worcester newspapers on microfilm at the Boston Public Library and emerged with new material about Barry's life. Mary Rostad produced the excellent maps. And fellow authors who shared research advice include Mitchell Zuckoff, Joe Pompeo, Michael Cannell, Cathryn Prince, Sarah Weinman, Allan Levine, and Jerry Aylward. I thank all of you for your contributions.

Hilary McMahon of Westwood Creative Artists is my agent and ally, and I'm grateful for her guidance, advice, and support. *A Gentleman and a Thief* is my third book with Amy Gash, executive editor at Algonquin Books, and her wisdom, insight, and encouragement have made me a better writer. Thanks to the rest of the team at Algonquin—Brunson Hoole, Elizabeth Johnson, Michael McKenzie, Travis Smith, and Brenna Franzitta—for their work on editing, design, and promotion. And thanks to my editors at HarperCollins Canada, Janice Zawerbny and Jim Gifford.

Kerry Oliver is my partner in true crime and in everything else. I'm grateful, every day, for her advice and patience, for her help with research and editing, and for her unshakable belief in what I do. She's my precious gem.

Wolfville, Nova Scotia

ARTHUR BARRY'S MAJOR HEISTS

NASSAU COUNTY, LONG ISLAND

1924

September 9: Nellie and Joshua Cosden, oil tycoon, Edwina and Louis Mountbatten, cousin of the Prince of Wales, Sands Point, $170,000 (A)

1925

October 4: Eva and Harvey Shaffer, real estate broker, Great Neck, $12,000 (S)

October 18: Thomas Hitchcock Sr., polo expert, Westbury, $900 (A)

November 7: Margaret and August Flamman, former Brooklyn district attorney, Kensington, $13,000 (A)

November 28: Margarita and John Phipps, businessman and lawyer, Westbury, $12,500 (S)

1926

August 3: Kate and Brewster Jennings, Standard Oil executive, Glen Head, $13,000 (S)

September 29: Margaret and Harold Talbott, Chrysler director, Manhasset, $23,000 (I)

1927

Early April: Marion and John Greenleaf, architect, Hewlett Bay Park, $10,000 (I)

April 2: Amelia and Robert Sealy, banker, Hewlett Bay Park, $2,500 (S)

April 8: E. M. Richardson, Sherwin-Williams director, Plandome, $4,500 (S)

May 5: Ada and William Tregoe, realtor, Great Neck, $4,000 (S)

May 29: Dorothea and Jessie Livermore, Wall Street investor, Regina and Harry Aronsohn, silk manufacturer, Kings Point, $100,000 (C)

WESTCHESTER COUNTY, NEW YORK

1922

February 28: Margaret and Henry Graves III, New York Trust Company executive, Ardsley, $62,000 (S)

1923

February 28: Ann and Duncan Fraser, heir to mining and steel fortune, Ardsley, $25,000 (S)

1924

March 25: Clara and Henry Brooks, telephone company executive, Ardsley, $1,000 (S)

November 11: Jessie and Marselis Parsons, president of Rye National Bank, Rye, $6,000 (A)

December 3: Greta and Donaldson Brown, vice president of General Motors, Irvington, $10,000 (A)

1925

May 13: Katherine and Dr. Joseph Blake, surgeon, Tarrytown, $15,000 (A)

1926

January 8: Dorothy and Roy Allen, vice president of Life Savers, Port Chester, $3,000 (A)

May 8: Charlotte and Frederick Wheeler, president of American Can, Rye, $30,000 (A)

June 8: Coster Steers, broker, Port Chester, $10,000 (A)

July 8: Madeleine and Alfred Berolzheimer, head of Eagle Pencil, Tarrytown, $10,000 (A)

August 1: Mabel and John Stilwell, utility company executive, Yonkers, $5,000 (A)

MANHATTAN

1925

September 30: Jessie, Woolworth heiress, and James Donahue, stockbroker, Plaza Hotel, $700,000 (A)

CONNECTICUT

1926

September 25: Jane and Duane Armstrong, retired shoe manufacturer, Greenwich, $30,000 (A)

October 25: Isabel and Percy Rockefeller, investor and nephew of Standard Oil founder John D. Rockefeller, Greenwich, $25,000 (A)

NEW JERSEY

1926

September 10: Mary and Matthias Plum, vice president of International Paper, Rumson, $50,000 (S)

(C) Convicted
(I) Indicted
(A) Admitted
(S) Suspected

Note: All values are as reported in the 1920s.

NOTES ON SOURCES

WE MET BY chance. I was researching con artists of the Jazz Age when I happened upon Arthur Barry's amazing story of glamour and deception, crime and punishment, love and redemption. One of the search engine hits was a link to a 1956 *Life* magazine feature that touted him as "the greatest jewel thief who ever lived." As I dug deeper, I was astounded to discover his brazen burglaries, how he hobnobbed with New York's elite as he cased their mansions, how he fooled millionaires, socialites, and even a future king of England. Here was a real-life gentleman thief who took from the rich and gave to himself, pocketing jewels worth millions of dollars. Barry had the charm of John Robie, Cary Grant's character in the Hitchcock classic *To Catch a Thief*, the ingenuity of Arsène Lupin, the good-guy burglar of the Netflix series *Lupin*, the chutzpah of Frank Abagnale, the slippery con man portrayed by Leonardo DiCaprio in *Catch Me If You Can*. I was hooked.

The *Life* magazine article by Robert Wallace, republished a couple of years later in *The Double Dealers: Adventures in Grand Deception*—an anthology of tales of frauds, scams, and swindles—was the starting point for my research. My next stop was journalist Neil Hickey's interviews with Barry for a pair of features in *American Weekly* magazine in 1959, which were expanded into the book *The Gentleman Was a Thief*, published in 1961. These sources, which recorded Barry's recollections of people, places, and events, provided invaluable insights as I re-created the master thief's life and exploits.

Much of his story, however, remained to be told. Barry regaled his interviewers with accounts of his most infamous heists but said nothing about dozens of other forays into the homes of the rich and famous. Sometimes his memory failed him, and sometimes he deliberately reinvented his past. Hickey's book and the earlier magazine features, for instance, make no mention of his prosecution for murder in 1922, after a fatal shooting outside a Connecticut dance hall. Eager to portray himself as a lone wolf, Barry downplayed his partnership with accomplice-turned-bitter enemy James Monahan.

Insider accounts of the police investigation that led to Barry's arrest in 1927, published less than a year later in *True Detective Mysteries* magazine, yielded fresh insights, as well as what appears to be the only complete text of Barry's confession. His lengthy interviews with New York *Daily News* crime reporter Grace Robinson in 1932 were the basis for an eight-part series that revealed "the intimate life story of Arthur Barry, prince of jewel thieves." The following year, King Features distributed seven installments of Anna Blake's account of her "Life of Love and Fear" as Barry's wife. Both series provided new information and made it possible to tell more of this story in the couple's own words.

The Newspapers.com and NewspaperArchive.com databases provided a trove of news coverage of Barry and his crimes. Most editions of the Worcester papers published in his time have yet to be scanned and were searched old-school, on microfilm. Census and other genealogical records available at Ancestry.com helped me to describe Barry's family and his early life in Worcester. Descriptions of the weather on specific days are based on newspaper reports and forecasts. All monetary figures expressed in today's values were converted using tools available through the website MeasuringWorth.com. I used press accounts and vintage photographs, postcards, and maps to capture the look and feel of Barry's world, from the bomb-cratered battlefields of France to the sumptuous estates of Long Island, from the dungeon-like cells of Sing Sing prison to the rustic New Jersey farm that became his refuge. Where I encountered glaring inconsistencies in news reports and other accounts, or discovered conflicting versions of conversations and events, I have noted these discrepancies in the text or in the endnotes.

Erik Larson, in a discussion of the sources he consulted as he researched and wrote *The Devil in the White City: Murder, Magic, and Madness at the*

Fair That Changed America, described endnotes as a map that readers can follow to verify facts and quotations or to find more information. "Anyone retracing my steps," the master of narrative nonfiction explained, "ought to reach the same conclusions" as he did.

The endnotes that follow are my road map to the story of jewel thief extraordinaire Arthur Barry.

ENDNOTES

PROLOGUE: PRINCE CHARMING

1   **A man in a tuxedo** Details of Barry's encounter with the Prince of Wales, his initial attempt to rob the Cosden mansion, and all quotations and actions not noted below are drawn from the most reliable account of these events: Anna Blake Barry, "My Life of Love and Fear as the Sweetheart and Wife of Arthur Barry, the World's Most Famous Jewel-Thief," *Atlanta Constitution*, January 29 and February 5, 1933. The story related also relies on the work of veteran New York journalist Grace Robinson, who interviewed Barry in 1932 about his night with the prince and the Cosden robbery. She also gathered "statements from persons who remember the incident well" and was confident these "friends out of Barry's past" had provided "the whole amazing story." See Arthur Barry, as told to Grace Robinson, "Barry Bares Rialto Bout with Wales," *Daily News* (New York), November 3, 1932. Neil Hickey, *The Gentleman Was a Thief: The Colorful Story of Arthur Barry, a 1920's Rogue* (New York: Holt, Rinehart & Winston, 1961), 8–16, provided many details but offers a different chronology of these events.

1   **the British actor Ronald Colman** The resemblance is noted in Robert Wallace, "Confessions of a Master Jewel Thief," in Alexander Klein, ed., *The Double Dealers: Adventures in Grand Deception* (London: Faber & Faber, 1958), 97, originally published as "Confessions of Master Jewel Thief," *Life*, March 12, 1956. Barry's eye and hair color were noted on a registration card for Arthur T. Barry, dated June 5, 1917, United States, Selective Service System, World War I Selective Service System Draft Registration Cards, 1917–1918. National Archives and Records Administration, Washington, DC, accessed via Ancestry.com.

2   **"that slender riotous island"** F. Scott Fitzgerald, *The Great Gatsby* (New York: Simon & Schuster, 1995), 9.

2   **was the guest of honor** The prince's activities during the 1924 visit are described in Philip Ziegler, *King Edward VIII: A Biography* (New York: Alfred A. Knopf, 1991), 130–35, and Ted Powell, *King Edward VIII: An American Life* (Oxford: Oxford University Press, 2018), 92–113. The fox hunt was reported in "Mackay Dinner and Dance for Prince at Harbor Hill Tonight to Be Elaborate," *Brooklyn Daily Eagle*, September 6, 1924.

2   **"Never before in the history"** Ziegler, *King Edward VIII*, 131.

2   **"one of the show places"** "Prince Is Guest of Pratts: Meets Long Island '400,'" *Brooklyn Daily Eagle*, September 1, 1924.

2   **upstaged by Clarence H. Mackay** "Mackay Dinner and Dance for Prince at Harbor Hill Tonight to Be Elaborate," and "Mackay Home a Fairyland in Wales' Honor," *Times Union* (Brooklyn), September 7, 1924.

2   **"A royal fete"** "New York Society Engrossed in Plans for Prince of Wales," *Evening Star* (Washington, DC), September 14, 1924.

2   **handed the prince the keys** Powell, *King Edward VIII*, 102. "Woodside," *Old Long Island* (blog), http://www.oldlongisland.com/2010/04/woodside.html?m=1, posted April 2, 2010, provides descriptions and vintage photographs of the estate. The Burden cars at the prince's disposal are noted in "Wales Not on All-Night Party in City, Aides Insist; Ridicule Threatening Note," *Brooklyn Daily Eagle*, September 5, 1924.

2   **Burden Palace** "Life of Prince Threatened in a Letter Mailed to Acting British Consul General Here," *Daily News*, September 5, 1924.

2   **a rambling, Colonial-style confection** Photographs of the mansion accompanied the news reports "Raffles Stalking Prince Seizes $100,000 in Gems at Cosden Home," *Daily News*, September 11, 1924, and "Pushed into Limelight by the Prince," *Brooklyn Daily Eagle*, September 12, 1924.

4   **"small but jolly"** "Wales Shows Lots of Dash in Polo Match after Another All-Night Dancing Session," *Brooklyn Daily Eagle*, September 4, 1924. This report confirmed that the Mountbattens and Jean Norton were staying with the Cosdens.

4   **"dark, handsome naval officer"** Hickey, *The Gentleman Was a Thief*, 14.

4   **his only commitment** "U.S. Polo Team Big Favorite in Game Today," *Times Union*, September 9, 1924.

4   **"He is here to play"** "Prince Is No 'Jazz Hound,' but Surely Loves Dancing," *Standard Union* (Brooklyn), September 5, 1924.

4   **"These Yank pressmen"** Ziegler, *King Edward VIII*, 131.

4   **"Prince Charming"** The moniker appeared in many American news accounts. See, for instance, "H.R.H. Attending Polo Matches Will Be Prince," *Indianapolis Star*, August 16, 1924, and "Wales the Man True to Ideals," *Times Dispatch* (Richmond, VA), September 14, 1924.

4   **"Would you marry"** Powell, *King Edward VIII*, 102.

4   **ARMY OF LOVELY WOMEN and "forgot decorum"** "Prince Scorns Guard at Race," *Daily News*, September 2, 1924.

5   **"a judge of that sort of thing"** "Barry Bares Rialto Bout with Wales."

5   **"Wales does things spontaneously"** "Wales Shows Lots of Dash in Polo Match after Another All-Night Dancing Session."

5   **"is that little lark still on?"** Blake Barry, "My Life of Love and Fear," *Atlanta Constitution*, February 5, 1933.

5   **"Hello, suckers!"** Lynn Yaeger, "Celebrating Texas Guinan, the Original 'Nasty Woman,'" Vogue.com (January 12, 2017), https://www.vogue.com/article/texas-guinan-20th-century-actress-nasty-woman.

5   **awning over the entrance** A photograph of the club's entrance is reproduced in "A Dry Manhattan," *A New Yorker State of Mind* (blog), March 18, 2015, https://newyorkerstateofmind.com/2015/03/18/a-dry-manhattan.

6   **"formidable woman"** David Castronovo, "Edmund Wilson's 1920s," *New England Review* 21, no. 4 (Fall, 2000): 104.

6   **"a gorgeous tamer"** Michael A. Lerner, *Dry Manhattan: Prohibition in New York City* (Cambridge, MA: Harvard University Press, 2007), 186.

6   **narrow, smoke-filled room** The club is described in Neal Gabler, *Winchell: Gossip, Power and the Culture of Celebrity* (New York: Alfred A. Knopf, 1995), 68.

6   **"a little fellow"** "Tex Guinan Tells How She Makes $100,000 A Year; Never Takes a Drink, and Says Folks Don't Go to Night Clubs to Imbibe Booze," *Brooklyn Daily Eagle*, December 18, 1927.

6   **"gay set is at its best"**   "Dry Locks Set for 14 Cabarets," *Daily News*, March 6, 1925.

6   **stashed its liquor**   Debby Applegate, *Madam: The Biography of Polly Adler, Icon of the Jazz Age* (New York: Doubleday, 2021), 200. Applegate notes contemporary references to Broadway as the Big Street and the surrounding area as the Roaring Forties.

6   **"a bacchanalian feast"**   Applegate, *Madam*, 200.

7   **"Princely Fun"**   "My Life of Love and Fear," *Atlanta Constitution*, January 29, 1933.

7   **"atmosphere of mystery"**   "Knockout Sends Pining Mother to Her Children," *Los Angeles Daily Times*, October 3, 1923.

7   **"many socially prominent New Yorkers"**   "Dry Locks Set for 14 Cabarets."

7   **Members of the house orchestra**   Arthur Barry described the Club Deauville visit in Hickey, *The Gentleman Was a Thief*, 9–13. A New York *Daily News* report later confirmed that the prince visited the club in 1924. See "Dry Locks Set for 14 Cabarets," *Daily News*, March 6, 1925.

8   **toured front-line trenches**   Ziegler, *King Edward VIII*, 48.

8   **"dressed faultlessly in evening clothes"**   "My Life of Love and Fear," *Atlanta Constitution*, January 29, 1933.

8   **traced the plates**   "Wales Not on All-Night Party in City, Aides Insist; Ridicule Threatening Note."

8   **"He went in disguise"**   "If Prince Cannot Go to Broadway, He Will Have Broadway Come to Him," *Buffalo Courier*, September 5, 1924.

9   **white silk gloves**   Hickey, *The Gentleman Was a Thief*, 15.

9   **pretend to be lost or drunk**   Wallace, "Confessions of a Master Jewel Thief," 100.

9   **worth almost $60 million today**   Hickey, *The Gentleman Was a Thief*, ix.

10   **"second-story man"**   For one of many examples of this moniker, see "$500,000 Raffles' Story," *Daily News*, July 3, 1927.

10   **"Prince of Thieves"**   See, for instance, "Arthur Barry's Own Story of His Life," *Daily News*, January 1, 1933.

10   **"Aristocrat of Crime"**   Barry is among the famous jewel thieves featured in Charles and Bonnie Remsberg, "The Aristocrats of Crime," *New York Times*, December 17, 1964.

10   **"the greatest jewel thief"**   Wallace, "Confessions of a Master Jewel Thief," 97.

CHAPTER 1: THE COURIER

13   **traveling alone on a southbound train**   Barry's recollections of his trips as a courier for Lowell Jack and his conversations with him are drawn from Neil Hickey, *The Gentleman Was a Thief: The Colorful Story of Arthur Barry, a 1920's Rogue* (New York: Holt, Rinehart & Winston, 1961), 17–21, and Robert Wallace, "Confessions of a Master Jewel Thief," in Alexander Klein, ed., *The Double Dealers: Adventures in Grand Deception* (London: Faber & Faber, 1958), 98–99, originally published as "Confessions of Master Jewel Thief," *Life*, March 12, 1956.

13   **"of the dangerous class"**   "Old Style Tramps Have Gone to Their Reward," *Berkshire Eagle* (Pittsfield, MA), January 13, 1923.

14   **"soup"**   The use of homemade nitroglycerin by safecrackers in the early 1900s is described in "The Ungentle Art of Burglary," *Scientific American* 94, no. 4 (January 27, 1906): 88, and James Forbes, "John the Yeggman." *Outlook* 98 (August 12, 1911): 823–28.

14   **extremely volatile**   See "The Manufacture of High Explosives," *Scientific American* 97, no. 26 (December 1907): 475–78; and Kat Eschner, "The Man Who Invented Nitroglycerin Was Horrified by Dynamite," *Smithsonian Magazine* (October 12, 2017), https://www.smithsonianmag.com/smart-news/man-who-invented-nitroglycerin -was-horrified-dynamite-180965192.

14   **Heart of the Commonwealth**   This account of the city's history is based on Margaret A. Erskine's *Worcester: Heart of the Commonwealth* (Woodland Hills, CA: Windsor Publications, 1981), 39–40, 74, 84, 86, 113–14.

14   **"immersed in politics"**   David McCullough, *John Adams* (New York: Simon & Schuster, 2008), 40.

16   **"the city's worst jobs"**   Timothy J. Meagher, *Inventing Irish America: Generation, Class, and Ethnic Identity in a New England City, 1880–1928* (Notre Dame, IN: University of Notre Dame Press, 2001), 42.

16   **When he married**   Marriage of Thomas Barry and Bridget Walsh, October 26, 1880, Massachusetts Vital Records, 1840–1911, New England Historic Genealogical Society, Boston, via Ancestry.com.

16   **Bridget Walsh, an Irish-born servant**   The 1880 US Census, taken shortly before the marriage, records her as a servant on a farm in Amherst, Massachusetts, a community to the west of Worcester.

16   **a studio photograph**   The image is posted on the Barry family's page on the Find a Grave website: https://www.findagrave.com/memorial/8495000/thomas-francis-barry.

16   **"the poor, workaday part"**   Arthur Barry, as told to Grace Robinson, "Barry Tells Own Story of Robber Feats," *Daily News* (New York), October 30, 1932. The Barry family's home addresses and Thomas Barry's employment were traced using the digitized collection of Worcester *City Directories*, available online from the Worcester Historical Museum: http://digitalworcester.com/node/4.

16   **sixth of the couple's nine surviving children**   Census returns identify nine children, and a headstone on the family's plot in Worcester's St. John Cemetery records the deaths of four more in infancy. A photograph of the headstone accompanies the entry for Thomas Francis Barry (1857–1932) on the Find a Grave website: https://www.findagrave .com/memorial/8495000/thomas-francis-barry.

17   **"the sweet-toned bell"**   Barry discussed being an altar boy and his parents' hopes he would enter the priesthood in "Barry Tells Own Story of Robber Feats." The family's Ward Street home was located just inside the northwestern boundary of Sacred Heart Parish. See the map in John F. McClymer, "'Rebellion against Priest': Making a Niche in a Late-Nineteenth-Century American City," *Massachusetts Historical Review* 10 (2008): 5.

17   **The calling attracted so many**   Meagher, *Inventing Irish America*, 88.

17   **Schoolhouse No. 4**   "Ward Street School-Millbury Street, Worcester, MA: U.S. National Register of Historic Places," https://www.waymarking.com/waymarks /WMMQ2G_Ward_Street_School_Millbury_Street_Worcester_MA.

17   **a smaller operation**   In 1910, Worcester Brewing Corporation was capitalized at $300,000 while Bowler Brothers' capitalization was $1 million. *Worcester Directory 1910*, 808 and 813, http://digitalworcester.com/node/14. Thomas Barry is identified as a brewery foreman in the 1920 census.

18   **"architectural monstrosity"**   "Worcester Three-Deckers MRA Amendment," National Register of Historic Places Registration Form, December 26, 1989, section 8, 2–3, https:// npgallery.nps.gov/NRHP/GetAsset/NRHP/64000305_text. Section 7, pages 3–4, notes that the Perry Avenue three-deckers were built between 1901 and 1910.

18   **"piazzas"**   All quotations in this paragraph are drawn from "Samuel N. Behrman (1893–1973) on Life in a Three-Decker," https://www.worcesterhistory.org/worcesters-history/worcesters-own/three-deckers.

18   **"fine and close-knit family"**   Wallace, "Confessions of a Master Jewel Thief," 98.

18   **"moderately alcoholic"** and **"no more than the usual amount of friction"**   Case File of Arthur Barry, New York State Department of Correctional Services, Auburn Correctional Facility Records, Inmate Case Files, Series W0006-77A (14610-77A). New York State Archives, Albany.

18   **"knew we'd be punished"**   "Barry Tells Own Story of Robber Feats."

19   **hauled before judges**   A list of Barry's juvenile offenses, as recorded in Worcester police files, was reproduced in "Barry's Record Here Recounted by Police," *Worcester Gazette*, June 10, 1927, and Barry, as told to Robinson, "Arthur Barry's Own Life Story: Jewel Thief Tells About His Exploits," *Daily News*, November 6, 1932.

19   **"putting the lights out of commission"**   "Smashing Lights," *Worcester Daily Telegram*, September 16, 1910. While he was identified in the newspaper's report as Edward Barry, the offense matches a vandalism conviction recorded by Worcester police.

19   **"a pretty bad boy"**   "Barry's Record Here Recounted by Police."

19   **"downfall"**   Wallace, "Confessions of a Master Jewel Thief," 98.

19   **started drinking beer and wine**   Barry described drinking, smoking, and gambling in his youth in Case File of Arthur Barry, New York State Department of Correctional Services, Auburn Correctional Facility Records, Inmate Case Files, Series W0006-77A (14610-77A).

19   **"crime flourished"**   Meagher, *Inventing Irish America*, 62.

19   **"an urgent demand"**   Herbert M. Sawyer, *History of the Department of Police Service of Worcester, Mass., from 1674 to 1900* (Worcester: Worcester Police Relief Association, 1900), 138–39, 149–50.

19   **"poverty, disorder, fights, and youth gangs"**   This description and the newspaper quotations that follow are drawn from William B. Meyer, "The Poor on the Hilltops? The Vertical Fringe of a Late Nineteenth-Century American City," *Annals of the Association of American Geographers* 95, no. 4 (December 2005): 780.

19   **shadowed a middle-aged couple**   Barry described his first burglary in Wallace, "Confessions of a Master Jewel Thief," 99.

20   **order a roast turkey dinner**   These prices were drawn from advertisements in the June 9, 1912, edition of the *Boston Globe*.

20   **"I wish I could remember"**   "Barry Tells Own Story of Robber Feats."

20   **"steal the British Crown Jewels"**   Kermit Jaediker, "America's Prince of Thieves," *Daily News*, November 18, 1956.

20   **"stubborn child"**   "Judge Stobbs Finds No Case Against the Man," *Worcester Daily Telegram*, August 6, 1913, and "Arthur Barry's Own Life Story: Jewel Thief Tells About His Exploits." The law originated in 1646 and was a remnant of the state's strict Puritan past that was not repealed until the 1970s. See John R. Sutton, "Stubborn Children: Law and the Socialization of Deviance in the Puritan Colonies," *Family Law Quarterly* 15, no. 1 (Spring 1981): 31–64, and Lawrence R. Sidman, "The Massachusetts Stubborn Child Law: Law and Order in the Home," *Family Law Quarterly* 6, no. 1 (Spring 1972): 33–58.

21   **a frantic Bridget Barry contacted**   "16-Year-Old Boy Puts Mother Out," *Worcester Evening Gazette*, September 26, 1913.

21   **breaking into the store**   Court Brief in *Worcester Daily Telegram*, October 1, 1913.

21   **a charge of breaking and entering**   "Three Are Defaulted," *Worcester Daily Telegram*, June 3, 1914.

CHAPTER 2: A "BIG-TIMER"

22   **Arthur bolted from the railyard**   This account of Barry's capture and his initial court appearance is drawn from Neil Hickey, *The Gentleman Was a Thief: The Colorful Story of Arthur Barry, a 1920's Rogue* (New York: Holt, Rinehart & Winston, 1961), 20–21, and "Captured After a Long Chase by the Police," *Berkshire Eagle* (Pittsfield, MA), August 15, 1914.

23   **an aging and forbidding building**   Erin Hunt, curator of the Berkshire County Historical Society in Pittsfield, confirmed the police station's location in 1914 and provided a photograph. Email communication with the author, November 9, 2021.

24   **six-by-ten-foot cell**   Mary Wilson, "Former Pittsfield Jail Opens Its Doors to the Homeless," WTEN/ABC News 10, Albany, NY, October 8, 2019, https://www.news10 .com/news/local-news/former-pittsfield-jail-opens-its-doors-to-the-homeless.

24   **no record of a Frank J. Walsh**   The court proceedings were recorded in "Has No Record," *Berkshire Eagle*, August 18, 1914; "To Look Up Record," *Berkshire Eagle*, August 20, 1914; and Hickey, *The Gentleman Was a Thief*, 21. The court file of the case does not appear to have survived. Email exchange between the author and John D. Lizzo, head account clerk, Pittsfield District Court, September 27, 2021.

25   **"of good appearance" and "a rheumatic cripple"**   "Worcester Youth Sent to Reformatory," *Berkshire Eagle*, August 25, 1914. Bridget Barry confirmed that Arthur's father was disabled in 1914 in a press interview: "Mother Will Not Aid New York Jewel Thief," *Boston Globe*, June 8, 1927.

25   **imposed the maximum sentence**   Samuel J. Barrows, "The Massachusetts Prison System," *New England Magazine* 8, no. 1 (March 1893): 42.

25   **"the end of his amateur days"**   "Jewel Thief and Lifer Began His Career Here," *Berkshire Eagle*, November 16, 1932.

25   **"ruthlessly shorn away"**   A former inmate described the intake procedures, including arriving in handcuffs, in "My Experiences as a Convict, by an Ex-Convict, Part I," *Cambridge Magazine* 2, no. 1, May 1896, 19–20. Photographs and drawings of the reformatory's exterior and interior appeared in Barrows, "The Massachusetts Prison System," 39, 42–47.

26   **Fingerprints were being hailed**   Fingerprint evidence had been used to solve crimes in the United States and Britain during the previous decade, and space for up to four fingerprint impressions had been added to the cards that recorded Bertillon measurements. Colin Beavan, *Fingerprints: The Origins of Crime Detection and the Murder Case that Launched Forensic Science* (New York: Hyperion, 2001), 185–94.

26   **"Correction of waywardness"**   "Citizens from the Scrap-Heap," *Boston Evening Transcript*, February 25, 1914.

26   **"influence of the home"**   "How Gardening Turns Bad Boys into Useful Citizens," *Austin American* (TX), September 2, 1914.

26   **"the hated bell"**   "My Experiences as a Convict, by an Ex-Convict Part I."

27 **workshops turned out** The workshops and the trades and educational training are described in Barrows, "The Massachusetts Prison System," 38–40.

27 **"school of letters"** *First Annual Report of the Bureau of Prisons of Massachusetts, 1916* (Boston: Wright & Potter Printing, 1917), 45, 64.

27 **"men who have fought"** "Prison Reform Discussed at Randall Club." *Fall River Globe* (MA), April 13, 1916.

27 **an array of subjects** *First Annual Report of the Bureau of Prisons of Massachusetts, 1916*, 65.

27 **inmates joined societies** "My Experiences as a Convict, by an Ex-Convict, Part II," *Cambridge Magazine* 2, no. 2 (June 1896): 109–10.

27 **"News from the Outside World"** See, for instance, *Our Paper* (Concord Junction, MA) 31, no. 1 (January 2, 1915).

27 **"pride in their criminal tendencies"** "Legislature Turns Down Bristol County Jail Bill," *Fall River Globe*, April 25, 1911.

27 **held about seven hundred** Inmate numbers and their offenses are reported in *First Annual Report of the Bureau of Prisons of Massachusetts, 1916*, 43, 49. There were 703 inmates in January 1915 and 733 in October of that year. Chaplain Walker reported the January figure in "Lowell," *Boston Globe*, January 9, 1914.

27 **serving time for burglary or theft** *First Annual Report of the Bureau of Prisons of Massachusetts, 1916*, 54.

27 **"a boy in short trousers"** "Legislature Turns Down Bristol County Jail Bill."

27 **"the education of criminals"** "Learned Crime in Prison," *Fitchburg Sentinel* (MA), November 17, 1910.

27 **"graduates"** See, for instance, "William Doyle in Court," *Boston Globe*, June 15, 1914.

28 **"most of their leisure time"** "Learned Crime in Prison."

28 **serving seven months** Hickey, *The Gentleman Was a Thief*, 22.

28 **"A man coming out of prison"** "Prison System 'Is Ridiculous,'" *Boston Globe*, February 9, 1915. The parole board's criteria for releasing reformatory inmates are described in "Citizens from the Scrap-Heap."

28 **visited him at Concord and assured them he was innocent** Hickey, *The Gentleman Was a Thief*, 21.

28 **a high school diploma** This is noted in Receiving Blotter: Arthur Barry (Inmate 80071), July 1, 1927, Sing Sing Prison, Inmate Admission Registers, 1842–1852, 1865–1971. New York State Department of Correctional Services, Series B0143, box 43, vol. 87. New York State Archives, Albany.

28 **a ten-dollar fine for drunkenness** "Barry's Record Here Recounted by Police," *Worcester Gazette*, June 10, 1927.

28 **walking with a girlfriend** "John W. Farden Informs Police He Is Dazzled by the Light of Electric Car," *Worcester Daily Telegram*, October 11, 1915.

28 **sent back to Concord** Arthur was arrested as a parole violator on September 26, 1916. Arthur Barry, as told to Grace Robinson, "Arthur Barry's Own Life Story: Jewel Thief Tells About His Exploits," *Daily News*, November 6, 1932. The parole violation is also noted in "Jewel Thief and Lifer Began His Career Here." Files on individual Concord inmates created between 1910 and 1935, including Arthur's, have not survived. See note appended to the finding aid for "Inmate Case Files, 1884–1929 (Massachusetts Reformatory)," Massachusetts Archives, Boston, http://chc.library.umass.edu /state-archives/2017/04/18/inmate-case-files-massachusetts-reformatory-concord-mass.

29 **"We do not attempt"** "Prison Reform Discussed at Randall Club."

29 **"the spirit of patriotism"** *Second Annual Report of the Bureau of Prisons of Massachusetts, 1917* (Boston: Wright & Potter Printing, 1918), 59.

29 **a major producer** The Bridgeport munitions plant and its contracts are described in Cecelia F. Bucki, "Dilution and Craft Tradition: Bridgeport, Connecticut, Munitions Workers, 1915–1919," *Social Science History* 4, no. 1 (1980): 105–24; "Connecticut Must Supply Arms of Nation and Draft Will Exempt Expert Crafts," *Bridgeport Times and Evening Farmer*, June 8, 1917; "Arms Co. Officials on Stand," *Bridgeport Times and Evening Farmer*, December 19, 1917; and Luke Mercaldo, "Remington's Allied Rifle Contracts During World War I," *Remington Society of American Journal* (Q2, 2012): 22–5, https://www.remingtonsociety.org/remingtons-allied-rifle-contracts-during-wwi.

30 **"terrific heat"** "From Cape Verde Islands, from the Follies Bergere, from Everywhere," *Hartford Courant*, July 1, 1917. This article and Alden Hatch, *Remington Arms in American History* (New York: Rinehart & Company, 1956), 221, describe the plant's security measures.

30 **an inspection staff** "A Visit to the Bridgeport Plant," in *A New Chapter in an Old Story* (New York: Remington Arms-Union Metallic Cartridge, 1912).

30 **rifles for the Russian army** Hatch, *Remington Arms in American History*, 220.

30 **paid high wages** Hatch, *Remington Arms*, 221, and "Patriotic vs. Unpatriotic Action," *Bridgeport Times and Evening Farmer*, August 27, 1917.

30 **registered for the draft** Registration card for Arthur T. Barry, dated June 5, 1917, United States, Selective Service System, World War I Selective Service System Draft Registration Cards, 1917–1918. National Archives and Records Administration, Washington, DC, accessed via Ancestry.com. Arthur described himself as "Inspector drop forge dept."

30 **"true age and background"** Hickey, *The Gentleman Was a Thief*, 22.

30 **ineligible for military service** The Selective Service Regulations, 1917, disqualified anyone "convicted of any crime designated as treason or felony, or an 'infamous' crime." Swarthmore College Peace Collection, "Military Classifications for Draftees, World War I (1917)," http://www.swarthmore.edu/Library/peace/conscientiousobjection/MilitaryClassifications.htm. The restriction was still in place in October 1918, when the chaplain of the Massachusetts Reformatory called for the "ancient law" banning felons to be repealed, to ensure that there were "no closed doors to any ex-prisoner who follows the straight road upon release." *Second Annual Report of the Bureau of Prisons of Massachusetts, 1917*, 59.

CHAPTER 3: FIRST-AID MAN

31 **something in the water** The bucket incident is described in James E. Pollard, *The Forty-Seventh Infantry: A History, 1917–1918, 1919* (Saginaw, MI: Seeman & Peters, 1919), 27.

31 **six-inch shells** *Princess Matoika*'s armament and troop-carrying capacity are described in "Attacked Twice by Submarines," *Herald and Review* (Decatur, IL), July 23, 1918.

32 **one of the sailors reckoned** "Hickman Youth Tells of Sea Battle," *Modesto Morning Herald* (CA), August 3, 1918.

32 **a recruiting station in Times Square** Neil Hickey, *The Gentleman Was a Thief: The Colorful Story of Arthur Barry, a 1920's Rogue* (New York: Holt, Rinehart & Winston, 1961), 22. Barry's enlistment date is recorded in US Department of Veterans Affairs,

BIRLS Death File, 1850–2010, Ancestry.com. His enlistment form is reproduced in Anna Blake Barry, "My Life of Love and Fear as the Sweetheart and Wife of Arthur Barry, the World's Most Famous Jewel-Thief," *Atlanta Constitution*, January 15, 1933. In a March 31, 2023, letter to the author, archives technician Lennox Welsh confirmed that the National Archives could not locate Barry's military records and that they may be among those lost in a 1973 fire at the National Personnel Records Center in St. Louis.

32   **did not tell his parents**   Hickey, *The Gentleman Was a Thief*, 34.

32   **his next of kin**   US Army Transport Service Arriving and Departing Passenger Lists, 1910–1939, Records of the Office of the Quartermaster General, 1774–1985, RG 92, microfilm roll 539, National Archives and Records Administration, College Park, MD, via Ancestry.com.

32   **a battery of written examinations**   A recruit described the tests in "Letter from Donald Tenney," *Lincoln Sentinel* (KS), June 13, 1918.

32   **dispatched to a base hospital**   Hickey, *The Gentleman Was a Thief*, 22.

32   **practiced carrying injured men**   Medical Corps training is described in "Letter from Donald Tenney." As a child, Barry later claimed, he had dreamed of becoming a surgeon. Arthur Barry, as told to Grace Robinson, "Barry Tells Own Story of Robber Feats," *Daily News* (New York), October 30, 1932.

32   **The largest contingent**   Edward S. Pearl, "WWI: Boot Camp in Charlotte," *Tar Heel Junior Historian* (Spring 1993), https://www.ncpedia.org/wwi-boot-camp-charlotte. Descriptions of the camp are also drawn from Jack Dillard, "Camp Greene—A WWI Crossroads for Thousands," *Charlotte Viewpoint*, November 11, 2012, http://www.charlotteviewpoint.org/article/2900/Camp-Greene-A-WWI-crossroads-for-thousands.

32   **a photographer's studio**   The photographs appear in Hickey, *The Gentleman Was a Thief*, and in Robert Wallace, "Confessions of Master Jewel Thief," *Life*, March 12, 1956.

32   **"possessed a wonderful personality"**   "Was Convict's Buddy in War," *Star-Gazette* (Elmira, NY), July 31, 1929.

33   **"cold waves of increasing severity"**   Charles F. Brooks , "The 'Old-Fashioned' Winter of 1917–18," *Geographical Review* 5, no. 5 (May 1918), 405, 408, 410.

34   **"a sea of mud"**   Pollard, *The Forty-Seventh Infantry*, 17–18. This is also the source of descriptions of the cold weather's impact on training, the poor sewage system, and the fire hazard.

34   **forgetting to shave**   Text of postcard sent from Charlotte to Milford, Ohio, postmarked September 15, 1918, in the author's collection.

34   **"army men and their home folks"**   Masthead statement in *Trench and Camp* (Camp Greene edition), October 29, 1917. An article in this issue, "Soldiers Entertained by Musical Company," reviewed the first of a series of performances by visiting vaudeville companies.

34   **"full of soldiers"**   Text of postcard sent from Charlotte to Philadelphia, postmarked May 16, 1918, in the author's collection. North Carolina became the first southern state to ban alcohol in May 1908. See "Prohibition, Bootlegging, and the Law in North Carolina," *Digital North Carolina Blog*, posted January 17, 2014, at https://www.digitalnc.org/blog/prohibition-bootlegging-and-the-law-in-north-carolina.

34   **field training resumed**   The regiment's final weeks before leaving for France are described in Pollard, *The Forty-Seventh Infantry*, 18–19, 22–24.

34   **the liner's camouflage paint**   The ship's description and history have been reconstructed from "Along the Waterfront," *San Francisco Examiner*, February 23, 1918;

"Princess Matoika Bound for Coast," *Honolulu Advertiser,* February 23, 1918; and "The Perils of the Sea," *Tipton Daily Tribune* (IN), March 9, 1918. Barry's departure on the transport on May 10 is confirmed in Records of the Office of the Quartermaster General, 1774–1985, RG 92, microfilm roll 539, National Archives and Records Administration, College Park, MD, via Ancestry.com.

35   **joined a convoy**   The voyage is described in Pollard, *The Forty-Seventh Infantry,* 26–27. Barry narrowly avoided two dangerous encounters with German submarines. On *Princess Matoika*'s next voyage to France in June 1918, its gunners sank a U-boat that attacked its convoy. A German sub torpedoed and sank a ship accompanying the transport the following month, on the return trip to the United States. See "Local Sailor Saw Covington When Torpedoed," *Public Ledger* (Maysville, KY), July 18, 1918; "Attacked Twice by Submarines," *Herald and Review* (Decatur, IL), July 23, 1918; and "Back on Dry Land Again," *Miltonvale Record* (KS), July 25, 1918.

35   **"I never saw so much water"** and **"They were all anxious"**   "Back on Dry Land," *Miltonvale Record,* June 27, 1918.

35   **Red Cross trains**   Pollard, *The Forty-Seventh Infantry,* 28 and "At Sea, July 26," *Miltonvale Record,* August 29, 1918.

35   **"Never before"**   "With Our Red Cross Base Hospitals in France," *Delaware County Daily Times* (Chester, PA), October 13, 1917.

35   **"rips, tears and lacerates"**   Justin Barr, Leopoldo C. Cancio, David J. Smith, Matthew J. Bradley, and Eric A. Elster, "From Trench to Bedside: Military Surgery During World War I Upon Its Centennial," *Military Medicine* 184 (November/December 2019): 216. Shelling accounted for an estimated 70 percent of wounds during World War I, compared to just 20 percent from gunshots.

35   **"the utter damnable wickedness"**   Leslie Buswell, *Ambulance Number 10: Personal Letters from the Front* (East Sussex, UK: Naval & Military Press, originally published 1916), 57, 60.

36   **reducing the risk of infection**   "Wounded Fighters Do Not Complain," *Twin Falls Weekly News* (ID), September 26, 1918.

36   **"A gloomy cavern"**   "Wounded American Soldiers Show Nerve of Veterans, Surgeons Say," *Washington Post,* December 16, 1917.

36   **"Ours come first"**   "Asbury Park Boy Tells of First Trip Over Top," *Asbury Park Press* (NJ), March 5, 1918.

36   **"It is one thing"**   Frank P. Sibley, "Brave New Englanders in Battle of the Marne," *Boston Globe,* August 25, 1918.

36   **"the most popular man"**   Robert Del Toro, "Fighting a War Without Rifles: Deconstructing the Image of the Unflappable Medic," *Voces Novae: Chapman University Historical Review* 10, no. 1 (2018): 1, https://digitalcommons.chapman.edu/cgi/viewcontent.cgi?article=1116&context=vocesnovae.

36   **Trench Rats**   "Letter from Donald Tenney."

37   **pinned down for hours**   "Maurice Casey Writes Mother of Receiving Slight Gas Burns," *Burlington Free Press* (VT), September 12, 1918.

37   **killed two stretcher bearers**   "91st Men Willingly Risked Lives to Save Comrades," *Spokesman-Review* (Spokane, WA), May 17, 1919.

37   **German biplanes strafed**   "Brooklyn Soldiers, with Hands Badly Torn, Held Grimly to Mortars and Shattered German Waves, Private Holt's Story of 2d Battle of the Marne," *Brooklyn Daily Eagle,* September 22, 1918.

37 **issued two weapons** "Letter from Donald Tenney."

37 **"A Red Cross"** "Townsend Brothers Write," *Record-Journal* (Meriden, CT), August 21, 1918.

38 **"It was simply hell"** "Battle of Sergy Was 'Simply Hell,'" *Washington Standard* (Olympia), November 6, 1918. Details of the battle have been drawn from "Americans Seeing Red," *Chattanooga Daily Times* (TN), August 1, 1918; "All France Lauds American Troops," *Philadelphia Inquirer*, August 1, 1918; "Vivid Account of Sergy Battle Given by Writer," *Winston-Salem Journal* (NC), August 1, 1918; and "Huns' Best Against Ours," *Yonkers Statesman* (NY), August 3, 1918.

38 **"Medical officers and enlisted men"** Pollard, *The Forty-Seventh Infantry*, 44.

38 **crawled on his hands and knees** Barry, as told to Robinson, "Arthur Barry's Own Life Story," *Daily News*, November 6, 1932.

38 **"always volunteered for hazardous duty"** "Lindy Aids Face Barry; Jafsie Next," *Daily News*, October 29, 1932.

38 **"extraordinary heroism in action"** Hickey, *The Gentleman Was a Thief*, 25.

39 **a barrage of shells** The attack is described in Pollard, 49, 52. Barry is listed among the regiment's casualties on page 131.

39 **suffered serious burns** Barry's injuries and treatments are described in Hickey, *The Gentleman Was a Thief*, 25. His temporary blindness was noted in Case File of Arthur Barry, New York State Department of Correctional Services, Auburn Correctional Facility Records, Inmate Case Files, Series W0006-77A (14610-77A). New York State Archives, Albany. Nursing care for gassed soldiers is described in Constance J. Moore, "Army Nurses Care for Mustard Gas Patients During WWI," *The Connection* (Army Nurse Corps Association newsletter), https://e-anca.org/History /Topics-in-ANC-History/Mustard-WWI.

39 **WOUNDED, DEGREE UNDETERMINED** "313 Casualties Announced in Overseas Army," *New York Times*, September 1, 1918. The list appeared in the *Atlanta Constitution*, Brooklyn's *Times Union*, and the *Democrat and Chronicle* of Rochester, New York, on the same day. The *Boston Globe* published the list, under the headline CASUALTIES AMONG NEW ENGLAND MEN, on August 27, 1918. Several of these lists record the date he was wounded as August 8.

39 **hopped aboard a train** The Paris spree is described in Hickey, *The Gentleman Was a Thief*, 25–26.

39 **"When you go to war"** Martin King, *Battlefield Medics: How Warfare Changed the History of Medicine* (London: Arcturus, 2021), 160.

39 **his name was withdrawn** Barry's biographer attributed the failure to prosecute to "a momentary breakdown in the army's clerical machinery." See Hickey, *The Gentleman Was a Thief*, 27.

40 **"Don't know why"** "Arthur Barry's Own Life Story."

40 **Barry's regiment was fortunate** Pollard, *The Forty-Seventh Infantry*, 59, 62–66, 68–70.

40 **"The men were doubtful"** Pollard, *The Forty-Seventh Infantry*, 71. The regiment's casualty figures are compiled on page 126.

40 **"came in mighty green"** George Seldes, "A Christmas Letter from a Soldier in Germany," *Buffalo Morning Express and Illustrated Buffalo Express*, January 12, 1919.

CHAPTER 4: THE LONG WATCH

41   **crossed scarred battlefields**   The march is described in James E. Pollard, *The Forty-Seventh Infantry: A History, 1917–1918, 1919* (Saginaw, MI: Seeman & Peters, 1919), 72–73, 76–79.

41   **billeted in Dümpelfeld**   Neil Hickey, *The Gentleman Was a Thief: The Colorful Story of Arthur Barry, a 1920's Rogue* (New York: Holt, Rinehart & Winston, 1961), 28.

42   **"It made a picture"**   "Letters from Our Soldier Boys," *Evening Kansan-Republican* (Newton, KS), June 12, 1919.

42   **Watch on the Rhine**   The term was being used by the beginning of 1919. See George H. Seldes, "A Christmas Letter from a Soldier in Germany," *Buffalo Morning Express and Illustrated Buffalo Express*, January 12, 1919.

42   **picked up enough German and French**   Arthur Barry, as told to Grace Robinson, "Galloping Dominos Took Barry Dough," *Daily News* (New York), November 4, 1932.

42   **a regime of training exercises**   Pollard, *The Forty-Seventh Infantry*, 79–80, and Dean A. Nowowiejski, *The American Army in Germany, 1918–1923: Success Against the Odds* (Lawrence: University Press of Kansas, 2021), 30–32.

43   **One American pilot**   "With the American Doughboys Who Are Guarding the Rhine," *Brooklyn Daily Eagle*, June 1, 1919.

43   **the Forgotten Fourth, the Hard Luck Division**   "4th Gives Pershing Rousing Welcome," *Boston Globe*, March 22, 1919.

43   **"War is hell"**   "From Pvt. R.A. Mullenix," *Daily Tribune* (Wisconsin Rapids, WI), March 20, 1919.

43   **impossible to fully enforce**   Nowowiejski, *The American Army in Germany*, 6, 33–34.

43   **Buying a glass of beer**   "With the American Doughboys Who Are Guarding the Rhine."

43   **"No man in American uniform"**   George Seldes, *Witness to a Century: Encounters with the Noted, the Notorious, and the Three SOBs* (New York: Ballantine Books, 1987), 112.

43   **"promenade with the blonde fräulein"**   Seldes, "A Christmas Letter from a Soldier in Germany."

43   **"Men in fighting men's uniforms"**   Seldes, *Witness to a Century*, 118.

43   **"As their armed forces demobilized"**   Margaret MacMillan, *Paris 1919: Six Months That Changed the World* (New York: Random House, 2003), 54.

44   **"growing spirit of dissatisfaction"**   Edwin L. James, "Soldiers on Rhine Beginning to Show Weariness of Army," *Pittsburgh Post-Gazette*, March 2, 1919.

44   **"When do we go home?"**   "May Be After Pershing," *Baltimore Sun*, March 19, 1919.

44   **had to march forty miles**   Descriptions of the Fourth Division review are drawn from Pollard, *The Forty-Seventh Infantry*, 80–82, and "4th Gives Pershing Rousing Welcome," *Boston Globe*, March 22, 1919.

44   **"their fine, clean records"**   "Pershing Inspects Fighting Divisions," *Philadelphia Inquirer*, March 16, 1919.

44   **"presented a brave spectacle"**   George Seldes, "Pershing Inspects Army of Million, Has Question and Word of Praise for Every Man with Wound Stripe," *St. Louis Globe-Democrat*, April 27, 1919.

45 **"a fever of excitement"** Pollard, *The Forty-Seventh Infantry*, 85.

45 **Fourth Division was rearmed** "Foch Ready by Tomorrow to Move Toward Berlin," *Hartford Courant*, June 20, 1919, and Pollard, *The Forty-Seventh Infantry*, 87.

45 **"unremitting military blow"** MacMillan, *Paris 1919*, 471.

45 **had to be inoculated** "Smallpox on Troop Ship; Men Isolated," *Brooklyn Daily Eagle*, July 28, 1919.

45 **disembarked at Hoboken** Records of the Office of the Quartermaster General, 1774–1985, RG 92, microfilm roll 207, National Archives and Records Administration, College Park, MD, via Ancestry.com.

45 **"the most upset aggregation"** "5,000 War Veterans, Vaccinated on Ship, Arrive from France," *New-York Tribune*, July 28, 1919.

45 **marched down Fifth Avenue** Frederick Lewis Allen, *Only Yesterday: An Informal History of the Nineteen-Twenties* (New York and London: Harper & Brothers, 1931), 10.

45 **"All the jubilation"** Seldes, *Witness to a Century*, 118.

45 **"honest and faithful service"** Barry, as told to Robinson, "Arthur Barry's Own Life Story: Jewel Thief Tells About His Exploits," *Daily News*, November 6, 1932. The date of Barry's discharge is recorded in US Department of Veterans Affairs, BIRLS Death File, 1850–2010, Ancestry.com. The form confirming his honorable discharge was reproduced in Anna Blake Barry, "My Life of Love and Fear as the Sweetheart and Wife of Arthur Barry, the World's Most Famous Jewel-Thief," *Atlanta Constitution*, January 15, 1933.

CHAPTER 5: SECOND-STORY MAN

49 **refused to hire Irish Catholics** Timothy J. Meagher, *Inventing Irish America: Generation, Class, and Ethnic Identity in a New England City, 1880–1928* (Notre Dame, IN: University of Notre Dame Press, 2001), 45–48, 99–103. The quotation appears on page 47.

49 **"Time and again I pleaded"** "Mother Will Not Aid New York Jewel Thief," *Boston Globe*, June 8, 1927.

49 **"The cost of living horror"** "The Government Did It; the Government Must Undo It." *New York Herald*, August 5, 1919.

49 **almost doubled since 1914** Frederick Lewis Allen, *Only Yesterday: An Informal History of the Nineteen-Twenties* (New York and London: Harper & Brothers, 1931), 5.

49 **looking for work in New York** "$75,000 Needed to Find Work for Soldiers," *New-York Tribune*, August 9, 1919.

50 **"Nothing is too good"** The cartoon was described in Allen, *Only Yesterday*, 8.

50 **rented an apartment** Neil Hickey, *The Gentleman Was a Thief: The Colorful Story of Arthur Barry, a 1920's Rogue* (New York: Holt, Rinehart & Winston, 1961), 2, 35. The Street View of 1940s New York online database includes photographs of the building in 1946: https://1940s.nyc/map/photo/nynyma_reco040_1_01946_0002#17.5/40.807603/-73.955927.

50 **"hard, cynical, ruthless"** Ernest H. Gruening, "New York: I. The City—Work of Man," in Daniel H. Borus, ed., *These United States: Portraits of America from the 1920s* (Ithaca, NY: Cornell University Press, 1992), 264–65.

50 **"It's a bad town"** F. Scott Fitzgerald, *This Side of Paradise* (New York: Charles Scribner's Sons, 1920), 233.

51   **"unprofitable and somehow disreputable"**   Robert Wallace, "Confessions of a
Master Jewel Thief," in Alexander Klein, ed., *The Double Dealers: Adventures in Grand
Deception* (London: Faber & Faber, 1958), 99, originally published as "Confessions of
Master Jewel Thief," *Life*, March 12, 1956.

51   **"The thought of violence"**   Arthur Barry, as told to Neil Hickey, "I Was the King of
Jewel Thieves," *American Weekly*, January 18, 1959.

51   **"climbs up porches and fire-escapes"**   Upton Sinclair, *Plays of Protest* (New York:
Mitchell Kennerley, 1912), 148.

51   **"clean-cut and sportsmanlike"**   Hickey, *The Gentleman Was a Thief*, 36.

51   **"any smart man"**   "Captured Barry Boasts He Stole 5 to 10 Million," *Brooklyn Daily
Eagle*, October 24, 1932.

51   **hopped aboard a northbound train**   Barry described his first jewel theft and how he
sold the stolen gems in Hickey, *The Gentleman Was a Thief*, 36–41, and Arthur Barry,
as told to Grace Robinson, "Barry Tells Own Story of Robber Feats," *Daily News* (New
York), October 30, 1932. A few details differ in the two accounts. Barry told the *Daily
News* that the first home he burgled was in Connecticut and that he netted only $1,000,
but he was in police custody at the time of the interview and may have been wary of
revealing information tying him to the crime.

52   **circulated a bulletin**   "Thefts Amounting to $27,500 Kept Secret by Police," *New-York
Tribune*, February 1, 1920.

52   **center of New York's diamond trade**   Murray Schumach, "Uneasiness Is Felt by
Merchants in the Diamond District," *New York Times*, October 4, 1977.

52   **"strangest jewelry exchange"**   "Wear Showcases on Hands, Carry Scales in Pockets,
Keep Books Under Hats," *Evening World* (New York), April 21, 1920.

53   **earned in a year**   "Increases for Teachers Are Demanded in Bill," *New-York Tribune*,
February 16, 1920.

53   **A factory worker**   George Moss, *America in the Twentieth Century* (Englewood Cliffs,
NJ: Prentice Hall, 1989), 97.

54   **"The mysterious burglar"**   "John H. Coyne's Home Visited by a Burglar," *Yonkers
Statesman*, November 23, 1920. At least six burglaries or attempted break-ins were
reported to Yonkers police that fall. See also "Daring Thieves Take Jewelry," *Yonkers
Herald*, October 7, 1920, and "South Yonkers Home Robbed," *Yonkers Herald*, October
14, 1920.

54   **"Burglars," his advertisements asserted, "consider Yonkers"**   Classified
advertisement for "Insurance," *Yonkers Herald*, March 22, 1920.

54   **"spacious pieces of property"**   "Vigilantes, with Patrols and Searchlights, to Guard
Ardsley," *New-York Tribune*, March 2, 1922.

54   **slipped into the mansion**   "Banker Thalmann's Home Robbed of $10,000 Gems," *Daily
News*, October 21, 1921.

54   **sightings of a prowler**   "Burglar Gets Gems While Family Dines," *New York Times*,
March 2, 1922.

54   **"excuse me, Mr. Graves"**   "Burglar Gets Gems While Family Dines," *New York Times*,
March 2, 1922. Other details of the burglary are drawn from "Burglar Steals $20,000
Jewels as Family Dines," *Evening World* (New York), March 1, 1922; "Raffles Steals
$62,000 in Gems as Family Dines," *Daily News*, March 2, 1922; and "Get $20,000 Gems
While Family Dines," *New York Herald*, March 2, 1922.

55   **organized a vigilance committee**   "Vigilantes, with Patrols and Searchlights, to Guard Ardsley," *New-York Tribune*, March 2, 1922.

55   **Gold Badge Squad**   "Glare of Headlights Cause of Fatal Crash, Coroner Finds," *Yonkers Herald*, March 22, 1922. This article is also the source of this account of the crash that killed Graves and Wilson.

55   **Volunteer Thug Hunters**   "Volunteer Thug Hunters Killed in Auto Crash," *Daily News*, March 22, 1922.

56   **identify Arthur Barry as the man responsible**   "Believe Livermore Gem Thief Got Nearly Million in County," *Yonkers Statesman*, June 15, 1927.

CHAPTER 6: A SIMPLE ASSAULT

57   **"Go, get them"**   The shooting and its aftermath were described in "Two N.Y. Gunmen Shoot Man After Dance Row Here," *Bridgeport Telegram*, April 14, 1922; "Wagner, Shot at Schwaben Hall, Not Expected to Live," *Bridgeport Times*, April 14, 1922; and "Aurilio Grilled by Coroner," *Bridgeport Times*, April 15, 1922.

58   **"members of a bootlegging ring"**   "Aurilio Grilled by Coroner."

58   **"sinking rapidly"**   "Wagner, Shot at Schwaben Hall, Not Expected to Live." His wounds were described in "Coroner's Report, Death of Peter A. Wagner, April 18, 1922," Connecticut State Library, State Archives Record Group 003, Records of the Judicial Department, Hartford County, Fairfield County Coroner's Reports, vol. 15 (1922), 250.

58   **"to avoid trouble"**   "Wagner Dead, Pal Slashed with Knife, Gang War Feared," *Bridgeport Telegram*, April 19, 1922; "Aurilio Grilled by Coroner"; and "Coroner's Report, Death of Peter A. Wagner," 250–53.

59   **"had an opportunity"**   "Warrant Charges Barry with First Degree Murder," *Bridgeport Times*, April 26, 1922. His arrest and denials of involvement in the shooting were also reported in "Arrest Barry in Dance Hall Murder," *Boston Globe*, April 26, 1922; and "Barry Denies Knowing Where Porter May Be," *Bridgeport Telegram*, May 5, 1922.

59   **He was so ill**   "Arrest Barry in Dance Hall Murder"; "Barry Still at Hospital, May Undergo Operation—No Trace of Joseph Porter," *Bridgeport Times*, May 1, 1922; "Police Sent to Take Barry into Custody," *Bridgeport Telegram*, May 3, 1922; and "Barry in Jail Until Monday," *Bridgeport Times*, May 4, 1922.

59   **"The hangman's noose"**   "Barry Waves Extradition," *Bridgeport Times*, April 29, 1922.

59   **"sat unconcerned" and "suave, debonair"**   "Arthur Barry, Held for Wagner Shooting, Bound Over," *Bridgeport Times*, May 8, 1922.

59   **"but not flashy"**   "Barry in Jail Until Monday."

59   **a Yale Law School graduate**   "Services Monday for George Mara," *Bridgeport Sunday Post*, May 1, 1966. Barry's parents' role in retaining Mara was noted in "Barry Still at Hospital, May Undergo Operation—No Trace of Joseph Porter."

59   **"imminent physical danger"**   "Coroner's Report, Death of Peter A. Wagner," 251–52; "Barry and Porter Held Responsible for Wagner's Death," *Bridgeport Times*, April 28, 1922; and "Coroner Phelan Holds Two for Wagner Shooting," *Bridgeport Telegram*, April 29, 1922.

60   **"He could not swear"**   "Arthur Barry, Held for Wagner Shooting, Bound Over," *Bridgeport Times*, May 8, 1922. Evidence presented at the hearing also was reported in "May Try Barry at Present Term of Criminal Court," *Bridgeport Telegram*, May 9, 1922. The unusual move to demand a preliminary hearing was noted in "Arthur Barry to Face Court Today on Murder Charge," *Bridgeport Telegram*, May 8, 1922.

60 **"The witnesses all exonerated me"** Arthur Barry, as told to Grace Robinson, "Glamor of Barry's 'Big Breaks' Gone," *Daily News* (New York), November 2, 1932.

60 **a charge of manslaughter** "Charge Against Barry Is Reduced to Manslaughter," *Bridgeport Telegram*, May 12, 1922, and "Change Accusation against Barry," *Bridgeport Times*, May 12, 1922.

60 **he remained locked up** "Arthur Barry Pleads Not Guilty—Bonds Set at $2,500," *Bridgeport Times*, May 16, 1922, and "271 Cases Investigated by Coroner," *Bridgeport Times*, June 13, 1922.

61 **pleaded guilty to simple assault** Docket Sheet, *State v. Arthur Barry, alias Arthur Cummings*, May Term 1922, and Judgment, *State v. Arthur Barry*, September 26, 1922, Fairfield County Superior Court, Case No. 4334.

61 **"got off"** "Light Sentence for Accused in Fatal Shooting," *Bridgeport Times*, September 26, 1922.

61 **crept along a dark corridor** The escape and security investigation were described in "Barry Saws Way Out of County Jail," *Bridgeport Times*, November 22, 1922, and "Investigate County Jail; Three Escape," *Bridgeport Times*, November 23, 1922.

62 **"my little prank"** Barry described the escape in "Glamor of Barry's 'Big Breaks' Gone."

62 **"one of the most daringly planned"** "Prisoner Flees Fairfield Jail," *New Britain Herald* (CT), November 22, 1922.

62 **a warrant for his arrest** "New Charge Against Barry to Be Larceny," *Bridgeport Times*, May 12, 1922; "More Prisoners Make Successful Break from Jail Here," *Bridgeport Telegram*, November 23, 1922; and "Livermore Bandit Made Jail Break Here, After Killing," *Bridgeport Telegram*, June 7, 1927.

62 **"I wasn't guilty"** "Glamor of Barry's 'Big Breaks' Gone."

CHAPTER 7: ALL THAT GLITTERS

64 **"Strange animals, statues and gold"** Thomas Hoving, *Tutankhamen: The Untold Story* (New York: Simon & Schuster, 1978), 87–88.

65 **"Picture a heap of jewels"** "Tomb Treasures of Tut-Ankh-Amen Beyond Reckoning," *New York Times*, February 18, 1923. The jewels and other treasures were described in Rebekah Bell, "Seven Ways King Tut Led One of History's Most Luxurious Lifestyles," *Robb Report*, August 18, 2016, https://robbreport.com/shelter/art-collectibles/slideshow /seven-ways-king-tut-led-one-historys-most-luxurious-lifestyles.

65 **only pharaoh's tomb discovered almost intact** "Times Man Views Splendors of Tomb of Tutankhamen," *New York Times*, December 22, 1922.

65 **broken into at least three times** "Carnarvon Tells of Wonders He Saw in Pharoah's Tomb," *New York Times*, February 19, 1923. Carter's discovery of discarded jewelry in the dust was noted in "Treasure Removed from Luxor Tomb," *New York Times*, December 22, 1922. The evidence of three incursions in ancient times was discussed in Hoving, *Tutankhamen*, 174–75.

66 **"In the beginning"** Stellene Volandes, *Jewels That Made History: 100 Stones, Myths & Legends* (New York: Rizzoli, 2020), 9.

66 **found in a Siberian cave** "Stone Bracelet May Have Been Made by Denisovans," *Archaeology*, May 7, 2015, https://www.archaeology.org/news//3270-150507-siberia -denisovan-bracelet.

66 **Julius Caesar . . . decreed** Victoria Finlay, *Jewels: A Secret History* (New York: Ballantine Books, 2006), 77–78.

66 **claimed the sole right** Volandes, *Jewels That Made History*, 14.

67 **"the most non-essential of luxury objects"** Eric Konigsberg, "Old School Jewelry Heists Are on the Rise—and Celebrities Are the Target," *Town & Country*, April 12, 2018, https://www.townandcountrymag.com/society/money-and-power/a19746799/jewelry-heists-celebrities.

67 **"One buys diamonds"** Aja Raden, *Stoned: Jewelry, Obsession, and How Desire Shapes the World* (New York: Ecco, 2015), 38.

67 **"Precious stones have a strange lure"** Paul Harrison, "Even Love Is Cause for Fewer Tears Than Costly Jewels," *Brooklyn Citizen*, December 5, 1926.

67 **a rare yellow-tinted Indian diamond** Wilkie Collins, *The Moonstone* (Hertfordshire, UK: Wordsworth Editions, 1993), 7–12, 41–42.

68 **"the devil's pet baits"** Arthur Conan Doyle, "The Adventure of the Blue Carbuncle," in *The Adventures of Sherlock Holmes* (London: Harper, 2009), 151–52.

68 **"worn sometimes with more love of display"** Agatha Christie, "The Jewel Robbery at the Grand Metropolitan," in *Triple Threat: Exploits of Three Famous Detectives: Hercule Poirot, Harley Quin and Tuppence* (New York: Dodd, Mead, 1943), 131.

68 **"Diamonds are trumps"** "Diamonds Helped Win the War, and Now Everybody's Wearing 'em," *New York Daily Herald*, January 11, 1920.

68 **"People who made money"** "Jewels Quaint and Rare," *Palm Beach Post*, March 14, 1920.

68 **"It is nothing short of hysteria"** Remsen Crawford, "The Revel of Luxury," *New York Times*, September 21, 1919.

68 **in return for a 128-pearl necklace** David Dunlap, "Commercial Real Estate; Cartier Spruces Up to Show Off Its Jewels in Style," *New York Times*, April 26, 2000.

68 **"For the new moneymakers in America"** Finlay, *Jewels*, 107.

69 **"bigger than the Ritz-Carlton Hotel"** F. Scott Fitzgerald, "The Diamond as Big as the Ritz," in Matthew J. Bruccoli, ed., *The Short Stories of F. Scott Fitzgerald* (New York: Scribner, 1989), 185.

69 **"lived like a young rajah"** Fitzgerald, *The Great Gatsby* (Simon and Schuster, 1995), 70–71. The gift of pearls is described on page 80.

69 **"dressed up like a pawnshop window"** "Even Love Is Cause for Fewer Tears Than Costly Jewels."

69 **locked away their jewelry** Polly Fergusson, "Wearing of Paste Jewelry Now in Vogue in Society," *Times Union* (Brooklyn), April 11, 1926.

69 **"All this money in jewels"** "$250,000 in Jewels Stolen in Beverly," *New York Times*, August 11, 1929.

69 **"If you must have jewels"** "Even Love Is Cause for Fewer Tears Than Costly Jewels."

CHAPTER 8: CLIENTS

70 **"The same methods"** "Robbers Get $10,000 Jewelry Loot in Ardsley-on-Hudson," *Yonkers Statesman*, March 1, 1923. The value of the jewels stolen was pegged at between $10,000 and $25,000 in "Burglars Make Big Hauls in Two Houses," *Daily Item* (Port

Chester, NY), March 1, 1923. Fraser's father, Charles D. Fraser, had made the family's fortune as an executive of Lake Superior Consolidated Iron Mines, Minnesota Iron Company, and a half dozen other firms. See *Directory to the Iron and Steel Works of the United States* (Philadelphia: American Iron and Steel Association, 1904), 76–78.

70   **"biggest year"**   "Daring Ladder Thief Here, Riddle to Police, Has Been Operating in City 5 Years," *Yonkers Herald*, June 12, 1926. Information on some of these burglaries was drawn from "Ladder Burglar Frightened Away," *Daily News* (New York), November 9, 1923; "Police on Lookout for Ladder Burglar," *Yonkers Herald*, November 12, 1923; and "Franklin Coe Home Entered by Thief," *Yonkers Herald*, November 16, 1923. Coe's ownership of *Town and Country* in 1923 was noted in "Franklin Coe, 68, Retired Publisher," *New York Times*, February 21, 1940.

71   **Yonkers police scrambled**   These measures were reported in "Police on Lookout for Ladder Burglar," *Yonkers Herald*, November 12, 1923; "Net Drawn Tighter on Ladder Burglar," *Daily News*, November 12, 1923; "Police Have Clue in Ferguson Burglary," *Yonkers Herald*, November 15, 1923; "'Ladder Burglar' Sought in Score of Yonkers Jobs," *Times Union* (Brooklyn), November 21, 1923; "Ladder Thief Eludes Police," *Yonkers Herald*, November 21, 1923; and "Daring Ladder Thief Here, Riddle to Police, Has Been Operating in City 5 Years," *Yonkers Herald*, June 12, 1926.

71   **"Traps have been laid"**   "Daring Ladder Thief Here."

72   **"determined to use their weapons"**   "Ardsley Park Residents Up in Arms Against Burglars," *Yonkers Statesman*, July 20, 1923.

72   **grabbed his army-issue Colt**   John Wheeler, "Cherchez La Femme," *Boston Globe*, January 19, 1951. Barry reportedly confessed to this robbery in 1927. See "Westchester Asks 'Loan' of Barry as Ladder Burglar," *Standard Union* (Brooklyn), June 15, 1927.

72   **the ladder burglar, however, was still at work**   Attempted burglaries in early 1924 were reported in "Ladder Burglar Now Operating in Nepperhan," *Yonkers Statesman*, March 14, 1924, and "Daring Ladder Thief Here, Riddle to Police, Has Been Operating in City 5 Years." The Brooks robbery was reported in "Police Hunting $1,000 Gem Thieves," *Daily News*, March 27, 1924.

72   **Barry had planned and executed**   "Believe Livermore Gem Thief Got Nearly Million in County," *Yonkers Statesman*, June 15, 1927. A Westchester assistant district attorney and a deputy sheriff who interviewed Barry in 1927 revealed that Barry robbed the home of Donald Markel on June 23, 1923, the Waitt residence in January 1924, and the Brooks home on March 25, 1924. See "Scarsdale Murder Laid to Gem Thief," *New York Times*, June 16, 1927.

72   **calling himself Arthur Gibson**   Barry never revealed why he chose Gibson to replace his old alias, Cummings. He may have seen the name in a newspaper while serving time at the Fairfield County Jail. An Arthur Gibson managed rental properties in Bridgeport, and his name frequently appeared in the classified columns of the *Bridgeport Telegram*, including an advertisement published days before Barry's escape. See "Houses for Sale," November 18, 1922. Or he may have read the obituary of a prominent Boston-area doctor with that name, who died earlier that year. See "Dr Arthur A. Gibson, 72, of Somerville Dead," *Boston Globe*, February 7, 1922.

73   **"the most elaborate of all"**   "The Casino Remodeled," *New York Times*, December 25, 1921. A description of the Casino in the early 1920s also appears in Stephen Wolf, "The Night Spot That Roared," *New York Times*, May 25, 2012.

73   **"A lot of wealthy women"**   Robert Wallace, "Confessions of a Master Jewel Thief," in Alexander Klein, ed., *The Double Dealers: Adventures in Grand Deception* (London:

Faber & Faber, 1958), 100, originally published as "Confessions of Master Jewel Thief," *Life*, March 12, 1956. Barry also described his casino visits in Neil Hickey, *The Gentleman Was a Thief: The Colorful Story of Arthur Barry, a 1920's Rogue* (New York: Holt, Rinehart & Winston, 1961), 1–3.

73 **"clients"** Wallace, "Confessions of a Master Jewel Thief," 97.

74 **One productive afternoon visit** Hickey, *The Gentleman Was a Thief*, 3.

74 **"about 80 percent preparation"** Arthur Barry, as told to Grace Robinson, "Barry, in Manacles, Explains 'Success,'" *Daily News*, November 1, 1932.

74 **"Preparedness and thorough planning"** Hickey, *The Gentleman Was a Thief*, 43.

74 **"my unwitting accomplices"** Arthur Barry, as told to Neil Hickey, "I Was the King of Jewel Thieves," *American Weekly*, January 18, 1959. His study of the society pages for news of the wealthy and leads on who owned expensive jewelry was also noted in Anna Blake Barry, "My Life of Love and Fear as the Sweetheart and Wife of Arthur Barry, the World's Most Famous Jewel-Thief," *Atlanta Constitution*, January 29, 1933.

74 **"I knew that Mrs. So-and-So"** Barry, as told to Robinson, "Barry Tells Own Story of Robber Feats," *Daily News*, October 30, 1932.

74 **"No use to make a visit"** "Barry, in Manacles, Explains 'Success.'"

74 **"old money"** Jack Smith, "The Membership You Weren't Allowed to Talk About Is Now Open to New Recruits," *Robb Report*, January 8, 2018, https://robbreport.com /lifestyle/sports-leisure/the-membership-you-werent-allowed-to-talk-about-is-now-open-to-new-recruits-2771295.

74 **"roster of fashionables"** H. L. Mencken, ed., *Americana 1926* (London: Martin Hopkinson, 1926), 274.

75 **claimed to have memorized** Hickey, *The Gentleman Was a Thief*, 4.

75 **A typical edition** *Social Register, New York, 1916, vol. 30, no. 1 (December 1915)* (New York: Social Register Association, 1915).

75 **a $4,000 luxury-class car** Sale prices and images of this Cadillac model as produced in the early 1920s are available at The Cadillac Database (Photo Pages): https://www .newcadillacdatabase.org/static/CDB/Dbas_txt/Phot_ndx.htm.

75 **"After a few cocktails"** "I Was the King of Jewel Thieves." He also described ingratiating himself with household staff in Hickey, *The Gentleman Was a Thief*, 4, 43–44.

75 **chatted up one servant** and **entered a home in Ardsley** Hickey, *The Gentleman Was a Thief*, 43–44.

76 **"Nine out of ten times"** Barry, as told to Robinson, "Arthur Barry's Own Life Story," *Daily News*, November 6, 1932.

76 **"Hide your jewels"** "Jewel Losses Debunked," *Daily News*, June 17, 1927.

76 **"swag"** Barry, as told to Robinson, "Barry Barred Fence as Gem Deal Crook," *Daily News*, November 5, 1932.

76 **"fences in those days"** Wallace, "Confessions of a Master Jewel Thief," 99.

76 **as many as fifty** "Barry, in Manacles, Explains 'Success.'"

76 **"looking for a bargain in jewels"** "Prominent People Buy Stolen Gems, Policemen Assert," *Brooklyn Daily Eagle*, June 19, 1927.

76 **"Jewels," Barry noted, "have strange careers"** "Barry Barred Fence as Gem Deal Crook."

76   **"I never missed an issue"**   "Barry Barred Fence as Gem Deal Crook." Barry mistakenly referred to the weekly as the *Jewelers' Guide*, "a periodical common in the Maiden Lane district," but no publication of that name was produced in New York's diamond district in the 1920s. Issues of the *Jewelers' Circular* published between 1917 and 1935 are available online: https://catalog.hathitrust.org/Record/006082689.

77   **at least a half million dollars' worth**   Hickey, *The Gentleman Was a Thief*, 6.

77   **"with enough ready cash"**   "Barry Barred Fence as Gem Deal Crook."

77   **kept them on as he rode the train and never handled a ladder**   "Barry, in Manacles, Explains 'Success.'"

77   **a night watchman**   "Arthur Barry's Own Life Story."

77   **"keeps male watch dogs"**   Barry, as told to Robinson, "Glamor of Barry's 'Big Breaks' Gone," *Daily News*, November 2, 1932.

77   **"This is only common sense"**   "Barry, in Manacles, Explains 'Success.'"

77   **"One can always depend"**   "Arthur Barry's Own Life Story."

77   **discovered a woodland path**   Hickey, *The Gentleman Was a Thief*, 43. The path Barry used may be part of Westchester County's South County Trailway, a hiking and cycling route that now runs alongside the Saw Mill River Parkway.

78   **"timed as carefully"**   "Barry, in Manacles, Explains 'Success.'"

78   **"practically child's work"**   "Barry, in Manacles, Explains 'Success.'"

78   **"These were of enormous help"** and **"I'm here to service"**   Hickey, *The Gentleman Was a Thief*, 44–45.

78   **"the work of a moment"** and **"and bending the hammer"**   "Barry, in Manacles, Explains 'Success.'"

CHAPTER 9: AMERICAN RAFFLES

79   **could mimic the accents**   This was noted in Neil Hickey, *The Gentleman Was a Thief: The Colorful Story of Arthur Barry, a 1920's Rogue* (New York: Holt, Rinehart & Winston, 1961), 4.

79   **"There were always so many people"**   "Jewel Thief Barry Tells His Methods," *Worcester Daily Telegram*, October 24, 1932.

79   **"came and went like moths"**   F. Scott Fitzgerald, *The Great Gatsby* (New York: Simon and Schuster, 1995), 43.

79   **"Cocktail in hand"** and **"the most bejeweled feminine necks"**   Arthur Barry, as told to Neil Hickey, "I Was the King of Jewel Thieves," *American Weekly*, January 18, 1959. Barry also described crashing garden parties in Robert Wallace, "Confessions of a Master Jewel Thief," in Alexander Klein, ed., *The Double Dealers: Adventures in Grand Deception* (London: Faber & Faber, 1958), 100, originally published as "Confessions of Master Jewel Thief," *Life*, March 12, 1956.

80   **donned a butler's uniform** and **put on a clerical collar**   "New Exploits of Society's Suave and Sinister 'Supper-Man,'" *Detroit Free Press*, November 30, 1930.

80   **"a cerebral crook"**   Hickey, *The Gentleman Was a Thief*, x, 3, 43.

80   **"His manners were impeccable"**   Wallace, "Confessions of a Master Jewel Thief," 97, 99.

80   **"An elegant devil"**   "I Was the King of Jewel Thieves."

80   **"Is that you, Paul?"**   Arthur Barry, as told to Grace Robinson, "Arthur Barry's Own Life Story," *Daily News* (New York), November 6, 1932.

80   **he left two cigarettes**   "Barry Predicts He Will Get Life as Four Termer," *Times Union* (Brooklyn), October 24, 1932.

80   **"just for the hell of it"**   "Arthur Barry's Own Life Story."

81   **"We don't forget people"**   "$2,000,000 Gem Thief, Fugitive for 3 Years, Is Caught in Jersey," *New York Times*, October 23, 1932. The break-in was reported in "Ladder Man Makes Big Haul in Raid on Doctor's Home," *Yonkers Statesman*, May 14, 1925. Blake's war service is noted in "Dr. Blake Marries Mrs. Mackay in Paris," *New York Times*, November 29, 1914. Barry's confession to the burglary was reported in "Scarsdale Murder Laid to Gem Thief," *New York Times*, June 16, 1927. Detectives suspected the burglar was a veteran, who returned the gems after learning of Blake's war record from press reports. See "Stolen Jewels Returned to Blake Home," *Mount Vernon Argus* (White Plains, NY), May 22, 1925.

81   **"Anyone who could afford"**   Kermit Jaediker, "How Burglary's Tom Edison Laughed at Window Locks," *Daily News*, November 25, 1956.

81   **"For what it's worth"**   "Cary Grant: A Class Apart—Quotable Cary," *American Masters*, PBS, May 25, 2005, https://www.pbs.org/wnet/americanmasters/cary-grant-quotable -cary/618.

81   **"One of my first commandments"**   "Arthur Barry's Own Life Story."

81   **"tact and courtesy"**   "Way to Rob Is, 'Be Nice,' Barry Holds," *Worcester Gazette*, June 9, 1927.

81   **"I sometimes thought"**   Hickey, *The Gentleman Was a Thief*, xi.

81   **"the first indication of disturbance"**   "Arthur Barry's Own Life Story." He mentioned the close call, when a bullet grazed his tie pin, in this article.

81   **"The great detective, Sherlock Holmes"**   "E.W. Hornung, Author of 'Raffles,' Dead," *New York Times*, April 8, 1921.

82   **"Why should I work"**   E. W. Hornung, "The Ides of March," in *The Collected Raffles Stories* (Oxford: Oxford University Press, 1996), 19.

82   **"the last Victorian hero"**   Clive Bloom, introduction to *The Collected Raffles Stories*, xxi.

82   **"the socially irreproachable hero"**   "'Raffles' for Talking Film," *New York Times*, October 20, 1929.

82   **"still one of the best-known"**   George Orwell, "Raffles and Miss Blandish," *Decline of the English Murder and Other Essays* (London: Penguin Books, 1965), 63.

82   **"I have nothing but my wits"**   Hornung, "The Ides of March," 7.

83   **"the table sparkled with their hoard"**   Hornung, "The Ides of March," 18.

84   **"the richly immoral"**   Hornung, "A Jubilee Present," in *The Collected Raffles Stories*, 150.

84   **"He will commit a burglary"**   Orwell, "Raffles and Miss Blandish," 66–67.

84   **"a part of headline language"**   A. J. Liebling, "Horsefeathers Swathed in Mink," *New Yorker*, November 22, 1947, 66.

84   **as early as 1922**   The earliest headline reference appears to be RAFFLES STEALS $62,000 IN GEMS AS FAMILY DINES, *Daily News*, March 2, 1922.

84   **The references puzzled Barry**   Hickey, *The Gentleman Was a Thief*, 78.

84   **"consummate daring and extraordinary nerve"**   Hornung, "The Ides of March," 8.

84   **"I think it gives one confidence"**   Hornung, "The Ides of March," 19.

84   **"infinitely the finest monarch"**   Hornung, "A Jubilee Present," 160.

85   **"an overwhelming show of force"**   Glenn Stout, *Tiger Girl and the Candy Kid: America's Original Gangster Couple* (New York: Mariner Books, 2021), 106. Stout describes the New York jewelry heists on pages 106–14, 127–33, and 138–48.

85   **"Pardon us"**   All quotations in this paragraph have been drawn from Charles Leerhsen, *Butch Cassidy: The True Story of an American Outlaw* (New York: Simon & Schuster, 2020), 9–17.

85   **"I had plotted and planned" and "urbane scoundrel"**   Peter Duffy, "City Lore: Willie Sutton, Urbane Scoundrel," *New York Times*, February 17, 2002.

85   **"You can't rob a bank"**   Steve Cocheo, "The Bank Robber, THE QUOTE, and the Final Irony," *ABA Banking Journal* 89, no. 3 (March 1997): 71.

85   **"insurance will cover this"**   Albin Krebs, "Willie Sutton Is Dead at 79; Bank Robber Got $2 Million," *New York Times*, November 19, 1980. Sutton's fame rested in part on a published comment he denied saying—that he robbed banks "because that's where they keep the money."

86   **"You got to hand it"**   David Grann, *The Old Man and the Gun and Other Tales of True Crime* (New York: Vintage, 2018), 3–4, 7, 13–14, 22–23.

86   **"His stage presence"**   Wallace, "Confessions of a Master Jewel Thief," 100.

CHAPTER 10: COSDEN AND MOUNTBATTEN

89   **"It was just before daybreak"**   Accounts of what Mountbatten saw and heard include Henry M. Paynter, Jr., "Hear Prince Guest at Cosden Home Night of Gem Robbery; Detectives See Heads of International Ring," *Buffalo Courier*, September 11, 1924; "Mountbattens Lose Jewelry Worth $10,000; Detectives Expect Speedy Arrest," *Daily News* (New York), September 11, 1924; "Cosden Theft Laid to 'Average Crook,'" *New York Times*, September 12, 1924; "Cosden Robbery Clue Is Expected to Bring Arrest Within 2 Days," *Times Union* (Brooklyn), September 12, 1924; and "Lady Louis Mountbatten: Jewel Loss 'Very Light,'" *Daily Telegraph* (London), September 12, 1924.

89   **New York's old-money families**   Sands Point estates of the 1920s were identified through a search of the website Old Long Island, at http://www.oldlongisland.com /search/label/Sands%20Point.

90   **an inheritance of $70 million**   Gustavus Myers, *History of the Great American Fortunes* (New York: Modern Library, 1936), 169.

90   **rented a house in Great Neck**   Maureen Corrigan, *So We Read On: How The Great Gatsby Came to Be and Why It Endures* (New York: Little, Brown, 2014), 112–18. A 1927 map published in the *New Yorker*, reproduced on page 119, locates the estate of the Cosdens' neighbor, Vincent Astor, on the western side of Sands Point, overlooking Hempstead Harbor.

90   **"the consoling proximity of millionaires"**   F. Scott Fitzgerald, *The Great Gatsby* (Simon & Schuster, 1995), 9–10.

90   **headed west and struck it rich**   Details of Cosden's rise in the oil industry and the properties he owned in 1924 are compiled from "'Game Josh' Cosden, Rubber Ball of Oil Industry, Dies at 59," *Oshkosh Northwestern*, November 18, 1940; "Joshua Cosden Dies on Train," *Fort Worth Star-Telegram*, November 18, 1940; "Unsettled Oil," *Time*,

November 17, 1930; "Big Spring," *Time*, April 10, 1933; Debbie Jackson and Hilary Pittman, "Throwback Tulsa: 'Prince of Petroleum' Left Towering Legacy," *Tulsa World*, March 23, 2017; and Larry O'Dell, "Cosden, Joshua Seney," *Encyclopedia of Oklahoma History and Culture*, https://www.okhistory.org/publications/enc/entry?entry=CO065.

90 **"Oil gushed up"** Winifred Van Duzer, "How the New-Rich Cosdens Nabbed the Prince," *Miami Tribune*, October 19, 1924.

90 **"No story-book hero"** "Auctioneer Will End Fabulous Cosden Saga," *Daily News*, November 13, 1940.

90 **"spirit of America"** "The Flame of Ambition," *Times* (Shreveport, LA), November 23, 1940.

91 **"small, dapper, energetic man"** Lemuel F. Parton, "Who's News Today?" *Indianapolis Star*, November 16, 1940.

91 **former estate of William Bourke Cockran** Betsy Silverstein, "Preserving a Piece of Sands Point History: The Cockran Barns," *Journal of the Cow Neck Peninsula Historical Society 2017/2018*, https://www.cowneck.org/william-bourke-cockran.

91 **one of the finest properties** This description of the estate is based on "Astor Buys Long Island Park for Home Sites; Will Put Up Dwellings for $15,000 to $30,000," *New York Times*, January 15, 1926, and Charles F. Shepard, "Port Washington Will Have Big Development This Spring," *Brooklyn Daily Eagle*, January 24, 1926. *Crimper* is described in "Edward B. McLean Buys Cosden Yacht," *Washington Times*, March 28, 1925.

91 **Castle Petroleum** "Life of Prince Threatened in a Letter Mailed to Acting British Consul General Here," *Daily News*, September 5, 1924.

91 **"Cosden has all the instincts"** Van Duzer, "How the New-Rich Cosdens Nabbed the Prince." On the writer, see "Winifred Van Duzer, a Newspaper Writer," *New York Times*, March 7, 1951.

91 **the playfully named Snob II** "French Horse Meets Kings of Turf at Belmont," *Daily News*, September 1, 1924.

91 **"Any millionaire can drive"** Van Duzer, "How the New-Rich Cosdens Nabbed the Prince."

91 **cartoon published in 1922** "How the Man from Oklahoma Rode into the '400,'" *Times Dispatch* (Richmond, VA), May 21, 1922.

92 **"a dear boy"** and **"a marvellous person"** Philip Ziegler, *Mountbatten: The Official Biography* (London: Collins, 1985), 54. The prince's complaints about his "rotten" family and life are quoted on page 55.

92 **"How I loathe my job"** Juliet Nicolson, *The Great Silence: Britain from the Shadow of the First World War to the Dawn of the Jazz Age* (New York: Grove, 2009), 181.

92 **"blazed in London society"** Ziegler, *Mountbatten*, 66.

92 **"close relation of the King of England"** Ziegler, *Mountbatten*, 71–73.

93 **"No one living enjoys less privacy"** P. W. Wilson, "The Prince of Wales Returns," *New York Times*, August 17, 1924.

93 **more than seventy journalists** The press attention is described in Ted Powell, *King Edward VIII: An American Life* (Oxford: Oxford University Press, 2018), 101–3.

93 **spotted boarding Crimper** "Prince Is No 'Jazz Hound,' but Surely Loves Dancing," *Standard Union* (Brooklyn), September 5, 1924.

93 **"entertained the prince in a quiet way"** "New York Society Engrossed in Plans for Prince of Wales," *Evening Star* (Washington, DC), September 14, 1924.

93   **almost as much time at the Cosdens'**   Van Duzer, "How the New-Rich Cosdens Nabbed the Prince."

93   **listed in the Social Register**   Van Duzer, "How the New-Rich Cosdens Nabbed the Prince."

93   **a staple of the newspaper society pages**   "Society at the Capital—News of the Resorts," *New-York Tribune*, January 30, 1921; "Round of Dances Marks Waning of Palm Beach Season," *New-York Tribune*, March 27, 1921; "Social Notes," *New York Herald*, September 20, 1921; "Society Notes," *New-York Tribune*, December 21, 1921; and "Social Notes," *New York Herald*, March 3, 1922. Neil Hickey, in *The Gentleman Was a Thief: The Colorful Story of Arthur Barry, a 1920's Rogue* (New York: Holt, Rinehart & Winston, 1961), 13, confirmed that Barry monitored news reports of the prince's visits with the Cosdens, as did Barry's wife in Anna Blake Barry, "My Life of Love and Fear as the Sweetheart and Wife of Arthur Barry, the World's Most Famous Jewel-Thief," *Atlanta Constitution*, January 29, 1933.

93   **one of the finest in the world**   "Jewels Quaint and Rare," *Palm Beach Post*, March 14, 1920.

93   **identical size and color**   "$7,000,000 Left to Art Museum," *The Sun* (New York), May 4, 1917, and "$4,557,904 Estate Left to Museum," *New York Herald*, July 4, 1918.

94   **bought one for his wife**   "Big Spring," *Time*, April 10, 1933.

94   **wearing the magnificent pearls**   See "Mrs. Joshua S. Cosden," *New-York Tribune*, July 29, 1922, and "How the Man from Oklahoma Rode into the '400.'"

94   **"a comfort and reassurance"**   Richard Hough, *Edwina: Countess Mountbatten of Burma* (London: Weidenfeld & Nicolson, 1983), 97. Ashley wore a strand in an image that appeared under the headline A GODDAUGHTER OF THE LATE KING in the *Tatler*, March 1, 1922, 289. Hough's book includes several photographs of her wearing pearls, even when she accompanied her husband on a fishing trip.

94   **Barry parked his Cadillac**   This account of the robbery is drawn from Hickey, *The Gentleman Was a Thief*, 13–16; Arthur Barry, as told to Grace Robinson, "Barry Bares Rialto Bout with Wales," *Daily News*, November 3, 1932; and Blake Barry, "My Life of Love and Fear," *Atlanta Constitution*, January 29 and February 5, 1933.

94   **returned from a dance**   "Investigators Believe Quarter Million Jewel Robbery Was Inside Job," *Buffalo Commercial*, September 11, 1924.

95   **five-room bedroom suite**   A floor plan of the Cosden and Mountbatten bedrooms was published in "Baffling Mr. Cosden and the $50,000,000 Somersault," *Philadelphia Inquirer*, December 21, 1930.

95   **worth a total of $130,000**   The value of the stolen Cosden gems was reported in "Cosdens and Mountbattens Bar Police and Reporters from Aiding Gem Search," *Brooklyn Citizen*, September 11, 1924, and "Cosden Theft Laid to 'Average Crook,'" *New York Times*, September 12, 1924. Lady Mountbatten's losses were itemized in "The Gem in the Shirt," *News Journal* (Wilmington, DE), September 15, 1924, and "The Long Island Jewel Robbery," *The Times* (London), October 13, 1924. The sum of money in her husband's wallet was reported in "Did Raffles or Slick Woman Thief Steal Costly Jewels of Prince of Wales Hosts?" *Brooklyn Daily Eagle*, October 5, 1924.

96   **sharing the front page**   See "Wales' Party Robbed of Jewels," *Washington Times* (DC), September 10, 1924; "Cosden Reports Jewel Robbery," *Indianapolis Times*, September 10, 1924; and "Lady Mountbatten's Jewels Stolen from J.S. Cosden Home on Long Island," *Ottawa Evening Citizen*, September 10, 1924.

96   **a photograph of Nellie Cosden** "Huge Gem Theft," *Daily News*, September 11, 1924.

96   **"two of the wealthiest families"** "Mystery Still Shrouds Theft at Cosden Home," *Evening Sun* (Baltimore), September 11, 1924.

96   **headlines around the world** The coverage is compiled in "General Press Cuttings September 1924 to April 1925, vol. V," MS62/MB/17/12, Mountbatten Papers: Press Cuttings of Edwina, Countess Mountbatten of Burma, in the Broadlands Archives, University of Southampton, UK.

96   **offered readers the lowdown** "Mountbatten Gem Mystery," *Daily Chronicle* (London), September 11, 1924, and "Lady Louis' Loss," *Daily News* (London). September 11, 1924.

96   **"social outcasts and parvenus"** Ziegler, *King Edward VIII*, 131–32.

96   **"There isn't any master criminal"** "Police Threaten to Break Secrecy in Probe into Cosden Gem Robbery," *Daily News*, September 12, 1924, and "L.I. Sleuths Start Cosden Robbery Probe," *Times Union*, September 11, 1924.

96   **a gang of international thieves** "Hear Prince Guest at Cosden Home Night of Gem Robbery; Detectives See Heads of International Ring."

96   **"a gentleman Raffles"** "Did Raffles or Slick Woman Thief Steal Costly Jewels of Prince of Wales Hosts?"

96   **"known to have visited"** "Sanford Confirms $50,000 Gem Theft," *New York Times*, October 2, 1924.

97   **dispatching a lone patrolman** "Cosdens and Mountbattens Bar Police and Reporters from Aiding Gem Search."

97   **"Not a jewel was lost"** "Wales Follows Hounds, Proved Expert Rider," *Buffalo Times*, September 11, 1924.

97   **"apparently unruffled"** and **"substantial clue"** "Arrest in Theft of Cosden Gems Expected Today," *Daily News*, September 11, 1924.

97   **an inside job** See "Cosden Home Robbed as Prince Is Feted," *Evening Sun*, September 10, 1924, and "Cosden Gem Theft Baffles Police; All Night Search," *Brooklyn Daily Eagle*, September 11. 1924.

97   **in an unlocked drawer** "Clue Found in Cosden Theft; Arrest Near," *Buffalo Enquirer*, September 12, 1924.

97   **an experienced professional** "$250,000 in Gems Are Stolen from Cosden L.I. Home," *Brooklyn Daily Eagle*, September 10, 1924.

97   **the Cosdens finally met** "Cosden Tells of Robbery," *New York Times*, September 17, 1924, and "Sanford Confirms $50,000 Gem Theft."

97   **"The trackers of criminals"** "$125,000 Insurance Paid in Mountbatten Gem Robbery," *San Francisco Examiner*, November 4, 1924.

97   **"very pinnacle of my success"** "Barry Bares Rialto Bout with Wales."

CHAPTER 11: THE PLAZA PEARLS

98   **stepped from a taxicab** Barry described how he stole the Donahue gems in Neil Hickey, *The Gentleman Was a Thief: The Colorful Story of Arthur Barry, a 1920's Rogue* (New York: Holt, Rinehart & Winston, 1961), 61–7.

98   **had given the Cosdens a foothold** Winifred Van Duzer, "How the New-Rich Cosdens Nabbed the Prince," *Miami Tribune*, October 19, 1924.

99 **"state of perfection"** "New Plaza Hotel Cost $12,500,000," *New York Times*, September 12, 1907.

99 **"New York's best address"** Stephen Birmingham, *The Right Places (For the Right People)*, (Guilford, CT: Lyons, 2016), 191.

99 **needed to pick a swank Manhattan hotel** F. Scott Fitzgerald, *The Great Gatsby* (New York: Simon & Schuster, 1995), 132–42. Narrator Nick Carraway also meets Jordan Baker for lunch at the hotel; see page 79.

100 **beachfront mansion in Palm Beach** and **summer retreat, in Southampton** "J.P. Donahue Dies; Poison Kills Broker" and "A Social Leader at Palm Beach," *New York Times*, April 24, 1931.

100 **"well-to-do in a modest way"** Grace Robinson, "Woolworths Fail to Clear Suicide," *Daily News* (New York), April 25, 1931.

100 **one-third of his $55 million estate** Gustavus Myers, *History of the Great American Fortunes* (New York: Modern Library, 1936), 711.

100 **Her tax assessment** "Woolworth Heiress Robbed at the Plaza of $750,000 in Gems," *New York Times*, October 2, 1925.

100 **a jaw-dropping $900,000** "Woolworths Fail to Clear Suicide" and John O'Donnell, "Woolworth Son-in-Law Dies a Mystery Suicide," *Daily News*, April 24, 1931.

101 **"attired like a regal princess"** Mary Cummings, "High Style in the Gilded Age: Jessie Woolworth Donahue," *Southampton History Museum Blog* (December 1, 2020), https://www.southamptonhistory.org/post/high-style-in-the-gilded-age-jessie-woolworth-donahue.

101 **an oversized glittering tiara** See, for instance, "Safe Blowers Get $150,000 Gems," *Daily News*, October 5, 1925.

101 **"Woolworth family jewels"** "Heroes of the Week," *New Yorker*, October 10, 1925, 6.

101 **"very fond of pearls"** "Woolworth Heiress Robbed."

101 **the royal family of Persia** "Woolworth Gem Thieves Are Experts," *Brooklyn Citizen*, October 3, 1925.

101 **"that finishes the necklace"** "Woolworth Heiress Robbed."

102 **suites of any size** "The Plaza Hotel: H. J. Hardenberg, Architect," *Architects' and Builders' Magazine* 9, no. 1 (October 1907): 14. The layout of the Donahue suite was described in "Enright Hunts Donahue Jewel Thief In Person," *Times Union* (Brooklyn), October 2, 1925.

102 **a ten-carat diamond** Descriptions of the major pieces stolen appeared in "Enright Hunts Donahue Jewel Thief In Person"; "Woolworth Heiress Robbed"; and "$683,000 Gem Theft Seen as Inside Job; $20,000 Reward Offer," *Brooklyn Daily Eagle*, October 2, 1925. The jewels taken are also described in *The People vs. Noel C. Scaffa*, 1925; New York County District Attorney Indictments, 1883–1951; REC 007; 162229; Municipal Archives, City of New York.

102 **"The easy way to tell"** Robert Wallace, "Confessions of a Master Jewel Thief," in Alexander Klein, ed., *The Double Dealers: Adventures in Grand Deception* (London: Faber & Faber, 1958), 102, originally published as "Confessions of Master Jewel Thief," *Life*, March 12, 1956.

103 **"Did you hide my jewels?"** "Police Probe Inside Job Theory in $1,000,000 Plaza Jewel Theft," *Daily News*, October 2, 1925.

104 **"the greatest coup in gem robberies"** "$683,000 Gem Theft Seen as Inside Job."

105 **consoling the shaken Donahues** "Woolworth Heiress Robbed."

105   **"tracing Wall Street bond thieves"**   "$300,000 in Gems Loot of Crooks in Chicago and Indianapolis, Ind.," *Brooklyn Daily Eagle*, October 3, 1925.

105   **"international thieves of high calibre"**   "Woolworth Gem Thieves Are Experts," *Brooklyn Citizen*, October 3, 1925. Details of the investigation are drawn from "Police Probe Inside Job Theory in $1,000,000 Plaza Jewel Theft"; "$683,000 Gem Theft Seen as Inside Job"; "Enright Hunts Donahue Jewel Thief In Person"; and "Woolworth Heiress Robbed."

105   **might embolden other crooks**   "$683,000 Gem Theft Seen as Inside Job" and "Police Probe Inside Job Theory in $1,000,000 Plaza Jewel Theft." For criticism of the delay in reporting the crime to police, see "Secrecy Clogs Police Hunt for Woolworth Jewel Loot," *Daily News*, October 3, 1925.

105   **"We know the jewels are gone"**   "Secrecy Clogs Police Hunt for Woolworth Jewel Loot."

105   **chided Donahue for wearing**   "Police Probe Inside Job Theory in $1,000,000 Plaza Jewel Theft."

106   **"several quarts"**   "Heroes of the Week" and "Of All Things," *New Yorker*, October 10, 1925, 6, 8.

106   **"a shrewd knowledge of pearls"**   "Woolworth Heiress Robbed."

106   **"It will be almost impossible"**   "Secrecy Clogs Police Hunt for Woolworth Jewel Loot." A photograph of the necklace accompanied this report.

106   **"a master criminal"**   "Police Soon to Have Photos of Every Pearl in String Stolen from Mrs. Donahue," *Standard Union* (Brooklyn), October 4, 1925.

CHAPTER 12: THE GREAT RETRIEVER

107   **Barry claimed a chair**   Unless otherwise noted, Barry's movements, conversations, and dealings with Scaffa are drawn from the account he gave to his biographer. Neil Hickey, *The Gentleman Was a Thief: The Colorful Story of Arthur Barry, a 1920's Rogue* (New York: Holt, Rinehart & Winston, 1961), 67–74.

107   **an Upper West Side landmark**   The hotel and lobby are described in Tom Miller, "Check Out the Hotel Endicott," Landmark West, https://www.landmarkwest.org /theywerehere/440-columbus-avenue.

107   **"most famed of U.S. private detectives"**   "Retriever in Trouble," *Time*, June 10, 1935.

107   **"smart enough to know"**   "Detecting Noel Scaffa, Crack Jewel Detective," *Daily News* (New York), April 28, 1935.

108   **the Great Retriever**   Gene Coughlin, "Hot Diamonds," *San Francisco Examiner*, May 1, 1949.

108   **recovered millions of dollars' worth**   "Millions in Gems Restored by Scaffa's Work," *New York American*, April 23, 1935. A clipping of the article appears in the Frank Costello Files, Federal Bureau of Investigation, File 87-30 Sub A, 55, https://archive.org/details /FrankCostelloFBI/Costello%2C%20Frank%20File%20%23%2087-30%20SUB.%20A /mode/2up.

108   **"If Scaffa couldn't get them"**   Hickey, *The Gentleman Was a Thief*, 76.

109   **Scaffa walked through the door**   The return of the gems to Coughlin and the interview at the district attorney's office was reported in "Get Donahue Gems; Mystery in Return as Deep as in Theft," *New York Times*, October 14, 1925, and "Donahue Jewels Regained, Arrest Is Believed Near," *Times Union* (Brooklyn), October 14, 1925.

110   **"hard but fair"**   "Ferdinand Pecora, Financial Prober," *Miami Herald*, December 9, 1971. Other biographical details are drawn from "Ex-Justice Ferdinand Pecora, 89, Dead," *New York Times*, December 8, 1971.

110   **Scaffa told them**   Scaffa's statement was reproduced in "Pecora Fails to Identify Jewel Thief," *Brooklyn Daily Eagle*, October 19, 1925; "Paid $65,000 to Get Donahue Gems Back," *New York Times*, October 21, 1925; and "Pecora Bares Astounding Transaction in Return of Donahue Gems," *Daily News*, October 21, 1925. Scaffa rounded up the amount paid to Barry to $65,000, $1,000 more than Barry recalled receiving, and this figure was widely reported in news coverage of the return of the jewels.

110   **He described Layton**   "Paid $65,000 to Get Donahue Gems Back."

110   **the name was Scaffa's invention**   Hickey, *The Gentleman Was a Thief*, 74.

110   **no record of Scaffa booking a room**   "Paid $65,000 to Get Donahue Gems Back."

110   **"A single double cross"**   Hickey, *The Gentleman Was a Thief*, 71.

111   **offered to turn in the thief**   Hickey, *The Gentleman Was a Thief*, 71.

111   **"sneak thief"**   "Get Donahue Gems; Mystery in Return as Deep as in Theft."

111   **"There will be no compromise"**   "Denies Donahue Bought Gems Back," *New York Times*, October 16, 1925.

111   **"No bargains with thieves"**   "Donahue Gems Not Returned as Rumors Die," *Times Union*, October 12, 1925.

111   **"The public is entitled to facts"**   "'The Great Jewel Robbery,' or 'The Unknown Man,'" *Daily News*, October 21, 1925.

111   **"What kind of law enforcement"**   "Why We Have Crime Waves," *Brooklyn Daily Eagle*, October 14, 1925.

111   **"won't it encourage other thefts"**   "Donahue Jewel Arrest Soon Predicted by Police; Case Like Cosden L.I. Robbery," *Times Union*, October 15, 1925. The possible offenses were also discussed in "No Move to Unmask Man of Mystery in Donahue Gem Return," *Brooklyn Daily Eagle*, October 14, 1925, and "Why We Have Crime Waves."

111   **"compounding" a felony**   The legal definition of the offense was reported in "Facts in Donahue Gem Theft Told to Grand Jury," *Brooklyn Daily Eagle*, October 21, 1925.

111   **launched a grand jury investigation**   "Donahues Appear at Grand Jury, Tell Gem Secret," *Times Union*, October 21, 1925.

112   **"As to the truth or falsity"**   "Donahue Gem Case Before Grand Jury," *New York Times*, October 22, 1925; "Doubts Scaffa Tale of Donahue Jewels," *New York Times*, October 23, 1925; and "Donahues Before Jury; Pecora Now Doubts Gem Tale," *Brooklyn Daily Eagle*, October 22, 1925.

112   **"a grave mistake"**   "Scaffa Tells Story of Return of Pearls," *Daily News*, October 23, 1925.

112   **Scaffa was indicted**   "Scaffa Indicted in Donahue Gem Case," *New York Times*, October 24, 1925. The grand jury's true bill and the indictment have survived: *The People vs. Noel C. Scaffa*, 1925; New York County District Attorney Indictments, 1883–1951; REC 007; 162229; Municipal Archives, City of New York.

112   **a bid to stamp out the practice**   "New Gem Theft Indictments Seen; Scaffa, On Bail, Plans Statement," *Daily News*, October 24, 1925.

112   **"issuing an open invitation"**   "Legislative Gem Probe Looms," *Daily News*, October 23, 1925.

112   **one of the missing Cosden gems**   "Scaffa Indicted in Donahue Gem Case." The ring's value was reported in "Mystery in Story That Cosden Gem Has Been Returned," *Brooklyn Daily Eagle*, January 8, 1925.

112 **continued to hunt for stolen jewels** See, for instance, "No Clue to Taylor Thief," *New York Times*, December 4, 1925, and "Col. Starr's Home Robbed of $20,000," *New York Times*, December 22, 1925.

113 **"The whole system smells"** "Scaffa the Great," *Daily Mirror*, April 26, 1935. Clippings of the article and cartoon appear in the Frank Costello Files, Federal Bureau of Investigation, File 87-30 Sub A, 119.

113 **"better than a total loss"** and **"accidentally found the jewels"** Robert Wallace, "Confessions of a Master Jewel Thief," in Alexander Klein, ed., *The Double Dealers: Adventures in Grand Deception* (London: Faber & Faber, 1958), 99–100, originally published as "Confessions of Master Jewel Thief," *Life*, March 12, 1956.

113 **An ex-con came forward** "Scotland Yard Aid Asked in Gem Theft," *New York Times*, October 29, 1925.

113 **the Donahues' maid and valet** "Gem Net Seen Snaring Two," *Daily News*, November 8, 1925.

113 **arrests were imminent** See, for instance, "Thrill Arrests for Gem Theft Still Missing," *Daily News*, November 9, 1925.

114 **a petty crook seeking attention** "Camden Prisoner Boasts of Part in Donahue Gem Haul," *Brooklyn Daily Eagle*, July 1, 1926.

114 **"bold rogue"** Morris Markey, "An Unsolved Mystery," *New Yorker*, December 12, 1925, 19.

CHAPTER 13: NIGHTLIFE PLUNGER

115 **"old quarrels, old love affairs"** "Fifth Anniversary of the Elwell Murder Finds It Listed as the Perfect Mystery," *New York Times*, June 12, 1925. Details of the crime scene are drawn from Jonathan Goodman, *The Slaying of Joseph Bowne Elwell* (New York: St. Martin's, 1988), 73–89, and "What Has Happened to Justice?: Was It Blind in Elwell Case, a Three-Year Mystery?" *Daily News* (New York), May 13, 1923.

115 **"concocted a murder mystery"** "Elwell, the Man of Many Masks," *New York Times*, June 20, 1920.

116 **Elwell's movements the previous night** Goodman, *The Slaying of Joseph Bowne Elwell*, 61–71, and "J.B. Elwell, Whist Expert and Race Horse Owner, Slain," *New York Times*, June 12, 1920.

116 **The contents of the home** "Elwell's Belongings to Be Auctioned," *New York Times*, October 2, 1920.

116 **rented the town house to Myrtle King** Arthur Barry, as told to Grace Robinson, "Galloping Dominos Took Barry Dough," *Daily News*, November 4, 1932. Bernard Sandler, a lawyer with offices on Broadway, was identified as the owner in "May Reopen Inquiry in Elwell Murder," *New York Times*, May 22, 1924.

116 **"I've been a gambler"** and **"I can no more resist"** "Galloping Dominos Took Barry Dough."

116 **"I took it easy at first"** Neil Hickey, *The Gentleman Was a Thief: The Colorful Story of Arthur Barry, a 1920's Rogue* (New York: Holt, Rinehart & Winston, 1961), 53.

116 **a $35,000 windfall** "Galloping Dominos Took Barry Dough."

116 **dropping $15,000 . . . in a single disastrous night** Hickey, *The Gentleman Was a Thief*, 54.

116   **a motley crew** Goldstein, Fallon, Crater, and other patrons of Barry's gambling house were identified in "Galloping Dominos Took Barry Dough."

116   **"where another man's bankroll came from"** Hickey, *The Gentleman Was a Thief*, 53–54. This is also the source of Barry's description of being chauffeured to craps games.

118   **bantamweight champion of the world** "Goldstein Wins Bantam Title from Lynch," *Daily News*, March 22, 1924, and "Bantamweight Championship Back in Brooklyn after Twenty-five Years," *Standard Union* (Brooklyn), December 20, 1924.

118   **disgraced doctor** Paul Drexler, "The Crimes of 'Dr. Grant,'" *San Francisco Examiner*, February 28, 2016, https://www.sfexaminer.com/news/the-crimes-of-dr-grant.

118   **would soon be sent to prison** "Fuller and McGee Win Sing Sing Paroles; Served Year for $4,000,000 Bucketing Frauds," *New York Times*, June 1, 1928.

118   **"most brazen of attorneys"** Gene Fowler, *The Great Mouthpiece: A Life Story of William Fallon* (New York: Bantam Books, 1946), 403. That Broadway actors attended Fallon's trials is mentioned on page 118, and Fallon's record of acquittals in homicide cases is on page 254. Fowler confirms Fallon's legal work for Rothstein, and this is also noted in Herbert Mitgang, *Once Upon a Time in New York: Jimmy Walker, Franklin Roosevelt, and the Last Great Battle of the Jazz Age* (New York: Cooper Square Press, 2003), 8. Carl Sifakis, *The Encyclopedia of American Crime* (New York: Facts on File, 1982), 244–45, provides an overview of Fallon's career.

118   **Good Time Joe** Stephen J. Riegel, *Finding Judge Crater: A Life and Phenomenal Disappearance in Jazz Age New York* (Syracuse, NY: Syracuse University Press, 2022), 16. Crater's reputation as "a big spender and skirt chaser" is noted in Mitgang, *Once Upon a Time in New York*, 24.

118   **"too busy dealing the chips"** "Galloping Dominos Took Barry Dough."

119   **"Seems the Elwell mystery"** "Galloping Dominos Took Barry Dough."

119   **"My philosophy was to live hard"** Hickey, *The Gentleman Was a Thief*, 7.

119   **"youth, wealth and celebrity were venerated"** Lucy Moore, "The Shape of Things to Come: What the 1920s Can Teach Us About the 2020s," *Globe and Mail* (Toronto), December 28, 2019, https://www.theglobeandmail.com/opinion/article-the-shape-of-things-to-come-what-the-1920s-can-teach-us-about-the.

119   **"A whole generation had been infected"** Frederick Lewis Allen, *Only Yesterday: An Informal History of the Nineteen-Twenties* (New York and London: Harper & Brothers, 1931), 94.

120   **"the grandest, gaudiest spree"** F. Scott Fitzgerald, "Early Success," in Edmund Wilson, ed., *The Crack Up* (New York: New Directions, 1956), 87.

120   **the Lost Generation** Carlos Baker, *Hemingway: The Writer as Artist*, 4th ed. (Princeton, NJ: Princeton University Press, 1972), 365.

120   **"We have been forced to live"** John F. Carter, "'These Wild Young People' by One of Them," *Atlantic Monthly* (September 1920), 301–4, https://wpscms.pearsoncmg.com/wps/media/objects/1693/1733989/documents/doc_d090.html.

120   **Irene Castle appeared on screen** Gary Dean Best, *The Dollar Decade: Mammon and the Machine in 1920s America* (Westport, CT: Praeger, 2003), 52.

120   **"More people were comfortably well-off"** John Kenneth Galbraith, *The Great Crash 1929* (Boston: Houghton Mifflin, 1988), 2.

121   **quadrupled during the decade** Allen, *Only Yesterday*, 163.

121   **"You can't go to town in a bathtub"** George Moss, *America in the Twentieth Century* (Englewood Cliffs, NJ: Prentice Hall, 1989), 97.

121   **"nightly miracle"**   Best, *The Dollar Decade*, 56–59.

121   **"We are lucky dogs"**   Sherwood Anderson, "Hello, Big Boy," *Vanity Fair*, July 1926, republished in Graydon Carter and David Friend, eds., *Bohemians, Bootleggers, Flappers, and Swells: The Best of Early Vanity Fair* (New York: Penguin, 2014), 244.

122   **"chief business of the American people"**   "The Press Under a Free Government," address to the Society of American Newspaper Editors in Washington, DC, January 17, 1925, https://coolidgefoundation.org/resources/the-press-under-a-free-government. For examples of Coolidge's concern for the soul of his prospering nation, see his remarks in *Time Capsule/1927: A History of the Year Condensed from the Pages of Time* (New York: Time, 1968), 10–11, and *Time Capsule/1929: A History of the Year Condensed from the Pages of Time* (New York: Time, 1968), 11.

122   **"It was that kind of time"**   Hickey, *The Gentleman Was a Thief*, 7.

122   **flying an airplane on the Sabbath**   H. L. Mencken, ed., *Americana 1926* (London: Martin Hopkinson, 1926), 83.

122   **"I am opposed to bobbed hair"**   Mencken, *Americana 1926*, 243.

123   **"almost complete incapacity for innocent joy"**   Mencken, "Maryland: Apex of Normalcy," in Daniel H. Borus, ed., *These United States: Portraits of America from the 1920s* (Ithaca and London: Cornell University Press, 1992), 165.

123   **depicting a helpless Uncle Sam**   The cartoon was reproduced in Dean Jobb, "Hell of a Racket: America Was Thirsty, and Canadians Like to Help," *Literary Review of Canada* 26, no. 9 (November 2018): 29.

123   **triple the number of licensed venues**   Daniel Okrent, *Last Call: The Rise and Fall of Prohibition* (New York: Scribner, 2010), 208 and Seth Kugel, "Tell Them Seth Sent You," *New York Times*, April 29, 2007. The number of licensed establishments before Prohibition is noted in Debby Applegate, *Madam: The Biography of Polly Adler, Icon of the Jazz Age* (New York: Doubleday, 2021), 109.

123   **a mere three minutes, ten seconds**   *Time Capsule/1923: A History of the Year Condensed from the Pages of Time* (New York: Time, 1967), 62–63.

123   **"When . . . does the Prohibition law"**   Michael A. Lerner, *Dry Manhattan: Prohibition in New York City* (Cambridge, MA: Harvard University Press, 2007), 1.

123   **"Gotham and Gomorrah"**   *Current Opinion*, April 1920, 423–24, quoted in Applegate, *Madam*, 8.

124   **"an orgy of graft, perjury, and corruption"**   Lerner, *Dry Manhattan*, 83.

124   **"It was a common sight"**   Edward Robb Ellis, *The Epic of New York: A Narrative History* (New York: Carroll & Graf, 2005), 517.

124   **"We knew of the millions"**   "The Tribune and Prohibition," October 12, 1925, in *A Century of Tribune Editorials* (Freeport, NY: Books for Libraries Press, 1970), 98.

124   **scrambled for the membership cards**   These precautions are noted in "Padlock Confronts 30 Leading Resorts," *New York Times*, October 21, 1925, and Lerner, *Dry Manhattan*, 153.

124   **"night mayor"**   See, for instance, "Mayor Jimmy Back, Touched by Welcome," *Daily News*, September 28, 1927.

124   **"speakeasies . . . eroded the boundaries"**   George Chauncey, *Gay New York: Gender, Urban Culture, and the Making of the Gay Male World, 1890–1940* (New York: Basic Books, 1994), quoted in David Rosen, *Prohibition New York City: Speakeasy Queen Texas Guinan, Blind Pigs, Drag Balls & More* (Charleston, SC: History Press, 2020), 46.

124   **"very highest and very lowest"**   Lerner, *Dry Manhattan*, 143.

124   **"where the underworld can meet"**   James Traub, *The Devil's Playground: A Century of Pleasure and Profit in Times Square* (New York: Random House, 2004), 84.

125   **check their guns at the door**   Rosen, *Prohibition New York City*, 48.

125   **"one of the city's leading public enemies"**   "Larry Fay Is Slain in His Night Club; Doorman Is Hunted," *New York Times*, January 2, 1933. This is also the source of the description of Fay's attire and car.

125   **"a nightlife plunger"**   Barry, as told to Robinson, "Barry Bares Rialto Bout with Wales," *Daily News*, November 3, 1932.

125   **"high and handsome"**   Fowler, *The Great Mouthpiece*, 172.

125   **Barry was a regular**   Barry's friendships with Fallon and Collins are noted in Hickey, *The Gentleman Was a Thief*, 9, 55.

125   **"One of the busiest swindlers"**   "'Dapper Don' Collins, Criminal, 1929," Criminal Accounts and Articles, Compiled by James Rodney Wood, Jr., Box 13, Folder 24, 55, Wood Detective Agency Records, 1865–1945, Harvard Law School Library, Historical & Special Collections. Other biographical details on Collins are drawn from Sifakis, *The Encyclopedia of American Crime*, 158–60, and Dean Jobb, "The Jazz Age Crimes of Dapper Don Collins," *Ellery Queen's Mystery Magazine* 161, nos. 5 and 6 (May/June 2023): 78, 111, 120, 171, 191–92.

125   **the Colossus of Rogues**   Fowler, *The Great Mouthpiece*, 354.

125   **blowing $500**   Hickey, *The Gentleman Was a Thief*, 6–7. The cost of a Model T Ford in 1925 was $260. George Moss, *America in the Twentieth Century* (Englewood Cliffs, NJ: Prentice Hall, 1989), 97.

125   **ten dollars for a pint of whiskey**   These prices are reported in "Padlock Confronts 30 Leading Resorts" and Lerner, *Dry Manhattan*, 142.

126   **chorus girls appearing in Broadway musicals**   Hickey, *The Gentleman Was a Thief*, 56. "Blossom Time" opened in September 1921. See "'Blossom Time' Is Charming with Its Schubert Melodies," *New York Herald*, September 30, 1921, and "Blossom Time," Internet Broadway Database, https://www.ibdb.com/broadway-show/blossom-time-2098.

126   **"One had only to announce"**   Allen, *Only Yesterday*, 275–76.

126   **"You see plenty of jeweled women"**   "Galloping Dominos Took Barry Dough." This is also the source of information on Barry's visit to Paris. His attempt to steal the diamond on display in Miami is also recounted in Hickey, *The Gentleman Was a Thief*, 46–49.

126   **"Why did I take up stealing?"**   "Cary Grant: A Class Apart—Quotable Cary," *American Masters*, PBS.org, May 25, 2005, https://www.pbs.org/wnet/americanmasters /cary-grant-quotable-cary/618.

127   **"I never bothered to save"**   Hickey, *The Gentleman Was a Thief*, 7.

127   **"a gay and hectic life"**   "Galloping Dominos Took Barry Dough."

CHAPTER 14: ANNA BLAKE

128   **"a fair microcosm"**   Jack Alexander, "District Leader—I," *New Yorker*, July 25, 1936, 25. Alexander noted the boundaries of the Eleventh Assembly District on page 21.

128   **they met in a barbershop**   The meeting was recorded in Neil Hickey, *The Gentleman Was a Thief: The Colorful Story of Arthur Barry, a 1920's Rogue* (New York: Holt, Rinehart & Winston, 1961), 50.

128 **"sudden, firm, and cordial"** Alexander, "District Leader—III," *New Yorker*, August 8, 1936, 18. Hines's claim to have shod forty thousand horses is noted in Alexander, "District Leader—I," 21.

129 **"hauled both bullets and bacon"** "'Jimmy' Is Back, and the Old 11th Is Mighty Glad," *Evening World* (New York), July 15, 1919.

129 **met again a couple of days later** Hickey, *The Gentleman Was a Thief*, 51.

130 **"Czar" and "one-man power to make and break"** "Hylan Men Join Fight on Murphy," *New-York Tribune*, August 15, 1921, and "Hines Men File Anti-Murphy Ticket Today," *New-York Tribune*, August 16, 1921. Hines described Murphy as an arrogant bully in "Tammany Alarmed, Is Likely to Put Tally on Ticket," *New York Times*, August 19, 1921.

130 **New York's most infamous crooks** Alexander, "District Leader—II," *New Yorker*, August 1, 1936, 20–22.

130 **"The name of Hines"** Alexander, "District Leader—II," 22.

130 **"promulgate and promote"** "For New Democratic Club," *New-York Tribune*, January 19, 1910.

130 **a membership of four thousand** "Tammany Leader Opposes Murphy; Police Picket Club," *New-York Tribune*, July 7, 1921.

130 **"The district leader is a Santa Claus"** Alexander, "District Leader—I," 22.

131 **"The payoff came"** Terry Golway, *Machine Made: Tammany Hall and the Creation of Modern American Politics* (New York: Liveright, 2014), 156.

131 **an organizer for the Cayuga Club** Stephen J. Riegel, *Finding Judge Crater: A Life and Phenomenal Disappearance in Jazz Age New York* (Syracuse, NY: Syracuse University Press, 2022), 51.

131 **up to six hundred people** "'Jimmy' Is Back, and the Old 11th Is Mighty Glad." The clubhouse is also described in "From Day to Day in Old New York," *Buffalo Enquirer*, March 29, 1924. The gambling allegation was reported in "Tammany Leader Opposes Murphy; Police Picket Club," *New-York Tribune*, July 7, 1921, and "Denies Gambling in Hines's Club," *Evening World*, August 15, 1921.

131 **It was there he met** Hickey, *The Gentleman Was a Thief*, 54, 80–81, lists Fallon, O'Farrell, and Goldstein as people Barry met at the club.

131 **sometimes represented Hines** See, for example, "Denies Gambling in Hines's Club."

131 **"the town's foremost Sherlock"** Gene Fowler, *The Great Mouthpiece: A Life Story of William Fallon* (New York: Bantam Books, 1946), 349.

131 **"intelligent, courteous and well-mannered"** "New Exploits of Society's Suave and Sinister 'Supper-Man,'" *Detroit Free Press*, November 30, 1930.

131 **fond of his fellow Irishman** Hickey, *The Gentleman Was a Thief*, 51.

131 **"The district leader . . . is able frequently"** Alexander, "District Leader—II," 18–19, 21. On Tammany Hall's corruption of the justice system, see also Herbert Mitgang, *Once Upon a Time in New York: Jimmy Walker, Franklin Roosevelt, and the Last Great Battle of the Jazz Age* (New York: Cooper Square Press, 2003), 37–38.

132 **"one of the best damned captains"** Hickey, *The Gentleman Was a Thief*, 56.

132 **"comfortably fixed financially"** Anna Blake Barry, "My Life of Love and Fear as the Sweetheart and Wife of Arthur Barry, the World's Most Famous Jewel-Thief," *Atlanta Constitution*, January 15, 1933. Details on Blake's birth, her parents, and her early life are drawn from birth, marriage, and census records available through Ancestry.com and cemetery records posted on the Find a Grave website, www.findagrave.com.

132 **blue-and-gold colors** "Reunion of Holy Cross Alumnae," *New York Times*, May 20, 1906. Other details about the academy are drawn from "Holy Cross Academy Marks Its 75th Year," *New York Times*, May 7, 1933, and Anna Peterson, "42d St. Academy to Mark Century," *New York Times*, May 4, 1958.

133 **"My uncle had great plans"** Blake Barry, "My Life of Love and Fear," *Atlanta Constitution*, January 15, 1933.

134 **"It's no use"** "Burned to Death Beneath His Auto," *Brooklyn Daily Eagle*, August 14, 1912.

134 **"We never 'settled down'"** "My Life of Love and Fear," *Atlanta Constitution*, January 15, 1933. The flat's size was reported in John O'Donnell, "Livermore Burglar Tells to Save Blonde," *Daily News* (New York), June 8, 1927.

134 **Three million women would join** George Moss, *America in the Twentieth Century* (Englewood Cliffs, NJ: Prentice Hall, 1989), 102.

134 **"the working wives' problem"** "Working Wives of the West: Society Still Frowns on Them in the World's Last Stronghold of a Leisured Gentry," *New York Times*, August 12, 1923.

135 **"No childish excitement can compare"** Mary Knight, *On My Own* (New York: Macmillan, 1938), 29.

135 **"A wonderful feat"** *Time Capsule/1923: A History of the Year Condensed from the Pages of Time* (New York: Time, 1967), 140.

135 **"this first-woman business"** "I'm Not a Torch-Bearer, Amelia Earhart Declares," *Toronto Daily Star*, December 12, 1932.

135 **strong support in Tammany-controlled districts** Golway, *Machine Made*, 228.

135 **more women than men were registered** "Day's Registration 131,676 in N.Y. City," *New York Herald*, October 11, 1922.

135 **Lady Astor of Harlem** "All Party Lines Forgotten at This Democratic Ball," *Evening World*, March 8, 1922.

135 **"public-spirited"** "Women Against the Boss," *New York Times*, August 31, 1921. See also "1,000 Women to Aid Hines Fight Murphy," *New York Times*, August 30, 1921, and "Women War On Murphy," *New York Times*, April 27, 1920.

136 **"by their first names"** Alexander, "District Leader—I," 22. The reference to "my people" appears on page 26.

136 **dispensed the goodies** Hickey, *The Gentleman Was a Thief*, 58–59.

136 **"Two, four, six, eight"** Alexander, "District Leader—I," 26. This description of the parade and picnic is also drawn from "5,000 Kiddies Guests of Monongahelas," *Evening World*, June 18, 1921; "Uncle Sam's Proposal to Liberty: At the June Walk," *Daily News*, June 19, 1921; "Ice Cream and Chawklit! Good Things Galore! And How the Boys Ate," *Daily News*, June 26, 1927; and "What Fun!" *Daily News*, June 22, 1930.

136 **getting out the vote** Election day duties are described in Alexander, "District Leader—I," 23.

137 **attend the Democratic State Convention** "My Life of Love and Fear," *Atlanta Constitution*, January 15, 1933.

137 **"constitutional liberties of all citizens"** "Democrats Name Smith Once More for Governor; Plank Condemns Klan," *Brooklyn Daily Eagle*, September 26, 1924.

137 **Frank Blake died** A funeral notice appeared in "Died," *New York Times*, October 4, 1924.

137   **met at the Monongahela Club**   Hickey, *The Gentleman Was a Thief*, 56. Blake said they were introduced at a house party in "My Life of Love and Fear," *Atlanta Constitution*, January 15, 1933.

137   **"might be a society doctor"**   "My Life of Love and Fear," January 29, 1933.

137   **"almost seems like Fate"**   "My Life of Love and Fear," January 15, 1933.

137   **spending weekends with Blake**   The Lake Ronkonkoma visits, Blake's comment to her sister, and Barry's help with her district captain's duties are noted in Hickey, *The Gentleman Was a Thief*, 58–59. A woman named Brown reportedly owned the cottage. See "$1,000,000 Gem Clue in Livermore Case," *New York Times*, June 8, 1927.

138   **a screened-in veranda**   A photograph of the bungalow accompanied the article "Livermore Thief's Love Traps Gang," *Daily News*, June 8, 1927.

138   **recruited to join a local lodge**   "Polite Crook, Robbed Many Homes, Caught at Ronkonkoma on Sunday," *Suffolk County News* (Sayville, NY), June 10, 1927.

138   **"the finest private house"**   William Kalush and Larry Sloman, *The Secret Life of Houdini: The Making of America's First Superhero* (New York: Atria Books, 2006), 163. The house is also described in Lisa Kaplan Gordon, "Harry Houdini's House Is About to Disappear from the Market," *Town & Country*, March 27, 2018, https://www .townandcountrymag.com/leisure/real-estate/g10202603/harry-houdini-house.

138   **"When I was with Arthur"**   "My Life of Love and Fear," *Atlanta Constitution*, January 15, 1933.

138   **"happy-go-lucky"**   "My Life of Love and Fear," January 15, 1933.

138   **"a little money of my own"**   Hickey, *The Gentleman Was a Thief*, 57.

139   **"Have you heard from the Prince"**   Blake recounted their conversation at the Deauville Club in "My Life of Love and Fear," January 29, 1933.

139   **encountered someone from Worcester**   Hickey, *The Gentleman Was a Thief*, 91–92.

139   **made his money from gambling**   "My Life of Love and Fear," January 15, 1933.

139   **"I deal in it a bit"**   Hickey, *The Gentleman Was a Thief*, 91–92.

139   **made his pile from bootlegging**   See references in F. Scott Fitzgerald, *The Great Gatsby* (New York: Simon & Schuster, 1995), 65, 114.

140   **"handsome, gay and kind"**   "My Life of Love and Fear," January 15, 1933.

140   **His real name appeared**   The marriage certificate was reproduced in "My Life of Love and Fear," January 15, 1933.

140   **"going-about-carousing set"**   John O'Donnell, "Two More Gem Robberies," *Daily News*, June 10, 1927.

CHAPTER 15: A SCHOLARLY COP

143   **"spectacular arrest"**   "Fires Three Shots at Auto Driver," *Times Union* (Brooklyn), April 24, 1923, and "Bullets Pursue Driver of Fleeing Auto, After Crash," *Brooklyn Daily Eagle*, April 25, 1923.

143   **had been with the police force**   He joined the force in 1921. See "Nassau Sleuths' Head Wins Success by Close Attention to His Duties," *Times Union*, July 29, 1925, and "Harold King, Famed Cop Hit by Scandal, Dies," *Newsday* (Long Island, NY), December 11, 1956.

143   **served overseas as a motorcycle courier**   King's wartime service was noted in his obituary in the *New York Herald Tribune*, December 11, 1956, reproduced at https://

www.findagrave.com/memorial/156755008/harold-r-king. King was sent to France with the 25th Balloon Company in June 1918. See RG 92, Records of the Office of the Quartermaster General, 1774–1985, National Archives at College Park; College Park, Maryland, passenger list of troopship *America*, which sailed from Newport News, VA on June 29, 1918, available online at Ancestry.com.

144   **a parade of petty criminals**   Cases King handled were reported in "Burglar Admits So Many Thefts Police Doubt Him," *New-York Tribune*, April 8, 1921; "Suspect Arrested in Slaying of Hempstead Woman; Partly Identified; Stories Conflict," *Times Union*, June 23, 1921; "Nassau Bandits Rob Brooklyn Man of $3,100," *Times Union*, January 4, 1922; "Stolen Motorcars Found; 2 Arrests," *Brooklyn Daily Eagle*, February 25, 1923; "Caught in Stolen Car; Confesses," *Brooklyn Daily Eagle*, June 3, 1923; and "Sees Cold Winter Ahead; Vet Seeks Jail Term," *Times Union*, December 24, 1923.

144   **"A suburb of Wall Street"**   John Gunther, *Inside U.S.A.* (London: Hamish Hamilton, 1947), 538.

144   **King was among the officers**   "Bank Bandits Had Local Tip, Police Say; after $30,000," *Brooklyn Daily Eagle*, April 5, 1924, and "Roads Are Hunted for Bank Bandits Who Killed Man," *Brooklyn Citizen*, April 5, 1924.

144   **"a police system in good working order"**   "Supervisors Act to Strengthen Police System," *Brooklyn Daily Eagle*, April 8, 1924.

144   **quit the Hempstead force**   "King—Smith," *Brooklyn Daily Eagle*, April 2, 1924

145   **hunting down car thieves**   "Political Gossip of Three L.I. Counties," *Times Union*, March 22, 1924; "Organize Motor Patrol," *Brooklyn Daily Eagle*, March 31, 1924; and "Mystery Motor Puzzles Police," *Brooklyn Daily Eagle*, September 5, 1924. His other investigations were reported in "Ten Men Are Arrested for Digging Bait in Sand," *Brooklyn Daily Eagle*, June 27, 1924; "Seven Persons Killed in Traffic Accidents," *Standard Union* (Brooklyn), October 13, 1924; "Thieves Get $3,000 Loot at A.L. Kramer's Home," *Times Union*, December 20, 1924; and "L.I.R.R. Bandit Still at Large," *Times Union*, January 14, 1925.

145   **identified a murder victim**   "Identify Nassau Murder Victim," *Times Union*, February 6, 1924.

145   **one of fifty-five deputies**   Jerry Aylward, *Nassau County Police Department* (Charleston, SC: Arcadia, 2019), 13.

145   **promoted to sergeant**   King was identified as a sergeant in press accounts of his cases beginning in late April 1925. See, for instance, "Children See Father Killed as Wife Fires," *Daily News*, April 28, 1925.

145   **King placed second**   "14 Policemen Dropped from Nassau List," *Brooklyn Daily Eagle*, June 23, 1925.

146   **"sheer ability and hard work"**   "Nassau Sleuths' Head Wins Success by Close Attention to His Duties." The timing of his appointment to lead the detective division is noted in "Long Island Political Brevities," *Times Union*, July 3, 1925.

146   **he was newly married**   "Social and Personal: King—Smith," *Times Union*, April 3, 1924. Lewis K. Smith, who worked on Wall Street and was on his way to meet a customer when a wagon crammed with explosives detonated, died of his injuries the following day. See "Explosion's Toll in Brooklyn-L.I. Increased to 15," *Brooklyn Daily Eagle*, September 17, 1920, and Beverly Gage, *The Day Wall Street Exploded: A Story of America in Its First Age of Terror* (New York: Oxford University Press, 2009), 161, 330.

146   **Nassau Sleuth**   "Nassau Sleuths' Head Wins Success by Close Attention to His Duties."

146 **King traced the car** "Slain Chauffeur's Taxi Sold by Man Assuming His Name," *Brooklyn Daily Eagle*, July 7, 1925. Details about Panella and the discovery of his body were reported in "Taxicab Driver Found Slain in Deserted Ruins," *Brooklyn Daily Eagle*, July 5, 1925.

146 **pieced together a troubling portrait** "Unbalanced by Blows on Head," *Kingston Daily Freeman* (NY), July 11, 1925.

146 **"at home in any drawing room" and "talk to you all day"** Kermit Jaediker, "Inspector King's Unfinished Business," *Daily News*, December 30, 1956.

146 **"scholarly cop"** "Proud Moment," *Daily News*, August 18, 1926.

147 **failed to catch Knapp** "Police Seek Man Who, They Say, Killed for Thrill of It," *Daily News*, January 24, 1926.

147 **King refused to give up** "Irwin Case Recalls Six-Year Search for Nassau Thrill Slayer," *Daily News*, May 16, 1937.

CHAPTER 16: THE PHANTOM

148 **startled to find a stranger** The robbery was described in "Acrobatic Thief Makes Eighth Big Haul on L.I.," *Times Union* (Brooklyn), November 9, 1925, and "Acrobatic Burglar Loots Eight Homes While Owners Dine," *Philadelphia Inquirer*, November 9, 1925. Background on the Monaelessers is drawn from the doctor's obituary, "Dr. Monaelesser, Medical Director," *Brooklyn Daily Eagle*, August 9, 1941

149 **lost diamond and emerald jewelry** "Porch Gang Left Clews in $11,700 Jewelry Robbery," *Brooklyn Daily Eagle*, October 5, 1925, and "$12,000 Gem Theft in Great Neck," *Daily News* (New York), October 5, 1925.

149 **"the Galloping Hitchcocks"** "The Galloping Hitchcocks," *New Yorker*, August 14, 1926, 17.

149 **the items were gone** "Famous Polo Player's L.I. Home Robbed," *Brooklyn Citizen*, October 19, 1925, and "Hitchcock Home Robbed of Gems," *Brooklyn Daily Eagle*, October 19, 1925.

149 **the work of the same man** "L.I. Dinner Thief Raids Lake Home at Kensington," *Brooklyn Daily Eagle*, November 10, 1925.

149 **suspect in each burglary** See "List of Homes Gibson Visited Stealing Gems," *Brooklyn Citizen*, June 9, 1927; "Barry Again Led to Looted Homes," *Times Union*, June 10, 1927; and "Barry Gang Got Gems of Society Folk," *Daily News*, June 10, 1927. Police suspected he had robbed the Monaelessers, but Barry denied he was responsible, then claimed he had acted as lookout and an accomplice had gone inside. See "Barry Visit Homes He Rifled of Gems," *Times Union*, June 12, 1927, and "Beware of Gunman, Barry Tells Police," *New York Times*, June 12, 1927.

149 **raiding Hitchcock's home** Barry revealed he was the Hitchcock burglar in Robert Wallace, "Confessions of a Master Jewel Thief," in Alexander Klein, ed., *The Double Dealers: Adventures in Grand Deception* (London: Faber & Faber, 1958), 101, originally published as "Confessions of Master Jewel Thief," *Life*, March 12, 1956.

150 **"belong to the same clubs"** "Gem Band Linked in Two Thefts," *Daily News*, October 6, 1925."

150 **how Barry entered** Details of the break-in and the evidence found at the scene were reported in "Burglar Gets $12,500 Gems in Great Neck," *Brooklyn Daily Eagle*, November 9, 1925, and "Acrobatic Burglar Loots Eight Homes While Owners Dine."

150 **in the running for an appointment** "Anderson Wants U.S. Judgeship," *Times Union*, November 17, 1925.

150 **as far away as Miami** "Thief Scales Walls," *Miami Herald*, November 9, 1925. See also Acrobatic Thief Calls at 8 Houses," *Evening Sun* (Baltimore), November 9, 1925, and "'Dinner Thief' Is Police Problem on Long Island," *Evening News* (Harrisburg, PA), November 9, 1925.

150 **"the agility of a human fly"** "'Dinner Thief' of Rare Jewels Eludes Long Island Police: Gem Chests of Eight Matrons Raided" *Atlanta Constitution*, November 9, 1925.

150 **"climbing up ledges, sills and shutters"** "New York Dinner Thief Makes Another Rich Haul," *Morning Post* (Camden, NJ), November 9, 1925.

150 **"stunt artists of the movies"** "Burglar Gets $12,500 Gems in Great Neck."

151 **Barry eventually confessed to the burglary** He admitted the Flamman break-in in "Barry Visit Homes He Rifled of Gems" and "Beware of Gunman, Barry Tells Police."

151 **Dinner Thief** The nickname bestowed by the Nassau County Police is noted in "Acrobatic Thief Makes Eighth Big Haul on L.I."

151 **"the thief entered the victim's houses"** "Lone Dinner Thief Active Once More," *Buffalo Evening News*, November 9, 1925. This report included the total value of the jewels taken in the thefts.

151 **the Phantom** "$25,000 Flatbush Holdup; Thief in Vanderbilt Home; Whitney Maid Routs thug," *Times Union*, December 9, 1925.

151 **cruised the highways and roads** "Gem Thief Patrol Guards L.I. Roads," *Times Union*, November 10, 1925. The possible posting of guards on estates was reported in "Acrobatic Burglar Loots Eight Homes While Owners Dine."

151 **"He believes the thief"** "Lone Dinner Thief Active Once More."

151 **$12,500 in jewels and valuables** The break-in and the items stolen were described in "$25,000 Robbery at Home of John S. Phipps," *Times Union*, November 28, 1925; "Raffles of Nassau Robs Phipps Home," *Standard Union* (Brooklyn), November 29, 1925; and "Agile 'Dinner Thief' Gets $25,000 Gems at Phipps Estate," *Brooklyn Daily Eagle*, November 29, 1925.

152 **sixty-six-room Georgian mansion** Debra Morgenstern Katz, "The Long Life of Old Westbury Gardens," *New York Times*, November 15, 1998. Photographs and a description of the estate appear in Paul J. Mateyunas, *Long Island's Gold Coast* (Charleston, SC: Arcadia, 2012), 54.

152 **"a power in financial circles"** His wealth was estimated at $100 million when he died in 1927. "Payne Whitney Dies Suddenly at Home," *New York Times*, May 26, 1927. The Greentree estate is described and depicted in Mateyunas, *Long Island's Gold Coast*, 32.

153 **"Thank God for that"** The attempted robbery was described in detail in "$25,000 Flatbush Holdup; Thief in Vanderbilt Home; Whitney Maid Routs thug."

153 **a suspect in the Phipps and Whitney burglaries** Barry was identified as a suspect in the Phipps robbery in "List of Homes Gibson Visited Stealing Gems"; "Barry Again Led to Looted Homes"; and "Barry Gang Got Gems of Society Folk." Similarities between the Whitney break-in and other "dinner thief" robberies were noted in numerous press reports, including "L.I. Dinner Burglar Enters Whitney Home," *Standard Union*, December 9, 1925, and "Dinner Thief Again Raids North Shore Area; Gets $5,000," *Brooklyn Daily Eagle*, April 8, 1927.

CHAPTER 17: "WELL-MANNERED BANDITS"

154 **"Were you at the opera?"** This account of the robbery and all quotations are drawn from the following news reports: "Thieves Chat with Yonkers Couple in Bed as They Take Diamonds, Leave Other Jewels," *New York Times*, August 2, 1926; "$5,000 in Jewels Taken in Robbery," *Yonkers Herald*, August 2, 1926; "Thieves Hold Couple in Bed at Gun Point and Escape with Gems," *Yonkers Statesman*, August 2, 1926; and "Ex-U.S. Officer Robbed of $5,000 by Bold Pair," *Daily News* (New York), August 2, 1926.

155 **an executive with a utility company** "Well Known Residents Who Were Victims of Robbers," *Yonkers Herald*, August 2, 1926, and "Mrs. B.W. Stilwell Dies, General's Mother," *New York Times*, June 23, 1942.

155 **"famous 'ladder burglar'"** "Burglar Gets Gems," *Miami Herald*, August 2, 1926.

155 **Fourteen prisoners in handcuffs** The escape was described in "Escapes on Way to Prison," *Boston Globe*, January 25, 1921. The car dealership burglary and Monahan's arrest were described in "'Duck' Monahan Sought as Chief of Jewel Gang," *Worcester Telegram*, June 10, 1927, and "Jimmie Monahan Shot and Captured Says He Posed as Judge Thayer's Son," *Worcester Evening Post*, July 7, 1927.

156 **"a tug on the handcuffs"** "Worcester Criminal Lived Like Prince," *Worcester Evening Post*, July 8, 1927. The police bulletin, announcing the reward and reproducing Monahan's mug shots and fingerprints, accompanied this news report. The bloodied handcuffs were described in the *Boston Globe*'s report, "Escapes on Way to Prison."

156 **"prepared to take any chance"** "Trap 'Boston Billy,' Shoot and Seize Him," *New York Times*, July 8, 1927.

156 **five foot eight** Monahan was described in "'Boston Billy' Caught, Wounded in Hot Chase; Wanted for L.I. Thefts," *Times Union* (Brooklyn), July 7, 1927.

156 **a slew of aliases** The names in addition to Boston Billy Williams—James Ward, James Thayer, James King—were recorded in "Receiving Blotter, Inmate 80134—Monahan, James F.", July 28, 1927, Sing Sing Prison Inmate Admission Registers, 1842–1971, New York Department of Correctional Services, Series B0143, Box 43, vol. 87. New York State Archives, Albany.

156 **"it would be a good joke"** "'Boston Billy' Boasts of Many Conquests; Denies Livermore Raid," *Times Union*, July 8, 1927.

156 **dressing as a woman and "were not entirely complimentary"** "'Duck' Monahan Sought as Chief of Jewel Gang."

156 **"gambling on the Lord's Day"** Monahan's criminal record was reported in "Trap 'Boston Billy,' Shoot and Seize Him" and "Latest Word on Monahan as Barry Pal," *Worcester Gazette*, June 10, 1927.

157 **"a street corner 'tough boy'"** "Police Use Barry Against Monahan," *Worcester Evening Post*, July 9, 1927.

157 **registered for the draft** Monahan listed the water meter factory as his employer when he filled out his draft form on September 12, 1918. World War I Draft Registration Cards, 1917–1918, M1509, National Archives and Records Administration, Washington, DC, accessed through Ancestry.com.

157 **"We palled around together"** "Trap 'Boston Billy,' Shoot and Seize Him."

157 **They were regulars** Their attendance at both venues was noted in John O'Donnell, "Girl Who Says She's Wife Held to Accuse Billy," *Daily News*, July 13, 1927. On the rink, see "Old Boxing Center on West Side Sold," *New York Times*, January 9, 1952.

157   **"the one place in the city"**   A classified advertisement for the Palace's dance hall appeared on page 16 of the *Daily News*, June 21, 1924.

158   **two jewel thieves might be better**   Barry claimed he was still working alone as late as 1925. See "Barry Again Makes Tour of Homes Robbed," *Brooklyn Citizen*, June 29, 1927.

158   **"If you're willing"**   Neil Hickey, *The Gentleman Was a Thief: The Colorful Story of Arthur Barry, a 1920's Rogue* (New York: Holt, Rinehart & Winston, 1961), 87. The location of the speakeasy is noted on page 81.

158   **"If you spoke quietly"**   Robert Wallace, "Confessions of a Master Jewel Thief," in Alexander Klein, ed., *The Double Dealers: Adventures in Grand Deception* (London: Faber & Faber, 1958), 103, originally published as "Confessions of Master Jewel Thief," *Life*, March 12, 1956.

158   **The Stilwell robbery was one of their first**   Barry's confession to the heist was reported in "Jewel Thief Admits Stilwell Residence Burglary Last Year," *Yonkers Statesman*, June 11, 1927; "Believe Livermore Gem Thief Got Nearly Million in County," *Yonkers Statesman*, June 15, 1927; and "15 More Robberies Admitted by Barry," *New York Times*, June 15, 1927.

158   **Sometimes they teamed up**   Barry described how the partnership worked in "Barry Identifies Houses He Robbed," *New York Times*, June 29, 1927.

158   **worming his way into high society**   Monahan and his methods were described in "Trap 'Boston Billy,' Shoot and Seize Him"; "Jewel Thief, 62, Dies in Poverty," *New York Times*, October 25, 1960; and "'Boston Billy' Boasts of Many Conquests; Denies Livermore Raid."

158   **"He had polished himself"**   "Trap 'Boston Billy,' Shoot and Seize Him."

159   **"business associates"**   Anna Blake Barry, "My Life of Love and Fear as the Sweetheart and Wife of Arthur Barry, the World's Most Famous Jewel-Thief," *Atlanta Constitution*, January 15 and February 5, 1933.

159   **"I can get any woman"**   "'Boston Billy' Boasts of Many Conquests; Denies Livermore Raid."

160   **a decision he would come to regret**   Biographer Neil Hickey reached this conclusion after his conversations with Barry. See Hickey, *The Gentleman Was a Thief*, 87.

160   **the mansion of bank president Marselis Parsons**   "Rye, N.Y. Burglar Gets $6000 to $7000 in Jewels," *Boston Globe*, November 13, 1924, and "$6,000 in Gems Stolen," *Gazette* (Montreal, QC), November 13, 1924. Parsons is identified as president of the Rye National Bank in "Comly Elected Vice-President of the Rye National Bank," *Daily Item* (Port Chester, NY), January 18, 1927.

160   **the home of Donaldson and Greta Brown**   "Rob G.M.C. Secretary," *Traverse City Record-Eagle* (MI), December 5, 1924; "$10,000 Gem Theft," *Daily News*, December 6, 1924; and "DuPont Company Names Directors," *Evening Journal* (Wilmington, DE), March 9, 1925. Barry confessed to the Parsons and Brown robberies in 1927. See "Believe Livermore Gem Thief Got Nearly Million in County" and "Scarsdale Murder Laid to Gem Thief," *New York Times*, June 16, 1927.

160   **the Port Chester home of Roy Allen**   "Second-Story Man at Work," *Ithaca Journal* (NY), January 15, 1926. Barry's admission to this burglary was reported in "Scarsdale Murder Laid to Gem Thief" and "Believe Livermore Gem Thief Got Nearly Million in County."

160   **returned to Rye to rob Frederick Wheeler**   The robbery was described in "Motor Burglars Make Jewel Haul at Wheeler mansion in Rye, N.Y.," *Brooklyn Daily Eagle*, May

8, 1926; "See Men Fleeing from Rye Home of Can Company Head, Police Won't Reveal Booty," *Daily Item*, May 8, 1926; and "Armed Crooks Menaced the Wheeler Family; Thought They Had Cut Phone Wire," *Daily Item*, May 10, 1926. Wheeler served as president of the golf association in 1918. See "U.S.G.A. Gives Ouimet War-Time Present," *Brooklyn Daily Eagle*, January 26, 1918.

160   **"Don't wake your husband"**   The robbery was described in "Well-Mannered Bandits Rob Home of Pencil King While He Sleeps," *Yonkers Statesman*, July 9, 1926, and "Burglars Take Jewels," *Times Union*, July 10, 1926. Barry confessed to robbing the Wheeler and Berolzheimer homes with Monahan in "Scarsdale Murder Laid to Gem Thief," "Believe Livermore Gem Thief Got Nearly Million in County," and "15 More Robberies Admitted by Barry." Information on the Berolzheimers (they later shortened the surname to Berol) was drawn from the obituary notice "Alfred Berol, 81, of Eagle Pencils," *New York Times*, June 16, 1974 and "Berol Era," in Kenneth L. Diem, Leonore L. Diem and William C. Lawrence, *A Tale Of Dough Gods, Bear Grease, Cantaloupe, and Sucker Oil: Marymere/Pinetree/Mae-Lou/AMK Ranch* (Moran, WY), University of Wyoming-National Park Service Research Center, 1986, http://npshistory.com /publications/grte/dough_gods/sec3.htm.

161   **grabbed an iron ladder**   The most detailed press account of the robbery was "Plum House Looted of $55,000 in Gems at Point of Guns," *Asbury Park Press* (NJ), September 11, 1926. Some news reports estimated jewelry worth as much as $75,000 was taken. See "Druggist Kills Wrong Man at Holdup, Claim," *Daily News*, September 11, 1926, and "$75,000 Gems Stolen from Seashore Home," *Philadelphia Inquirer*, September 11, 1926.

161   **"It is of grave importance"**   "The Statesman Says—," *Yonkers Statesman*, August 9, 1926.

CHAPTER 18: THE ROCKEFELLER GEMS

162   **Diamonds sparkled**   This description of the robbery and the investigation is based on Neil Hickey, *The Gentleman Was a Thief: The Colorful Story of Arthur Barry, a 1920's Rogue* (New York: Holt, Rinehart & Winston, 1961), 83–85; "Rockefeller Home Thief Has Ladder," *Daily Item* (Port Chester, NY), October 26, 1926; "Rockefellers' Gems Stolen by Lone Thief," *Daily News* (New York), October 27, 1926; "Thief Enters Percy A. Rockefeller's Home at Greenwich and Takes Valuable Jewels," *New York Times*, October 27, 1926; "P. Rockefeller Home Robbed as Family Dines," *Chicago Tribune*, October 27, 1926; and "Jewelry Burglar Robs Rockefeller Greenwich Home," *Hartford Courant*, October 27, 1926.

162   **made headlines across North America**   US and Canadian papers that carried Associated Press and other wire service reports of the burglary included "Percy Rockefeller's Home Robbed as Family Dines," *San Francisco Examiner*, October 27, 1926; "Rockefeller Jewels Stolen," *Pittsburgh Daily Post*, October 27, 1926; "Lone Burglar Gets Rockefeller Gems," *Montreal Star*, October 27, 1926; and "Rockefeller Home Robbed," *Leader-Post* (Regina, SK), October 27, 1926.

162   **estimated at $100 million**   "Two Americans Lead List of World's Twelve Richest Men," *Daily News*, October 7, 1926. Biographical information on Percy and the Rockefeller family is drawn from Ron Chernow, *Titan: The Life of John D. Rockefeller* (New York: Vintage, 2004), 132, 226, 233, 337, 375–76, 632.

162   **"A capitalist of first magnitude"**   "Percy Rockefeller, Financier, Is Dead," *Boston Globe*, September 26, 1934.

163   **"Scions of Millions"**   *Baltimore Sun*, April 24, 1901.

163   **"I didn't buy any of them"**   "Rockefellers' Gems Stolen by Lone Thief," *Daily News*, October 27, 1926. On the value of the stolen gems, see also "Rockefeller Gem Robbery Unsolved," *Daily News*, October 29, 1926, quoting the $25,000 figure. An earlier estimate of $20,000 appeared in "Rockefeller Jewel Thief Left No Clues," *Journal* (Meriden, CT), October 27, 1926.

163   **the work of the burglar**   "Jewelry Burglar Robs Rockefeller Greenwich Home," *Hartford Courant*, October 27, 1926; "P.A. Rockefeller's Home Robbed," *Lexington Herald-Leader* (KY), October 29, 1926; and "Thief Enters Percy A. Rockefeller's Home at Greenwich and Takes Valuable Jewels," *New York Times*, October 27, 1926.

163   **swiped $30,000 in jewels**   "Greenwich Gem Thief Gets Rich," *Daily Item*, September 27, 1926. Barry was reported to have confessed to the Armstrong robbery in "Robberies Total $800,000," *Hartford Courant*, July 8, 1927. Armstrong's business background was noted in "Shoe Firm Founder's Rites Will Be Here," *Democrat and Chronicle* (Rochester, NY), October 30, 1931. The mansion was described in "Suit Over Residence Sale," *Hartford Courant*, October 29, 1926, and "A 'Very English' Citadel Could Possibly Be Your Subsequent Dwelling in Greenwich," *Luxury Homes News*, April 5, 2021, https://luxuryhomesnews .com/a-very-english-citadel-could-possibly-be-your-subsequent-dwelling-in-greenwich.

163   **avoided the spotlight**   "Percy A. Rockefeller of New York Dies," *Boston Globe*, September 25, 1934.

163   **"one of the outstanding country residences"**   Lee E. Cooper, "Percy Rockefeller Mansion to be Razed; Estate Once Insured Against Earthquakes," *New York Times*, February 25, 1938.

163   **the highest per capita income**   Phyllis A. S. Boros, "'Great Estates' Explores Greenwich's Gems of the Past," *Connecticut Post*, March 17, 2014, https://www.ctpost .com/news/article/Great-Estates-explores-Greenwich-s-gems-of-the-5324286.php. Greenwich's development as a country retreat for the wealthy is explored in Jacqueline Weaver, "Project Documents the Era of Greenwich's Great Estates," *New York Times*, November 2, 1986.

163   **fine art and antiques**   "Rockefeller Art Will Be Actioned," *New York Times*, February 9, 1938, and "Art Works Bring $10,562," *New York Times*, March 12, 1938.

163   **"mortal dread of earthquakes"**   "Percy Rockefeller Carried Million in 'Quake Insurance," *Daily Item*, February 25, 1938. The house was described in "Rockefeller Home to Fall Before Wreckers' Crew," *Daily Item*, February 24, 1938, and Robert E. Tomasson, "End of the Era for Lavish Estates," *New York Times*, September 14, 1986.

164   **a major quake rattled Connecticut**   It occurred in May 1791, causing minor damage, and was strong enough to be felt as far away as New York City and Boston. "Largest Earthquake in Connecticut," *ConnecticutHistory.Org*, May 16, 2020, https:// connecticuthistory.org/largest-earthquake-in-connecticut-today-in-history-may-16.

164   **a bob-haired flapper wielding an umbrella**   See, for instance, "Burglar Chased from Home by Woman," *Akron Beacon Journal*, October 29, 1926, and "Evicts Burglar," *Muncie Evening Press*, November 3, 1926.

164   **hired the renowned William J. Burns**   Hickey, *The Gentleman Was a Thief*, 85.

165   **"impromptu venture"**   Barry described the robbery in Hickey, *The Gentleman Was a Thief*, 83–85. While Hickey claimed the crime was still unsolved in the 1960s, press reports suggested Barry confessed to the break-in as early as 1927. See "Robberies Total $800,000"; "Just Some of Gem Thief's Victims!" *Daily News*, June 9, 1927, and "15 More Robberies Admitted by Barry," *New York Times*, June 15, 1927.

CHAPTER 19: "THAT SLENDER RIOTOUS ISLAND"

166   **"Stop there, or I'll shoot!"**   The incident was described in Neil Hickey, *The Gentleman Was a Thief: The Colorful Story of Arthur Barry, a 1920's Rogue* (New York: Holt, Rinehart & Winston, 1961), 87–88. Hickey recorded the location as Little Neck, a community that straddled the boundary with Queens; the portion falling within Nassau County was officially renamed Great Neck in 1928. See Joan Brown Wettingfeld, "Little Neck: The Evolution of a Village," *QNS*, July 9, 2003, https://qns.com/2003/07 /little-neck-the-evolution-of-a-village.

167   **netted more than $13,000**   The homes were in the communities of Plandome, Westbury, and Center Island. See "List of Homes Gibson Visited Stealing Gems," *Brooklyn Citizen*, June 9, 1927 "Barry Again Led to Looted Homes," *Times Union* (Brooklyn), June 10, 1927; and "Barry Gang Got Gems of Society Folk," *Daily News* (New York), June 10, 1927. These articles identified Barry and Monahan as suspects in all three robberies, as well as the break-in at the Jennings home.

167   **climbed onto a porch roof**   "Porch Climber Loots Jennings Home of $14,000," *Brooklyn Daily Eagle*, August 3, 1926.

167   **almost quadrupled in size**   "Roster Nassau County Police," in Henry J. Lee, ed., *The Long Island Almanac and Year Book 1927* (Brooklyn, NY: Brooklyn Daily Eagle, 1927), 190–91. A total of 192 officers are listed.

167   **a roster of at least fourteen**   This is the number of men who posed for a photograph of the detective bureau in September 1925. The photo was reproduced in Jerry Aylward, *Nassau County Police Department* (Charleston, SC: Arcadia, 2019), 15.

167   **"The sweeping reorganization"**   "Nassau's New Police Curb Crime," *Daily News*, January 24, 1926.

167   **two-seater Model Ts**   Photographs of the patrol cars appeared in *Nassau County Police Department*, 13, 16.

167   **"far-flung stretches"**   "Nassau's New Police Curb Crime."

167   **passed his captain's exam**   "5 Men Qualify as Captains of Nassau Police," *Brooklyn Daily Eagle*, August 16, 1926.

168   **"Proud Moment"**   *Daily News*, August 18, 1926.

168   **broke into the summer home**   Barry later confessed to the crime. See "Barry Visits Homes He Rifled of Gems," *Times Union*, June 12, 1927.

168   **newspaper magnate Ralph Pulitzer**   He was publisher of the *World* from 1911 to 1930. "Ralph Pulitzer Died in New York; Rites Tomorrow," *St. Louis Star-Times*, June 15, 1939.

168   **a businessman from Dayton**   Background on Talbott's business career and his polo playing on Long Island were drawn from "Harold E. Talbott's Death a Loss to Nation and City," *Dayton Daily News*, March 3, 1957, and "Harold Talbott, Ex-Secretary of Air, Dies," *St. Louis Globe-Democrat*, March 3, 1957.

168   **from a prominent Philadelphia family**   These biographical details were drawn from "Mrs. John B. Thayer: Dies on 32d Anniversary of Her Husband's Death on Titanic," *New York Times*, April 15, 1944, and "Heiress to Hunt Lions Where Roosevelt Did," *New York Times*, November 13, 1924.

169   **hobbled from the start**   The theft, Scaffa's role, and King's investigation were reported in "Talbotts Robbed of $32,000 Gems," *Times Union*, October 9, 1926; "Detectives Probe $25,000 Gem Theft at Talbott Home," *Brooklyn Daily Eagle*, October 9, 1926; "Rob

Woman's Home of $23,000 in Gems," *New York Times*, October 9, 1926; and "$23,000 Gems Fly; Dog Barks in Vain," *Daily News*, October 9, 1926.

169 **still facing trial**   Scaffa stood trial the following month. See "Scaffa On Trial in Gem Theft Case," *New York Times*, November 9, 1926.

169 **he acted as lookout**   "Beware of Gunman, Barry Tells Police," *New York Times*, June 12, 1927.

169 **offer of a reward**   "Peggy's $23,000 Gem Collection Lost This Time," *Daily News*, October 11, 1926.

169 **banker and philanthropist**   Information on the Jonases was drawn from "Nathan Jonas Dies, Noted Philanthropist," *Brooklyn Daily Eagle*, October 18, 1943.

169 **acting alone**   Barry later insisted he did not take part. See "Barry Visits Homes he Rifled of Gems."

169 **"Back into that room!"**   This account of the Jonas break-in is based on the following press reports: "Burglar in Home of Nathan S. Jonas Loses Nerve, Flees," *Times Union*, November 29, 1926; "Burglar Holds Up N.S. Jonas in Home, but Nerve Fails Him," *Brooklyn Daily Eagle*, November 29, 1926; "Nathan Jonas Faces Burglar with Gun, Who Gets No Loot," *Standard Union* (Brooklyn), November 29, 1926; and "Burglar Pays Visit to Home of Nathan Jonas," *Brooklyn Citizen*, November 29, 1926.

171 **"It was his business"**   Anna Blake Barry, "My Life of Love and Fear as the Sweetheart and Wife of Arthur Barry, the World's Most Famous Jewel-Thief," *Atlanta Constitution*, January 15, 1933.

171 **a man armed with a revolver**   The encounter was described in "Nassau 'Dinner Burglar,' Faced by Woman, Flees," *Times Union*, March 23, 1927, and "Nassau's Famous 'Dinner Burglar' At Work Again," *Brooklyn Daily Eagle*, March 23, 1927. William Couchman was identified as the holder of a seat on the New York Stock Exchange in "New High Level for U.S. Steel," *Buffalo Evening News*, June 18, 1926. The Couchman house was described in "Buys Handsome Home in Plandome Section," *Brooklyn Daily Eagle*, October 28, 1926.

171 **got a good look at him**   "Barry to Accuse Monahan Today of Murder, Theft," *Times Union*, July 11, 1927.

171 **helped to plan the attempted robbery**   "Barry Identifies Houses He Robbed," *New York Times*, June 29, 1927.

171 **the home of banker Robert Sealy**   The watch was described in "Find Seeley Gems on Livermore Trio," *Times Union*, June 6, 1927.

171 **joined the long list**   They were identified as suspects in both burglaries in "Livermores Tell Jury of $90,000 Holdup in Home," *Brooklyn Daily Eagle*, June 9, 1927.

171 **the home of E. M. Richardson**   Details of the burglary appeared in "Dinner Thief Again Raids North Shore Area; Gets $5,000," *Brooklyn Daily Eagle*, April 8, 1927; "Dinner Thief Gets $4,500 Gems," *Times Union*, April 8, 1927; "Dinner Burglar Gets $3,000 Gems," *Times Union*, April 9, 1927; and "$4,500 Jewels Go as Family Dines," *Daily News*, April 9, 1927.

171 **only Monahan had gone inside**   "Barry Identifies Houses He Robbed."

171 **a seventy-pound safe**   Details of the theft were reported in "Thieves Steal Safe with $10,000 Gems from Nassau Home," *Brooklyn Daily Eagle*, April 22, 1927, and "Burglars Get Rich Haul in Mineola Home," *Brooklyn Citizen*, April 22, 1927.

171 **lugged it a short distance**   Barry described removing and opening the safe in "Barry Identifies Houses He Robbed."

171   **"up against a blank wall"**   King's description of the stalled investigation appeared in
       Elvin N. Edwards, as told to Isabel Stephen, "How We Caught 'Boston Billy'—$1,000,000
       Crook," *True Detective Mysteries* 9, no. 2 (May 1928): 45–46. The reference to file drawers
       of reports appears on page 44.

172   **"Shoot him on sight"**   "Hunt Dinner Thief with Machine Gun," *Times Union*, April
       13, 1927. The squad was also described in "Dinner Thief Takes Night Off as Police Hunt
       Him," *Times Union*, April 14, 1927, and "Special Squad on Lookout for Nassau Robber,"
       Brooklyn Citizen, April 13, 1927.

172   **stuffing his pockets with jewelry**   The robbery was reported in "L.I. Gem Burglar Foils
       Gun Guard," *Times Union*, May 5, 1927, and "'Breakfast Burglar' Gets $4,000 in Gems,"
       Brooklyn Daily Eagle, May 6, 1927.

CHAPTER 20: THE MASTERPIECE

173   **Two ghostlike figures approached**   This account of the robbery is assembled from
       Barry's recollections of events and dialogue, published in: Arthur Barry, as told to Grace
       Robinson, "Barry Tells Own Story of Robber Feats," *Daily News*, October 30, 1932; Barry,
       as told to Robinson "Glamor of Barry's 'Big Breaks' Gone," *Daily News*, November 2,
       1932; Robert Wallace, "Confessions of a Master Jewel Thief," in Alexander Klein, ed., *The
       Double Dealers: Adventures in Grand Deception* (London: Faber & Faber, 1958), 102–4,
       originally published as "Confessions of Master Jewel Thief," *Life*, March 12, 1956; Arthur
       Barry, as told to Neil Hickey, "I Was the King of Jewel Thieves," *American Weekly*,
       January 18, 1959, 9, 18–19; and Hickey, *The Gentleman Was a Thief: The Colorful Story
       of Arthur Barry, a 1920's Rogue* (New York: Holt, Rinehart & Winston, 1961), 95–103.
       Information and quotations added from news reports and other sources are cited in the
       endnotes that follow.

174   **"There has been no expense spared"**   Illustrated real estate brochure reproduced in
       "When 'Silvermore' Was For Sale," Old Long Island, November 4, 2009, http://www
       .oldlongisland.com/2009/11/when-silvermore-was-for-sale.html. Other details about
       the estate are drawn from "Jesse Livermore Buys $250,000 Estate of Late Senator Palmer
       at Great Neck," *New-York Tribune*, May 22, 1921, and "Sale of Livermore King's Point
       Home Brings $222,000," *Brooklyn Daily Eagle*, June 30, 1933.

174   **one of the largest and most expensive**   The yacht is described in Tom Rubython, *Jesse
       Livermore—Boy Plunger: The Man Who Sold America Short in 1929* (London: Myrtle
       Press, 2015), 280–83.

174   **awarded the Order of Leopold**   "King Decorates Lindy," *Daily News*, May 29, 1927.
       Lindbergh's flight and his reception in Europe is described in A. Scott Berg, *Lindbergh*
       (New York: Berkley Books, 1999), 114–49.

174   **"sight at a distance"**   *Time Capsule/1927: A History of the Year Condensed from the
       Pages of Time* (New York: Time, 1968), 187–88.

174   **"as if a photograph"**   Kenneth Whyte, *Hoover: An Extraordinary Life in Extraordinary
       Times* (New York: Alfred A. Knopf, 2017), 325.

174   **hit his twelfth home run**   "The Year Babe Ruth Hit 60 Home Runs," Baseball-Almanac
       .com, https://www.baseball-almanac.com/feats/feats12c.shtml and *Time Capsule/1927*,
       164–65.

174   **a seven-year legal battle**   The case was summarized in *Time Capsule/1927*, 48–62.

175 **"no finer, charitable and congenial"** "Harry Aronsohn Dies in N.Y.," *Morning Call* (Paterson, NJ), July 7, 1945. Other biographical information on the couple is drawn from "Mrs. Aronsohn Buried," *Passaic Daily Herald* (NJ), April 10, 1916, and "Important Change in Silk Operation," *News* (Paterson, NJ), November 23, 1921. Paterson is referred to as "Silk City" in "Another Addition to the Silk City's Factories," *Morning Call*, March 10, 1908.

175 **"You may need this"** This comment to Aronsohn was reported in "$100,000 Holdup at Livermores Leaves No Clue," *Brooklyn Daily Eagle*, May 30, 1927.

176 **"We are sorry, indeed"** Elvin N. Edwards, as told to Isabel Stephen, "How We Caught 'Boston Billy'—$1,000,000 Crook," *True Detective Mysteries* 9, no. 2 (May 1928): 46.

177 **The revolver Barry was holding** Barry later claimed he was unarmed, but Jesse Livermore told the police he saw a revolver and flashlight in his hand. See "Barry Tells Own Story of Robber Feats."

177 **accepted Barry's offer of a cigarette** "How We Caught 'Boston Billy,'" 47.

178 **"magician of finance"** "Stock Magician Quits Retreat and Gives Curb Market Thrill," *Evening Star* (Washington, DC), April 7, 1922. His rapid rise on Wall Street and his 1907 coup were described in Freeman Tilden, "'War Brides'—and Bridegrooms," *Evening Star*, November 28, 1915, and "Boy Plunger," *Time*, December 9, 1940.

178 **"The first requisite to success"** "Jesse Livermore Comes Back with Another Million," *Evening World* (New York), January 10, 1917.

178 **investors and brokers took notice** See, for instance, "Shorts Make Heavy Dives," *Washington Herald*, March 18, 1920; "Less Bear Pressure on Wall Street Stock List," *Evening Star*, May 9, 1920; and "Stock Market Again Dull," *Washington Herald*, June 30, 1920.

178 **"a stock market god"** Rubython, *Jesse Livermore—Boy Plunger*, xiii.

178 **made a $4 million killing** "Livermore Makes $4,000,000 Coup," *St. Louis Globe-Democrat*, April 12, 1927.

178 **"not only without fear"** Edward V. Riis, "Livermore Theft Riddle to Police," *Times Union* (Brooklyn), May 31, 1927.

178 **the young businessmen and clerks** Grace Robinson, "L.I. Thieves Get $100,000," *Daily News*, May 30, 1927.

178 **she never called her husband Pops** Jesse Livermore noted this—and praised his wife's "courage and presence of mind" as she manipulated Barry into returning the rings—in "Livermore Theft Riddle to Police."

179 **"a Broadway beauty"** "Jesse Livermore Reported Wed to Broadway Beauty," *Evening World*, December 3, 1918.

179 **"a way with words"** Rubython, *Jesse Livermore—Boy Plunger*, 211.

179 **loot worth at least $60,000** "$100,000 Holdup at Livermores Leaves No Clue," *Brooklyn Daily Eagle*, May 30, 1927. Barry later estimated the rings were worth as much as $35,000 each. See "Barry Tells Own Story of Robber Feats."

179 **"such good sports"** "How We Caught 'Boston Billy,'" 47.

179 **"The Livermore place was burglarized"** King described his arrival at the Livermore estate, the interview, and his initial reaction to the witness accounts of the robbery in "How We Caught 'Boston Billy,'" 46–47, 98.

180 **"one of the most sensational thefts"** "$100,000 Holdup at Livermores."

180   **"quiet but firm politeness"**   "Livermores Robbed of $100,000 in Gems at Point of
      Pistols," *New York Times*, May 30, 1927.

180   **"dainty in their methods"**   "L.I. Thieves Get $100,000."

180   **snapped up the offbeat story**   "Polite Thugs Get $90,760," *Lansing State Journal* (MI),
      May 30, 1927; "Polite Burglars Return Rich Loot," *Spokesman-Review* (Spokane, WA),
      May 30, 1927; "'Friendly' Pair Rob House of $100,000," *Fort Worth Star-Telegram*, May
      30, 1927; and "Polite Duo Get $100,000 Livermore Gems," *San Francisco Examiner*, May
      30, 1927.

180   **held to Regina Aronsohn's head**   "L.I. Thieves Get $100,000."

181   **threatened to shoot Dorothea Livermore**   "L.I. Thieves Get $100,000" and "Livermores
      Robbed of $100,000."

181   **"experts in their line"**   "Livermores Robbed of $100,000."

181   **"bold robbers hardly ever linger"**   "L.I. Thieves Get $100,000."

181   **doubted it was the work**   "Livermores Robbed of $100,000."

181   **"Police do not recognize"**   "Livermore Theft Riddle to Police."

181   **gifts of expensive jewelry**   Rubython, *Jesse Livermore—Boy Plunger*, 211–12.

181   **transferred to a vault**   "L.I. Thieves Get $100,000."

181   **questioning the estate's servants**   "How We Caught 'Boston Billy,'" 99.

181   **suspected a third man was involved**   "$100,000 Holdup at Livermores."

181   **claimed to have seen five people**   Robinson, "Bobbed Blonde Seen in Livermore Theft,"
      Daily News, May 31, 1927.

182   **"just what to make of it"**   "Livermore Theft Riddle to Police."

182   **"There were so many similarities"**   "How We Caught 'Boston Billy,'" 98.

182   **"the 'gentleman burglars' of fiction"**   "Livermores Robbed of $100,000."

182   **"I am kind-hearted" and "my masterpiece"**   "Barry Tells Own Story of Robber Feats."

CHAPTER 21: THE TRAP

185   **often slowed to a crawl**   Barry's frustration with the train's slow progress, his last
      meeting with Monahan at Penn Station, the planned vacation with Blake, and his
      resolve to stop stealing are recorded in Neil Hickey, *The Gentleman Was a Thief: The
      Colorful Story of Arthur Barry, a 1920's Rogue* (New York: Holt, Rinehart & Winston,
      1961), 104–9. Monahan's handover of package of jewelry and Blake's attire were described
      in "Confesses Theft of Livermore Gems," *New York Times*, June 7, 1927.

185   **box containing unsold jewelry**   The contents were itemized in "2 Men and Woman
      Held in Theft of Livermore Gems," *Brooklyn Daily Eagle*, June 6, 1927, and "Confesses
      Theft of Livermore Gems."

186   **"My first job"**   "Livermore Theft Clew," *Daily News* (New York), June 3, 1927.

186   **"coming to see you again"**   "Livermore Gets Warning Letter," *New York Times*, June 2,
      1927, and "Livermore Guard Doubled by Threat," *Times Union* (Brooklyn), June 2, 1927.

186   **the work of cranks**   "Livermore Theft Clew."

186   **An anonymous call**   The call and speculation over what police were told was reported
      in "Livermore Gem 'Squeal' Near in Fight Over Girl," *Brooklyn Daily Eagle*, June 1,
      1927; "Livermore Jewel Clue Given Police," *Standard Union* (Brooklyn), June 1, 1927;

"Livermores Fear Kidnapping of Sons," *Times Union*, June 2, 1927; "Livermore Theft Mystery Deepens," *Yonkers Herald*, June 2, 1927; and "Livermore Theft Clew."

187 **"talked out of his turn"** Grace Robinson, "Squealer Tip Speeds Livermore Gem Hunt," *Daily News*, June 2, 1927.

187 **The gang's headquarters** "Double Livermore Guard," *Daily News*, June 2, 1927.

187 **"was being closely watched"** "Tail Livermore Suspect," *New York Times*, June 3, 1927.

187 **"the most important clew"** "Livermore Theft Clew."

187 **a $5,000 reward** The insurance company's deal with O'Farrell was noted, Hickey, *The Gentleman Was a Thief*, 104, and John O'Donnell, "Society Raffles in Net," *Daily News*, June 7, 1927.

187 **"super-sleuth" and "the vicar of a smart suburban parish"** Alissa Keir, "Snapshots," *Daily News*, August 19, 1931.

187 **One of his childhood buddies** "V. O'Farrell Dies; Noted Detective," *New York Times*, October 8, 1932.

188 **"vile and threatening language" and "excellent police duty"** O'Farrell's New York Police Department disciplinary and conduct record was summarized in "Re: Valerian J. O'Farrell, Information Concerning," memorandum dated March 30, 1933. Federal Bureau of Investigation Records—Val O'Farrell, 1933–1956, FBI Series 36 Box 1 Folder 1 File No. 62-28367, #1–11, March 7, 1933–March 15, 1956. Special Collections and University Archives, Raynor Memorial Libraries, Marquette University, Milwaukee, WI.

188 **"first class thief catchers"** "Val O'Farrell Faces Trial," *New York Sun*, August 19, 1911.

188 **"one of the best detectives"** "Detective Shake-Up Arouses Corrigan," *New York Times*, May 3, 1911.

188 **he was demoted** "Detective Shake-Up Arouses Corrigan"; "Spite, O'Farrell Says," *New York Times*, September 2, 1911.

188 **accused of taking a $1,000 bribe** "Try Policeman O'Farrell," *New York Times*, August 19, 1911.

188 **allowed to retire** "Detective O'Farrell Out," *New York Times*, January 21, 1912.

188 **"There was more money"** "V. O'Farrell Dies." This comment is also recorded in "Snapshots."

188 **an early headline-grabbing coup** "Says Thieves Gave $25,000 Gems Back," *New York Times*, February 24, 1914.

188 **to catch pilfering employees** *The American Cloak and Suit Review* 8, no. 3 (September 1914), 257.

188 **beating and intimidating** "Accuse Private Detectives," *New York Times*, January 26, 1913.

188 **impersonating a federal agent** The misconduct of these operatives is noted in "Val O'Farrell," memorandum dated March 3, 1933, Federal Bureau of Investigation Records—Val O'Farrell, 1933–1956.

188 **after a client absconded** "Val O'Farrell in Bankruptcy Suit," *New York Sun*, May 30, 1919.

188 **rounding up the wayward sons** "V. O'Farrell Dies; Noted Detective."

189 **"the Klondike"** "The Ropers," *New Yorker*, April 27, 1929, 34.

189 **a twelve-room home** "Snapshots."

189 **a scuffle broke out** "Advent of Woman Signal for Fight," *New York Herald*, May 29, 1923, and "Gems Lost in Raid, Says Miss Gomez," *New York Times*, May 29, 1923.

189   **sued him for perjury and fraud**   "Val O'Farrell Sued for Divorce 'Fraud,'" *New York Times*, August 13, 1921, and "Secret Hearing Held in O'Farrell Case," *New York Herald*, April 20, 1921.

189   **"pretty shady"**   "Memorandum," March 27, 1933, Federal Bureau of Investigation Records—Val O'Farrell, 1933–1956.

190   **"unsavory"**   "Memorandum for the Director," May 19, 1937, FBI Records—Val O'Farrell, 1933–1956.

190   **"his name in print"**   "Snapshots."

190   **"flush and spending money"**   O'Donnell, "Livermore Thief's Love Traps Gang," *Daily News*, June 8, 1927.

190   **"Bit by bit"**   "New Exploits of Society's Suave and Sinister 'Supper-Man,'" *Detroit Free Press*, November 30, 1930.

190   **worked his contacts**   Elvin N. Edwards as told to Isabel Stephen, "Trapping 'Boston Billy'—$1,000,000 Crook," *True Detective Mysteries* 9, no. 3 (June 1928): 20.

190   **a woman phoned his office**   The tip, O'Farrell's call to the Nassau County Police, and King's order to delay the train are described in Hickey, *The Gentleman Was a Thief*, 112.

190   **"Are you Arthur Gibson?"**   The arrest was described in Hickey, *The Gentleman Was a Thief*, 109–10; Edwards, as told to Isabel Stephen, "How We Caught 'Boston Billy'—$1,000,000 Crook," *True Detective Mysteries* 9, no. 2 (May 1928): 102–3; "Livermore Gems Found on Suspect," *Times Union*, June 6, 1927; and "Find Seeley Gems on Livermore Trio," *Times Union*, June 6, 1927. Photographs of the station grounds appeared in Dale Spencer and Janet Rischbieter, *Lake Ronkonkoma* (Charleston, SC: Arcadia, 2015). 94.

CHAPTER 22: OWNING UP

192   **"sneeringly and sullenly refused"**   King described the overnight interrogation in Elvin N. Edwards, as told to Isabel Stephen, "How We Caught 'Boston Billy'—$1,000,000 Crook," *True Detective Mysteries* 9, no. 2 (May 1928): 104. The firsthand accounts of King and district attorney Edwards presented in this article are the main source of this account of Barry's questioning and admissions. Additional details about the interrogation are drawn from in "Six Gem Thefts Bared; Livermore Arrests Made," *Brooklyn Daily Eagle*, June 6, 1927; "2 Men and Woman Held in Theft of Livermore Gems," *Brooklyn Daily Eagle*, June 6, 1927; "Find Seeley Gems on Livermore Trio," *Times Union* (Brooklyn), June 6, 1927; "Livermore Gems Found on Suspects," *Times Union*, June 6, 1927; and "Confesses Theft of Livermore Gems," *New York Times*, June 7, 1927.

192   **"nonchalant and at ease"**   "Livermore Loot Vanishes with Gang's Leader," *Brooklyn Daily Eagle*, June 7, 1927.

192   **"without any rough treatment"**   "King Lauds Nassau Police at Uniondale Coffee Party," *Times Union*, February 29, 1928. Use of the interrogation method was also denied in "'Third Degree' Is Taboo with Nassau County Police," *Brooklyn Daily Eagle*, February 26, 1928.

193   **"arrived at the scene of violent crimes"**   "This Month's Contributors," *True Detective Mysteries* 9, no. 2 (May 1928), 8.

193   **"seldom use bulldog tactics"** and **"an impenetrable fog of mystery"**   "How We Caught 'Boston Billy,'" 44, 105.

194   **faced them across his desk**   Edwards described his impressions of Barry and Blake and King's identification of the stolen ring in "How We Caught 'Boston Billy,'" 104–6.

194   **"I reeled back"**   Anna Blake Barry, "My Life of Love and Fear as the Sweetheart and Wife of Arthur Barry, the World's Most Famous Jewel-Thief," *Atlanta Constitution*, February 5, 1933.

194   **"how *could* you do this to me?"**   These exchanges, the threat to charge Blake, and Barry's offer to confess appeared in "How We Caught 'Boston Billy,'" 106.

195   **after holding out for fifteen hours**   "Livermore Thief Implicates Aide," *Times Union*, June 7, 1927.

195   **"Tell me the whole story"**   Neil Hickey, *The Gentleman Was a Thief: The Colorful Story of Arthur Barry, a 1920's Rogue* (New York: Holt, Rinehart & Winston, 1961), 113.

195   **"very touching way"**   The full confession was reproduced in "How We Caught 'Boston Billy'—$1,000,000 Crook," 107–8. Extracts appeared in Hickey, *The Gentleman Was a Thief*, 113–14; "Confesses Theft of Livermore Gems"; and John O'Donnell, "Livermore Burglar Tells to Save Blonde," *Daily News* (New York), June 8, 1927.

195   **a check of his fingerprints**   "Confesses Theft of Livermore Gems."

195   **"as still and white"**   "How We Caught 'Boston Billy'—$1,000,000 Crook," 107.

195   **identify any of the pieces**   The identification process was described in "Gibson Arrest Reveals Many Gem Robberies," *Standard Union* (Brooklyn), June 7, 1927; "Confesses Theft of Livermore Gem," and "$1,000,000 Gem Clue in Livermore Case," *New York Times*, June 8, 1927.

196   **"I see that little ring"**   "Livermore Thief Implicates Aide."

196   **"frighten you too much"**   "Livermore Burglar Tells to Save Blonde."

196   **Guards allowed them to kiss**   O'Donnell, "Livermore Thief's Love Traps Gang," *Daily News*, June 8, 1927. The meeting was also noted in "Confesses Theft of Livermore Gems."

196   **"I'm sorry that I got you into this"**   "Livermore Burglar Tells to Save Blonde."

196   **"I am going to confess"**   Blake Barry, "My Life of Love and Fear," *Atlanta Constitution*, February 5, 1933.

196   **"clean as a whistle"**   O'Donnell, "Admits $1,000,000 Thefts," *Daily News*, June 9, 1927.

196   **"notable piece of police work"**   Quoted in an editorial page note in the *Times Union*, June 14, 1927.

196   **might soon be closed**   See "Livermore Suspect Seized; Gems Found," *New York Times*, June 6, 1927, and "Gibson Arrest Reveals Many Gem Robberies," *Standard Union*, June 7, 1927.

196   **Barry "did not want a lawyer"**   "Link Gem Suspect to L.I. Theft Ring," *Times Union*, June 7, 1927.

197   **named "Bill Williams" as his accomplice**   "Confesses Theft of Livermore Gems."

197   **dispatched to the Times Square Hotel**   "$1,000,000 Gem Clue in Livermore Case."

198   **Monahan's idea**   Hickey, *The Gentleman Was a Thief*, 113–14; "Confesses Theft of Livermore Gems"; and "Livermore Thief Implicates Aide."

198   **"the real brains of our team"**   "How We Caught 'Boston Billy'—$1,000,000 Crook," 106.

198   **Monahan as the brains**   "Livermore Crook Shows Detectives Looted L.I. Homes," *Brooklyn Daily Eagle*, June 9, 1927.

198 **"My boy"** "Gem Robber Balks at Tour of Crimes," *New York Times*, June 10, 1927.

198 **"BOSTON BILLY" GANG** "$1,000,000 Gem Clue in Livermore Case."

198 **"master-mind"** "Million Dollar Gem Thefts Go to Jury Today," *Daily News*, June 13, 1927.

198 **"jewel bandit leader"** "Livermore Loot Vanishes with Gang's Leader," *Brooklyn Daily Eagle*, June 7, 1927.

198 **"lays the whole robbery plot"** "Livermore Loot Vanishes with Gang's Leader."

198 **"He told the truth"** Edwards as told to Stephen, "Trapping 'Boston Billy'—$1,000,000 Crook," *True Detective Mysteries* 9, no. 3 (June 1928), 20–21.

199 **front-page news** See "Held for Holdup," *The Wichita Eagle* (KS), June 7, 1927; "Second Man Held in Jewel Theft," *Courier-Journal* (Louisville, KY), June 7, 1927; "'Gentleman Bandit' Has 3 Homes; Entertained Long Island's Elite," *Salt Lake Telegram* (UT), June 8, 1927; "Livermore Jewel Robber Confesses Looting Mansion," *West Palm Beach Post* (FL), June 7, 1927; "Second Arrest Is Made," *Nebraska State Journal* (Lincoln), June 7, 1927; "Second Arrest Made in Livermore Robbery," *Joplin Globe*, (MO) June 7, 1927.

199 **the highest circulation** The *Daily News* became the highest-circulation American paper in 1923. Leo McGivena (and others), *The News: The First Fifty Years of New York's Picture Newspaper* (New York: News Syndicate, 1969), 106, 119.

199 **"Nothing that is not interesting"** Willard G. Bleyer, *Main Currents in the History of American Journalism* (Boston: Houghton Mifflin, 1927), 423.

199 **"Lay emphasis on romantic happenings"** Donald L. Miller, *Supreme City: How Jazz Age Manhattan Gave Birth to Modern America* (New York: Simon & Schuster, 2014), 349.

199 **"the pursuit of elusive news"** Walter Trohan, "Capital Circus," *Daily News*, December 20, 1961.

199 **"outstanding jewel thieves"** "Livermore Thief's Love Traps Gang."

200 **"for further developments"** O'Donnell, "Society Raffles in Net," *Daily News*, June 7, 1927.

200 **BARRY GANG GOT GEMS** *Daily News*, June 10, 1927.

200 **JUST SOME OF GEM THIEF'S VICTIMS!** *Daily News*, June 9, 1927.

200 **"The robber who stole suavely"** "Livermore Thief's Love Traps Gang"; O'Donnell, "'Just One More' Caught Gem Thief," *Daily News*, June 11, 1927.

200 **she posed for photographers** See, for instance, "Loves $1,000,000 Raffles," *Brooklyn Daily Eagle*, June 9, 1927. The dog's name is noted in O'Donnell, "Admits $1,000,000 Thefts," *Daily News*, June 9, 1927.

200 **"I love him and will keep on doing so"** "Admits $1,000,000 Thefts."

200 **"matronly"** and **"almost maternal affection"** "Livermore Thief's Love Traps Gang."

200 **"elderly sweetheart"** "Police Work on Two More Gem Thefts," *Brooklyn Daily Eagle*, June 10, 1927.

200 **King revealed Blake's ties** "Livermore Loot Vanishes with Gang's Leader" and "Confesses Theft of Livermore Gems."

200 **"never been an active worker"** $1,000,000 Gem Clue in Livermore Case."

200 **"I would rather say nothing"** "Link Gem Suspect to L.I. Theft Ring," *Times Union*, June 7, 1927.

201 **"I've struggled to keep this home together"** "Barry's Mother Unable to Help Admitted Thief," *Worcester Daily Telegram*, June 8, 1927.

201 **"Whatever he has done"** "Local Man Held In $100,000 Theft," *Worcester Daily Telegram*, June 7, 1927.

201 **doing time in a Connecticut prison** "Barry to Fight Against Going to Bridgeport to face Charge of Murder," *Worcester Daily Telegram*, April 26, 1922.

201 **broke a finger** For instance, "Resume Hunt for Monahan in Barry Case," *Worcester Gazette*, June 11, 1927.

201 **"sumptuous mansion"** "Society Raffles in Net."

201 **a winter home in Palm Beach** See, for instance, "Find Livermore Thief, Not Gems," *Yonkers Herald*, June 9, 1927.

201 **"liveried chauffeur"** "Livermore Thief's Love Traps Gang."

201 **"New England mob"** "$1,000,000 Gem Clue in Livermore Case."

201 **"a life of gentlemanly ease"** "'Just One More' Caught Gem Thief."

CHAPTER 23: ONLY HIGH-CLASS WORK

202 **"first day of real summer"** "1 Heat Victim First Day of Real Summer," *Daily News* (New York), June 10, 1927. The courthouse was described in "Nassau County's New Court House in Mineola," *Brooklyn Daily Eagle*, April 23, 1900; "Laying the Corner Stone," *Times Union* (Brooklyn), July 13, 1901; "The Corner Stone Laid," *Times Union*, July 14, 1901; and "Nassau's New Courthouse," *New-York Tribune*, August 26, 1901.

202 **looked cool and confident** This description of Barry is based on the photo that accompanied John O'Donnell's story "Two More Gem Robberies," *Daily News*, June 10, 1927, and a second photo, taken that day, in the author's collection.

202 **"walked out with the air"** "Barry's Gem Trip Becomes Holiday with Sweetheart," *Brooklyn Daily Eagle*, June 10, 1927. This article noted the hours-long delay to the start of the tour.

204 **"tour of the lost diamonds"** "Barry's Gem Trip Becomes Holiday with Sweetheart."

204 **"along a path of plunder"** "Two More Gem Robberies."

204 **"a visit to the *Social Register*"** O'Donnell, "Admits $1,000,000 Thefts," *Daily News*, June 9, 1927.

204 **"a student out on a necking party"** "Two More Gem Robberies."

204 **"Stand back"** This description of the visit to the Shaffer home is based on the following news reports; "Two More Gem Robberies"; "Gem Robber Balks at Tour of Crimes," *New York Times*, June 10, 1927; "Police Work on Two More Gem Thefts," *Brooklyn Daily Eagle*, June 10, 1927; and "Barry's Gem Trip Becomes Holiday with Sweetheart."

204 **pleaded guilty the previous day** His guilty pleas on June 8 were reported in the press and recorded in *The People of the State of New York v. Arthur Barry*, Case No. 4236, County Court of Nassau County, Mineola, NY.

204 **realized he risked being charged** King confirmed that this was Barry's reason for halting the crime scene visits in "Barry's Gem Trip Becomes Holiday with Sweetheart."

205 **"I know he's terrible"** "Two More Gem Robberies."

205 **relied on these outings** This point was made in "Barry Brought to Westchester for Questioning in Murder of Policeman and Local Robberies," *Daily Item* (Port Chester, NY), June 22, 1927.

205 **"Ladies' hats"** "Beware of Gunman, Barry Tells Police," *New York Times*, June 12, 1927.

205 **"a week-end guest visiting a hostess"** O'Donnell, "Raffles Leads Police Over His Gem Loot Trail," *Daily News*, June 12, 1927.

205 **he acted as lookout** "Barry Picks Out L.I. Homes He and His Pal Robbed," *Brooklyn Daily Eagle*, June 12, 1927.

205 **"only did high class work"** "Beware of Gunman, Barry Tells Police."

205 **A gold badge and a string of rosary beads** "Badge of Deputy Sheriff Found on Thief May Be a Clue to County Robbers," *Yonkers Herald*, June 10, 1927, and "New Clue in Gem Robberies Here," *Yonkers Herald*, June 18, 1927. Steers's occupation is noted in "Coster Steers Funeral Set for Tomorrow," *Daily Item*, April 24, 1952.

206 **"committed so many robberies"** "Jewel Thief Admits Stilwell Residence Burglary Last Year," *Yonkers Statesman*, June 11, 1927.

206 **stopped by Sergeant Jack Harrison** Background on Harrison and the shooting is drawn from the following news reports: "2 Bandits Murder Scarsdale Officer and Flee in Motor," *Brooklyn Daily Eagle*, July 19, 1923. "Police Officer Is Slain at Scarsdale by Thieves," *Yonkers Herald*, July 19, 1923; "Copper Killed by Auto Thief," *Star-Gazette* (Elmira, NY), July 19, 1927; and "Policeman Slain by Gunmen; Kin Vows Vengeance," *Daily News*, July 20, 1923.

206 **"shoot a cop"** Monahan's admissions to Barry were reported in "Scarsdale Murder Laid to Gem Thief," *New York Times*, June 16, 1927.

206 **losing his cap** "Cop Slain in 1923 by 'Boston Bill,' Declares Barry," *Brooklyn Daily Eagle*, June 15, 1927.

206 **"We have very little evidence"** "Scarsdale Murder Laid to Gem Thief."

206 **"a hard man to take alive"** O'Donnell, "Raffles Leads Police over His Gem Loot Trail," *Daily News*, June 12, 1927.

206 **"He's a desperate man"** "Beware of Gunman, Barry Tells Police."

207 **"You've got to be careful"** "'Boston Billy' Accuses Barry," *Yonkers Herald*, June 21, 1927, and "Letter Says Barry Killed Policeman," *New York Times*, June 18, 1927.

207 **"squealing"** "Barry Removed to County Jail as Threat Is Feared," *Brooklyn Daily Eagle*, June 15, 1927, and "Machine Guns Guard Livermore Crook," *Times Union*, June 14, 1927.

207 **Edwards agreed to send Barry** Court orders approving tours of crime scenes in Westchester and Nassau Counties note that Barry "may render great aid and assistance" to the investigations of the Livermore and other robberies. The orders were filed as *The People of the State of New York v. Arthur J. Gibson, also known as Arthur J. Barry*, Case No. 4261, County Court of Nassau County.

207 **The route was kept secret** The security measures were reported in "Barry Is Spirited to Westchester," *Times Union*, June 22, 1927, and "Barry Points Out 22 Homes He Robbed," *New York Times*, June 23, 1927.

207 **crisscrossed the county** The tour was described in "Barry Came to Identify Home Here," *Yonkers Herald*, June 23, 1927, and "15 More Robberies Admitted by Barry," *New York Times*, June 15, 1927.

207 **"I want to thank you"** "Barry Points Out 22 Homes He Robbed" and "Barry Gentleman Burglar, Meets Gentleman He Robbed," *Times Union*, June 23, 1927. Biographical information on Mallory is drawn from "Robert Mallory Jr. Dies," *Brooklyn Daily Eagle*, December 2, 1929.

208 **"the most successful robber"** "Jewel Losses Debunked," *Daily News*, June 17, 1927.

208   **"a string of robberies"**   "Man-Hunt for 'Boston Billy' Rivals Search for Chapman,"
Times Union, June 21, 1927.

208   **"admitted other robberies so readily"**   "Gem Robber Admits Nine More Thefts," *New
York Times*, June 9, 1927.

208   **"society friends"**   "Jewel Losses Debunked."

208   **also preying on Long Island homes**   "Livermore Crook Shows Detectives Looted
L.I. Homes," *Brooklyn Daily Eagle*, June 9, 1927, and "Gem Robber Admits Nine More
Thefts."

208   **His share of the take**   "$80,000 Gem Loot Total, Says Barry," *Times Union*, June 16,
1927.

208   **"could have made a better living"**   "New Clue in Gem Robberies Here," *Yonkers
Herald*, June 18, 1927.

208   **"he might have participated"**   "Barry Identifies Houses He Robbed," *New York Times*,
June 29, 1927. This tour was also reported in "Barry Is Taken on New Tour of Burglary
Scenes," *Brooklyn Daily Eagle*, June 29, 1927.

208   **they walked sixty paces**   The route from the jail to the courthouse and the interiors of
the courtroom were described in "Nassau County's New Court House in Mineola" and
"Laying the Corner Stone."

209   **"the dry judge"**   "'Dry Judge' Finds Drunkenness Cheap," *New York Times*, February
1, 1931, and "Justice L.J. Smith Dies Unexpectedly," *New York Times*, June 9, 1932.
This description of Lewis is based on his World War I draft registration form and a
photograph published in "What Has Happened to Justice: Second Degree Rewarded
Mother-in-Law Slayer," *Daily News*, March 20, 1927.

209   **a minimum sentence of fifteen years**   Lewis E. Lawes, *Life and Death in Sing Sing*
(London: John Long, 1929), 24, 26.

209   **"The Court then imposes sentence"**   The sentencing hearing was described in "Barry,
Gem Thief and Ladder Burglar Gets 25-Year Sentence," *Yonkers Herald*, July 1, 1927,
and "Barry in Sing Sing to Serve 25 Years," *Times Union*, July 1, 1927. The sentence was
imposed for the burglary conviction. A notation on the court file shows Barry received
a suspended sentence on the second count, larceny. *The People of the State of New York
v. Arthur Barry*, Case No. 4236, County Court of Nassau County.

209   **struck a deal**   "Jewel Losses Debunked."

209   **no more than thirty years**   "Gem Robber Admits Nine More Thefts."

209   **"Severity of punishment"**   "'Third Degree' Is Taboo with Nassau County Police,"
Brooklyn Daily Eagle, February 26, 1928, and "King Lauds Nassau Police at Uniondale
Coffee Party," *Times Union*, February 29, 1928.

210   **"charges enough against him"**   "15 More Robberies Admitted by Barry."

210   **Percy Rockefeller's Owenoke estate**   "Admits $1,000,000 Thefts" and "15 More
Robberies Admitted by Barry."

210   **"still looking for his confederate"**   "Barry Sentenced to Serve 25 Years," *Times Union*,
July 1, 1927.

210   **Anna Blake ran up to them**   This scene was described in "Barry, Gem Thief and
Ladder Burglar Gets 25-Year Sentence" and other press reports. "Barry Sentenced to 25
Years for Livermore Theft," *Brooklyn Daily Eagle*, July 1, 1927, reported that Barry and
Blake met in Edwards's office before he was sentenced.

210 **"I am usually very calm"** Anna Blake Barry, "My Life of Love and Fear as the Sweetheart and Wife of Arthur Barry, the World's Most Famous Jewel-Thief," *Atlanta Constitution*, February 5, 1933.

210 **"I went to pieces"** Blake Barry, "My Life of Love and Fear," *Atlanta Constitution*, February 12, 1933.

210 **"I'll be an old man"** "New York Gives Barry 25 Years," *Worcester Daily Telegram*, July 2, 1927.

CHAPTER 24: UP THE RIVER

211 **jammed into a car between two other prisoners** "Barry Sentenced to Serve 25 Years," *Times Union* (Brooklyn), July 1, 1927.

211 **"up the river"** The phrase originated in the 1890s. See the entry for Sing Sing in Encyclopedia.com, https://www.encyclopedia.com/places/united-states-and-canada /us-political-geography/sing-sing#3401803869.

211 **"sure to strike terror"** "Sing Sing Prison No Longer Drably Grim," *Daily News*, December 12, 1926.

211 **"limp and dejected"** Lewis E. Lawes, *Life and Death in Sing Sing* (London: John Long, 1929), 70.

212 **"This way"** The steps for processing Sing Sing's new arrivals were described in Lawes, *Life and Death in Sing Sing*, 70–76.

212 **asked him dozens of questions** Receiving Blotter for Arthur Barry, July 1, 1927, in Sing Sing Prison, Inmate Admission Registers, 1842–1852, 1865–1971, New York Department of Correctional Services, B0143, New York State Archives, Albany, via Ancestry.com. Lawes noted the clerks' preference for questioning lifers and the reasons new inmates gave for breaking the law in *Life and Death in Sing Sing*, 71–73.

213 **"There is only harshness"** and **"Little cubbyholes of cold stone"** Lawes, *Life and Death in Sing Sing*, 48. The cells are described on pages 76–77.

213 **"a dead man's grave"** James McGrath Morris, *The Rose Man of Sing Sing: A True Tale of Life, Murder, and Redemption in the Age of Yellow Journalism* (New York: Fordham University Press, 2003), 268–69.

213 **"the devil himself"** Lawes, *Life and Death in Sing Sing*, 77–78.

213 **"My God!" he exclaimed. "It's inhuman!"** Denis Brian, *Sing Sing: The Inside Story of a Notorious Prison* (Amherst, NY: Prometheus Books, 2005), 124.

213 **"no matter how hardened"** Lawes, *Life and Death in Sing Sing*, 76.

214 **new inmates remained in isolation** The settling-in routines for new inmates and the prison jobs available are noted in Lawes, *Life and Death in Sing Sing*, 77–85.

214 **"You take the back door"** Hurley described the arrest in "'Boston Billy' Boasts of Many Conquests; Denies Livermore Raid," *Times Union*, July 8, 1927. Description of Hurley is based on "'Boston Billy's' Captor No 'Story Book' Sleuth; Lets His Results Talk," *Brooklyn Daily Eagle*, July 11, 1927; and a photograph that appeared in "Bandit's Nemesis," *Times Union*, July 10, 1927.

215 **"an ace detective"** "Nassau Police Official Takes Life with Gun," *Daily News*, December 19, 1956.

215 **had been on his trail** Sheraton described his search for Monahan and how he teamed up with Hurley in "When Justice Triumphed: A Detective's Long Search," *Pittsburgh Sun-Telegraph*, February 21, 1941.

215   **The wound was minor**   Monahan's wound was described in "Shot Fells Boston Billy, Noted L.I. Jewel Crook, After Gun Duel with Cops," *Brooklyn Daily Eagle*, July 7, 1927.

215   **"I'd be better off"**   "Livermore Robber Shot at Sound View by N.Y. Detective," *Journal* (Meriden, CT), July 7, 1927.

215   **"facetious and scornful"**   Elvin N. Edwards as told to Isabel Stephen, "Trapping 'Boston Billy'—$1,000,000 Crook," *True Detective Mysteries* 9, no. 3 (June 1928): 86.

215   **"society racket"**   "'Boston Billy' Boasts of Many Conquests."

215   **"Barry is a rat"**   "'Boston Billy' Blandly Denies Thefts," *Times Union*, July 8, 1927.

215   **"grudge work on his part"**   "Trap 'Boston Billy,' Shoot and Seize Him," *New York Times*, July 8, 1927.

216   **"is obviously scared"** and **"afraid of 'burning'"**   "'Boston Billy' Boasts of Many Conquests."

216   **"cold, debonair, wise-cracking"**   "Boston Billy Deals for Mercy," *Daily News*, July 9, 1927.

216   **"If I had a little hacksaw"**   "Not Guilty Is Williams Plea," *Yonkers Herald*, July 8, 1927.

216   **"If I put those two men"**   "'Boston Billy' Boasts of Many Conquests."

216   **"Dapper Gem Thief"**   "Barry Goes from Prison to Testify in Williams' Case," *Daily Item* (Port Chester, NY), July 11, 1927. A photograph of his arrival appeared under the headline LIVERMORES DESCRIBE GEM ROBBERS, *Brooklyn Citizen*, July 12, 1927.

216   **"tickled to death about it"**   "Woman Identifies Monahan as Thief," *Times Union*, July 9, 1927.

217   **devouring pints of ice cream**   "Seek Indictment of 'Boston Billy,'" *Yonkers Herald*, July 14, 1927. On the heatwave, see "Heat Kills 9 More in a Day," *Daily News*, July 16, 1927.

217   **"It doesn't pay"**   "'Boston Billy' Case Put to Grand Jury," *New York Times*, July 12, 1927.

217   **"mixed up with women"**   "Williams Is Identified as Burglar," *Daily Item*, July 13, 1927.

217   **"a mighty good time"**   Wilbur E. Rogers, "Genuine Story-Book Crook with Polished Personality Is 'Boston Billy' Williams," *Brooklyn Daily Eagle*, July 9, 1927.

217   **did not recognize him**   "Barry Now Dodges Facing His Ex-Pal in L.I. Robberies," *Brooklyn Daily Eagle*, July 12, 1927.

217   **identified him as the armed man**   "Call 'Boston Billy' Couchman Robber," *New York Times*, July 10, 1927, and "Jonas Identifies Monahan as Thief," *Times Union*, July 13, 1927.

217   **"worthless without corroboration"**   "Conviction Seems Certain as Jonas Identifies Billy," *Brooklyn Daily Eagle*, July 14, 1927.

217   **the grand jury indicted him**   "'Boston Billy' faces 17 Additional Counts," *New York Times*, July 16, 1927.

217   **imprisoned for life**   "Seek Indictment of 'Boston Billy,'" *Yonkers Herald*, July 14, 1927, and "Will Seek Life Term for 'Boston Billy,'" *New York Times*, July 15, 1927.

217   **committed in their jurisdiction**   "Barry to Accuse Monahan Today of Murder, Theft," *Times Union*, July 11, 1927.

217   **threatening to indict him**   "'Boston Billy' Faces Inquiry in Murder," *New York Times*, July 9, 1927.

217   **identified him as the gunman**   "'Boston Billy' Identified by Three as Killer in Bridgeport Dance Hall," *Brooklyn Daily Eagle*, July 20, 1927. The electric chair did not replace executions by hanging in Connecticut until 1936. See "Connecticut Abandons Old Hanging Machine Which Jerked Its Victims into Air—Branded 'Most Humane,'" *Independent* (St. Petersburg, FL), May 6, 1936.

218   **"other prosecuting authorities"** and **"easy to get out of"**   "Trapping 'Boston Billy'—
       $1,000,000 Crook," 86–87.

218   **"I'll go crazy here"**   "Boston Billy Is Placed in Solitary Confinement as Key Is Found in
       Cell," *Brooklyn Daily Eagle*, July 20, 1927, and "Foil 'Boston Billy' in Jail-Break Plot," *New
       York Times*, July 21, 1927. The likelihood that Barry could hear his screams was noted in
       "'Boston Billy's' Escape Foiled; Filed Spoon into Key in Cell," *Times Union*, July 20, 1927.

218   **set fire to his mattress**   "Boston Billy Trial Off Until Monday," *New York Times*, July
       22, 1927, and "Boston Billy Haggard, Wins Delay," *Daily News*, July 22, 1927.

218   **"glassy eyed and shaking"**   "'Boston Billy' Williams Tries to Set Jail on Fire and Goes
       on Hunger Strike," *Brooklyn Daily Eagle*, July 21, 1927.

218   **a possible plea of insanity**   "Look for an Insanity Plea by Williams; Examination
       Planned," *Yonkers Herald*, July 22, 1927. The results were reported in "Alienists for State
       Test 'Boston Billy's' Sanity," *Brooklyn Daily Eagle*, July 23, 1927.

218   **Grim headlines predicted**   See, for instance, "'Boston Billy' Guilty; May Get 80 Years,"
       New York Times, July 26, 1927. The guilty plea was also reported in "Boston Billy Williams
       Pleads Guilty to Livermore Thefts," *Yonkers Herald*, July 25, 1927. Court records confirm
       the guilty pleas related to the Aronsohn robbery: *The People of the State of New York v.
       James F. Monahan*, Case No. 4276, County Court of Nassau County, Mineola, NY.

218   **sparked a brief treasure hunt**   "$60,000 Necklace Flung Away by Boston Billy Now
       Sought as Part of Livermore Loot," *New York Times*, August 1, 1927.

219   **"tantamount to life in prison"**   "Sentence Billy Williams to 50 Years in Sing Sing Cell,"
       Yonkers Herald, July 28, 1927.

219   **eligible to apply for early release**   His parole date—March 20, 1969—was recorded in
       Receiving Blotter for James Francis Monahan, July 28, 1927, in Sing Sing Prison, Inmate
       Admission Registers.

219   **abandon bids to put him on trial**   "'Boston Billy' Williams Starts Serving Half
       Century Sentence in Sing Sing Prison for Long Island Robbery," *Yonkers Herald*, July
       29, 1927, and "May Prosecute Williams Here," *Yonkers Herald*, July 30, 1927.

219   **blew kisses**   "Boston Billy's Farewell," *Brooklyn Daily Eagle*, July 29, 1927.

219   **"Beau Brummel of house breakers"**   "Boston Billy Pleads Guilty," *Daily News*, July 26,
       1927.

219   **"dirty rat"**   The complete poem was published in "'Boston Billy' Pleads Guilty to
       Livermore Theft," *Times Union*, July 25, 1927.

219   **locked up in Sing Sing**   "Barry Re-Enters Sing Sing," *Times Union*, July 27, 1927.

CHAPTER 25: SING SING

220   SQUEALER IN PERIL   *Daily News* (New York), July 28, 1927.

220   **"I won't be here long"**   "Boston Billy's Escape Boast Doubles Guards at Sing Sing,"
       Brooklyn Daily Eagle, July 30, 1927.

220   **considered transferring Barry**   "To Keep Monahan From Barry," *Times Union*
       (Brooklyn), July 28, 1927.

220   **"the state's ugliest criminals"**   "Crime: Dannemora, Auburn," *Time*, August 5, 1929,
       https://content.time.com/time/magazine/article/0,9171,737601,00.html.

220   **Siberia**   The nickname is noted in "Warden Blames Outbreak at Dannemora on
       Lifers Sent There as Punishment," *Brooklyn Daily Eagle*, July 23, 1929, and Denis Brian,

Sing Sing: The Inside Story of a Notorious Prison (Amherst, NY: Prometheus Books, 2005), 113.

221   **Lawes ordered that Barry be released**   "Squealer Freed from Solitary," *Daily News*, August 22, 1927.

221   **"Few men's minds"**   Lewis E. Lawes, *Life and Death in Sing Sing* (London: John Long, 1929), 81.

221   **"Most labor is hard"**   "The Case of Arthur Barry," *Daily Item* (Port Chester, NY), July 8, 1927.

221   **"dark and troubled souls"**   "Makes Prison Yard 'a Thing of Beauty,'" *New York Times*, October 19, 1924.

221   **"to keep her from starvation and want"**   James McGrath Morris, *The Rose Man of Sing Sing: A True Tale of Life, Murder, and Redemption in the Age of Yellow Journalism* (New York: Fordham University Press, 2003), 242–43. The gardens and Chapin's efforts to build them are described on pages 305–12.

221   **"You can imagine"**   Morris, *The Rose Man of Sing Sing*, 310.

222   **"When he gave me an order"**   Arthur Barry, as told to Grace Robinson, "Arthur Barry's Own Life Story," *Daily News*, November 6, 1932. Barry described himself as superintendent of Chapin's greenhouse.

222   **"Shirking . . . will not be tolerated"**   Morris, *The Rose Man of Sing Sing*, 312.

222   **he convinced the warden**   Neil Hickey, *The Gentleman Was a Thief: The Colorful Story of Arthur Barry, a 1920's Rogue* (New York: Holt, Rinehart & Winston, 1961), 117. A photograph of the aviary appears in Guy Cheli, *Sing Sing Prison* (Portsmouth, NH: Arcadia, 2003), 112. Chapin's friendship with the Houdinis is noted in Morris, *The Rose Man of Sing Sing*, 324, 327, 344.

222   **superintendent of the greenhouse**   Hickey, *The Gentleman Was a Thief*, 117. The building's construction during his time in Sing Sing is confirmed in "Prison Aviary Gets Pets Soon," *Yonkers Statesman*, December 10, 1929.

222   **called Barry "son"**   Anna Blake Barry, "My Life of Love and Fear as the Sweetheart and Wife of Arthur Barry, the World's Most Famous Jewel-Thief," *Atlanta Constitution*, February 12, 1933.

222   **"country club for criminals"**   "'Good Old Days' Seen Dawning in Sing Sing Again," *Daily News*, January 3, 1927. Movies, recreation time, and other privileges granted to inmates were described in *Life and Death in Sing Sing*, 92–99; "Convicts Not 'Bad,' Warden Declares," *New York Times*, October 26, 1928; and "Sing Sing Cuts Movie Shows, Since Cells Are More Livable," *New York Times*, August 15, 1929. Lawes's challenge to his critics was noted in Edward Kavanaugh, "Feeding 1,675 Daily Makes Warden Lawes of Sing Sing Really a 'Big Hotel Man': No Coddling of Prisoners Discovered There," *Brooklyn Daily Eagle*, June 5, 1927.

223   **"Treat a man like a dog"**   Lawes, *Life and Death in Sing Sing*, 84.

223   **a Grade A man**   The grading system and visiting privileges were described in Lawes, *Life and Death in Sing Sing*, 90.

223   **"a powerful incentive"**   Lawes, *Life and Death in Sing Sing*, 90.

223   **"Stay out of trouble"**   Hickey, *The Gentleman Was a Thief*, 116.

223   **"determined to be a model prisoner"**   Arthur Barry, as told to Neil Hickey, "Love On Borrowed Time," *American Weekly*, January 25, 1959, 20.

223   **Blake visited every week**   Hickey, *The Gentleman Was a Thief*, 116.

223   **no barriers or screens**   Chapin described his visits with female admirers in Morris, *The Rose Man of Sing Sing*, 320. A photograph of the visiting room in the 1920s appears in Cheli, *Sing Sing Prison*, 48.

223   **"lived for the day"**   Blake Barry, "My Life of Love and Fear," *Atlanta Constitution*, February 12, 1933.

223   **"trying to obtain his freedom"**   "'Boston Billy' Guilty; May Get 80 Years," *New York Times*, July 26, 1927.

223   **"the prison nine"**   "Giants Show 'Em How It's Done," *Daily News*, September 1, 1927.

223   **"gazed with envious eyes"**   "Giants Beat the Sing Sing Team," *Yonkers Herald*, September 1, 1927.

223   **was allowed to listen**   "Convicts Listen to Fight," *New York Times*, September 23, 1927.

224   **toured the prison**   Cheli, *Sing Sing Prison*, 59 and James Cannon, "Sophisticates of C.C.N.Y. Clown in Sing Sing Chair," *Daily News*, December 28, 1927.

224   **received a gift package**   "Sing Sing Gifts to All Prisoners," *Times Union*, December 25, 1927.

224   **"fill the great gaps"**   Hickey, *The Gentleman Was a Thief*, 117.

224   **fifteen thousand books**   "Move Sing Sing Library," *New York Times*, August 21, 1929. Book titles and subjects are drawn from *Sing Sing Prison: Library Catalogue* (Ossining, NY: Sing Sing Prison, 1901).

224   **"a bad influence"**   Lawes, *Life and Death in Sing Sing*, 97.

224   **"the malodorous march"**   Lawes describes the daily routine in Lawes, *Life and Death in Sing Sing*, 88–94.

224   **"the smallest area"**   Edward H. Smith, "Old Sing Sing Cells Round Out a Century," *New York Times*, August 21, 1927.

224   **heated, well-lit cells**   The new cells were described in "Old Sing Sing Cells Round Out a Century" and "Sing Sing Prison No Longer Drably Grim," *Daily News*, December 12, 1926.

226   **an inside job**   See, for instance, "Barry's Sweetheart Aids Grand Jury Case Against Boston Billy, Gem Bandit," *Brooklyn Daily Eagle*, July 12, 1927, and "Livermore Driver Sought; He Loved Society Woman," *Daily News*, July 14, 1927.

226   **"a dive for criminals"**   "Jewel Thief Denies Kane Acted as Aide," *New York Times*, January 29, 1929.

226   **"I'm going to fight"**   "Long Island Society Long a Prey to 'Boston Billy' Gang," *Kenosha News* (WI), December 24, 1928. Sheraton's hunt for Kane was reported in "Kane Nabbed as Last Livermore Jewels Robber," *Brooklyn Citizen*, December 23, 1927; "Livermore Thief, Hunted 2 Years, Caught in West," *Brooklyn Daily Eagle*, December 23, 1928; and "When Justice Triumphed: Detective Tells Inside Story of Trailing the Livermore Gem Gang," *Daily News*, February 17, 1929.

226   **Monahan had given a statement**   "Eddie Kane Denies Aiding L.I. Robbers," *Times Union*, December 22, 1928, and "Held as Third Thief in Livermore Raid," *New York Times*, December 23, 1928.

226   **mandatory in felony cases**   The ruling and its impact was reported in "Appeals Court Voids 9,000 Convictions," *New York Times*, November 21, 1928, and "Appeals Court Rules 9,000 in Jail Illegally," *Democrat and Chronicle* (Rochester, NY), November 21, 1928. Years later, Barry claimed he had studied law books at Sing Sing and had discovered the flaw in his conviction on his own. He planned to apply for release five

years into his sentence, when a statute of limitations on burglary and larceny would expire and he could no longer be prosecuted a second time. The potential legal problem was identified in the press months before the Court of Appeals ruling, however, making it unlikely Barry stumbled upon it on his own. Hickey, *The Gentleman Was a Thief*, 117–18. Examples of early press coverage of the issue include "Holds Law Dispensing With Indictments Void," *New York Times*, February 12, 1928, and "Several Hundred Illegally in Jail," *Brooklyn Daily Eagle*, February 12, 1928.

226   **"a most ridiculous mess"**   "Serious as Well as Ridiculous," *Daily Argus* (White Plains, NY), November 22, 1928.

226   **casually puffing a cigarette**   "Nassau Police Guard Convict Gem Witness," *Standard Union* (Brooklyn) December 28, 1928. Barry's departure from Sing Sing was reported in "Writ to Bring Barry Before Nassau Jury," *Times Union*, December 26, 1928. His refusal to testify against Kane was noted in "Barry Indicted in Livermore Case," *Brooklyn Daily Eagle*, December 29, 1928, and "Guns Bristle as Convict Faces Livermore Gem Quiz," *Daily News*, December 29, 1928.

226   **Kane's only crime**   Hickey, *The Gentleman Was a Thief*, 92–4.

227   **Four indictments**   "Kane Indicted in Livermore Home Robbery," *Standard Union*, December 29, 1928. The joint indictments are filed as *The People of the State of New York v. Edgar Kane and Arthur Barry*, Case Nos. 4900, 4901, 4902, and 4903, County Court of Nassau County, Mineola, NY.

227   **sentenced him to twenty-five years**   "Livermore Thief Gets 25-Year Term," *Times Union*, January 24, 1929, and "Livermore Jewel Thief Gets 25-Year Term," *Brooklyn Daily Eagle*, January 24, 1929.

227   **acknowledged for the first time**   "Pedigree, Arthur Barry," January 23, 1929, *The People of the State of New York v. Edgar Kane and Arthur Barry*, Case No. 4900.

227   **"Didn't you tell me" and an honest and reliable employee**   "Monahan Denies Kane Had Part in Livermore Theft," *Times Union*, January 29, 1929. The detail about Monahan remaining handcuffed while he testified was reported in "Rout Gunmen from Court as Convict Testifies in Trial of Gem Theft Suspect," *Brooklyn Daily Eagle*, January 29, 1929.

227   **the jury acquitted**   "Kane Acquitted, Is Rearrested," *New York Times*, January 30, 1929, and "Kane Acquitted, Three Other Cases Will Be Dropped," *Times Union*, January 30, 1929. Kane pleaded guilty in Connecticut a few months later to carrying a concealed weapon and received a sentence of three and a half to five years in prison. "Gun Toter Sent to Jail by Judge at Bridgeport," *Journal* (Meriden, CT), May 21, 1929.

227   **On his way back**   "Escape Attempt Foiled By Shots," *Yonkers Herald*, January 29, 1929, and "'Boston Billy' Fails in Dash for Liberty," *New York Times*, January 30, 1929.

227   **nothing more than a ruse**   "Kane Acquitted, Three Other Cases Will Be Dropped," *Times Union*, January 30, 1929.

228   **to relieve overcrowding**   The prison population was at record-high levels at the beginning of 1929, and transfers to other prisons to relieve overcrowding were common. See "Dangerous Prisoners Taken from Sing Sing," *Brooklyn Daily Eagle*, August 9, 1928, and "1,850 at Sing Sing a Record," *New York Times*, March 23, 1929. Barry's admission to Auburn on December 30, 1928, was recorded in Auburn Prison Inmate Record Cards, 1915–1970, Series B1222, Box 3, card for Arthur Barry, inmate no. 43077, New York State Archives, Albany.

228   **wrangled a meeting with Warden Lawes**   "My Life of Love and Fear," *Atlanta Constitution*, February 12, 1933.

228   **recommend that he serve his time**   "Livermore Thief Gets 25-Year Term." His return
to Auburn was reported in "'Boston Billy's' Pal Guarded in Prison Shift," *Brooklyn Daily
Eagle*, January 31, 1927.

CHAPTER 26: BREAKOUT

231   **crouched in a stairwell**   Barry described the escape and his flight to New York City in
press interviews and in his biography. Descriptions and quotations, unless otherwise
noted, are drawn from: "Arthur Barry's Life Story," *Daily News* (New York), October 31,
1932; Robert Wallace, "Confessions of a Master Jewel Thief," in Alexander Klein, ed., *The
Double Dealers: Adventures in Grand Deception* (London: Faber & Faber, 1958), 104–8,
originally published as "Confessions of Master Jewel Thief," *Life*, March 12, 1956; Arthur
Barry, as told to Neil Hickey, "Love on Borrowed Time," *American Weekly*, January 25,
1959, 20, 22; and Neil Hickey, *The Gentleman Was a Thief: The Colorful Story of Arthur
Barry, a 1920's Rogue* (New York: Holt, Rinehart & Winston, 1961), 125–58. Barry also
described the escape in "Newark Man Held as Kidnaper," *Herald-News* (Passaic, NJ),
October 24, 1932.

231   **former medical student**   "N.Y. Man Caused Riot at Auburn, Asserts Warden," *Times
Union* (Brooklyn), August 10, 1929.

231   **young hoodlum from Rochester**   "4 Convicts Elude Auburn Pursuit; Governor Acts,"
Brooklyn Daily Eagle, July 29, 1929. Photographs of Small and Caprico accompanied the
article "City Thugs Blamed in Auburn Break," *Daily News*, July 30, 1929.

231   **"I'll kill you for that"**   Osborne described the ambush in "Charge Barry, Small Used
Guard as Shield," *Daily News*, December 15, 1932. The guard suffered "irritation and
inflammation" to his eyes but soon recovered his sight: "Capt. Osborn Will Not Lose
His Eyesight," *Advertiser-Journal* (Auburn, NY), July 30, 1929.

232   **"Come on, you fellows"**   "Voice Fails Small Asking for Mistrial," *Daily News*,
December 20, 1932. More than two decades later, Barry claimed he was the one who
incited the riot, shouting: "We're breaking out! If anybody wants to come along, come
now!" See Wallace, "Confessions of a Master Jewel Thief," 105. Barry repeated the
claim in Hickey, *The Gentleman Was a Thief*, 141. Small, however, was the only escapee
identified as urging other inmates to join the escape in press accounts of the riot and the
trials that followed.

232   **the iron-barred gate**   A photograph of the gate, taken shortly after the escape, was
published alongside the article "Auburn Convicts Quiet, but Sullen," *Democrat and
Chronicle* (Rochester), July 29, 1929.

232   **inmate from Buffalo**   Details on Pawlak are drawn from "Buffalo Convicts' Records
Bared; Pawlak, Escaped, Criminal in Youth," *Buffalo News*, July 29, 1929, and "New
Panel Drawn for Convicts' Trial," *Buffalo News*, November 21, 1929.

232   **"Open that gate"**   "Prison Guard Says Pawlak Clubbed Him," *Buffalo Times*, November
23, 1929. A photograph of a guard unlocking the gate with the large key appeared in
Eileen McHugh, *Auburn Correctional Facility* (Charleston, SC: Arcadia, 2010), 104.

233   **the oldest prison**   Details of Auburn's history and its eponymous system have been
compiled from McHugh, *Auburn Correctional Facility*, 8–10; "Lawrence Van Gelder,
"Prison Has History of Riot and Reform," *New York Times*, November 5, 1970, and
Norval Morris and David J, Rothman, eds., *The Oxford History of the Prison: The
Practice of Punishment in Western Society* (New York: Oxford University Press, 1995),
117–22.

234   **"very cruel and very shocking"**   Richard Moran, *Executioner's Current: Thomas Edison, George Westinghouse, and the Invention of the Electric Chair* (New York: Knopf, 2002), 25. The execution of William Kemmler is described on pages 3–18.

234   **a familiar routine**   The Auburn routine and the first-grade designation were described in Ralph Record, "Marching Horde in Auburn Prison Described as Grim Army in Gray," *Star-Gazette* (Elmira, NY), January 13, 1930. Barry's assignment to the cabinetmaking shop was noted in Hickey, *The Gentleman Was a Thief*, 124, 131. His designation as a first-grade inmate is recorded in New York State Department of Correctional Services, Auburn Correctional Facility Records, Auburn Prison Inmate Record Cards, 1915–1970, Series B1222, Box 3, card for Arthur Barry, inmate no. 43077, New York State Archives, Albany.

234   **He wrote scores of letters**   Auburn censors logged 104 outgoing letters written by Barry between March 1929 and his escape four months later. Auburn Prison—Inmate Records, Series B1225, Correspondence and Report File Relating to Inmate Escapes and Captures, 1927–1934. New York State Archives, Albany.

234   **"In these pigeonholes"**   Record, "Dust Gathers on Men's Souls in Century-Old Auburn Cells," *Ithaca Journal* (NY), January 14, 1930.

234   **a new, modern cellblock**   "Plan New Cells at Prison," *New York Times*, June 30, 1929. The prison population as of July 1, 1929, was noted in Record, "Money Spent on Criminals Might Better Be Spent on Them as Children," *Star-Gazette*, January 24, 1930.

234   **Grievances festered**   Prison conditions were described in "Dust Gathers on Men's Souls in Century-Old Auburn Cells" and "Crime: At Leavenworth," *Time*, August 12, 1929, https://content.time.com/time/subscriber/article/0,33009,732737,00.html. The amount apportioned for food per inmate had not changed since 1868. See George W. Alger, "The Revolt of the Convicts," *Atlantic*, May 1930, 690, https://cdn.theatlantic.com/media/archives/1930/05/145-5/132416780.pdf.

234   **"living death"**   Victor F. Nelson, *Prison Days and Nights* (Garden City, NY: Garden City Publishing, 1936), 4.

235   **"mixed with the bad"**   "Four Men at Large After Auburn Break; Two Probes Started," *Times Union*, July 29, 1929. The number of convicted killers and rapists was noted in "Money Spent on Criminals Might Better Be Spent on Them as Children."

235   **"used to no little luxury"**   James C. Young, "Overcrowding Blamed for Prison Outbreaks," *New York Times*, July 28, 1929. The effect of harsher sentences imposed under the Baumes Laws was noted in "Osborne's Prison Reforms Recalled by Auburn Break," *Brooklyn Daily Eagle*, July 29, 1929.

235   **"We could not kiss"**   Anna Blake Barry, "My Life of Love and Fear as the Sweetheart and Wife of Arthur Barry, the World's Most Famous Jewel-Thief," *Atlanta Constitution*, February 12, 1933. A photograph of the visiting room appears in McHugh, *Auburn Correctional Facility*, 44.

235   **Blake complained of pain**   The car accident, cancer diagnosis, and Barry's escape plans were recounted in Hickey, *The Gentleman Was a Thief*, 88–89, 124–31.

235   **"I felt the overpowering desire"**   "Love on Borrowed Time."

236   **"I picked out a couple"**   "Captured Barry Boasts He Stole 5 to 10 Million," *Brooklyn Daily Eagle*, October 24, 1932. The ballfield meetings were also described in Hickey, *The Gentleman Was a Thief*, 127–28.

236   **to visit him on July 16**   Visitor cards for Mrs. A Barry, July 16 and 17, 1929. Auburn Prison—Inmate Records, Series B1225, Correspondence and Report File Relating to Inmate Escapes and Captures, 1927–1934.

236   **"Step on the gas"**   "Four Men at Large After Auburn Break; Two Probes Started,"
       Times Union, July 29, 1929.

236   **"it's a terrible thing"**   "Mother's Plea Wins Pawlak's Mercy in Prison Getaway,"
       Buffalo News, July 31, 1929. When he described the escape decades later, Barry claimed
       he pointed his rifle at Reese and did most of the talking after they entered the car. See
       Wallace, "Confessions of a Master Jewel Thief," 106, and Hickey, *The Gentleman Was a
       Thief*, 144.

237   **"intended putting me out of the way"**   "Reese Near Death in Convict Dash, Saved by
       Wallet," *Advertiser-Journal*, July 31, 1929. Barry later insisted that no shots were fired
       and that their plan had been to release Reese unharmed. See Wallace, "Confessions of a
       Master Jewel Thief," 106 and Hickey, *The Gentleman Was a Thief*, 145.

237   **"I figured I would last"**   Wallace, "Confessions of a Master Jewel Thief," 106. The
       break-in, the clothing taken, and the discarded uniforms were also noted in "Fonda's
       Suspect a Fugitive But Not from Auburn Prison," *Advertiser-Journal*, July 31, 1929.

238   **a 1926 Franklin**   "Escaped Convicts Sought Here," *Daily Item* (Port Chester,
       NY),   July 30, 1929. The car was described in a memo dated July 29, 1929, and filed
       in Auburn Prison—Inmate Records, Series B1225, Correspondence and Report File
       Relating to Inmate Escapes and Captures, 1927–1934.

238   **"the fastest car over the road"**   "Its Most Enthusiastic Owners Are Those Who Have
       Tried the Others" (advertisement), *Saturday Evening Post*, March 6, 1926, 168.

239   **named for an ancestor**   Henry Fonda, as told to Howard Teichmann, *My Life* (New
       York: New American Library, 1981), 21.

239   **encountered several more troopers**   "Newark Man Held as Kidnaper," *Herald-News*,
       October 24, 1932, and Hickey, *The Gentleman Was a Thief*, 155–56.

240   **Black Sunday or Terror Sunday**   The term *Black Sunday* appeared in several
       newspaper reports, including "2 on Trial Today for Auburn Riot; May Draw Life," *Daily
       News*, December 12, 1932. *Terror Sunday* may have been a local name for the incident
       and appeared in "Brophy Asks Barry Sent to Auburn," *Syracuse Herald*, November 2,
       1932. Details of the riot are drawn from "Four Armed Auburn Convicts Elude Pursuit
       After Gun Battle and Fire as Governor Demands Cause of Riots," *Brooklyn Daily
       Eagle*, July 29, 1929; "Two Convicts Killed, Several Men Wounded, Four Escape in
       Armed Mutiny of 1,700 Auburn Prisoners Led By Lifers," *Poughkeepsie Eagle-News*,
       July 29, 1929; "Four Men At Large After Auburn Break; Two Probes Started," *Times
       Union*, July 29, 1929; "Two Buffalo Prisoners Are Dead, One Hunted, After Riot at
       Auburn," *Buffalo News*, July 29, 1929; "Auburn Convicts Quiet, but Sullen," *Democrat
       and Chronicle*, July 30, 1929; and "Convicts Continue Noise," *New York Times*, July 30,
       1929.

240   **falling stock prices**   Examples are "Market Takes 'Technical Drop' on 10 P.C. Cash,"
       Brooklyn Daily Eagle, July 29, 1929, and "Stock Market Under Pressure," *Times Union*,
       July 29, 1929.

240   **"a sweeping and thorough investigation"**   "Full Probe of Riot Demanded by
       Roosevelt," *Democrat and Chronicle*, July 30, 1929.

240   **"revolt, sabotage, death"**   "Crime: Dannemora, Auburn," *Time*, August 5, 1929, https://
       content.time.com/time/magazine/article/0,9171,737601,00.html.

240   **photograph was already on the front page**   "Four Armed Auburn Convicts Elude
       Pursuit After Gun Battle" and "Four Men at Large After Auburn Break."

240   **seemed to be in print**   "Convicts Riot, Put Torch to Auburn Prison; 1,700 Battle Guards
       Five Hours, Wounding 4; Two Mutineers Killed, 4 Escape Over Wall," *New York Times*,

July 29, 1929, and "Two Convicts Killed, Several Men Wounded, Four Escape in Armed Mutiny of 1,700 Auburn Prisoners Led By Lifers."

240   **ringleader**   "Convicts Riot, Put Torch to Auburn Prison."

240   **"most notorious"**   "Arthur Barry Stole $80,000 Livermore Gems and Confessed," *Brooklyn Daily Eagle*, July 29, 1929.

240   **"I stood for a moment"**   Blake Barry, "My Life of Love and Fear," *Atlanta Constitution*, January 15, 1933.

CHAPTER 27: REFUGE

241   **"perpetrated by one man"**   "$250,000 in Jewels Stolen in Beverly," *New York Times*, August 11, 1929. A photograph of the Hutchinson mansion appeared in "Scene of Gem Burglary and Victims," *Brooklyn Daily Eagle*, August 12, 1929.

242   **a fifty-dollar reward**   Telegrams sent by warden Edgar Jennings, July 29 and August 7, 1929. Auburn Prison—Inmate Records, Series B1225, Correspondence and Report File Relating to Inmate Escapes and Captures, 1927–1934. New York State Archives, Albany.

242   **"a criminal of some kind"**   Galen Campbell to Jennings, December 15, 1929; Acting Warden to Campbell, December 17, 1929; Campbell to Auburn Prison, December 21, 1929; John Cornell to Auburn Prison, December 28, 1929. Auburn Prison—Inmate Records, Series B1225, Correspondence and Report File Relating to Inmate Escapes and Captures, 1927–1934.

242   **"bold marauder"**   "$25,000 Gem Theft! Hunt Jailbreaker Barry," *Daily News*, August 11, 1929. The other crimes were reported in "Convicts Seize Payroll," *Daily News*, August 3, 1929; "$8,000 Gem Theft Blamed on Barry," *Daily News*, August 16, 1929; and Martin Sommers, "$75,000 Gem Haul in L.I. Robbery Laid to Barry," *Daily News*, August 19, 1929.

242   **confessed to the Hutchinson theft**   "Hutchinson Jewel Thief Confesses, Clears Barry," *Daily News*, August 28, 1929.

242   **"a terror phantom"**   "Rich in Fear of Barry's Coming Back," *Daily News*, August 10, 1929.

242   **"I know about cauterizing wounds"**   "Arthur Barry's Life Story," *Daily News*, October 31, 1932. In this article, Barry claimed the bullet had not been removed more than three years after he was shot.

243   **willing to remove the bullet**   Neil Hickey, *The Gentleman Was a Thief: The Colorful Story of Arthur Barry, a 1920's Rogue* (New York: Holt, Rinehart & Winston, 1961), 167. In other accounts, he claimed a doctor in Albany treated him for the bullet wound soon after the escape. See, for instance, "Barry Lived in Ease Off Gem Theft Loot," *New York Times*, October 24, 1932.

243   **"Hold me"**   She recounted these events, conversations, and her thoughts in Anna Blake Barry, "My Life of Love and Fear as the Sweetheart and Wife of Arthur Barry, the World's Most Famous Jewel-Thief," *Atlanta Constitution*, January 15, February 12, 1933. Barry's biographer claimed Blake's reunion with Barry was at the apartment the night he arrived from Albany, but it seems unlikely they would have risked meeting there so soon after the escape. See Hickey, *The Gentleman Was a Thief*, 161–63.

243   **on the lookout for both him and Blake**   "Crime Haunts Here Combed for Two Auburn Fugitives," *Standard Union* (Brooklyn), July 30, 1929, and "Edwards Hunts Barry's Sweetie in Prison Break," *Daily News*, August 1, 1929.

243 **"The air was full of tips"** Theodore Prager, *Police Reporter* (New York: Duell, Sloan & Pearce, 1957), 154.

243 **police caught up with Blake** Hickey, *The Gentleman Was a Thief*, 166–67. Police surveillance of Blake was also noted in "New Exploits of Society's Suave and Sinister 'Supper-Man,'" *Detroit Free Press*, November 30, 1930.

244 **"Every time I went anywhere"** Blake Barry, "My Life of Love and Fear," *Atlanta Constitution*, February 19, 1933.

244 **"I was so ill"** "My Life of Love and Fear," February 12, 1933.

244 **tried to rob a garage** "Woman Shot Dead as Police Seize Thug," *New York Times*, November 13, 1929, and "Mother Dies in Gun Battle," *Daily News*, November 13, 1929.

244 **picked up Joe Caprico** "Man Held on Coast as Auburn Desperado," *New York Times*, December 28, 1929, and "Auburn Rioter Is Back," *Buffalo News*, January 24, 1929.

244 **"Go to hell"** "Crime: Again, Auburn," *Time*, December 23, 1929, https://content.time .com/time/magazine/article/0,9171,738294,00.html. Pawlak's arrest was reported in "Police Wound Auburn Lifer in Gun Fight," *Buffalo Times*, September 11, 1929.

244 **"brief and precarious liberty"** "Senseless Jail Breaks," *Democrat and Chronicle* (Rochester), December 30, 1929.

245 **"There's no safer place"** "Jewel Robber Surprised by Treatment in N.J. Jail," *Central New Jersey Home News* (New Brunswick), October 25, 1932.

245 **ventured outside for a nighttime walk** Barry's routines during his stay in the East Side apartment were noted in Hickey, *The Gentleman Was a Thief*, 167.

245 **"I do not intend"** "My Life of Love and Fear," *Atlanta Constitution*, January 22, 1933.

245 **dyed his hair a lighter shade** Barry made these changes to his appearance, his biographer noted, while he was hiding out in New York City in 1929. Hickey, *The Gentleman Was a Thief*, 167.

245 **"dapper appearance and quiet manner"** "2 Auburn Fugitives Sought in New York," *New York Times*, July 30, 1929.

245 **"murderous break for liberty"** "$25,000 Gem Theft! Hunt Jailbreaker Barry."

245 **Gentleman Bandit** Chapman's crimes were documented in H. Paul Jeffers, *Gentleman Gerald: The Crimes and Times of Gerald Chapman, America's First "Public Enemy No. 1"* (New York: St. Martin's, 1993).

245 **the new "super-criminal"** Ama Barker, "Barry, the New Gerald Chapman," *Daily News*, August 25, 1929.

245 **"cold and calculating"** "When Justice Triumphed: Detective Tells Inside Story of Trailing the Livermore Gem Gang," *Daily News*, February 17, 1929.

246 **"one of the most dangerous"** "New Exploits of Society's Suave and Sinister 'Supper-Man.'" Rogers, who earned the nickname because of his slovenly appearance, was in and out of prison for most of the 1920s. Details of his criminal career are drawn from "Payroll Robber Gets 15 Years," *Yonkers Herald*, December 12, 1925; "Police Get No Trace of Rogers, Notorious Crook, Parole Beneficiary," *Brooklyn Daily Eagle*, February 2, 1926; "'Bum' Rogers' Plea of Guilty Entails Sentence for Life," *Ithaca Journal* (NY), December 3, 1926; and Ruth Reynolds, "Tom Marshall Reviews the Tombs Parade," *Daily News*, November 18, 1928.

246 **"an element of surprise"** Hoover's comments, *Time* magazine's observation, and the joke about booking upper-floor rooms were drawn from *Time Capsule/1929: A History of the Year Condensed from the Pages of Time* (New York: Time, 1968), 17–18, 215–16, 218.

CHAPTER 28: MR. AND MRS. TONER

247 **"my heart was in my mouth"** Descriptions of their lives in New Jersey and all quotations in this chapter, unless otherwise noted, are drawn from Blake's first-person accounts of her life, published as a series in several newspapers in 1933. See Anna Blake Barry, "My Life of Love and Fear as the Sweetheart and Wife of Arthur Barry, the World's Most Famous Jewel-Thief," *Atlanta Constitution*, January 15, 22, 29, February 12, 19, 26, 1933.

247 **"a city teeming with activity"** Kenneth T. Jackson, *Crabgrass Frontier: The Suburbanization of the United States* (New York: Oxford University Press, 1985), 277.

247 **accepting a diamond ring** "Will Probe Gift of 5 Karat Sparkler to Police Official," *Morning Call* (Camden, NJ), July 4, 1927, and "Gets Newark Police Post," *New York Times*, July 20, 1927.

248 **"instances improper reception of money"** *Brex v. Smith*, 104 N.J. Eq. 386 (N.J. 1929) 146 A. 34.

248 **"the most corrupt police"** Mark A. Stuart, *Gangster No. 2: Longy Zwillman, the Man Who Invented Organized Crime* (Washington, DC: Lyle Stuart, 1985); quoted in Scott M. Deitche, *Garden State Gangland: The Rise of the Mob in New Jersey* (Lanham, MD: Rowman & Littlefield, 2018), 23. Zwillman is the subject of chapter 3 of Deitche's book.

248 **the Hoover Apartments** Alfred Albelli, "Barry Vault Hunted for Lindy Ransom," *Daily News* (New York), October 26, 1932.

248 **"a rather quiet, unexciting life"** The apartment and Blake's frequent visits to New York were also described in Hickey, *The Gentleman Was a Thief*, 167–68, 171.

249 **a squeegee salesman** Hickey, *The Gentleman Was a Thief*, 168.

249 **"Don't you remember me, Art?"** Barry also claimed he had bribed a policeman in "Barry Predicts He Will Get Life as Four Termer," *Times Union* (Brooklyn), October 24, 1932.

249 **"I thought it was curtains"** "Newark Man Held as Kidnaper," *Herald-News* (Passaic, NJ), October 24, 1932.

250 **"Where is Barry?"** "New Exploits of Society's Suave and Sinister 'Supper-Man,'" *Detroit Free Press*, November 30, 1930.

250 **"his bland air of unconcern"** "Mr. Colman's Raffles and Some Others," *New York Times*, August 3, 1930. The movie debuted in New York City in July 1930. See "New Films on Broadway," *New York Times*, July 20, 1930.

250 **"You can't help liking him"** "The Screen: The Amateur Cracksman Again," *New York Times*, July 25, 1930.

250 **"the delicate touch of a surgeon"** "The Screen: From the Viennese," *New York Times*, July 23, 1932.

250 **"The lady stood beside me"** "Cinema: The New Pictures," *Time*, August 1, 1932, https://content.time.com/time/magazine/article/0,9171,744077,00.html.

250 **"figured it was safer to stay"** "Jewel Robber Surprised by Treatment in N.J. Jail," *Central New Jersey Home News* (New Brunswick), October 25, 1932.

250 **Gothic Revival–style mansion** Alfred Albelli, "Woman Tipped Barry Off as Lindy Slayer," *Daily News*, October 31, 1932. A photograph of the building appeared in "Barry's Newark Hideout," *Daily News*, October 31, 1932.

251   **"hob-nobbed with the police"**   Arthur Barry, as told to Grace Robinson, "Arthur Barry's Own Life Story," *Daily News*, November 6, 1932.

252   **a fan of detective magazines**   "Captured Barry Boasts He Stole 5 to 10 Million," *Brooklyn Daily Eagle*, October 24, 1932, and "Jewel Robber Surprised by Treatment in N.J. Jail." The cover of the *True Detective Mysteries* issue appeared in a photograph that accompanied "2 Lindy Aids Face Barry; Jafsie Next," *Daily News*, October 29, 1932.

252   **"two mashers following me"**   Hickey, *The Gentleman Was a Thief*, 172.

252   **"a good place to live"**   "Barry Lived in Ease Off Gem Theft Loot," *New York Times*, October 24, 1932.

252   **"A splendid young fellow"**   "Barry Grilled Hard as Lindy Kidnap Suspect," *Daily News*, October 24, 1932. Information about Reuter and his dealings with Barry, unless cited below, are drawn from Cpl. Samuel J. Leon, "Continued Investigation on Arthur T. Barry in Reference to His Connection with Lindbergh Kidnaping and Abduction Case," New Jersey State Police *Report*, October 24, 1932. New Jersey State Police Museum and Learning Center, West Trenton, NJ.

253   **"A perfect gentleman"**   Barry, as told to Robinson, "Barry Tells Own Story of Robber Feats," *Daily News*, October 30, 1932. A photo of the Reuter homestead accompanied this article.

253   **a disabled war vet**   "Barry Lived in Ease Off Gem Theft Loot."

253   **"A small, thin blonde"**   "Barry Grilled Hard as Lindy Kidnap Suspect" and "Grill Raffles on Lindy Case After Capture," *Morning Post* (Camden, NJ), October 24, 1932.

253   **"so handy around the house"**   "Barry Grilled Hard as Lindy Kidnap Suspect."

253   **"I disclosed to her all the details"**   Arthur Barry, as told to Neil Hickey, "Love on Borrowed Time," *American Weekly*, January 25, 1959, 22.

253   **"Everything was peaceful"**   Blake's time at the farm was also described in Hickey, *The Gentleman Was a Thief*, 169–70. Drawing water from a well was noted in Arthur Barry, as told to Grace Robinson, "Arthur Barry's Own Life Story," *Daily News*, November 6, 1932.

253   **not much of a carpenter or mechanic**   "Famous Jewel Thief Quizzed by Police on Lindbergh Kidnaping," *Central New Jersey Home News*, October 24, 1932.

253   **"The hardest money I ever earned"**   The note was reproduced in Blake Barry, "My Life of Love and Fear," *Atlanta Constitution*, January 15, 1933.

253   **kept it for the rest of her life**   Blake's reaction to the note and Barry's work on the hydroelectric plant were noted in Hickey, *The Gentleman Was a Thief*, 170–71.

253   **"the life of every party"**   "Grill Raffles on Lindy Case After Capture."

254   **"I enjoyed my stay there"**   "Jewel Robber Surprised by Treatment in N.J. Jail."

254   **"a great political future"**   "Barry's Vault Is Hunted for Lindy Ransom."

254   **"skirting too near the danger line"**   Barry's biographer later claimed he agreed to run and was being groomed for a future run for election as township clerk. See Hickey, *The Gentleman Was a Thief*, 173.

254   **struck Losey as odd**   "$2,000,000 Gem Thief, Fugitive for 3 Years, Is Caught in Jersey," *New York Times*, October 23, 1932. Losey is identified as Andover's mayor in "Mayor G.E. Losey Dies," *New York Times*, June 7, 1934.

254   **pulled a slick jewel heist**   Barry was linked to robberies in Connecticut, in Westchester County, and on Long Island in the latter half of 1930. See "See Work of Barry in Greenwich

Robbery," *New York Times*, July 13, 1930; "See 'Boston Billy' in New Robberies," *Times Union*, August 5, 1930; "$80,000 Jewels Stolen in Mamaroneck Home; Series of Thefts Laid to Notorious Crooks," *New York Times*, August 5, 1930; "Fingerprinting Yacht Guests in $60,000 Jewel Theft," *Daily News*, August 6, 1930; "Broker's Wife Robbed of $25,000 Jewelry," *New York Times*, August 14, 1930; and "$50,000 Gems Gone as Butler Vanishes," *New York Times*, December 5, 1930.

254 **BARRY'S BACK, PROBABLY** "Dinner Burglar in $26,000 Comeback," *Daily News*, July 5, 1930.

255 **"cat-footed thief"** "Seek Master Thief in New Gem Robbery," *New York Times*, July 5, 1930.

255 **"Barry is too clever a thief"** "Gem Thief Not Barry, Thinks Nassau Sleuth," *Brooklyn Daily Eagle*, July 6, 1930. The victims' attendance at the Talbott's party was mentioned in "L.I. Gem Theft Sleuths Hunt Barry, Convict," *Brooklyn Daily Eagle*, July 5, 1930.

255 **"You'd think Arthur Barry and his mob"** "Thief Grabs Vanderbilt 240-Diamond Heirloom," *Daily News*, January 25, 1932. The weekday circulation of the *Daily News* stood at 1.3 million copies in 1930. See Leo McGivena (and others), *The News: The First Fifty Years of New York's Picture Newspaper* (New York: News Syndicate, 1969), 189.

255 **"for a second helping"** The *Daily Mirror*'s articles on Barry were quoted in Hickey, *The Gentleman Was a Thief*, 173–75.

CHAPTER 29: THE EAGLET

256 **issued a bulletin** The timing of the first Associated Press report of the kidnapping is noted in Thomas Doherty, *Little Lindy Is Kidnapped: How the Media Covered the Crime of the Century* (New York: Columbia University Press, 2020), 15, 38. The text of the bulletin appeared in Frances R. Mears, "Crime and Punishment," in *Breaking News: How the Associated Press Has Covered War, Peace, and Everything Else* (New York: Princeton Architectural Press, 2007), 68.

256 **"We were all startled"** Alfred Albelli, "Barry Vault Hunted for Lindy Ransom," *Daily News* (New York), October 26, 1932. Barry later said he was unsure whether he heard the news the night of the kidnapping or when he read the next morning's papers. Blake, however, believed he learned about it on the car radio, and she recounted the comment that the kidnapper should be hanged. See Anna Blake Barry, "My Life of Love and Fear as the Sweetheart and Wife of Arthur Barry, the World's Most Famous Jewel-Thief," *Atlanta Constitution*, February 19, 1933.

256 **LINDBERGH BABY KIDNAPPED FROM HOME** "Lindbergh Baby Kidnapped from Home of Parents on Farm Near Princeton; Taken from His Crib; Wide Search On," *New York Times*, March 2, 1932.

257 **LINDY'S BABY KIDNAPED** *Daily News*, March 2, 1932.

257 **"Somebody's kidnapped the Lindbergh baby!"** "Barry Grilled Hard as Lindy Kidnap Suspect," *Daily News*, October 24, 1932.

257 **350 million people worldwide** Doherty, *Little Lindy Is Kidnapped*, 8.

257 **"the nation's No. 1 hero"** *Time Capsule/1932: A History of the Year Condensed from the Pages of Time* (New York: Time, 1968), 66.

257 **became known as the Eaglet** This nickname was noted in "Lindbergh Baby Kidnaped from His Home at Night," *Daily News*, March 2, 1932.

257   **"the most famous baby"**   "Lindy's Baby Kidnaped," *Daily News*, March 2, 1932.

257   **"since Booth shot Lincoln"**   *Time Capsule/1932*, 66–67.

258   **"the most outrageous thing"**   *Time Capsule/1932*, 67.

258   **four hundred reporters and photographers**   Ludovic Kennedy, *The Airman and the Carpenter: The Lindbergh Kidnapping and the Framing of Richard Hauptmann* (New York: Viking, 1985), 84–85.

259   **"penetrated the thickest skin"**   Ishbel Ross, *Ladies of the Press: The Story of Women in Journalism by an Insider* (New York: Harper & Brothers, 1936), 220.

259   **"more than sixscore millions"**   "This Week in America: Kidnapping Stirs Nation," *New York Times*, March 6, 1932.

259   **left behind few clues**   These clues were described in "Child Stolen in Evening," *New York Times*, March 2, 1932; "Known Facts in Abduction," *Daily News*, March 3, 1932; A. Scott Berg, *Lindbergh*, (New York: Berkley, 1999), 243, 245; and *Time Capsule/1932*, 67–68. The Lindbergh dog was described in Dr. John F. Condon, *Jafsie Tells All!: Revealing the Inside Story of the Lindbergh-Hauptmann Case* (New York: Jonathan Lee, 1936), 29.

259   **"the child is in gut care"**   The note was reproduced in Berg, *Lindbergh*, 244.

259   **KIDNAPPING WAVE SWEEPS THE NATION**   *New York Times*, March 3, 1932.

259   **kept track of kidnappings for ransom**   "Six States in Drive Against Kidnapping," *New York Times*, March 2, 1932.

259   **"There were so many kidnappings"**   David Stout, *The Kidnap Years: The Astonishing True History of the Forgotten Kidnapping Epidemic That Shook Depression-Era America* (Naperville, IL: Sourcebooks, 2020), xv.

260   **"snatch racket"**   See, for example, "Will New Jersey Meet This New Challenge in the Lindbergh Case?" *Morning Post* (Camden, NJ), April 12, 1932.

260   **"organized on an unprecedented scale"**   R. L. Duffus, "Kidnapping: A Rising Menace to the Nation," *New York Times*, March 6, 1932. On the fast-track effort to pass what became known as the Lindbergh Law, see "Kidnapping of Baby Speeds Federal Law," *New York Times*, March 2, 1932.

260   **"atrocious and shameful crime"**   These editorials were reproduced in "Editorials Stress Need of New Laws," *New York Times*, March 3, 1932.

260   **"90 percent entertainment"**   Joe Pompeo, *Blood & Ink: The Scandalous Jazz Age Double Murder That Hooked America on True Crime* (New York: William Morrow, 2022), 135.

260   **"a final affront to American civilization"**   "Shall We Declare Martial Law," *Daily Mirror* (New York), March 3, 1932, quoted in Doherty, *Little Lindy Is Kidnapped*, 42.

260   **"wealth, prominence and high standing"**   Fred Pasley, "Kidnappings—When Gangs Rule," *Daily News*, March 3, 1932.

260   **RAFFLES AND GIRL HUNTED IN KIDNAPPING**   The article was quoted in Neil Hickey, *The Gentleman Was a Thief: The Colorful Story of Arthur Barry, a 1920's Rogue* (New York: Holt, Rinehart & Winston, 1961), 175–76.

261   **"stamped with the technique"**   "Lindbergh to Pay $50,000; Expects Baby by Night," *Daily News*, March 3, 1932.

261   **the only fingerprint police recovered**   Berg, *Lindbergh*, 242–43.

261   **"nearly broke my heart"**   Blake Barry, "My Life of Love and Fear," *Atlanta Constitution*, February 19, 1933.

261 **"crack man-hunter"** Val O'Farrell, "Inside Job, Ace Sleuth Warns Lindy," *Daily News*, March 5, 1932. The artist's depiction of the crime appeared under the headline HOW KIDNAPERS MADE OFF WITH LONE EAGLE'S BABY IN DARING PLOT, *Daily News*, March 3, 1932.

262 **"It made me ill"** "My Life of Love and Fear," *Atlanta Constitution*, February 19, 1933. The building, completed in 1930, was described in Leo McGivena (and others), *The News: The First Fifty Years of New York's Picture Newspaper* (New York: News Syndicate, 1969), 178–85.

262 **"Barry might have been guilty"** "Sailor Away Kidnap Night, Pal Says, Shattering Alibi," *Daily News*, March 6, 1932. Blake, however, later claimed she received a retraction. See "My Life of Love and Fear," *Atlanta Constitution*, February 19, 1933.

262 **"I am more and more inclined"** O'Farrell, "Little Lindy in No Danger, Says Sleuth," *Daily News*, March 6, 1932.

263 **might recognize him** Blake noted their concerns that someone would recognize Barry from the republished photographs in "My Life of Love and Fear," *Atlanta Constitution*, February 19, 1933.

263 **stopped more than one hundred times** Berg, *Lindbergh*, 247.

263 **"No story was too fantastic"** "All Clues Prove Futile," *New York Times*, March 4, 1932.

263 **"Have you gottit the money"** Condon, *Jafsie Tells All!*, 74. Condon's dealings with the kidnapper were also described in Berg, *Lindbergh*, 254–67.

264 **appeared on the cover of *Time*** The magazine's May 2, 1932, edition.

264 **BABY DEAD** *Daily News*, May 13, 1932.

264 **WHO KILLED LINDY'S BABY?** Doherty, *Little Lindy Is Kidnapped*, 90.

CHAPTER 30: LINDBERGH SUSPECT

267 **"the actual kidnapper of the baby"** Report of Lt. Arthur T. Keaten, New Jersey State Police *Report*, July 19, 1934. New Jersey State Police Museum and Learning Center, West Trenton, NJ.

267 **"Lindbergh took me off the front page"** Alfred Albelli, "Barry Kidnap Plots Bared," *Daily News* (New York), October 24, 1932. The informer's claims were recorded in a 1934 report on the Lindbergh case compiled by the New York office of the Division of Investigation, which was renamed the Federal Bureau of Investigation in 1935. *Summary Report: Kidnaping and Murder of Charles A. Lindbergh Jr.*, N.Y. File 62-3057, February 16, 1934, Box 3, Borowitz Crime Ephemera: Lindbergh Kidnapping Collection, Kent State University Libraries, Special Collections and Archives, Kent, OH.

267 **"an underworld source"** "$2,000,000 Gem Thief, Fugitive for 3 Years, Is Caught in Jersey," *New York Times*, October 23, 1932.

267 **"like men adrift in mid-ocean"** "Raffles Defies Police to Find Lindbergh Link," *Morning Post* (Camden, NJ), October 26, 1932. Brex's position and title in 1932 were noted in "Drastic Police Shift Ordered in Newark," *New York Times*, August 2, 1934.

268 **"That's the man . . . who owes me"** "$2,000,000 Gem Thief."

268 **"a hard character"** "Barry Grilled Hard as Lindy Kidnap Suspect," *Daily News*, October 24, 1932. Losey noted his reluctance to help trap Barry in this article. His wife's death and young family were recorded in "Mayor G.E. Losey Dies," *New York Times*, June 7, 1934.

268 **"I felt the guns against my side"** Barry described the arrest in Arthur Barry, as told to Grace Robinson, "Arthur Barry's Own Life Story," *Daily News*, November 6, 1932. Other details have been drawn from G. Earle Joline, "Seen and Heard," *Daily Record* (Long Branch, NJ), October 26, 1932, and "Master Criminal Is Caught Near Andover," *New Jersey Herald* (Newton), October 27, 1932, quoted in "Recent Art Thefts Recall County's 'Gentleman Thief,'" *New Jersey Herald*, July 30, 2011, https://www.njherald.com/story /news/2011/07/31/recent-art-thefts-recall-county/3971414007. Press reports claiming Barry was armed—for instance, "$2,000,000 Gem Thief, Fugitive for 3 Years, Is Caught in Jersey"—were false; the arresting officers found no weapons in his possession. See Cpl. Samuel J. Leon and Cpl. William F. Horn, "Apprehension of Arthur T. Barry, Jewel Thief, Woodport-Andover Road, Byram Township, Sussex County, N.J. re: his possible implication in the Lindbergh Case," NJSP *Report*, October 22, 1932. NJSP Museum and Learning Center.

269 **"America's most notorious jewel thief"** Jack Miley, "Barry, Master Gem Thief, Seized as Suspect in Lindy Kidnaping," *Daily News*, October 23, 1932.

269 **"the slickest second-story man"** "National Affairs: Barry Trapped," *Time*, October 31, 1932, https://content.time.com/time/subscriber/article/0,33009,769708,00.html.

269 **"suave robber"** "$2,000,000 Gem Thief."

269 **DOES BARRY ARREST SOLVE KIDNAPING?** "Barry, Master Gem Thief," *Daily News*, October 23, 1932.

269 **"I couldn't believe it"** Anna Blake Barry, "My Life of Love and Fear as the Sweetheart and Wife of Arthur Barry, the World's Most Famous Jewel-Thief," *Atlanta Constitution*, February 26, 1933.

269 **"It makes me sick"** "Sweetie Certain Barry's Kidnap Alibi Will Stand," *Daily News*, October 24, 1932.

269 **"a terrible thing"** "Jewel Robber Surprised by Treatment in N.J. Jail," *Central New Jersey Home News* (New Brunswick), October 25, 1932.

269 **"I can account for every minute"** "Raffles Defies Police," *Morning Post*, October 26, 1932.

269 **"I never brought a ladder"** Albelli, "Barry Linked with Jafsie," *Daily News*, October 25, 1932.

270 **"I haven't had my fingers in anything"** "Barry Lived in Ease Off Gem Theft Loot," *New York Times*, October 24, 1932.

270 **"I've never done anything worse"** Albelli, "Barry Vault Hunted for Lindy Ransom," *Daily News*, October 26, 1932.

270 **"I am convinced he kidnaped"** Albelli, "Woman Tipped Barry Off as Lindy Slayer," *Daily News*, October 31, 1932. Albelli was sent to Newark the night of the kidnapping and spent three months hanging out in New Jersey speakeasies and gambling dens, looking for sources and tips. Leo McGivena (and others), *The News: The First Fifty Years of New York's Picture Newspaper* (New York: News Syndicate, 1969), 205.

271 **"he did not take it"** "Barry Grilled Hard as Lindy Kidnap Suspect," *Daily News*, October 24, 1932.

271 **"We questioned Barry"** "Barry Lived in Ease Off Gem Theft Loot."

271 **"A distinctly Barryesque touch"** The columns were "O'Farrell Traces Barry's Moves to Lindy Ransom Deal," *Daily News*, October 25, 1932; "O'Farrell Clues Bind Closer About Barry," *Daily News*, October 26, 1932; and "Locate Barry's 'Other Woman,' O'Farrell Urges," *Daily News*, October 27, 1932.

272 **"Barry had no connection whatsoever"** Sgt. A. Zapolsky and Cpl. Leon, "To the home of Dr. John F. Condon, Decatur Avenue, Bronx, N.Y. for the purpose of showing him photograph of Arthur T. Barry, Notorious Gem Thief, who was apprehended on the night of October 22nd, 1932, at the farm of Otto Reuter, Byram Township, Sussex County, N.J.," NJSP *Report*, October 25, 1932. NJSP Museum and Learning Center.

272 **collected a pair of Barry's shoes** Cpl. Horn, "Further Investigation of Arthur T. Barry regarding any connection he might have with the Lindbergh Case," NJSP *Report*, October 26, 1932. NJSP Museum and Learning Center.

272 **had never met or seen him** Sgt. E.A. Haussling, "Inspection of Arthur Barry by Mr. and Mrs. Ollie Whateley," NJSP *Report*, October 28, 1932. NJSP Museum and Learning Center. Their encounter with Barry was reported in "Fail to Identify Barry," *New York Times*, October 29, 1932.

272 **to see Barry in person** Cpl. Leon and Cpl. Horn, "The transporting of Dr. John F. Condon from his home in the Bronx, N.Y. to the Newark Police Headquarters for the purpose of identifying Arthur T. Barry and Ann Blake who is supposed to be Barry's wife," NJSP *Report*, November 2, 1932. The number of men in the lineup was noted in "Barry Faces New Quiz," *Times Union* (Brooklyn), November 3, 1932.

272 **"A dapper, intelligent-looking young chap"** Details of Condon's encounter with Barry and their discussions, unless otherwise noted, are drawn from Dr. John F. Condon, *Jafsie Tells All!: Revealing the Inside Story of the Lindbergh-Hauptmann Case* (New York: Jonathan Lee, 1936), 210–11. Condon's father, a stonecutter, emigrated from Ireland and settled in the Bronx. See page 15.

272 **"The man I gave the money to"** "Jafsie Is Unable to Pick Barry," *Evening Star* (Washington, DC), November 2, 1932. Barry's look of relief was noted in this report. Condon noted the bump on the man's thumb in *Jafsie Tells All!*, 44, 93, 222.

272 **"I'd never mistake the man"** "Jafsie Vindicates Barry and Both Have a Good Cry," *Daily News*, November 3, 1932.

273 **satisfied there was no evidence** "Barry Fears a Revengeful Death in Jail," *News* (Paterson, NJ), October 25, 1932, and "Raffles Defies Police to Find Lindbergh Link," *Morning Post*, October 26, 1932. After "an exhaustive investigation . . . concerning Barry in connection with the Lindbergh case," a state trooper noted in an internal report, it was clear the jewel thief "had no part in same." Report of Lt. Keaten, NJSP *Report*, July 19, 1934. New Jersey State Police Museum and Learning Center, West Trenton, NJ.

273 **"the prize police catch"** "Captured Barry Boasts He Stole 5 to 10 Million," *Brooklyn Daily Eagle*, October 24, 1932.

CHAPTER 31: CELEBRITY CROOK

274 **struck a match and held it** A photograph of this moment appeared over the caption, "The Intimate Life Story of Arthur Barry" in the *Daily News*, October 30, 1932.

274 **"the most dangerous criminal in America"** Arthur Barry, as told to Grace Robinson, "Barry Tells Own Story of Robber Feats," *Daily News*, October 30, 1932.

275 **more than 1.6 million readers** The paper's Sunday circulation in 1930 was noted in Leo McGivena (and others), *The News: The First Fifty Years of New York's Picture Newspaper* (New York: News Syndicate, 1969), 189.

275 **covered the biggest cases of the '20s** Ishbel Ross, *Ladies of the Press: The Story of Women in Journalism by an Insider* (New York: Harper & Brothers, 1936), 7, 277–79.

Robinson's coverage of the Hall-Mills cases was documented in Joe Pompeo, *Blood & Ink: The Scandalous Jazz Age Double Murder That Hooked America on True Crime* (New York: William Morrow, 2022), 169, 173, 177, 181, 185, 214, 224, 230.

275   **"small, slim, frail in build"**   Ross, *Ladies of the Press*, 270. Robinson's career path and high salary were noted on pages 279–80.

276   **"an iron-willed wisp"**   McGivena, *The News*, 282.

276   **"I'm not a bad fellow"**   Ross, *Ladies of the Press*, 270–71.

276   **a swing through Europe**   The trip and her coverage of the inauguration were described in McGivena, *The News*, 224–25, 282–85.

276   **"I lost my voice"**   Notation on clipping of 1956 *Life* magazine feature "Confessions of Master Jewel Thief," in Grace Robinson Papers, Series I. Research Files, 1902–1982. Box 4, "Barry, Arthur, Jewel Thief," Folder 33. American Heritage Center, University of Wyoming, Laramie. Blake noted that her husband smoked "one cigarette after another" in Anna Blake Barry, "My Life of Love and Fear as the Sweetheart and Wife of Arthur Barry, the World's Most Famous Jewel-Thief," *Atlanta Constitution*, February 12, 1933. Robinson referred to the number of guards and the closed windows in Barry, as told to Robinson, "Barry, in Manacles, Explains 'Success,'" *Daily News*, November 1, 1932.

276   **"Barry's good looks & finesse"**   Handwritten note dated January 3, 1976, in Grace Robinson Papers, Series I. Research Files, 1902–1982, Box 4, Folder 33.

277   **"I always consulted the stars"**   Barry, as told to Robinson, "Arthur Barry's Own Life Story," *Daily News*, November 6, 1932. The advertisement appeared in the paper's November 5 edition.

277   **"why Barry was such an enigma"**   "Barry, in Manacles, Explains 'Success.'"

277   **"anybody with a head could pull them"**   Barry, as told to Robinson, "Glamor of Barry's 'Big Breaks' Gone," *Daily News*, November 2, 1932.

277   **"It sounds like bragging"**   Barry, as told to Robinson, "Barry Bares Rialto Bout with Wales," *Daily News*, November 3, 1932.

277   **crashed one of the Long Island galas**   Ross, *Ladies of the Press*, 275–76.

278   **"must be the record of another Barry"**   Barry, as told to Robinson, "Arthur Barry's Own Life Story," *Daily News*, November 6, 1932.

278   **"pal"**   See, for instance, Barry, as told to Robinson, "Barry Barred Fence as Gem Deal Crook," *Daily News*, November 5, 1932.

278   **"Barry is the type of criminal"**   "Arthur Barry's Own Life Story." The dog's name was noted in Blake Barry, "My Life of Love and Fear," *Atlanta Constitution*, January 15, 1933.

278   **"The career of the great Barry"**   "Glamor of Barry's 'Big Breaks' Gone."

278   **"lies a hell on earth"**   Barry, as told to Robinson, "Barry Tells Own Story of Robber Feats," *Daily News*, October 30, 1932.

279   **a word every second**   Walter R. Mears, "A Brief History of AP," in *Breaking News: How the Associated Press Has Covered War, Peace, and Everything Else* (New York: Princeton Architectural Press, 2007), 411.

279   **page-one treatment**   "Escaped Convict Cleared in Lindbergh Baby Case," *Fort Worth Star-Telegram*, October 24, 1932; "Gem Thief Cleared in Lindy Kidnapping but Held by Police," *Wausau Daily Herald* (WI), October 24, 1932; "Convict Cleared of Lindy Charge," *Evening Herald* (Klamath Falls, OR), October 24, 1932; and "Cultivated Convict Freed of Suspicion in Kidnapping," *Elizabethton Star* (TN), October 24, 1932.

279   **So did their colleagues**   "Police Check Suspect of Kidnapping," *Winnipeg Tribune*, October 25, 1932, and "Barry, Modern U.S. Raffles, Caught in N.J.," *Vancouver Province*, October 23, 1932 .

279   **A Reuters wire service report**   "Arrest of Suspect in Lindbergh Baby Case," *Liverpool Post and Mercury* (UK), October 24, 1932.

279   **"Barry admits that he is a thief"**   "Lindbergh Baby Suspect," *Daily Telegraph* (London), October 27, 1932.

279   **a report sent via wireless**   "Notorious Gem Thief Caught in N.J. After Underworld Tip," *New York Herald* (Paris), October 24, 1932.

279   **L'ÉTONNANTE CARRIÈRE D'ARTHUR BARRY**   "Les présomptions s'accumulent sur le redoubtable gangster auteur possible du rapt de Hopewell," *Paris-midi*, October 24, 1932.

279   **Gangsterführer**   "Die Lindbergh-Affäre taucht wieder auf," *Die Stunde* (Vienna), October 29, 1932.

279   **Letters poured into**   "Lindy Aids Face Barry; Jafsie Next," *Daily News*, October 29, 1932.

279   **showed him admiring the ring**   "Gentleman Gem Thief Jailed," *Asbury Park Press* (NJ), October 25, 1932.

279   **"success and glory"**   The newsreel filming and Barry's comments were reported in "Cops Find Clues in Letter Cache to Tie Up Barry," *Daily News*, October 28, 1932; "Barry, Long Sought Gem Thief, Gets Into Movies for $75 Cash," *Herald-News* (Passaic, NJ), October 28, 1932; and "Jewel Thief Poses for Sound Pictures," *Courier-News* (Bridgewater, NJ), October 28, 1932.

280   **"a few hundred dollars richer"**   "Mrs. Mills Fleeing When Killed After Hall, Mott Hears," *New York Herald*, October 28, 1922. Suspicions that Gibson had received money were noted in Pompeo, *Blood & Ink*, 99.

280   **"helped to pay legal fees"**   Ellen Poulsen, "Crime Does Not Pay—Serialized Morality Tales of the 1930s," Writers of Wrongs, January 27, 2017, http://www.writersofwrongs .com/2017/01/crime-does-not-pay-serialized-morality.html.

280   **covered the legal fees**   A. Scott Berg, *Lindbergh*, (New York: Berkley Books, 1999), 304 and Jeremy W. Peters, "Paying for News? It's Nothing New," *New York Times*, August 6, 2011.

280   **"$25.00 and a couple of gowns"**   "Crime Does Not Pay—Serialized Morality Tales of the 1930s."

281   **"The fact about crime news"**   Silas Bent, *Ballyhoo: The Voice of the Press* (New York: Horace Liveright, 1927), 42, 212.

281   **"any prominence, or indeed any notice"**   The debate appeared in "Crime and the News," *New York Times*, November 1, 1932; "Publishing Crime News," *New York Times*, November 2, 1932; and "Crime News a Benefit," *New York Times*, November 4, 1932.

281   **"The world was really sitting pretty"**   Bryan B. Sterling and Frances N. Sterling, comps. and eds., *A Will Rogers Treasury: Reflections and Observations* (New York: Crown, 1982), 202.

282   **"a new kind of criminal appeared"**   Lew Louderback, *The Bad Ones: Gangsters of the '30s and Their Molls* (Greenwich, CT: Fawcett Publications, 1968), 7.

282   **"robbed no one but the monied men"**   Bryan Burrough, *Public Enemies: America's Greatest Crime Wave and the Birth of the FBI, 1933–34* (New York: Penguin, 2004), 21.

282   **"Banks, after all"**   Louderback, *The Bad Ones*, 11.

282 **"I don't look like a thug"** "Barry, in Manacles, Explains 'Success.'"

283 **"Modern Robin Hood"** *Daily Journal* (Vineland, NJ), October 26, 1932.

283 **"I only robbed the rich"** "Captured Barry Boasts He Stole 5 to 10 Million," *Brooklyn Daily Eagle*, October 24, 1932.

CHAPTER 32: A FAIR TRIAL

284 **"Be brave"** "Police Army Guards Barry Back to Jail," *Daily News* (New York), November 6, 1932. This article described the motorcade route and the heavy police presence during the transfer from Newark to Grand Central Terminal. The extradition order was noted in "2 Auburn Prison Guards on Way to Bring Back Barry," *Syracuse Herald*, November 4, 1932; "Barry Due Back in Auburn Cell This Afternoon," *Daily News*, November 4, 1932; and "Barry in Chains," *Daily News*, November 5, 1932.

285 PRINCE ARTHUR OFF TO HIS IRON PALACE *Daily News*, November 6, 1932.

285 **how many packs of cigarettes** "Barry Back in Cell in Auburn Prison; Fled During Riot," *Democrat and Chronicle* (Rochester), November 7, 1932.

285 **he did not look up** "Barry Gets Old Number," *New York Times*, November 7, 1932.

285 **recommendations for modernizing** Sam A. Lewisohn, chair, *Report by Commission to Investigate Prison Administration and Construction, Presented to the Legislature of the State of New York*, February 15, 1931 (New York State, 1931). The new buildings and other changes were reported in "Auburn Prison Force Tightens Precautions," *New York Times*, December 3, 1930; "New York Seeks to Remedy Cause of Riots at Auburn," *Dunkirk Evening Observer* (NY), April 17, 1931; and "Auburn Prison's Golf Course Called Great Aid to Morale," *Buffalo News*, December 3, 1931.

285 **"No longer is he housed"** "Arthur Barry Segregated in Auburn Cell," *Syracuse Herald*, November 7, 1932.

285 **Security was heavier** Security measures in the visiting room were noted in "Wife Returns to Auburn to Mother Barry," *Syracuse Herald*, November 27, 1932.

286 **"I was astonished to see"** Anna Blake Barry, "My Life of Love and Fear as the Sweetheart and Wife of Arthur Barry, the World's Most Famous Jewel-Thief," *Atlanta Constitution*, February 26, 1933. Photographs and descriptions of the uniforms appear in Eileen McHugh, *Auburn Correctional Facility* (Charleston, SC: Arcadia, 2010), 36–37.

286 **"fitting a square peg"** *Report by Commission to Investigate Prison Administration and Construction*, 4.

286 **a battery of interviews and examinations** The reports and comments cited are drawn from New York State Department of Correctional Services, Auburn Correctional Facility Records, Inmate Case Files, Series W0006-77A (14610-77A), Case File of Arthur Barry. New York State Archives, Albany.

286 **"Auburn prison's collection of bad men"** "Big Korney Moved to Clinton Prison," *Buffalo News*, June 20, 1933.

287 **"Barry made tools of them all"** Martha Martin, "Barry on the Spot for Double-Cross in Auburn Break," *Daily News*, October 30, 1932. The threats to his life were also noted in "Barry Due Back in Auburn Cell This Afternoon," *Daily News*, November 4, 1932; "2 Auburn Prison Guards on Way to Bring Back Barry"; and "Watch Barry's Wife as Auburn Gets Him Back," *Daily News*, November 13, 1932.

287 **"assaulting and shooting officer"** Auburn Prison Inmate Record Cards, 1915–1970, Series B1222-77 Box 3, Record Card for Arthur Barry. Auburn Correctional Facility Records, New York State Archives.

287 **"leader"** and **"brains"** "2 Auburn Prison Guards on Way to Bring Back Barry" and "Brophy Asks Barry Sent to Auburn," *Syracuse Herald*, November 2, 1932.

287 **"He is absolutely innocent"** "Broke, Barry Asks Court for Counsel," *Daily News*, November 27, 1932.

287 **"If his trial is fair"** "Wife Returns to Auburn to Mother Barry," *Syracuse Herald*, November 27, 1932.

287 **could not get a fair trial** "Auburn Convicts to Face Court Monday," *Democrat and Chronicle*, December 9, 1932.

287 **"run wild with gun, knife and torch"** "Biggest Auburn Prison Riot Was Three Years Ago Today," *Democrat and Chronicle*, December 11, 1932.

287 **"I can expect a hometown verdict"** Letter reproduced in Blake Barry, "My Life of Love and Fear," *Atlanta Constitution*, February 12, 1933.

288 **Security was tight** "Pair's Trial for Part in Prison Riot Opens Today," *Democrat and Chronicle*, December 12, 1932. Barry's successful bid to appear in the courtroom in street clothes was noted in "21 Convicts in Auburn for Riot Trial," *Syracuse Herald*, December 14, 1932.

289 **"How's your business going"** "Small Pleads His Own Case in Riot Trial," *Daily News*, December 14, 1932.

289 **"the proverbial intuition of a woman"** "Barry's Wife Aids in Picking Jurors in Trial for Riot," *Brooklyn Daily Eagle*, December 14, 1932. The composition of the jury was noted in "21 Convicts in Auburn for Riot Trial" and "Witnesses at Convict Trial Begin Story," *Democrat and Chronicle*, December 15, 1932.

289 **"pay attention to the testimony"** Small's tactics and these exchanges were reported in "Guard Swears Small Struck Him in Riot," *Syracuse Herald*, December 15, 1932; "Witnesses at Convict Trial Begin Story"; and "Prison Guard Names Small in Felon Riot," *Daily News*, December 16, 1932.

289 **Guards took the witness stand** This account of the evidence is drawn from "Guard Swears Small Struck Him in Riot," *Syracuse Herald*, December 15, 1932; "Charge Barry, Small Used Guard as Shield," *Daily News*, December 15, 1932; "Prison Guard Names Small in Felon Riot"; "Guards Swear Small, Barry Led in Rioting," *Press and Sun-Bulletin* (Binghamton, NY), December 16, 1932; "Small Is Identified as Aiding Barry Break," *New York Times*, December 17, 1932; "Guard Admits Studying for Barry Trial," *Daily News*, December 17, 1932; "Voice Fails Small Asking for Mistrial," *Daily News*, December 20, 1932; "Felon Scores Riot Judge in Mistrial Plea," *Daily News*, December 20, 1932; and "Wife of Barry Told to Leave Counsel Table," *Democrat and Chronicle*, December 21, 1932.

290 **"incompetent, irrelevant, and immaterial"** "Small Charges Court Unfair in Riot Trial," *Syracuse Herald*, December 21, 1932.

290 **"forgotten man at the bottom"** Amity Shlaes, *The Forgotten Man: A New History of the Great Depression* (New York: Harper Perennial, 2008), 127–28.

290 **"original forgotten man"** "Small-Barry Jury to Get Case Today," *Daily News*, December 23, 1932.

290 **"I've tried to give these men"** "Jury Out in Small-Barry Rioting Case," *Syracuse Herald*, December 23, 1932. The jury's review of the guards' evidence was noted in "Jury Is Deadlocked in Barry-Small Case," *New York Times*, December 24, 1932.

291 **"Those two words"** Blake Barry, "My Life of Love and Fear," *Atlanta Constitution*, February 26, 1933.

291 **"the height of error"** The judge's comments and the reactions of Barry and Blake were reported in "Small and Barry Acquitted of Aiding Riot at Auburn," *Times Union*,

December 24, 1932; "Barry and Small Acquitted in Auburn Rioting," *Syracuse Herald*, December 24, 1932; and "Felon-Lawyer in New Fight for Freedom," *Syracuse Herald*, December 25, 1932.

291 **"perversion of justice"** "Perverted Justice," *New York Times*, December 26, 1932.

291 **"You can't blame the juryman"** "Beer Bill Futile, Mulrooney Holds," *New York Times*, December 30, 1932.

291 **"We both were so happy"** "My Life of Love and Fear," *Atlanta Constitution*, February 26, 1933.

291 **"Since his escape"** "Barry's Plea Adds 7 Years to His Term," *Syracuse Herald*, February 14, 1933.

291 **penciled in a new release date** New York State Department of Correctional Services, Central Depository. Inmate Summary Cards (circa 1925–1992), Series 21833, Summary Card for Arthur Barry. New York State Archives.

CHAPTER 33: "MY LIFE OF LOVE AND FEAR"

292 **"the first enthralling account"** Advertisement in the *Atlanta Constitution*, January 14, 1933.

292 **"Behind this daring figure"** Anna Blake Barry, "My Life of Love and Fear as the Sweetheart and Wife of Arthur Barry, the World's Most Famous Jewel-Thief," *Atlanta Constitution*, January 15, 1933. The series ran weekly until February 26, 1933.

292 **an impressive list of Jazz Age luminaries** David Nasaw, *The Chief: The Life of William Randolph Hearst* (New York: Houghton Mifflin, 2000), 323. The *Tribune*'s circulation in 1934 was noted in Russell James Hammargren, "The Impact of Radio on the Newspaper: A Study of a Developing Conflict Between Two Agencies of Mass Impression from 1920 to 1934," master's thesis, University of Minnesota, 1934, 138. The *Constitution*'s circulation of about 96,000 in 1933 was noted in *The Constitution Publishing Company, by Atlantic Newspapers Inc., Successor on Consolidation, Petitioner, v. Commissioner of Internal Revenue, Respondent, Reports of the Tax Court of the United States*, vol. 23 (1954–55), 21.

294 **"slanderers"** "My Life of Love and Fear," January 15, 1933.

294 **"straight as a die"** Blake Barry, "My Life of Love and Fear," *Atlanta Constitution*, January 15, 1933.

294 **"If Arthur had not signed"** "My Life of Love and Fear," February 12, 1933.

294 **"That happiness we enjoyed"** "My Life of Love and Fear," February 26, 1933.

294 **"We knew it could not last"** "My Life of Love and Fear," January 15, 1933.

294 **"The gray future will find him changed"** "My Life of Love and Fear," February 26, 1933.

CHAPTER 34: HARD TIME

297 **"tantamount to being outdoors"** Jack Meddoff, "Nation's Economy to Set Pace for Crime, Says Attica Warden," *Buffalo News*, August 7, 1946. Conditions for inmates in segregation in New York prisons in the 1930s also were described in "Felon-Lawyer in New Fight for Freedom," *Syracuse Herald*, December 25, 1932.

297 **"rigid, strict and hopeless solitary confinement"** Charles Dickens, *American Notes for General Circulation* (New York: Harper and Brothers, 1842), 39.

298 **"those who stood the ordeal better"** *In Re Medley* (1890), 134 U.S. 160, https://caselaw .findlaw.com/us-supreme-court/134/160.html.

298 **"buried alive"** Nathaniel Penn, "Buried Alive: Stories from Inside Solitary Confinement," *GQ*, March 2, 2017, https://www.gq.com/story/buried-alive-solitary -confinement. This is the source for the effects of solitary confinement and examples of coping strategies that follow.

298 **"It's an awful thing, solitary"** Atul Gawande, "Hellhole," *New Yorker*, March 30, 2009, https://www.newyorker.com/magazine/2009/03/30/hellhole.

299 **"He has nothing to do"** "Przybyl's Isolation in Prison Protested," *Buffalo News*, February 14, 1931.

299 **desperate to escape the unit** "Confession of Murder Found to Be Untrue," *Democrat and Chronicle* (Rochester), July 21, 1931.

299 **"Five killed themselves"** "Two Eden Bandits Waive Extradition," *Buffalo News*, May 8, 1935.

299 **"I wonder if I can go through"** Arthur Barry, as told to Grace Robinson, "Glamor of Barry's 'Big Breaks' Gone," *Daily News*, November 2, 1932.

299 **he paced back and forth** Letter reproduced in Anna Blake Barry, "My Life of Love and Fear as the Sweetheart and Wife of Arthur Barry, the World's Most Famous Jewel-Thief," *Atlanta Constitution*, January 22, 1933.

299 **"Am feeling O.K."** Letter dated November 14, 1932, reproduced in Blake Barry, "My Life of Love and Fear," *Atlanta Constitution*, January 15, 1933.

299 **I have tried my darndest** Reproduced in "My Life of Love and Fear," February 26, 1933.

300 **flew into nighttime rages** The assault on Diaz is described in Neil Hickey, *The Gentleman Was a Thief: The Colorful Story of Arthur Barry, a 1920's Rogue* (New York: Holt, Rinehart & Winston, 1961), 194. The incident and punishment are confirmed in Auburn Prison Inmate Record Cards, 1915–1970, Series B1222-77 Box 3, Record Card for Arthur Barry. Auburn Correctional Facility Records, New York State Archives, Albany.

300 **a wing of dungeon-like cells** The cells and conditions were described in "Auburn Prison Population Up to 1,400 Total," *Democrat and Chronicle*, April 15, 1937.

300 **"ice boxes"** A former Auburn inmate defined the prison slang in "Larkman Will Ask State for Redress," *Buffalo News*, December 20, 1933.

300 **to end his time in segregation** Hickey, *The Gentleman Was a Thief*, 194–95.

CHAPTER 35: "NO DICE"

301 **"Nothing has been spared"** Wilbur G. Lewis, "Attica Prison to Be Convicts' Paradise," *New York Times*, August 2, 1931. Descriptions of the prison are drawn from this article and "Comforts of Modern Metropolitan Hotel Found at New Attica Prison," *Buffalo News*, July 22, 1931; Sam A. Lewisohn, chair, *Report by Commission to Investigate Prison Administration and Construction, Presented to the Legislature of the State of New York*, February 15, 1931 (New York State, 1931), 35–36, 38–42; and Tom Wicker, *A Time to Die* (New York: Quadrangle/New York Times Book Co,. 1975), 34–35.

302 **decried the money spent** *Report by Commission to Investigate Prison Administration and Construction*, 40–42, and Frederick A. Storm, "Remedy Is Seen for Ills of Prison in Segregating Trouble-Making Inmates," *Star-Gazette* (Elmira, NY), March 24, 1931.

302 **only seven inmates tried to flee** Jack Meddoff, "Nation's Economy to Set Pace for Crime, Says Attica Warden," *Buffalo News*, August 7, 1946.

302 **"Attica takes as much pride"** "Attica Prison to Be Convicts' Paradise."

302 **carolers from local churches** "Gifts to Prisoners Deluge Censors," *Democrat and Chronicle* (Rochester), December 24, 1937.

303 **"more or less as a privilege"** "Attica Prison to Be Convicts' Paradise."

303 **"We frequently have trouble"** "Attica Prison Overcrowded, Warden Says," *Democrat and Chronicle*, January 10, 1937. The overcrowding and need for a new cellblock was also reported in "Attica Prison Cells Will End Jail Crowding," *Star-Gazette*, June 4, 1931; "Attica Prison Near Capacity," *New York Times*, March 13, 1932; and "Contracts Are Let for Attica Prison Cells," *Buffalo News*, July 2, 1937.

303 **"putting them in tents"** "Warden Says Prison Requires More Cells," *Buffalo News*, January 8, 1937.

303 **slept on cots in corridors** "Prison Is Crowded," *Buffalo News*, November 12, 1937.

303 **tear gas was used** "Attica Convicts Riot; Damage Is Reported," *New York Times*, December 8, 1932, and "Attica Prison Row Quelled by Tear Gas," *New York Times*, December 10, 1932.

303 **"were as effectively removed"** Wicker, *A Time to Die*, 33.

303 **a charity ward in Long Island's Meadowbrook Hospital** "Gem Thief's Friend Dies with His Secret," *New York Times*, April 30, 1940. The detective posted at her bedside was reported in "Anna Blake Dies and Keeps Secret," *Kingston Daily Freeman* (NY), April 30, 1940. Her admission to a charity ward was confirmed in "To Bring 'Gentleman Crook' Back for Another L.I. Trial," *Newsday* (Melville, NY), November 8, 1949.

304 **"Lake Ronkonkoma's treasure trove"** "Gems Laborers Dug Up $50,000 of Barry's Loot," *Daily News*, March 10, 1933. Other details of the discovery are drawn from "'Buried Treasure' Believed Loot of Barry; Gems Missing from Discarded Jewelry," *New York Times*, March 9, 1933; "Crowd Joins Hunt for $1,000,000 Loot," *Evening Star* (Washington, DC), March 10, 1933; and "May Be Barry Jewels," *Brooklyn Daily Eagle*, March 11, 1933.

304 **King consulted Fifth Avenue jewelers** "Would Question Wife of Barry," *Times Union* (Brooklyn), March 10, 1933.

304 **"No dice"** "Gem Thief's Friend Dies with His Secret." King's suggestion that Blake could leave the reward money to her heirs was noted in Grace Robinson, "Parole Barry, Jewel Bandit, After 21 Years," *Daily News*, November 9, 1949.

304 **A guard approached Barry** How Barry learned of Blake's death and the decision to allow him to attend the funeral were described in Neil Hickey, *The Gentleman Was a Thief: The Colorful Story of Arthur Barry, a 1920's Rogue* (New York: Holt, Rinehart & Winston, 1961), 197–98.

305 **appearing in the evening papers** For instance, "Jewel Cache Secret Kept in Face of Death," *Buffalo News*, April 29, 1940.

305 **"the trusted wife of Arthur Barry"** "Arthur Barry's Anna Dies, Silent on Cache," *Daily News*, April 30, 1940. Robinson's article recorded the time of Blake's death.

305 **two guards accompanied him** Details of the funeral home visit were drawn from Hickey, *The Gentleman Was a Thief*, 198–99.

305 **covered the funeral expenses** Noted in "Barry May Escape New Prison Term," *New York Times*, November 17, 1949.

305 **"All my heart's love"** Fred Menagh, "The 'Daringest Gem Thief' Trusted a Blonde," *Miami Herald*, May 26, 1940. The letter was also quoted in Anna Blake Barry, "My Life of Love and Fear as the Sweetheart and Wife of Arthur Barry, the World's Most Famous Jewel-Thief," *Atlanta Constitution*, February 26, 1933.

305 **were eager to pitch in** "Inmates Aid Red Cross," *Star-Gazette*, June 26, 1940, and "Prisoners Put $1,000 Into Bonds," *New York Times*, February 19, 1942. The

five-cents-a-day pay rate was noted in "Prisoners Help Navy Fund Drive," *Democrat and Chronicle*, October 14, 1942.

305   **a leader of the fundraising efforts**   Bea Jones, "Barry Here to Face '27 Charges," *Newsday*, November 16, 1949.

305   **"The only regret we have"** and **more than $6,000 in war bonds**   "Service Award Is Given Prison for Work in War," *Buffalo News*, September 24, 1943. The unspecified "cotton product" the men made was noted in "Attica Prison Flag-Ceremony Set Tomorrow," *Democrat and Chronicle*, September 22, 1943.

306   **"While the inmates themselves"**   "Attica's Inmates Contribute 1000 Pints of Blood," *Buffalo News*, August 13, 1942. The inmates' request for the mobile unit was reported in "School 44 Pupils Active in Red Cross Activities," *Democrat and Chronicle*, April 2, 1942.

306   **"Well, let's just say"**   Norman Howden, "Attica Gifts Mainstay of Blood Center," *Democrat and Chronicle*, January 8, 1949. The photograph, described as the image of Attica inmates to appear in the press, accompanied the article, headlined PRISON IS THEIR STOPPING PLACE . . . BUT THEY'RE IN RED CROSS GALLON CLUB.

307   **without a single disciplinary infraction**   "Barry Here to Face '27 Charges." Only a fraction of Attica's inmate records for the period have been preserved, and Barry's file appears to have been among those destroyed. New York State Archives, Researcher Services Unit, email to author, March 14, 2023. The scope of the collection is described in Attica Correctional Facility Inmate Case Files (1940–2004), Series W0005, New York State Department of Correctional Services, New York State Archives, Albany, https://iarchives.nysed.gov/xtf/view?docId=ead/findingaids/W0005.xml.

307   *Exemplary*   Ben White and Art Smith, "Barry Out, Goes First to Wife's Grave," *Daily News*, November 23, 1949.

307   **in charge of the prison laundry**   "Barry Here to Face '27 Charges."

307   **the ten thousandth inmate**   "10,000th Inmate Admitted by Attica Prison," *Buffalo News*, February 16, 1948.

CHAPTER 36: "EASY COME, EASY GO"

309   **"There's nothing much I can say"**   "Barry, Society Jewel Thief, Is Released and Rearrested," *Evening Star* (Washington, DC), November 15, 1949. Details of his release and rearrest were also reported in Bob Hollingsworth, "Fabulous Gem Thief Returning for Trial," *Newsday* (Melville, NY), November 15, 1949, and Bea Jones, "Barry Here to Face '27 Charges," *Newsday*, November 16, 1949.

309   **something Barry wanted to see**   "Jewel Thief Gets Look at World After 17 Years," *Press and Sun-Bulletin* (Binghamton, NY), November 16, 1949.

309   **He filed a court action**   Val Duncan, "Old Con Loses Law Tilt for Liberty After 20 Years in Stir," *Newsday*, February 14, 1948.

309   **"for some time"**   "1929 Auburn Riot Leader Seeks Parole," *Syracuse Herald-Journal*, July 26, 1949.

309   **"evil ghosts of his wild old days"**   Ben White, "Gem Artist Out, Ghosts Lie in Wait," *Daily News*, November 16, 1949.

309   **"God knows I have paid"**   Neil Hickey, *The Gentleman Was a Thief: The Colorful Story of Arthur Barry, a 1920's Rogue* (New York: Holt, Rinehart & Winston, 1961), 203.

310   **"hardworking, gregarious, and meticulous"**   Sydney C. Schaer, "Frank Gulotta Dies; Was Judge and DA," *Newsday*, December 12, 1989. Details of his military and legal

careers also have been drawn from "Frank A. Gulotta, 82, Ex-New York Justice," *New York Times*, December 12, 1989, and "Nassau DA Quits, Gulotta Appointed," *Daily News*, July 1, 1949.

311   **"hard-driving and gutsy"**   Jerry Rosa, "Final Farewell to Gulotta's Dad," *Daily News*, December 13, 1989.

311   **The indictments accused Barry**   *The People of the State of New York v. Arthur Barry*, Case Nos. 4279, 4280, 4281, 4900, 4902 and 4903, County Court of Nassau County, Mineola, NY.

311   **"I don't know what I can do"**   "Paroled Jewel Thief Faces Old Counts," *Ithaca Journal* (NY), November 9, 1949.

311   **resigned in disgrace**   Alexander Feinberg, "King, Ex-Police Inspector, Indicted In Nassau County Bribery Inquiry," *New York Times*, September 26, 1945, and "Jury Clears King of Bribe Charge; Nassau Court Audience Applauds," *New York Times*, January 31, 1946.

311   **passed away in 1946**   "Elvin Edwards Rites," *New York Times*, July 24, 1946.

311   **died of a stroke**   "Obituary," *Daily News*, October 8, 1934, and "Milestones," *Time*, October 15, 1934.

311   **"My life has been a failure"**   "Jesse Livermore Ends Life in Hotel," *New York Times*, November 29, 1940.

311   **King's replacement as chief of detectives**   "Pinnell to Retire from Nassau Post," *New York Times*, December 18, 1961.

311   **"so much as a cuff link"**   White, "Out-at-Last Barry May Stay Out," *Daily News*, November 17, 1949.

311   **"It was easy come, easy go"**   Leo P. Hanning, "Barry Pleads Guilty; May Go Free," *Newsday*, November 17, 1949.

312   **"If you laugh when you win"**   "Barry Here to Face '27 Charges."

312   **"Barry is a changed man"**   "Nassau D.A. Asks Freedom for Barry," *Syracuse Herald-Journal*, November 17, 1949.

312   **"if the man hasn't learned his lesson"**   "Barry May Escape New Prison Term," *New York Times*, November 17, 1949.

312   **"Barry easily could double"**   "Barry Here to Face '27 Charges."

312   **"a respected citizen, a leader"**   Duncan, "Barry Free, His 19 Jail Years Balance Exploits as Prince of Jewel Thieves," *Newsday*, November 23, 1949.

312   **"conscientious, honest, and fair"**   "Officialdom Eulogizes Collins; Funeral Services on Monday," *Newsday*, December 6, 1952.

312   **"Though you may have spent"**   "Suspended Sentence for Barry, Gem Thief," *New York Times*, November 23, 1949.

312   **about sixty dollars in his pocket**   Barry's departure and the visit to Blake's grave were described in White and Art Smith, "Barry Out, Goes First to Wife's Grave," *Daily News*, November 23, 1949.

CHAPTER 37: AN HONEST MAN

313   **The job paid fifty dollars a week**   Robert Wallace, "Confessions of Master Jewel Thief," *Life* 40, no. 11 (March 12, 1956): 121.

313   **"The townspeople began to accept me"**   Arthur Barry, as told to Neil Hickey, "Love on Borrowed Time," *American Weekly*, January 25, 1959, 22.

314 **"I never thought"** "Confessions of Master Jewel Thief," 136. Photographs of Barry carrying the daily deposit to the bank and counting banknotes at the till appeared on pages 121 and 136.

314 **published in a Tennessee paper** "Country's Super Thief Ready to Go Straight," *Knoxville Journal* (TN), December 18, 1949.

314 **"as notorious for their charm"** "America's 'Gentlemen' Crooks," *The World's News* (Sydney, Australia), July 5, 1952.

314 **"Wonder how many film companies"** Jack Altshul, "Heads and Tales," *Newsday* (Melville, NY), December 8, 1949.

315 **"the No. 1 criminal of the age"** Henry Lee, "Mystery of the Master Criminal," *Coronet* 33, no. 1 (November 1952): 39–43. See Lawrence Elliott's feature, "Flying Saucers: Myth or Menace," 47–54, and Anne Fromer, "The Many Lives of Pope Pius XII," 71–86. The magazine's readership figure was noted on page 140.

315 **"Getting on the cover of Life"** Erika Doss, ed., *Looking at LIFE Magazine* (Washington: Smithsonian Institution Press, 2001), 3. The subscription and readership figures for 1956 appear on page 105.

315 **A THIEF WHO STOLE $10 MILLION IN JEWELS** "Confessions of Master Jewel Thief," 121–22, 124, 127–28, 130, 133–36.

317 **"pseudo-scientific pieces"** David Nasaw, *The Chief: The Life of William Randolph Hearst.* (Boston: Houghton Mifflin, 2000), 387. Story examples mentioned here are based on the magazine's August 20, 1961, issue.

317 **"Those felonies stand"** Barry, as told to Hickey, "I Was the King of Jewel Thieves," *American Weekly*, January 18, 1959, 8–9, 18–9. The second feature was "Love On Borrowed Time," *American Weekly*, January 25, 1959, 20, 22.

317 **"the most successful jewel thief"** Hickey, *The Gentleman Was a Thief: The Colorful Story of Arthur Barry, a 1920's Rogue* (New York: Holt, Rinehart & Winston, 1961), ix.

317 **had broken into journalism** Hickey, *Adventures in the Scribblers Trade: The Most Fun You Can Have* (Bloomington, IN: iUniverse, 2015), vii, 17–26; Hickey, "The Author of 'Lolita,'" *American Weekly*, October 4, 1959, 16–17; and Hickey, "Paul Newman: Different Kind of Bird," *American Weekly*, November 22, 1959, 12–13.

318 **"Only a criminal with a sense of irony"** and **"in an age of rascals"** Hickey, *The Gentleman Was a Thief*, x, xi.

318 **Monahan's death in 1960** "Jewel Thief, 62, Dies in Poverty," *New York Times*, October 25, 1960.

318 **"lone wolf"** Hickey, *The Gentleman Was a Thief*, 42, 87. Monahan had been identified as Barry's accomplice in *Life* magazine. See Wallace, "Confessions of Master Jewel Thief," 128.

318 **published in Britain** Hickey, *The Gentleman Was a Thief: The Colorful Story of Arthur Barry, a Rogue of the 1920s* (London: Frederick Muller, 1962).

318 **"Smooth thieves like Arthur Barry"** Emanuel Perlmutter, "Lone-Wolf at Work," *New York Times*, July 9, 1961.

318 **"extremely happy that Barry is successful"** Jack Setters, "Interesting Story of Great Jewel Thief," *Nashville Banner*, October 6, 1961.

318 **"This true story reads like fiction"** "Story of a Celebrated Rogue," *Sioux City Journal* (IA), September 10, 1961.

319 **"remorse or repentance"** Leon C. Metz, "The Gentleman Was a Thief," *El Paso Times* (TX), August 27, 1961.

319   **"Barry appears almost heroic"**   Ed Kelly, "Grand Larceny as It Is Done in Grand Manner," *Buffalo News*, August 12, 1961.

319   **"There is no censure"**   "Lone-Wolf at Work."

319   **went head-to-head**   Ira Cain, "PM East-PM West New ABC-TV Offering," *Fort Worth Star-Telegram*, July 3, 1961.

319   **"It's TV that's fresh and new"**   "'PM East' & 'PM West,'" *Broadcasting: The Businessweekly of Television and Radio*, June 26, 1961, 12–13, https://worldradiohistory .com/Archive-BC/BC-1961/1961-06-26-BC.pdf.

319   **Streisand, an early guest**   Mike Wallace, with Gary Paul Gates, *Between You and Me: A Memoir* (New York, Hyperion, 2005), 233–39.

319   **reinvented himself as a freelance writer**   John Lardner, "The Lexicographers in Stir," *New Yorker*, December 1, 1951, 101–2, 104–6, 109–16, 119–25.

319   **posed as messengers delivering flowers**   "$500,000 Gem Robber Chief Gets 8–16 Year Term, Pal 30," *Daily News*, March 23, 1932.

319   **"the two men took quiet satisfaction"**   Percy Shain, "How Crime Doesn't Pay—Taught by 2 Alumni," *Boston Globe*, July 25, 1961. No recording of the episode has survived.

320   **"only about 10 percent"**   Thomas J. Hynes, "Arthur T. Barry; His Biography Was a Bestseller," *Worcester Telegram*, July 17, 1981. The lineup of guests for Episode 266 of Season 2 of the show was noted in "On the Air," *Evening Sun* (Baltimore), November 16, 1964. No recording of the program appears to have survived.

EPILOGUE: UNCLE ARTIE

321   **"I don't know what he did"**   Author's telephone interview with Sean Galliher, March 3, 2023. All quotations from Galliher have been taken from this interview.

322   **"We loved him"**   Author's telephone interview with Mary Schumacher, February 28, 2023. This interview is the source of all quotations from Schumacher.

323   **"As you can see"**   Ben White, "Out-at-Last Barry May Stay Out," *Daily News* (New York), November 17, 1949.

323   **"To a thief"**   Bill Mason, with Lee Gruenfeld, *Confessions of a Master Thief: The Astonishing True Story of a High-Society Cat Burglar* (New York: Villard Books, 2003), ix. See also "Changing Style of Crime," *New York Times*, October 22, 1973.

323   **"big lawns and Cadillacs"**   "The Good Life," *Time*, February 28, 1949, https://content .time.com/time/magazine/article/0,9171,799825,00.html. When Dennis was nabbed after shifting his operations to Beverly Hills, Hollywood took notice and turned his exploits into a movie, *The Great Jewel Robber*, released in 1950. See "Story of Raffles at the Palace," *New York Times*, August 4, 1950.

323   **feature on jewel thieves**   Charles and Bonnie Remsberg, "The Aristocrats of Crime," *New York Times*, December 27, 1964.

323   **flooded her Instagram account**   Eric Konigsberg, "Old School Jewelry Heists Are on the Rise—And Celebrities Are the Target," *Town & Country*, April 12, 2018, https://www.townandcountrymag.com/society/money-and-power/a19746799 /jewelry-heists-celebrities.

324   **supported disabled vets and their families**   This description of the organization is drawn from "Blind Lawyer Heads Order of Purple Heart," *Kenosha News* (WI), August 24, 1963; "Purple Heart Charter Is Open for First Time Since '59," *Standard-Speaker*

(Hazelton, PA), December 2, 1963; and "Purple Heart Plans Parties," *Standard-Speaker*, December 12, 1963.

324 **served on the executive** "Purple Heart," *Boston Globe*, October 20, 1963.

324 **"his work for and with veterans"** "Former Jewel Thief Named Worcester's Veteran of the Year," *Boston Globe*, November 12, 1975. The parade and dinner were described in J. Victor Fontaine, "Parade to Highlight Nov. 11 Rites Tuesday," *Worcester Sunday Telegram*, November 9, 1975.

324 **Harold King, died of a stroke** "H.R. King Is Dead; Long a Detective," *New York Times*, December 11, 1956.

324 **killed himself with his .38-caliber** "Nassau Police Official Takes Life with Gun," *Daily News*, December 19, 1956.

325 **fifty-three when he died** "Scaffa, Jewelry Retriever, Dead," *New York Times*, September 1, 1941; "Scaffa Cleared, Donahue Case Stays Mystery," *Daily News*, May 20, 1928; and "Scaffa Gets Six Months in Gem Lie," *Daily News*, September 17, 1935.

325 **wiped out in the Depression** Larry O'Dell, "Cosden, Joshua Seney (1881–1940)," *The Encyclopedia of Oklahoma History and Culture*, https://www.okhistory.org /publications/enc/entry?entry=CO065.

325 **"Society's greatest gambler"** John O'Donnell, "Woolworth Son-In-Law Dies a Mystery Suicide," *Daily News*, April 24, 1931. The Donahue family disputed the official ruling of suicide. See "J.P. Donahue Dies; Poison Kills Broker," *New York Times*, April 24, 1931, and Grace Robinson, "Woolworths Fail to Clear Suicide," *Daily News*, April 25, 1931.

325 **outlived him by four decades** "Mrs. Jessie Donahue Dies; Woolworth's Daughter, 82," *New York Times*, November 4, 1971.

325 **was convicted in 1939** "Jimmy Hines Dead; Ex-Tammany Chief," *New York Times*, March 26, 1957.

325 **an array of offenses** Inmate Record Card of James Francis Monahan, New York State Department of Correctional Services, Clinton Correctional Facility Record Cards, Series B0097-77. New York State Archives, Albany.

325 **insane or had died** See "'Boston Billy's' Loot May Never Be Found; Insane," *Daily Item* (Port Chester, NY), May 15, 1928, and "Long Island Society Long a Prey to 'Boston Billy' Gang," *Kenosha News*, December 24, 1928. References to his death in prison appeared in "Barry, Society Jewel Thief, Is Released and Rearrested," *Evening Star* (Washington, DC), November 15, 1949, and White, "Gem Artist Out, Ghosts Lie in Wait," *Daily News*, November 16, 1949.

325 **scooped up and imprisoned** "Death Winds Up Career of Famed Jewel Thief," *Boston Globe*, October 26, 1960.

325 **"an old, embittered, befogged man"** West Peterson, "Boston Billy Williams: He Woke the Women Up," *Saga: The Magazine for Men* 23, no. 5 (February 1962), 101.

325 **"just ready for the taking"** "Notorious Jewel Thief of '20s Dies Here at 62," *Worcester Telegram*, October 24, 1960.

326 **"flawless attire and courtly manner"** "Jewel Thief, 62, Dies in Poverty," *New York Times*, October 25, 1960.

326 **"mingled gracefully"** "Milestones," *Time*, November 7, 1960, https://content.time .com/time/subscriber/article/0,33009,826738,00.html.

326 **"the problem of wayward youth"** Robert Wallace, "Confessions of Master Jewel Thief," *Life* 40, no. 11 (March 12, 1956): 121–22.

326 **He spoke to church groups** Thomas J. Hynes, "Arthur T. Barry; His Biography Was a Bestseller," *Worcester Telegram*, July 17, 1981.

326 **"a rather gallant burglar"** The encounter was described in Arthur Barry, as told to Neil Hickey, "Love on Borrowed Time," 22 and Hickey, *The Gentleman Was a Thief: The Colorful Story of Arthur Barry, a 1920's Rogue* (New York: Holt, Rinehart & Winston, 1961), 207–8.

326 **"to get sodden drunk"** "People," *Time*, December 9, 1935, https://content.time .com/time/magazine/article/0,9171,847596,00.html. The shooting, Jesse Livermore Jr.'s recovery, and the outcome of Dorothea Livermore's prosecution were reported in "Jesse Livermore Jr. Shot by Mother in Liquor Row," *New York Times*, November 30, 1935; "Court Frees Mother of Young Livermore," *New York Times*, March 26, 1936; and "People," *Time*, March 9, 1936, https://content.time.com/time/magazine /article/0,9171,770123,00.html.

327 **puttering in the yard** Details of Barry's death have been based on the author's interview with Sean Galliher, March 3, 2023, and "Arthur T. Barry; His Biography Was a Bestseller."

327 **"I am not good at drawing morals"** "Confessions of Master Jewel Thief," 136.

INDEX